Chet Atkins

Chet Atkins

The Greatest Songs of Mister Guitar

Mark S. Reinhart

McFarland & Company, Inc., Publishers
Jefferson, North Carolina

ALSO BY MARK S. REINHART

The Batman Filmography, 2d ed. (McFarland, 2013)

Abraham Lincoln on Screen: Fictional and Documentary Portrayals on Film and Television, 2d ed. (McFarland, 2009; paperback 2012)

Frontispiece: Chet Atkins with his 1959 Gretsch Chet Atkins Country Gentleman electric guitar, circa 1970.

LIBRARY OF CONGRESS CATALOGUING-IN-PUBLICATION DATA

Reinhart, Mark S., 1964–
Chet Atkins : the greatest songs of Mister Guitar / Mark S. Reinhart.
    p.   cm.
Includes bibliographical references and index.

ISBN 978-0-7864-7852-1 (softcover : acid free paper) ∞
ISBN 978-1-4766-1783-1 (ebook)

1. Atkins, Chet—Criticism and interpretation.
2. Country music—History and criticism.
3. Atkins, Chet—Discography.   I. Title.

ML419.A83R45 2014   787.87'1642092—dc23   2014031486

BRITISH LIBRARY CATALOGUING DATA ARE AVAILABLE

© 2014 Mark S. Reinhart. All rights reserved

No part of this book may be reproduced or transmitted in any form or by any means, electronic or mechanical, including photocopying or recording, or by any information storage and retrieval system, without permission in writing from the publisher.

On the cover: Chet Atkins with a Gibson Chet Atkins Country Gentleman electric guitar, 1990

Printed in the United States of America

McFarland & Company, Inc., Publishers
Box 611, Jefferson, North Carolina 28640
www.mcfarlandpub.com

For my parents and fellow Chet Atkins fans,
Larry and Sally Reinhart

Table of Contents

Acknowledgments
ix

Introduction
1

One Life, Six Strings
5

The Greatest Songs
Arranged Chronologically
27

Appendix: The Songs
Alphabetically
199

Bibliography
203

Index
205

Acknowledgments

Obviously, an analysis and appreciation of the most successful and noteworthy recordings of Chet Atkins could not exist without the man who created those recordings. So my first and biggest thank you must be delivered beyond our earthly realm— I would like to thank Mister Guitar himself for the incredible musical legacy that he has left to the world. Chet, you will always be my biggest musical hero, and I am proud to offer this book as a personal tribute.

I would also like to thank my father, Larry Reinhart, a fine guitar player in his own right, who introduced me to Chet's music before I had even started grade school. Because of Dad, I grew up listening to Chet and learning to play the guitar myself, and these pursuits have brought immeasurable joy to my life. Thanks, Dad.

I want to thank some other members of my family as well. My mother Sally Reinhart has always enjoyed Chet's music, too, and a number of times she made sure that we had great seats for Chet shows in and around our hometown. Also, she has always been kind enough to be a great audience for us whenever we play our guitars as much like Chet as we can. Thanks, Mom.

And I would like to thank my wife, Jill, my sons Taylor and Keaton, and my daughter, Jenna, for their ongoing support of all of my creative projects. I was able to take Jill to see Chet perform live on one occasion, so she got the chance to witness his musical genius firsthand. Unfortunately, my kids never got this chance, but they have still appreciated Chet's music enough over the years to allow some of his songs to make it onto their iPod playlists. Thanks, Jill, Taylor, Keaton and Jenna—it means a lot to me that you have welcomed Chet into our family's music mix.

I would like to thank Tom Redmond, the creator and administrator of the official Chet Atkins website, misterguitar.us, for his support of this project. Tom's site is a wonderful resource for all Chet fans, and his message board, known as the "Chetboard," is a perfect forum to allow all of those fans to stay in contact. All throughout the process of writing this book, I have been consulting with Chetboard members about many aspects of Chet's recording history. Everyone has been supportive of my work, and willing to share their knowledge of all things Chet with me—so my thanks go out not only to Tom, but also to all of the Chetboarders out there.

In fact, there are several Chet experts I first met through the Chetboard that ended up having a direct influence on the creation of this book—so I would like to thank them by name. In 2013, writer John Chintala authored an exhaustive compilation of Chet's musical work, *Chet Atkins: A Complete Guide to "Mister Guitar."* Both John's excellent research and direct correspondence with me were a huge help in writing this book. The same can be said about the well-known fingerstyle guitarist/author Craig Dobbins, who over the years had the privilege of working directly with Chet and several of Chet's close musical associates. Craig was kind enough to share his insights regarding Chet's musical career with me. Thank you, John and Craig—I hope both of you will feel that this book honors Chet's memory as much as your fine work has.

Introduction

Allow me to tell you a little bit about myself and my admiration for Chet Atkins. It really is no exaggeration for me to say that I have been an avid fan for most all of my life. My father, Larry Reinhart, introduced me to Chet's music before I had even started grade school. In fact, some of my earliest memories are of sitting with Mom and Dad in our living room, watching Chet play guitar on television. Mom and Dad even took me to see Chet perform in and around our hometown of Columbus, Ohio, a few times when I was a kid.

Chet was not the only guitarist I heard back then. Dad had played the instrument ever since he was a young man, so in addition to listening to Chet himself, I got to hear Dad's great Chet-inspired picking. This led me to be transfixed by the guitar before I was anywhere near big enough to hold a full-size one. I wore out more than a few toy plastic guitars before I decided to start learning how to play the instrument.

In fact, playing the guitar quickly became one of my major passions. By the time I was in my teens, three musical artists in particular had led me to want to become a professional singer/guitarist—those artists were Chet (of course!), the Beatles and the Monkees. I realize that I might well have just raised a few eyebrows by putting the Monkees in this list.

Still, I'll stand steadfastly by my love for Chet, The Beatles and the Monkees, and I'll point out the common thread that connected them—their use of electric guitars made by the Gretsch company. Chet's decades-long endorsement of Gretsch would become one of the major highlights of his career, and it led to the Beatles' lead guitarist George Harrison using Chet Atkins Gretsch models during the band's early years. Harrison never formally endorsed Gretsch, but his use of the company's guitars led many other 1960s musicians to use them as well, including the Monkees. In fact, The Monkees *did* formally endorse Gretsch after they had become so successful—in 1966 and 1967, the company manufactured a Monkees model guitar. "That Great Gretsch Sound" was the company's longtime slogan, and as far as I was concerned, Chet, the Beatles and the Monkees were three artists who proved that slogan to be true beyond the shadow of a doubt.

The look and the sound of the Gretsch electric guitars that Chet, the Beatles and the Monkees were playing ended up captivating me as much as Chet's playing had when I first heard him. As my musical career progressed, I felt that I just *had* to have my own Gretsch. In the early 1980s, I bought a 1969 Chet Atkins Nashville model, and it became the guitar that I used more than any other over the years. I became a decent flatpicking guitarist, certainly good enough to confidently accompany my own singing. I never even came close to being able to approximate Chet's fingerpicking style—but even though my level of talent on the guitar was far removed from that of my biggest musical hero, I was very proud to be playing a Gretsch that bore his name. In fact, I used the guitar so much that I bought another 1969 Nashville in 2001 so that I could have a second one for backup.

On June 30, 2001, I was driving to a local music store in Columbus to pick up that guitar after it had first been set up for me. As I was driving, I heard on the radio that Chet had passed away, and the news hit me just about as hard as the death of a beloved family member would have. I called Mom and Dad, and they felt Chet's loss every bit as keenly as I had. We had never tried to arrange a face-to-face meeting with Chet, so it might sound strange to you that his passing affected us so deeply. I guess that the best explanation I can offer for this is that we had been touched by Chet's music in a way that made a face-to-face meeting unnecessary—that music had been such a major part of our lives for so long that Chet somehow *was* just like family to us. Time has not lessened this connection in any way, and Dad and I still think of Chet fondly every time that we pick up our own guitars to play.

And in the years since Chet passed, I have picked up my guitars more times than I can count. I've worked regularly in several bands in the central Ohio area, but the work that has meant the most to me is with a band that I formed in the mid–1990s called Rich Meaty Taste. In spite of our decidedly silly name, we've made a lot of music that I am very proud of. In mid–2001, we put together an American musical history program called *Songs of America*, and since then we've performed the show for many thousands of people at civic concerts, patriotic events and school assemblies. Chet's work had a big influence on me while we were crafting *Songs of America*, because he had covered so many of the songs that we decided to include in the program.

(By the way, I should point out that as we put together the show, we knew that it would be strange if a band called Rich Meaty Taste was performing many of the greatest musical works in U.S. history—so we've always booked the program as "RMT Presents *Songs of America*." But to both our amusement and embarrassment, every now and again the full band name does get connected to the show.)

Over the years, the band has also worked on recording a wealth of original material. Our third CD entitled *Thank You So Much*, was released in 2006, and it included "American Song," a number I wrote for the *Songs of America* program about our love for our country's musical history. It also included a song that I wrote to honor the two guitarists closest to my heart. That song was an instrumental called "For Dad and Chet"—at one point in the song, I quoted a few notes from two of Chet's most famous recorded works, "Country Gentleman" and "Black Mountain Rag."

In addition to becoming a singer/guitarist, I also decided to become an author—my first two books *Abraham Lincoln on Screen* (2009) and *The Batman Filmography* (2013). After those two works were finished, I realized that I wanted to bring my musical interests and my writing interests together and create a book about my biggest musical hero, Chet Atkins.

But this does not mean that this book is solely about me finding a way to bring two of my greatest passions together—I really believe this is a book that Chet's legacy richly deserves. There are a number of wonderful books about Chet, and I own every one of them. But none of these books provide a detailed study of Chet's incredible work as a recording artist.

Introduction

The book you are now holding is meant to be that study—it is an analysis and appreciation of the most successful and noteworthy recorded songs of Chet Atkins. It chronicles the highlights of Chet's over 50-year tenure as a guitarist, singer, songwriter, and record producer, and this chronicle reveals a body of work that is truly unmatched in the history of modern musical entertainment.

Here is one thing that the book is *not*. It is not a complete Chet Atkins discography. The amount of material that Chet recorded during his career is nothing short of extraordinary—between the mid–1940s and the late 1990s he released around 100 albums, as well as over 100 singles. Of course, all of those releases add up to a mountain of individual songs. If I had tried to provide a rundown of every Chet album and every Chet single, and every last song on those albums and singles, I would have ended up writing a book that would have a *lot* longer. Worse yet, I would have ended up writing a book that did not allow me to really focus on Chet's most important recorded songs, the ones that best capture his genius.

And I'm happy to report that there are a number of excellent sites on the Internet that provide complete Chet Atkins discographies. So if you wish to study a more comprehensive list of Chet recordings than this book provides, you will have to look no farther than your computer.

Here are a few more things that the book is not. It is not any kind of in-depth personal biography of Chet. And it is not a guitar instruction book—though it discusses certain elements of Chet's guitar technique, it is much more about listening to Chet than it is about studying up to play like him. And it is not about the recordings that featured Chet in the capacity of sideman or non-performing producer—I feel that Chet's admirers around the world, myself included, are far more interested in what he accomplished as a star performer than what he accomplished while he was attending to those background roles.

Our journey through Chet's greatest recorded songs starts with a look at Chet's life and career, his most well-known guitars, his playing style, and his recording practices. We work our way through Chet's over half-century as a recording artist, closely examining 137 of his songs that serious Chet fans and music critics consider to be among his absolute best.

I should say a few words about the selection process of those songs. A project such as this cannot be completed without at least some degree of subjectivity, but I want to let you know that I did not just rely on my own personal tastes to complete this task. I consulted with a number of very knowledgeable Chet fans to get their opinions on just which of his recorded songs *they* considered to be his greatest and most important. Hopefully you will find most all of your favorites in here. But I have to admit, it is entirely possible that I might not have included a recorded song of Chet's that you feel is absolutely essential—after all, Mister Guitar's music is so incredible that one could convincingly argue for the greatness of literally hundreds upon hundreds of his songs.

One Life, Six Strings

The Life and Career

How does history remember Chet Atkins? Well, most encyclopedic works begin their summation of his life and career by stating he was a "country guitarist." Of course, using these words to describe Chet is by no means completely wrong—after all, he began his career as a guitarist playing country music, and as that career went on for decade after decade, he continued to play country music.

But this description is also *far* from right, because calling Chet a "country guitarist" does not come even slightly close to capturing the essence of this man who covered such an astonishing amount of musical ground. Yes, Chet played country, but he also played jazz, blues, pop, rock, classical, easy listening and gospel—and he played these styles with an authority that made *all* of them his own.

I suppose that it would come across as a bit confusing if these encyclopedic works elected to describe Chet as a "country/jazz/blues/pop/rock/classical/easy listening/gospel guitarist." And since country music was the style that got him started and helped to keep him going for so long, I guess I should just accept the standard description of him as a "country guitarist." But this is *my* book about Chet Atkins, so I'm now going to offer my own description of him.

Chet Atkins was a giant of the guitar, a player so versatile that he could never really be confined to any one particular musical style. In fact, his talent as a guitarist was *so* amazing that his name literally became synonymous with his instrument. Millions of people around the world knew him by his nickname of "Mister Guitar," and his endorsement deals with the Gretsch and Gibson companies led to the manufacture of untold numbers of Chet Atkins model guitars. The musical legacy that Chet Atkins left to the world is both profound and everlasting—because just as long as there are people on this earth who enjoy playing the guitar and listening to guitar music, there is going be an audience for his genius.

Of course, geniuses have to come into this world the regular way just like the rest of us. On June 20, 1924, Chester Burton Atkins was born to parents James Arley Atkins and Ida Sharp Atkins on the Atkins' 50-acre farm near the town of Luttrell, Tennessee. The Atkins family was a very musically talented clan. In addition to maintaining his family's farm, James worked as a music teacher, a piano tuner and an evangelistic singer. Also, all of Chester's siblings sang and played musical instruments. Chester's oldest sibling was his half-brother Jim, who was 12 years his senior. Jim was a talented guitarist, and young Chester's fascination with the guitar began when he first listened to his half-brother play.

This fascination deepened when Chester visited Knoxville, Tennessee, with his mother when he was six years old. In Knoxville, he happened to see a blind man singing and playing the guitar for loose change on the streets of the city. This street performer had a profound effect on Chester—he made the boy want to be a musician more than anything else in the world.

Around this time, Jim left Luttrell to live with the boys' Uncle Joe in Nebraska. There Jim got his first noteworthy job as a musician—he was hired to play guitar on radio station KMMJ. Chester missed Jim, but he was thrilled that his half-brother was finding success in the field of music. Chester resolved that like Jim, he would become a musician and play on the radio. Sadly, not long after Jim left, Chester had to say goodbye to another member of his family—his parents divorced in 1931, and his father moved away from Luttrell.

Chester continued to keep an eye out for any chance he might have to mold himself into a musician. His mother remarried in 1932, and his stepfather Willie Strevel ended up in possession of an old Sears and Roebuck Silvertone guitar. Chester convinced Willie to give that guitar to him in a trade. (The boy had two guns that had wound up belonging to him, and he gave them to Willie for the guitar.)

Chester also managed to get ahold of a beat-up fiddle from Uncle Joe. The boy soon learned to play that fiddle, and he used it to give his first-ever public performances. The most memorable of these was Chester's very first public performance, which took place at his school when he was just ten years old. At that performance, he played the traditional folk song "Wildwood Flower" for the school's entire student body. At all of Chester's early performances, his older brother Lowell accompanied him on guitar.

Unfortunately, Chester had to deal with major health issues when he was young—he suffered from asthma, which many times became so acute that he was forced to miss school. When Chester was eleven years old, his condition became so grave that his parents feared he might die. Chester's father decided to take the boy to live with him at his home near Columbus, Georgia—the hope was that Georgia's drier climate would improve the boy's health. This change of climate ended up working, and Chester's asthma problems lessened considerably.

Chester spent a year and a half in Georgia, and during that time he constantly worked on improving his guitar skills—it was then that he discovered that he would rather fingerpick the instrument's strings when he played instead of strumming them with a standard flat pick. He also started to come to the decision that the guitar would be his main instrument, not the fiddle.

Since his asthma had improved, Chester was able to return home to Luttrell—but he had grown so accustomed to being in Georgia that he continued to go back there to live for long stretches. One thing that Chester loved about living at his father's home was that he could listen to his father's radio. The reception was much better than any radio Chester could have listened to in Luttrell, so he had a whole new world of music and entertainment that he could be taking in.

At this time, Jim's musical career was progressing extremely well, and he was featured as a singer on the popular radio program *National Barn Dance* broadcast nationwide by WLS in Chicago, Illinois. Chester got to hear his half-brother on the radio for the first time, and he was so inspired by Jim's success that he worked even harder at honing his own musical skills. When he was fifteen years old, Chester heard a performer on the radio that ended up being an even *bigger* inspiration to him than Jim had been—a program called *Boone Country Jamboree* broadcast by WLW in Cincinnati, Ohio, featured singer/guitarist Merle Travis.

Merle played the guitar with a fingerpicking style that he had learned from guitarists in his home state of Kentucky when he was a young man. Picking his guitar's strings with his thumb and index finger, Merle could play a song's melody, and at the same time accompany that melody with rhythmic patterns played on the guitar's lower strings. The guitar pick that Merle used to play this style was a thumbpick, the kind of pick that is molded to fit around a player's thumb. When Merle fingerpicked the guitar while using a thumbpick, it sounded like two guitarists playing together, one handling the melody and another providing accompaniment. And Merle could quickly shift from fingerpicking to single-note soloing, since his thumbpick could also be used just like a regularly held flatpick.

Hearing Merle play struck Chester like a bolt of lightning—he had found the style of guitar playing that he had been looking for ever since he had begun to seriously devote himself to the guitar. Fingerpicking opened up a much wider realm of musical possibilities on the guitar than flatpicking alone ever could—it allowed a guitarist to play a number of different musical parts at the same time, much like the way pianists could on *their* instrument. Chester's musical path was clear now—he diligently worked on developing his own style of guitar playing based on Merle's fingerpicking style. That style would have such a profound, lasting influence on Chester that it would be impossible to figure out just how many thumbpicks he would go through over the next six decades.

Of course, there were musicians other than Travis who continued to influence Chester. Jim worked with guitarist Les Paul during the late 1930s, playing rhythm guitar and singing lead vocals in the Les Paul Trio. Les' flashy, innovative solo playing made quite an impression on Chester—Chester infused his own style with some of Les' flash, and this served as a nice counterpoint to the self-accompanying fingerstyle playing he had picked up from Travis.

Chester's skill as a guitarist was growing by leaps and bounds—when he was sixteen, he even got to realize his dream of playing on the radio just like his half-brother had done so many times. A preacher who was a friend of Chester's father gave radio sermons on the Columbus, Georgia, station WRBL, and he had Chester perform gospel songs on the guitar during several of his broadcasts. Chester even got his first fan letter from the performances he did on WRBL.

After completing his sophomore year of high school in Georgia, Chester decided that it was time to leave school for good and devote himself to his musical career full-time. He returned to Tennessee, and he got a job playing fiddle for the duo of Bill Carlisle and Archie Campbell, who performed on Knoxville radio station WNOX. In addition to doing radio shows with Carlisle and Campbell, Chester did numerous live performances with the duo at cities and towns throughout the eastern part of Tennessee. Chester was eighteen years old, and he was now officially a professional musician.

WNOX would end up being the place that really set Chester's career in motion. Not long after Chester had been hired to fiddle for Carlisle and Campbell, the station's program director, Lowell Blanchard, heard the young man play the guitar. Blanchard immediately recognized Chester's talent on the instrument and hired him as WNOX's staff guitarist. Chester was given access to the station's music library, and he devoted himself to building his repertoire.

While learning new tunes to play for WNOX, he heard recordings by the European jazz guitarist Django Reinhardt for the first time. Reinhardt had been seriously burned in a fire when he was eighteen years old, and the fingers on his left hand (his fretting hand) were so badly injured that doctors believed he would never play guitar again. But Django did indeed find a way to return to the guitar—he used only the index and middle fingers of his left hand for all of his solo work. Django's blindingly fast, musically complex playing brought him much acclaim during the 1930s and 1940s. It also made a great impression on Chester, so much so that he began working elements of the guitarist's style into his own playing.

Sometime in the early 1940s, Chester traveled to New York City to visit Jim, who at the time was regularly performing on bandleader Fred Waring's nationally broadcast NBC radio program. Chester got to spend several unforgettable days with his half-brother taking in the sights and sounds of the Big Apple. As Chester prepared to say goodbye to Jim and return to Tennessee, Jim surprised him with a once-in-a-lifetime gift. Jim owned a Gibson L-10 acoustic guitar that had originally been manufactured specifically for Les Paul in 1938, and he gave this guitar to Chester. For the first time in his life, Chester owned a truly high-quality guitar—he loved playing it so much that he would use it to record some of his greatest early songs, and he would keep it for the rest of his life.

WNOX had been very good to Chester, but he felt that it was time to set his sights much higher than the success he had found in east Tennessee. Merle Travis had left WLW in Cincinnati, and the station was looking for a performer to replace him. Jim helped Chester to get an audition at WLW, and the station hired him. Chester moved to Cincinnati to start his new job, but unfortunately, WLW was not happy with his playing—the station fired him after only six months because they felt he was not country-sounding enough.

Even though Chester's stint at WLW ended up being a disappointment, he made personal and professional connections there that would last his entire life. First and most importantly, he met Leona Johnson, who performed on WLW with her twin sister, Lois, in a singing duo. Chester and Leona fell in love, and they married in 1946.

Also, he forged a very close personal and musical bond with guitarist Henry "Homer" Haynes and mandolinist Kenneth "Jethro" Burns at WLW. Chester had first met Homer and Jethro when they were all working at WNOX, but it was while they were all living together in Cincinnati that their friendship became so deep-rooted. Homer and Jethro performed together in a country comedy duo, but they were also first-rate musicians. They were huge fans of Django Reinhardt just like Chester was, and the trio began to create music that was inspired by the guitarist. Over the next few years, they would record quite a few of their Django-inspired songs—and several these songs would end up being regarded as some of Chester's greatest recordings of all time. (Incidentally, Chester's connection to Jethro ended up going beyond just music and friendship—it actually became family when Jethro married Leona's twin sister, Lois.)

Chester left Cincinnati and took a job with radio station WPTF in Raleigh, North Carolina, but he didn't stay there for long. Country music star Red Foley had been picked to replace Roy Acuff as the host of the Grand Ole Opry concert series/radio program in Nashville, Tennessee, and Chester was able to arrange an audition with Red to become part of the star's backing band. Red was very impressed with Chester's guitar playing, so much so that he hired Chester to go to Nashville with him to perform on the Opry.

The Grand Ole Opry was the pinnacle of country music success—the Opry was first broadcast by the Nashville radio station WSM in the 1920s, and by the late 1930s it had become so successful that portions of it were broadcast nationwide by NBC Radio. In 1943, the Opry had moved to its permanent home in the Ryman Auditorium in downtown Nashville, leading the city to become known as "the country music capital of the world." Chester was going to get to appear on the Opry, and Nashville was sure to offer him other musical opportunities. Chester had finally made the big time—or so he thought.

But it turned out that Chester hadn't made it over all of the bumps on his road to success just yet. Red had promised Chester that he would be given solo guitar segments during the nationwide-broadcast portions of the Opry, but these segments ended up making very little impression on the boisterous Opry crowd. Consequently, the Opry's advertising sponsors ordered Chester's segments cut from the show. Chester was so distraught by this decision that he quit Red's band altogether.

Nashville did end up offering Chester another notable musical opportunity right after he quit working with Red—he had his first official recording session as a solo artist in the city. Chester recorded two songs, "Guitar Blues (Pickin' the Blues)" and "Brown Eyes Cryin' in the Rain," for the Nashville-based label Bullet Records. The songs were released as a 78 single in 1946, but they achieved very little success in terms of sales or airplay.

Chester's first stint in Nashville had come to an undistinguished end—he left the city and took a job at radio station WRVA in Richmond, Virginia. Unfortunately, this job turned out to be yet another short-lived one—while Chester was at WRVA his asthma returned, and it flared up so badly that he could not work. The station let him go, and his once-bright future as a musician seemed to have gone dark.

Chester regained his musical footing when he took a job at radio station KWTO in Springfield, Missouri. His demeanor and his musical style fit in well with the station, and he gave many live performances throughout the station's listening area that were very well-received. The move to Missouri gave Chester and Leona the chance to enjoy some financial and domestic stability for the first time in their marriage—there Leona gave birth to their first and only child, a daughter named Merle, in March 1947.

Chester's time in Missouri gave him a new name as well as a daughter. KWTO executive Si Siman was the first person to call Chester "Chet," and the nickname caught on so well with everyone that it quickly became Chester's professional name. Siman was so impressed with Chet's talent that he began to work on securing the guitarist a recording contract. But Chet's time at KWTO came to a very unexpected end—Siman took a long vacation from the station, and while he was away another station executive fired Chet for not sounding country enough.

By now, Chet had made enough of a name for himself as a guitarist that it did not take him long to find a new job. He was hired to work for the western bandleader/vocalist Shorty Thompson at radio station KOA in Denver, Colorado. This job would also be short-lived, but this time around, the circumstances that led Chet out of his current assignment were favorable. Chet had been contacted by a representative of Stephen H. Sholes, RCA Victor's director of country music operations—the label was interested in signing Chet to a recording contract because they hoped they could mold him into their own version of Merle Travis, who at the time was racking up hit after hit for Capitol Records. In the summer of 1947, Chet left

Shorty and KOA so that he could do his first recording session for RCA in Chicago, Illinois.

Chet recorded eight songs at his August 11, 1947, session held at the RCA Victor Studio in Chicago. Since RCA was trying use Chet to emulate Merle Travis's hits, five of the songs recorded that day were vocal numbers. Chet was definitely stepping out of his comfort zone for the label—he was first and foremost a guitarist, not a lead-singing frontman. But if RCA was willing to give him a contract, he was willing to try to be a frontman.

The songs that featured Chet on vocals were by no means bad, but they were by no means captivating either—they basically proved that Chet's main strength as a performer was not in his singing. The songs recorded that day that really stood out were the guitar instrumentals that he himself had written. But in the end, *none* of the songs that Chet recorded ended up selling well when RCA released them as 78 singles. Despite this lack of commercial success, Steve Sholes and RCA recognized Chet's great potential as an artist, so they resolved to find ways to keep working with him.

In late 1947, Steve had Chet travel to New York City so that he could play guitar for a variety of recording sessions that were being held at RCA's studios there. The label was stockpiling new recordings because it seemed certain that the American Federation of Musicians would be going on strike against the major American record companies at the beginning of the next year, which meant that musicians would not consent to doing any new studio work. (This strike did come to pass, and it lasted through almost all of 1948.)

While Chet was in New York City, Steve also had Chet do two sessions of his own for RCA. These sessions yielded eight songs, five of them Chet-sung vocal numbers and three of them instrumentals. All of the songs featured one particularly noteworthy supporting musician—Chet's half-brother Jim played rhythm guitar on them. Again, none of Chet's recordings ended up selling well when RCA released them as 78 singles, so his prospects as a solo recording artist did not seem to be particularly good.

Worse yet, RCA's general interest in Chet did nothing to keep him working in the short term, because the American Federation of Musicians strike kept him from being able to do any kind of studio work for the label for all of 1948. Out of employment options, Chet returned to WNOX in Knoxville, and he was so depressed over his dreams of stardom coming to an end that he considered quitting show business. But it turned out that Chet's star was just about to rise—the popular family singing group the Carter Sisters decided to move to WNOX, and there Chet formed an official musical partnership with them that would propel his career to new heights.

The Carters consisted of sisters Anita, Helen, June, and their mother Maybelle, and their traditional, acoustic-based country sound provided a perfect musical landscape for Chet's inventive guitar playing. The team of "The Carter Sisters, Mother Maybelle and Chet Atkins" became so popular at WNOX that they were able to earn a substantial amount of money by making personal appearances throughout the station's listening area. The act was so successful that in mid–1949, KWTO in Springfield, Missouri lured them away from WNOX with a lucrative financial offer. Once at KWTO, they enjoyed the same level of acclaim that they had found at KNOX. Chet also got to re-establish ties with all of his friends at KWTO after being fired from the station so unceremoniously two years earlier.

Eventually, KWTO proved to not be a big enough market for the popularity of the Carters and Chet either—WSM invited them to Nashville to become members of the Grand Ole Opry. For a short time, it seemed that Opry success was going to elude Chet once again, because the Nashville local musicians union had demanded that the Carters join the Opry without Chet—the union felt that the Carters should draw from the wealth of backing musician talent already in the city. So ironically, the very city that Chet would bring so much positive change to over the coming decades originally tried to keep him from coming to town. But fortunately for both Chet and Nashville, the Carters held firm—they decreed that they would not come to Nashville unless Chet was with them. The union relented, so the Carters and Chet moved to Nashville and joined the Opry in mid–1950.

This time around, Chet really *had* made the big time. His success with the Carters was so great that he made the decision to purchase his first truly world-class guitar. In 1950, Chet had the renowned guitar maker John D'Angelico of Brooklyn, New York, build him a D'Angelico Excel. Chet himself installed two pickups on the guitar so it could be used as an electric as well as an acoustic instrument.

Chet's growing success was not just confined to his work with the Carters—his career as a solo artist was finally beginning to win recognition. Several of the Django Reinhardt-inspired instrumentals he had recently recorded with Homer and Jethro had been released as 78 singles by RCA Victor, and these instrumentals garnered a decent amount of sales and airplay. Chet-penned numbers like "Gallopin' on the Guitar" recorded in February 1949 and "Main Street Breakdown" recorded in October 1949 were reaching a much wider audience than any of his previous recordings had—and this put Chet well on his way to building a fan base that would stick with him for decades.

In fact, "Gallopin' on the Guitar" ended up being so well-received that its title was used to bill Chet himself for a number of years. Many of his early to mid–1950s singles were released under the billing "Chet Atkins and His Galloping Guitar." And Chet's first-ever album also tied into the "Galloping Guitar" moniker—in 1953, RCA released a collection of eight of his recordings on 10-inch record format entitled *Chet Atkins' Gallopin' Guitar*. Needless to say, "Gallopin' on the Guitar" was one of the numbers that was prominently featured on this album—the song closed out its second side.

Ironically, the act that was responsible for bringing Chet to Nashville started to wind down not long after they had made their move to the city. The team of The Carter Sisters, Mother Maybelle and Chet Atkins began performing together less and less frequently during the early 1950s. This change in their performance schedule was by no means an indication of their lack of popularity. On the contrary, the Carters and Chet both enjoyed continued success together and apart, but their careers had simply started moving in different directions. Chet's popularity as a solo performer was on the rise, and the Carters had to structure their careers around their own busy family schedule. So as Chet started to make Nashville his home, he also started to see that his future as a musician would not be tied to the Carters or anyone else—he truly was a solo act, and a very potent one at that.

During this time period when Chet was first becoming widely recognized as a renowned solo performer, he also was achieving success in another realm of the music world—his accomplishments as a songwriter were quite impressive. He continued to write songs throughout his career that were every bit as memorable as "Gallopin' on the Guitar" and "Main Street Breakdown,"—this point will be made abundantly clear by the substantial number of Chet-penned numbers examined throughout this book.

One of the most obvious signs that Chet was achieving a considerable level of success was that his first large-scale fan club had been established. Margaret Fields and her husband, Don, had been big fans of Chet's ever since the late 1940s, and they convinced him to let them start the Chet Atkins Fan Club. The club ran from 1950 until 1960, and during that time it held eight conventions in Nashville—these conventions were attended not only by Chet's most ardent fans, but also by Chet. The club also produced a newsletter called *Gallopin' Guitar News* which gave Chet the opportunity to keep members informed about his many different musical projects. Most of the newsletter's issues have survived to the present day, and they provide a fascinating glimpse into some of the most exciting and productive years of Chet's career.

In fact, it could be argued that the 1950s were *the* most exciting and productive years of Chet's career. Chet himself offered evidence to support this viewpoint—in his 2001 autobiography *Chet Atkins: Me and My Guitars*, Chet stated "I believe this period, the early to mid–1950s, was my most productive time." He elaborated on this, saying "I was at the peak of my abilities, playing with authority and confidence, and all the different guitar sounds and types of music I'd listened to jelled into a style I knew was my own."

There are many of Chet's recordings from this period that could also be offered up to support Chet's belief that he had reached a truly special moment in his career during the 1950s—but we really only need to pick one to drive this point home. In March 1953, Chet recorded an instrumental he had co-written with the well-known songwriter Boudleaux Bryant called "Country Gentleman." "Country Gentleman" was an irresistibly jaunty number that Chet fans loved from the moment it was first released as a single, and it would continue to grow in stature over the years. In fact, it eventually became so popular with Chet's fans that it basically became his unofficial theme song.

Chet's growing success led him to enter into a guitar endorsement deal that would have a hugely positive effect on his career for the next quarter century. In early 1954, the Gretsch Company contacted Chet through their guitarist/designer Jimmie Webster to see if he would consider officially endorsing their company. Gretsch and Chet came to an agreement to design Gretsch electric guitar models that would bear Chet's name—and after the release of those models, they would then become the instruments that Chet would always use for recordings and personal appearances.

Throughout that year, Gretsch and Chet worked on designing their guitars, and the instruments they would come up with would turn out to be a resounding success. The Gretsch 6120 Chet Atkins Hollow Body model and the Gretsch 6121 Chet Atkins Solid Body model were released before the end of the year, and they sold extremely well right out of the gate. The 6120 was the model that Chet was directly involved in designing, and it ended up being the more popular of the two models.

In late 1954, Chet recorded the song that would end up being his first hit record. That song was "Mister Sandman," a number that had been a number one hit for the female vocal quartet the Chordettes earlier that same year. Chet's recording of the song didn't reach the very top of the charts like the Chordettes' version did, but it still caught on with the public very well—it reached the number 13 spot on the U.S. country single charts in early 1955.

And Chet had another hit record right on the heels of "Mister Sandman"—he recorded a guitar duet of the song "Silver Bell" with one of RCA Victor's biggest stars, singer/guitarist Hank Snow. In the spring of 1955, that record reached the number 15 spot on the U.S. country single charts. After all his years of hard work, Chet had finally reached a level of success that could really only be summed up through the use of one particular word—and that word was "star." Chet Atkins was now a star, and he would continue to be one for many, many years to come.

The relatively new medium of television played a major role in helping to establish Chet as a star. In the mid–1950s, several country music TV programs endorsed by the Grand Ole Opry were created, and Chet performed on them. One of these programs, *Stars of the Grand Ole Opry*, was originally filmed on 35mm color film—so pristine, motion picture-quality copies of that program are still in existence. Chet appeared on the program a number of times—so it is possible for present-day Chet fans to seek out film clips of him in his early glory, playing some of his most well-known songs on his newly manufactured Gretsch guitars.

Chet would make so many television appearances over the next four decades that they would become a treasure trove of Chet history that rivaled the size and scope of his recorded work. For example, Chet recorded a version of a song entitled "The Poor People of Paris (Jean's Song)" that became his first single to appear on the U.S. pop single charts. (Incidentally, this success offered further evidence that his fan base was continuing to grow well beyond just country music fans.) Chet played the number when he appeared on several television programs during the 1950s—these appearances included the ABC Television Network program *The Purina Grand Ole Opry* on April 28, 1956, and the NBC Television Network program *The Today Show* on April 4, 1957. Copies of those shows are also still in existence.

In addition to Chet's career as a musician taking off, his career as a music producer was also beginning to grow by leaps and bounds. Steve Sholes, RCA Victor's director of country music operations, had been relying on Chet to contract musicians for many of the label's Nashville sessions—Chet even began producing some of these sessions if Sholes could not attend them himself. Before too long, Chet's duties as a producer for RCA had become every bit as important as his activities as a musician for the label.

By the mid–1950s, rock and roll music had begun its phenomenal rise to popularity, and the style was well on its way to completely changing the landscape of popular music. Of course, Chet was keenly aware of this change—in fact, he ended up playing a part in launching the career of Elvis Presley, the performer who was at the center of the rock and roll revolution. Chet helped to organize Elvis's first-ever session for RCA Victor after the singer had been signed to the label. That session was held at RCA's Nashville studio on January 10, 1956, and it produced "Heartbreak Hotel," Elvis's first-ever number one hit on the U.S. pop charts. Chet played rhythm guitar on that record as well.

The incredible success that the signing of Elvis Presley had brought to RCA Victor in the mid–1950s ended up being the catalyst for some major changes to the label's corporate structure. Steve Sholes had overseen Elvis's move to the label, which naturally led to Steve's prestige within the company taking a quantum leap. Consequently, on September 1, 1957, RCA promoted Steve to head of the label's pop singles division. Since Chet had been working as Steve's assistant for the past five years helping to organize and produce the label's sessions held in Nashville, he was given Steve's old job.

Chet's tenure as the head of RCA's Nashville division was astonishingly successful and influential. He directed many of the country artists he produced to adopt a more polished, pop style on their records, and these records sold so well that they ended up giving birth to a new style of country music known as the "Nashville Sound." This blending of country and pop styles forever changed the face of country music, and helped to keep the genre commercially viable in the wake of the rock and roll revolution.

Steve and Chet's increased clout at RCA led them to be able to convince the label to build a stand-alone studio for their Nashville recording sessions. Since 1954, RCA's first Nashville studio had been located in rented space inside of the Methodist Television, Radio & Film Commission. Not surprisingly, it had become increasingly difficult over the years for RCA to maintain their Nashville studio at that site. After all, musicians and record producers were used to working into the late hours of the night, and perhaps having an alcoholic drink or two while they worked—this was obviously not a working environment that sat well with a Methodist organization.

Chet helped RCA to design the new studio, which was located in downtown Nashville. The studio would eventually become known as "RCA Studio B" after RCA built a second Nashville studio in 1964—but during the first years of its existence, it was simply known as "RCA Studios." Chet would oversee the production of countless records made by his RCA artists at the studio—and a *lot* of these records turned out to be big hits. Incidentally, more than a few of these records featured Chet playing supporting guitar parts. But luckily for those people who were fans of Chet's work as a solo act, he would still continue to make his own music at RCA Studios as well.

In 1958, Chet's song "Country Gentleman" actually *did* become an official moniker for him. That year, Gretsch released a new guitar model called the Chet Atkins Country Gentleman. The Chet Atkins Country Gentleman was manufactured by Gretsch until 1981, when Chet left Gretsch to enter into an endorsement deal with the Gibson Guitar Corporation. Then Gibson manufactured its own version of the Chet Atkins Country Gentleman until 2005. In 2007, the Atkins family licensed Chet's name back to Gretsch, and the company again began manufacturing their original version of the Chet Atkins Country Gentleman. So, well over 60 years after the initial release of the song "Country Gentleman," you can *still* buy a brand-new guitar bearing the song's name.

Chet had a few singles that had made the charts, but as time went on, his albums became the true focal point of his recording career. LPs such as *Chet Atkins in Three Dimensions* (1955), *Finger-Style Guitar* (1956), and *Hi-Fi in Focus* (1957) featured songs from an incredibly wide range of musical styles. These albums sold well, and very much helped to solidify his reputation as a world-class guitarist.

By the late 1950s and early 1960s, Chet's albums weren't just selling well, they were selling *very* well. His 1958 release *Chet Atkins at Home* climbed to number 21 on the U.S. album charts, giving him his first-ever charting LP. His 1960 release *Teensville* reached the number 16 spot on the U.S. album charts, giving Chet his second charting LP. And then his 1961 release *Chet Atkins' Workshop* climbed to number

7 on the U.S. album charts, making it his highest-charting album of all time, and only one to ever break the top ten.

Chet's success did not lead him to become complacent in terms of the musical projects that he took on—on the contrary, he kept on working to broaden his musical horizons by playing as many different styles as he could. Also, he constantly experimented with new guitar and recording technology. For example, on many of the songs found on *Teensville*, Chet used a modified DeArmond foot-operated pedal on the recording that ended up being the forerunner of the modern wah-wah pedal. Chet adapted a DeArmond volume pedal by replacing the pedal's volume potentiometer that controlled loudness with a tone pot that moved from extreme bass to extreme treble. When the pedal was moved, it gave Chet's guitar a crying sound similar to that of a trumpet note being muted and then unmuted. Chet's modified pedal was the first of its kind ever used with an electric guitar.

By the time that Chet had gained widespread fame as a guitarist, he was primarily known as an electric player—however, he had always maintained a keen interest in the acoustic guitar as well. That interest led him to want to learn more and more about the nylon-string acoustic guitar, an instrument commonly referred to as a "classical guitar" since it was often used for the playing of classical music works. Since Chet had always been a fingerstyle guitarist, his playing translated extremely well to the fingerpicking techniques normally used by classical guitar players. Consequently, he began devoting an increasing amount of his playing time to the classical guitar.

In late 1959, Chet decided to record an entire album of songs that featured him playing the classical guitar. He chose to title the album *The Other Chet Atkins* since it showcased an aspect of his playing that was markedly different from his electric work. His distinguished tenure as a nylon-string acoustic guitarist had only just begun with this particular album—he would use classical guitars for many of his recordings and performances throughout the rest of his career.

Chet's mystique was given an unexpected boost by the incredible success of The Beatles when the band first came to the United States in early 1964. The Beatles had been fans of Chet for years, especially the band's lead guitarist, George Harrison. This admiration ended up manifesting itself in Harrison's choice of guitars. In early 1963, right as the Beatles began to achieve their spectacular success, Harrison decided to make a major upgrade to his guitar arsenal—he purchased a Gretsch Chet Atkins Country Gentleman, and he favored using this model through much of 1964. But the Country Gentleman was not the only Chet Gretsch model that Harrison ended up becoming attached to—in late 1963 he purchased a Gretsch Chet Atkins Tennessean, and he frequently used this model throughout 1964 and 1965.

Of course, this meant that untold numbers of guitarists all over the world were seeing Harrison playing Gretsch guitars bearing Chet's name, so sales of Chet Atkins Gretsch models exploded in the mid–1960s. Harrison and the Beatles never ended up officially endorsing Chet Gretsches, but they really didn't have to—their use of those guitars turned out to be a huge unofficial advertisement for both the Gretsch Company and Chet himself.

In late 1965, Chet returned this favor by recording an entire album of Beatles songs entitled *Chet Atkins Picks on the Beatles*. The record featured Chet performing 12 instrumental versions of numbers written by Lennon and McCartney. Chet did not elect to perform any Harrison-written Beatle songs on this particular album, but

Harrison still ended up having a connection to the project—he penned the liner notes, in which he highly praised Chet's talent and the manner in which Chet had interpreted some of his band's songs.

The Beatles might have taken the music world by storm, but Chet's career was still moving along at a wonderful clip. In 1965, he had a top five country hit with his recording of "Yakety Axe," a guitar interpretation of his good friend Boots Randolph's saxophone instrumental "Yakety Sax." And he began a practice of recording excellent collaborative albums with a variety of prestigious artists—the first of these artists included Hank Snow, Arthur Fiedler and the Boston Pops, and Jerry Reed.

Of course, Chet's relationship with singer/songwriter/guitarist Jerry Reed went far beyond just the two of them recording a few albums together. Jerry's skill as a guitarist was every bit as great as his skill as a singer/songwriter—in fact, he was an *incredibly* gifted fingerstyle player, very much on the same level with Chet. The bond that Chet and Jerry shared through being two of the world's great fingerstyle guitarists led them to forge an incredibly successful musical partnership with one another—and this partnership would end up lasting all the way from the early 1960s through the late 1990s. After signing Jerry to RCA Victor in 1964, Chet produced a number of Jerry's recordings that became chart-topping hits. And Chet recorded dozens of Jerry's guitar compositions for his own albums.

It should be noted that the relationship between Chet and Jerry went beyond being just a mutually beneficial musical partnership—they also became very close personal friends, and both men would cherish that friendship for the rest of their lives.

Jerry also helped Chet to pair up with another one of his most trusted musical partners, guitarist Paul Yandell. Paul had been regularly working with Jerry since 1970, and Chet quickly became every bit as impressed by Paul's talent as Jerry had been. In fact, Paul would end up regularly working with Chet from the early 1970s all the way until the end of Chet's career. Simply put, Paul became Chet's right-hand man—not only did he provide steady accompaniment for Chet at countless recording sessions and live appearances for more than two decades, but he also became one of Chet's closest friends.

In addition to all of the work Chet was doing recording his own music and the music of his many RCA Victor artists, Chet still found the time to regularly make concert and television appearances. For example, during the 1960s and 1970s Chet toured with two of his close musical collaborators, saxophonist Boots Randolph and pianist Floyd Cramer—they hit the road together to perform a series of concerts known as "The Music Masters." And Chet performed on a myriad of television shows ranging from the PBS show *Evening at Pops* (where he performed with Arthur Fiedler and the Boston Pops) to the country music/comedy show *Hee Haw*. Chet's great popularity as a live performer provided him with the opportunity to travel all over the world throughout his career—public demand for his talent sent him not only around the United States, but also to many other countries.

By the late 1960s, Chet began pulling in quite a few awards for his work as a guitarist. In 1967, the Country Music Association named him Instrumentalist of the Year at the organization's first-ever awards ceremony. And the National Academy of Recording Arts and Sciences presented Chet with his first Grammy award in 1968—his album *Chet Atkins Picks the Best* won the Grammy Award for Best Pop Instrumental Performance. Over the years, Chet would receive many more awards from both of these institutions.

In 1973, Chet was presented with what was perhaps the most prestigious award of his career when he was inducted into the Country Music Hall of Fame. He was the youngest person to ever have received that honor. Chet had been a star for almost two decades now, but he was well on his way to becoming a legend.

But all of the good work he had been doing for the past twenty years certainly came at a price—in fact, over the years Chet had been working so hard as both a recording executive and a performing artist that he had been feeling more and more burned out. In 1973, things finally came to a head for Chet when he was diagnosed with colon cancer. He underwent surgery for his condition, and that surgery was successful. But he still felt that in light of the health problems he had faced, it was time for him to step away from the power position he had maintained at RCA Victor and to focus more on his own musical pursuits.

In 1974, Chet wrote his autobiography, *Country Gentleman*, with author Bill Neely. The book was an entertaining read, but it did not focus on the particulars of his incredible musical career nearly as much as it did on stories relating to his rural past. And of course, the book could not possibly have covered all of Chet's finest moments as a musician, because many of those moments were still yet to come.

Chet continued making collaborative albums with other artists, and some of those albums turned out to be among the very best he ever created. His two records with the legendary guitarist Les Paul, *Chester and Lester* (1976) and *Guitar Monsters* (1978), were commercially and critically very well-received. Another of Chet's wonderful collaborative albums was the 1980 release *Reflections*, which he did with the famed singer/guitarist Doc Watson.

By the early 1980s, he had decided that it was time to sever his ties with RCA Victor. This could not have been an easy decision for Chet—after all, he had been with RCA as an artist for about 35 years, and his staggeringly successful executive tenure with the label had led to the creation of country music's world-famous Nashville Sound. In other words, Chet had revolutionized country music both as an artist and a producer of other artists while he was with RCA—so it must have been hard for him to walk away from the company that he had shared so many musical triumphs with.

But walk away he did. Simply put, Chet felt that RCA had grown to be less supportive of his eclectic musical projects. For example, in 1981 he made an excellent collaborative album with the legendary jazz guitarist Lenny Breau entitled *Standard Brands*, and the label did almost nothing to promote that album's release. So he decided to find a new label, one that he felt would truly get behind his work. The label that Chet chose was Columbia Records, and he signed with them in 1983. On the whole, Chet's years with Columbia would certainly not be as prolific or groundbreaking as his long tenure with RCA had been. But Chet's time at Columbia would still produce a number of recordings that were every bit as wonderful as his best RCA recordings.

Chet's switch from RCA to Columbia was not the only major change he was making in his musical life. He had also decided to end his quarter-century relationship with Gretsch and sign an endorsement deal with Gibson. The main reason Chet left Gretsch was that the company was not interested in an idea for a new style of guitar that he had come up with. Over the years, Chet had devoted more and more of his playing time to the classical guitar during his concert appearances—and the problems he had encountered with a classical in terms of amplification and feedback had led him to want to create a new kind of guitar. This new guitar would be a solidbody, nylon-string classical outfitted with a built-in pickup—such a guitar would play much like a standard classical, and be able to be amplified with minimal feedback problems much like an electric.

Gretsch had no interest in developing or manufacturing Chet's solidbody acoustic guitar. Chet then took his idea to Gibson, and they *were* interested in its potential. So Chet left Gretsch for Gibson, and together they began work on building and marketing Chet's new instrument. In early 1982, this guitar model was ready to be unveiled to the public—it was named the Chet Atkins CE, the "CE" being an acronym for "classical electric." The CE was quickly embraced by nylon-string players, so it enjoyed strong sales upon its release. But no one was happier with the guitar model than Chet—he would regularly play and record with it for years to come.

In 1983, Chet fans Jim Ferron and Mark Pritcher formed an organization known as the Chet Atkins Appreciation Society. The Chet Atkins Appreciation Society provided fans with a means to share their enthusiasm for their musical hero—in 1983, it began regularly publishing a newsletter entitled *Mister Guitar*, and in 1985, it began holding yearly conventions in Nashville that Chet attended. (Since Chet's passing the organization has remained active, working to preserve and promote his legacy.)

Throughout his life, Chet had regretted never having any formal higher education. So in the early 1980s he lightheartedly created a C.G.P. degree for himself, which he said stood for "Certified Guitar Player." While the C.G.P. designation might have started as a bit of an in-joke, it stuck with Chet for the rest of his career—he was billed as "Chet Atkins C.G.P." on most all of his Columbia albums, and toward the end of his life he even awarded C.G.P. degrees to several of his guitarist friends.

Chet had been very interested in recording a new jazz album during the last few years he was with RCA Victor, but the label's lack of enthusiasm for his more musically ambitious projects kept that album from ever being made. Once Chet moved from RCA to Columbia, a label that was excited to support his new musical ventures, he was given the freedom to put his jazz album back at the top of his "to do" list. The album he made was entitled *Stay Tuned*, and it was essentially a musical summit meeting between Chet and a number of the 1980s' most prominent jazz and rock guitarists—it featured him performing duets with players such as George Benson, Earl Klugh, and Mark Knopfler.

Stay Tuned would very much end up being a blueprint for many of the albums that Chet recorded for Columbia—on these albums, Chet would collaborate with a variety of younger musicians from a wide spectrum of musical styles. Chet was seen as a legendary elder statesman by the entire music industry now, and there was no shortage of up-and-coming artists who were anxious to add a duet recording with Chet Atkins to their resume.

Chet might have been looking to the future by working with a variety of younger performers on many of his Columbia albums, but he very much looked to the past when he started working with famed author/radio personality Garrison Keillor. Garrison was the host of the popular radio show *A Prairie Home Companion* produced by Minnesota Public Radio, and in 1986 Chet began regularly performing on the show. Chet admired Garrison's talent both as an author and as a radio host, and performing on *A Prairie Home Companion* very much reminded him of his early years playing live on the radio. Chet's involvement with *A Prairie Home Companion* ended up being beneficial to his career in that it introduced the show's huge number of listeners, many of whom had never heard of him before, to his music.

The growing popularity of cable television during the 1980s also helped Chet to reach a new generation of music fans. The country music-oriented Nashville Network debuted in early 1983, and its programming schedule consisting of music videos, taped concerts and talk shows perfectly lent itself to Chet's talents. Consequently, Chet appeared on dozens upon dozens of Nashville Network-produced shows from the network's very first year up to the end of his own career.

Even with all of the great success Chet had achieved by playing the guitar at such a high level of skill, he never lost sight of the fact that playing the guitar at *any* level of skill was a joy. His simple love of the guitar was evidenced by the wealth of instructional guitar material he created over the years. For example, in 1986 Chet and his longtime musical collaborator John Knowles designed an informative book and video set for beginning guitarists entitled *Get Started on Guitar*. (John was the talented fingerstyle guitarist/arranger who arranged Chet's 1974 Grammy-winning version of the Scott Joplin song "The Entertainer.") The set's video featured Chet playing with two teenagers who had recently taken up the guitar, and showing them many of the basics of the instrument.

And in 1996, Chet made an instructional book and video set for much more advanced guitarists entitled *The Guitar of Chet Atkins*. This set's video featured Chet both playing and teaching a number of songs that he had arranged and recorded over the years. Watching Chet informally explaining elements of his guitar technique was a real treat for any serious fan.

Toward the end of his career, Chet's penchant for making collaborative albums with other artists continued. His last albums for Columbia included great records made with Jerry Reed, Dire Straits frontman Mark Knopfler, country superstar Suzy Bogguss, and Australian guitar virtuoso Tommy Emmanuel. And the awards kept right on coming—he won more than a few Grammys for his Columbia work, and in 1993 he was honored with a Grammy Lifetime Achievement Award.

Sadly, while Chet was making his album with Tommy entitled *The Day Finger Pickers Took Over the World*, his health took a serious downturn when he was again stricken with cancer—doctors had discovered a tumor in his brain. Chet's health never allowed him to fully resume his musical activities after *The Day Finger Pickers Took Over the World* was released in 1997. He would perform live a few more times over the next two years before his battle with cancer really began to overtake him—but for the most part, his incredible musical career was over.

Before his life ended, Chet was able to bestow one more amazing gift on his longtime fans. He wrote a book entitled *Chet Atkins: Me and My Guitars* with his longtime friends, authors Michael and Russ Cochran. The lavishly illustrated book focused on Chet's many musical accomplishments and the different guitars that he used to achieve them. *Chet Atkins: Me and My Guitars* was published in the spring of 2001, just a few months before Chet's passing.

Chet died on June 30, 2001, at the age of 77, and countless people around the world mourned the loss of the man who had so long been known as Mister Guitar. His funeral was held at Nashville's Ryman Auditorium, where Chet had performed for many Grand Ole Opry audiences over the years, and his eulogy was delivered by Garrison Keillor. Of course, there was a wealth of music performed at the service, including a medley of some of Chet's most famous songs played by his close friends, guitarists Paul Yandell, Steve Wariner, and Vince Gill.

Any summary of Chet's life and career would not be complete without this final observation. Chet was a brilliant musician, but even more importantly, the life he lived proved beyond the shadow of a doubt that he was a man of extraordinary intelligence and kindness. The world is undoubtedly a better place because Chet Atkins, both the musician and the man, was here with us for a while.

The Most Important Guitars

No examination of Chet Atkins' recording career would be complete without an in-depth discussion of the specific guitars that he used the most over the decades. The first of these guitars was his Gibson L-10 acoustic. This guitar was given to Chet by his older half-brother Jim, who worked with Les Paul during the late 1930s playing rhythm guitar and singing lead vocals. The L-10 had been made specifically for Les in 1938, and Jim had convinced Les to give it to him in a trade. In the early 1940s, Jim committed an act of generosity that benefitted not only his younger half-brother, but also millions of music fans all over the world—he gave the L-10 to Chet, and Chet loved playing the guitar so much that he used it to record some of his greatest early songs. The L-10 can be heard on classics such as "Canned Heat," "Main Street Breakdown" and "Gallopin' on the Guitar."

Chet outfitted the L-10 with a removable DeArmond pickup, so the guitar could basically be used as either an acoustic or electric instrument. For example, both "Canned Heat" and "Main Street Breakdown" were recorded by miking up the guitar and not using the pickup—so naturally, the guitar had the sound quality of a straight-up acoustic guitar. But on "Gallopin' on the Guitar" the pickup *was* used, so the guitar sounded very much like an electric.

As good as the L-10 sounded with the DeArmond pickup, Chet felt that he needed a guitar that was truly designed to be an electric instrument—that is, a guitar with a pickup permanently mounted on its body. So in the mid–1940s, Chet purchased a Gibson L-7 acoustic guitar, and then he purchased a Gibson P-90 pickup to install on the instrument. Chet himself ended up performing this installation. Once Chet started performing live with the electrified L-7, he noticed that audiences seemed to respond better to his playing than they did when he was playing an acoustic guitar—this led him to favor using an electric for more and more live performances and recording sessions. The L-7 can be heard on a number of Chet's important early recordings, including "I've Been Working on the Guitar" and "Dizzy Strings."

After Chet found resounding success performing with the Carter Sisters in the late 1940s, he made the decision to purchase his first truly world-class guitar. In 1950, Chet had the renowned guitar maker John D'Angelico of Brooklyn, New York, build him a D'Angelico Excel. Chet himself installed two pickups on the guitar, a Bigsby and a Gibson P-90, so that it could be used as an electric as well as an acoustic instrument. The Excel can be heard on most all of the recording Chet did between early 1951 and mid–1954.

In early 1954, the Gretsch Company contacted Chet through their guitarist/designer Jimmie Webster to see if he would consider endorsing their company. Gretsch and Chet came to an agreement to design Gretsch electric guitar models that would bear Chet's name—and after the release of those models, they would then become the instruments that Chet would always use for recordings and personal appearances.

Throughout that year, Gretsch and Chet worked on designing their guitars, and the instruments they would come up with would turn out to be a resounding success. The Gretsch 6120 Chet Atkins Hollow Body model and the Gretsch 6121 Chet Atkins Solid Body model were released before the end of the year, and they sold extremely well right away. The 6120 was the model that Chet was directly involved in designing, and it ended up being the more popular of the two models.

The first Gretsch guitar that Chet regularly used was a modified 1955 6120—this modified version had uncut f-holes, so it was actually much less of a true "hollow body" guitar than a standard 6120. Chet's 6120 had two output jacks that allowed the guitar's treble and bass strings to be plugged into their own separate inputs. (The instrument's pickups were wired in a manner that sent the treble strings' signal to one jack, and the bass strings' signal to the other.) This guitar was the one that Chet used on the songs recorded for his 1954 album *A Session With Chet Atkins*.

Chet also used the guitar on several of the songs he laid down at his first-ever stereo recording session on July 24, 1958, including "Swanee River" and "I'm Forever Blowing Bubbles." Obviously, this guitar was an ideal instrument for a stereo recording session—the guitar's treble strings (G, B, and high E) could be sent to one channel, and its bass strings (low E, A, and D) could be sent to the other. When played back in stereo, this "split guitar" effect created a highly unusual listening experience—the notes Chet played on the 6120 bounced between the left and right speakers like some sort of sonic ping pong ball.

Once Chet signed his endorsement deal with Gretsch, he constantly recorded with that brand of guitar—but it should be pointed out that he did not use only one *specific* Gretsch, because over the years the company supplied him with many different guitars. There were definitely a few Gretsches that he used much more than others—but even still, there is no way of knowing just which Gretsch he might have used on many of the songs discussed in this book. If I have found reliable evidence about Chet using a particular guitar on a particular recording, I will be using that evidence—but if not, my discussion of Chet's choice of guitars on a great number of his recordings will have to remain non-specific.

In 1958, Gretsch released a new Chet electric guitar model known as the Chet Atkins Country Gentleman. The Country Gentleman was named after Chet's landmark 1953 song, and it featured a mahogany finish and uncut f-holes. The model quickly became a big seller for the company, and it just as quickly became Chet's instrument of choice—he began recording with Country Gentleman guitars right after the model was first introduced.

In 1959, Chet received a new Country Gentleman from Gretsch, and this particular guitar became the instrument that he used on more of his recordings than any other guitar. Chet's 1959 Country Gentleman was equipped with a slightly wider neck than the neck of a standard Country Gentleman—the wider neck model of the guitar was eventually put into regular production by Gretsch. Chet would regularly use his 1959 Country Gentleman for recordings and personal appearances all the way up until 1980, when he ended his endorsement deal with Gretsch. (Incidentally, photos of Gretsch Chet Atkins Country Gentleman models were featured on the covers of the original vinyl releases of Chet's classic albums *Chet Atkins in Hollywood* and *Mister Guitar*.)

We should take just a moment to note that there was another Gretsch Chet Atkins electric guitar model released in 1958. That model was called the Chet Atkins Tennessean, and it was essentially an economy version of the 6120 Chet Atkins Hollow Body. Chet rarely played the Tennessean model, but it still became a big seller for Gretsch because Beatles lead guitarist George Harrison regularly used the guitar throughout 1964 and 1965.

Since Chet's endorsement deal with Gretsch lasted all the way from the mid–1950s until 1980, almost half of his career was spent playing that brand. But even during his Gretsch years, Chet regularly used a number of non–Gretsch guitars. The reason for this was simple. During the years that Chet endorsed the company, he had maintained a keen interest in refining his acoustic playing—and since Gretsch was primarily a manufacturer of electric guitars, Chet had to use acoustic guitars built by companies other than Gretsch to pursue this interest.

Chet's interest in acoustic guitars led him to want to learn more and more about the nylon-string acoustic guitar, an instrument commonly referred to as a "classical guitar" since it was often used for the playing of classical music works. And since Chet had always been a fingerstyle guitarist, his playing translated extremely well to the fingerpicking techniques normally used by classical guitar players. Consequently, he began devoting an increasing amount of his playing time to the classical guitar. Chet first recorded with one in 1955 when he made his initial excursion into the realm of classical music for his landmark album *Chet Atkins in Three Dimensions*.

In late 1959, Chet decided to take his love for the classical guitar to a whole new level—he began work on an entire album of songs that featured him playing the instrument. He chose to title the album *The Other Chet Atkins* since it showcased an aspect of his playing that was markedly different from his electric work. Interestingly, the classical guitars Chet would have used to record the album were not the finest of instruments—the first classical guitars that he bought for himself in the 1950s were ones that were built by relatively undistinguished guitar makers. In the years to come, he would end up playing classical guitar every bit as much as he played electric—and of course, this change in his playing focus would lead him to acquire a number of extremely high-quality classical guitars. But his first full-length foray into classical guitar playing was accomplished with decidedly ordinary guitars.

The first truly well-crafted classical guitar that Chet owned was a Juan Estruch. Chet acquired the guitar in the early 1960s, and he used it to record a number of songs on his 1964 album *My Favorite Guitars*. Chet would use his Juan Estruch on the majority of the classical guitar recordings he made over the next few years.

Chet used another acoustic guitar that he had acquired in the early 1960s on *My Favorite Guitars* as well. That instrument was a Del Vecchio Dinamico resonator guitar Chet had received from Nato Lima. Nato was a guitarist from Ceará, Brazil, who played in a well-known guitar duo known as Los Indios Tabajaras—the other half of that duo was Nato's brother Antenor. The success of Los Indios Tabajaras reached all the way to the United States in late 1963, when their recording of the popular Mexican song "Maria Elena" became a top ten hit. (Incidentally, Chet had recorded that same song a few years earlier—it appeared on the album, *The Other Chet Atkins*.) In the liner notes Chet wrote for *My Favorite Guitars*, Chet did not refer to this guitar as a Del Vecchio—instead, he called it his "Los Indios Tabajaras guitar."

We should take just a moment to discuss a resonator guitar. A resonator is an acoustic guitar that has one or more spun metal cones built into the guitar's sound board. These cones produce a resonator's sound, which is considerably louder than the sound produced by a standard acoustic guitar with a single completely hollow soundhole. Chet loved the sound made by his Del Vecchio so much that he would periodically record with it throughout the rest of his career. He normally played this guitar with its strings tuned up a half step from standard tuning, so from low to high its tuning was F-Bb-Eb-Ab-C-F. (Incidentally, Chet would own several different Del Vecchios over the years, but his Nato Lima Del Vecchio remained the one that he favored the most.)

In the early 1970s, Chet met Kentucky luthier Hascal Haile, and Hascal ended up building a number of classical guitars for him. In 1975, Hascal built one for Chet that featured ornate inlay work created by DiAnne Patrick—this instrument was the one that Chet played on his 1976 duet with Dolly Parton "Do I Ever Cross Your Mind." Chet used Hascal's guitars on a number of his other recordings as well, including his 1980 collaborative album with Doc Watson entitled *Reflections*.

During all of the years that Chet was with Gretsch, the company continued to modify its Chet Atkins models. For example, the 6120 Chet Atkins Hollow Body was completely redesigned in 1962. The new version of the 6120 very much resembled a Country Gentleman in that it had a thin body and uncut f-holes. And then in 1966, Gretsch renamed the redesigned 6120 Nashville. There was no difference between the redesigned 6120 and the Nashville other than this name change. During the 1960s, Chet would periodically play a new 6120 or a Nashville—but these guitar models did not impress him enough to give up regularly using his older Gretsch models—especially his 1959 Country Gentleman.

Toward the end of Chet's years with Gretsch, several *completely* new Chet Atkins electric guitar models were released. In 1971, Chet worked with Gretsch to design the Super Chet, which was undoubtedly one of the fancier guitars the company had produced. For example, the model featured a wider variety of tone controls than any of the earlier Chet Gretsches had. And in 1976, Chet and Gretsch designed a still fancier model known as the Chet Atkins Super Axe, which featured built-in effects units such as a phase shifter. During the 1970s, Chet occasionally used these new models for concert or television appearances—but again, they did not impress him enough to stop regularly using his older Gretsch models.

In the early 1980s, Chet's career was very much in the throes of change. He had left RCA Victor for Columbia Records, because Columbia was much more receptive to the new musical projects that he wanted to undertake. Also, Chet had decided to end his quarter-century relationship with Gretsch and sign an endorsement deal with the Gibson Guitar Corporation.

The main reason why Chet left Gretsch was that the company was not interested in an idea for a new style of guitar that he had come up with. Over the years, Chet had devoted more and more of his playing time to the classical guitar during his concert appearances—and the problems he had encountered with a classical in terms of amplification and feedback had led him to want to create a new kind of guitar. This new guitar would be a solidbody, nylon-string classical outfitted with a built-in pickup—such a guitar would play much like a standard classical, and be able to be amplified with minimal feedback problems much like an electric.

In the late 1970s, Chet had worked up a prototype of this new guitar design with help from Hascal Haile. Hascal had built a classical guitar neck that ran the entire length of the guitar—in other words, it was basically a guitar with no body. Chet attached a pickup to this strange-looking instrument, and the result of his efforts was a guitar that could prove that his idea of a solidbody acoustic was indeed a feasible one.

Chet showed this prototype to Gretsch, but the company had no interest in developing or manufacturing a solidbody acoustic guitar. Chet then took the prototype to Gibson, and they *were* interested in its potential. So Chet left Gretsch for Gibson, and together they began work on building and marketing Chet's solidbody acoustic. In early 1982, this guitar model was ready to be unveiled to the public—it was named the Chet Atkins CE, the "CE" being an acronym for "classical electric." The CE was quickly embraced by nylon-string players, so it enjoyed strong sales upon its release. But no one was happier with the guitar model than Chet—he would regularly perform and record with it for years to come.

In the early 1990s, the well-known guitar builder Kirk Sand designed a new classical electric guitar, and Chet liked the instrument so much that he persuaded Gibson to add it to its product line. The guitar was named the Chet Atkins Studio Classic, and Chet immediately began using it every bit as much as he used the CE.

When Chet left Gretsch for Gibson, the Chet-inspired guitar model names that Gretsch had been using for over two decades came with him. So in 1986, Gibson first released its version of the Country Gentleman. The Gibson Country Gentleman looked quite similar to its Gretsch counterpart, but there were substantial differences between the two guitar models. For example, the Gretsch Country Gentleman had uncut f-holes, and the Gibson Country Gentleman had open f-holes—so the Gibson model was much more of an acoustic/electric guitar than the Gretsch model was. Chet would use the Gibson Country Gentleman for performing and recording from the mid–1980s all the way until the end of his career.

We should mention several of Chet's most historically significant guitar amplifiers. In the early 1950s, Illinois musician/electronics repairman Ray Butts designed a guitar amp that he dubbed the EchoSonic. The amp was equipped with a built-in tape loop that recorded the signal from a guitar and played it back a fraction of a second later—this gave the guitar's sound a pronounced slap-back/echo effect. In 1954, Ray traveled to Nashville to show Chet the EchoSonic, and Chet was so impressed with the amp that he immediately started using it for selected live appearances and recording sessions—the EchoSonic can be heard on Chet's 1954 recording of "Mister Sandman."

Far and away the important guitar amplifier of Chet's career was his 1954 Standel 25L15 outfitted with a 15-inch JBL speaker. These tube amps were built by engineer Bob Crooks, the founder of Standel—and only fifty were ever made. Amazingly, the Standel 25L15 was basically the only amplifier Chet used for recording from the mid–1950s until the mid–1990s. Considering the fact that this amp delivered Chet's guitar sound on countless classic recordings made over a period of four decades, it is certainly no exaggeration to say that it is one of the most important guitar amplifiers in the history of *all* recorded music.

A Few Words About the Guitar and Recording Technology

Since this book contains so many discussions about the manner in which Chet used the guitar, I'll lay out the bare essentials of the instrument as a starting point.

A standard guitar has six strings, and they are tuned from low (the thickest string) to high (the thinnest string) E-A-D-G-B-E. The strings are tuned by turning the machine heads at the top of the guitar's neck. (The machine heads are often called a variety of other names, including "tuning keys.") Since there are two strings tuned to E, the way that they are differentiated from one another is to call the low one "low E" and the high one "high E." Over the years, Chet used a variety of different tunings on his recordings—so the book will contain many tuning discussions.

To change the pitch of the strings, guitarists push down on them on the guitar's fingerboard, which is the term for the top of the guitar neck where the strings are. The guitarist pushes the strings down in between the guitar's frets—the frets are the raised elements used to form the multiple lines running across a guitar's fingerboard. Frets are usually made of thin strips of metal. On a guitar, each fret represents a semitone in the standard western system of music where an octave is made up of twelve semitones. The higher a string is pushed down on the fingerboard, the higher the tone of that string will be.

Also, Chet often used a capo to change the tuning of his guitar. A capo is a device that fits around the neck of a guitar in order to clamp down the strings and raise their pitch. A capo shortens the playable area of the strings, because the strings are completely deadened behind the spot where they are capoed. We will make note of the recordings in this book where Chet used a capo.

Chet played acoustic and electric guitars. An acoustic guitar is a hollow-bodied instrument that uses one or more sound holes located near the middle of its body to amplify the sound of its strings. An electric guitar relies on a sound-capturing device known as a pickup to capture the sound of its strings. That sound is then run through an amplifier, which has speakers much like the ones found on a stereo system or a television. And there will be a fair amount of additional guitar terminology used in our discussion of Chet's greatest recorded songs.

Since Chet's over 50-year recording career spanned from the post–World War II era to the end of the twentieth century, the story of his recorded works runs in tandem with the story of the evolution of modern recording technology. When he made his first recordings as a young, up-and-coming guitarist in the mid–1940s, all recording studios consisted of little more than a single performance room equipped with a relatively small number of microphones. These microphones were all connected to a single audio recording device—so any musical performance that was recorded needed to have all of its musicians playing together in one take, from the first note of the recording to the last.

During the 1940s, magnetic tape recorders became the standard for commercial recording—and over the years, technological breakthroughs in magnetic tape recording allowed more and more separate tracks to be incorporated into a recorded song. In other words, musicians could record a song on tape, and that tape could be rewound and played back so that other musical parts could be added to the song.

This meant that not all of the musicians featured on a song had to play together in one take, from the first note of the recording to the last—new musical parts could be added to a recorded song minutes, hours, days, weeks or even *years* after that song was first recorded.

And in the last half of the twentieth century, digital recorders expanded the capabilities of multitrack recording technology even further—in fact, there was really no limit to how many separate tracks could be used on a song when it was recorded digitally.

Chet made good use of expanding multitrack recording technology throughout his career. By the mid–1950s, Chet had installed recording equipment in the garage of his first Nashville home—so Chet could begin recording a song at RCA's Nashville studios, and then take the master tape of that recording home in order to work on it further in *his* studio. Once Chet began this practice of working on his recordings at home on his own time, there would be no way of knowing whether the majority of a particular recording was done at RCA, or at his home studio.

In early 1958, Chet and his family moved to a new home in Nashville, and he equipped the basement of that home with all of his guitar and recording gear. Chet lived in this home for the rest of his life, and he would work there for the rest of his as well. He still would record songs at studios either owned or contracted by his record label (RCA until the early 1980s, and then Columbia Records for the rest of his career)—then he would take the master tapes of those recordings home in order to work on them further in his own studio. Again, this meant that there would be no way of knowing whether the majority of a particular recording was done at his label's studio, or at his home studio.

A note about recording formats: Most all of the release numbers listed in the book denote vinyl releases, because Chet's recording career fell almost entirely within the age of that particular format—indeed, only his very last few recordings were issued on compact disc instead of vinyl. Of course, many of Chet's classic albums that were originally released on vinyl have since been re-released on compact disc—but the book's credit information covers only original releases, not re-releases. Also, it should be pointed out that even though Chet's music was periodically released on magnetic tape formats such as reel-to-reel, 8-track, and cassette as well as vinyl, the book's credit information does not include those short-lived secondary formats.

THE GREATEST SONGS
Arranged Chronologically

"Guitar Blues (Pickin' the Blues)"

Composer: Chet Atkins. **Producer:** Jim Bulleit. **Musicians:** Chet Atkins (guitar), Louis Innis (rhythm guitar), Roy Lanham (rhythm guitar), Jack Shook (rhythm guitar), Ernie Newton (bass), Dutch McMillin (clarinet). **Location and Date of Recording:** WSM Studio B, Nashville, Tennessee, summer 1946. **Original Release:** Bullet 617 (Bullet 78 single, 1946).

The incredible solo recording career of Chet Atkins officially kicked off with a session at WSM's Studio B in Nashville, Tennessee, in the summer of 1946. At the session, the songs "Guitar Blues (Pickin' the Blues)" and "Brown Eyes Cryin' in the Rain" were recorded for the small Nashville-based label Bullet Records. Bullet released the songs as a 78 single, and although they achieved very little initial success, they now hold the distinction of being the first recorded material officially released under Chet's name.

Interestingly, this release came before there really even *was* a "Chet Atkins"— the billing on the single read "Chester Atkins and the All-Star Hillbillies." In 1946, Chet was still known by his given name of Chester because the nickname of "Chet" had not yet been bestowed on him. That nickname would be given to him the following year, when he was working at KWTO in Springfield, Missouri. (KWTO executive Si Siman was the first person to call Chester "Chet," and the nickname caught on so well with everyone that it quickly became Chester's professional name.)

Despite the way in which the single was originally billed, there was really nothing "hillbilly" at all about it. "Guitar Blues (Pickin' the Blues)" was by far its more compelling offering—the song was an instrumental written by Chet that featured him serving up a hearty helping of bluesy fingerpicking. "Brown Eyes Crying in the Rain" also featured Chet on guitar, but only sparingly—the song was a pleasant but unremarkable pop-flavored number that featured a lead vocal by one of the session's rhythm guitarists, Jack Shook.

Chet never made a definitive statement regarding what specific guitar he played on this session. He did state that he used his Gibson L-10 acoustic on a number of his later 1940s sessions, so it is likely he used that guitar on this session as well.

At any rate, in "Guitar Blues (Pickin' the Blues)" Chet plays in standard tuning, and he has a capo on his guitar at the 3rd fret. He plays the song out of the key of A, but the capo makes it sound as if he is playing out of the key of C. Accompanied by rhythm guitars, clarinet and bass, Chet skillfully delivers straight-ahead blues patterns that are far closer in spirit to blues, jazz and pop recordings of the 1940s than they are to country music recordings of that same time period. The cosmopolitan vibe of the recording is further driven home when Chet steps back for a moment to let clarinetist Dutch McMillan play a soulful, jazzy solo.

Incidentally, it should be noted that there are two recordings featuring Chet as a solo artist in existence that actually pre-date the release of this Bullet single. The songs "Why Don't You Leave Me Alone" and "Empty Slippers" were recorded by Chet at the WNOX Studio in Knoxville, Tennessee, in the mid–1940s. While Chet did not write either of these agreeable but decidedly unmemorable country tunes, he sang

Chet Atkins with his Gibson L-10 acoustic guitar at WRVA, Richmond, Virginia, 1946.

lead and played solo guitar breaks on them. These recordings were transferred to acetate disc for safekeeping, but they would not be officially released to the public for about 60 years. The tracks finally saw the light of day when they were included as bonus tracks on the Chet Atkins CD set *Mister Guitar: The Complete Recordings 1955–1960* released by Bear Family Records in 2004.

"Canned Heat"

Composer: Chet Atkins. **Producer:** Stephen H. Sholes. **Musicians:** Chet Atkins (guitar), George Barnes (rhythm guitar), Harold Siegel (bass), Charles Hurta (fiddle), Augie Klein (accordion). **Location and Date of Recording:** RCA Studio C, Chicago, Illinois, August 11, 1947. **Original Release:** RCA Victor 20-2472 (RCA Victor 78 single, 1947).

Chet's August 11, 1947, recording session at the RCA Victor Studio in Chicago, Illinois, was a truly historic one. It was his very first session for the record label, so it marked the beginning of an incredibly successful partnership which would last for well over three decades. The session was produced by RCA's director of country music operations Stephen H. Sholes, who had handled the arrangements for Chet to be signed to the label.

RCA had decided to sign Chet to a recording contract because they hoped they could mold him into their own version of singer/guitarist Merle Travis, who at the time was racking up hit after hit for Capitol Records. Of course, Merle's incredible guitar fingerpicking style was Chet's number one musical influence, so Chet had the "guitarist" part of this equation down pat. The "singer" part of the equation would not be as easy for him to master—he simply was not the kind of lead-singing frontman that Merle was. Still, Chet was willing to try to step up and be that kind of frontman if RCA was going to give him a contract, so five of the eight songs recorded at the session featured Chet singing lead.

The songs that featured Chet on vocals were by no means bad, but they were by no means very captivating either—they basically proved that Chet's main strength as a performer was not in his singing. The songs recorded that day that really stood out were the guitar instrumentals that he himself had written. Chet used his Gibson L-10 acoustic guitar for all of the session's songs, and that guitar's wonderful tone really helped to bring the instrumentals to life.

In fact, one of these instrumentals would become one of his most well-known early recordings. "Canned Heat" was a fast-paced number that showcased Chet's dazzling fingerpicking technique, a technique that had now actually surpassed that of Merle's. The recording was released on a 78 single in late 1947 under the billing "Chet Atkins and His Colorado Mountain Boys." (The reason the single was billed in this manner was because shortly before RCA Victor had brought Chet to Chicago to record, he had been working in Denver, Colorado, with the western bandleader/vocalist Shorty Thompson.)

On "Canned Heat," Chet plays out of the key of A in standard tuning, and he is backed by accordion, fiddle, rhythm guitar, and bass. Accordionist Augie Klein and fiddler Charles Hurta also take brief solo breaks during the song as well. The song is built around a basic pattern that uses the chords of A, D, and E—in other words, its structure is essentially no different from countless other country and blues songs of the time. What makes the song so special is Chet's playing—he pulls out all the stops, delivering a wealth of driving fingerpicking that includes both melody and self-accompaniment. He also includes playful runs on his lower strings (he even quotes "Yankee Doodle" on one of these runs), and musically adventurous single-note solos.

In fact, it is worth noting that several of the passages in these solos are obviously inspired by another of Chet's musical heroes, the European jazz guitarist Django Reinhardt. Django's blindingly fast, musically complex playing had a profound effect on Chet's work—"Canned Heat" was among the first of Chet's recordings that paid homage to Django, and it would be far from the last.

"Bug Dance"

Composer: Chet Atkins. **Producer:** Stephen H. Sholes. **Musicians:** Chet Atkins (guitar), George Barnes (rhythm guitar), Harold Siegel (bass), Charles Hurta (fiddle), Augie Klein (accordion). **Location and Date of Recording:** RCA Studio C, Chicago, Illinois, August 11, 1947. **Original Release:** RCA Victor 20-2692 (RCA Victor 78 single, 1947).

Another of the Chet-written guitar instrumentals recorded at Chet's first session for RCA Victor, "Bug Dance" was an infectious, leisurely tempoed swing number that allowed Chet to sit back in his comfort zone and let his musical virtuosity shine. Like "Canned Heat," the recording was released on a 78 single by RCA under the billing "Chet Atkins and His Colorado Mountain Boys." "Bug Dance" was structured around basic blues patterns out of the key of E, but it moved beyond being a straight-ahead blues number by including a second chord pattern that threw in a jazzy-sounding C chord.

Again playing his Gibson L-10 acoustic guitar and backed by accordion, fiddle, rhythm guitar, and bass, Chet locks in the groove of the song with his solid fingerpicking. He then he takes several jazzy single-note solo breaks that perfectly compliment the overall bright nature of the recording. Accordionist Augie Klein and fiddler Charles Hurta also take solo breaks, and they keep perfectly in step with the relaxed feel that Chet's guitar has established.

None of the eight songs that Chet recorded during his first RCA session ended up becoming hits, including "Canned Heat" and "Bug Dance," but they showed enough promise to keep the label working with Chet. They might not have found their own version of Merle Travis—but in the long run, they would realize that they had found an artist who was very special in his own right.

"I've Been Working on the Guitar"

Composer: Traditional. **Producer:** Charles Grean. **Musicians:** Chet Atkins (guitar), Jim Atkins (rhythm guitar), Charles Grean (bass), Buck Lambert (fiddle), Joe Biviano (accordion). **Location and Date of Recording:** RCA Studio 1, New York City, New York, November 19, 1947. **Original Release:** RCA Victor 20-2876 (RCA Victor 78 single, 1948).

RCA's director of country music operations Stephen H. Sholes felt that Chet was an artist with great potential even though his first records for the label did not sell well. So in late 1947, Sholes had Chet travel to New York City so that he could play guitar for a wide variety of recording sessions that were being held at RCA's studios there. The label was stockpiling new recordings because it seemed certain that the American Federation of Musicians would be going on strike against the major American record companies at the beginning of the next year, which meant that musicians would not consent to doing any new studio work. (This strike did come to pass, and it lasted through almost all of 1948.)

While Chet was in New York City, Sholes also had Chet do two sessions of his own for RCA. These sessions were produced by Charles Grean, who also played bass on all of the songs recorded during the sessions. The two sessions yielded eight songs, five of them Chet-sung vocal numbers and three of them instrumentals. All of the songs featured one particularly noteworthy supporting musician—Chet's older half-brother Jim played rhythm guitar on them.

The first of the two sessions was held on November 11, and none of the four songs that were recorded at that session turned out to be particularly memorable. At the second session held on November 19 another four songs were recorded—Chet used his newly purchased Gibson L-7 electric guitar on all of them. Two songs from the November 19 session *did* turn out to be very memorable ones, both of them catchy, high-energy instrumentals.

The first of these was "I've Been Working on the Guitar," an uptempo, guitar-driven version of the traditional song "I've Been Working on the Railroad." Like Chet's earlier RCA recordings, "I've Been Working on the Guitar" was released on a 78 single under the billing "Chet Atkins and His Colorado Mountain Boys."

Playing his Gibson L-7 electric in standard tuning with a capo on the 3rd fret, Chet is backed by accordion, fiddle, rhythm guitar, and bass. He starts out by fingerpicking the song's melody and a simultaneous accompanying pattern in the key of C, but the capo makes it sound as if he is playing out of the key of E-flat. As the song speeds along, Chet takes a number of solos infused with many nimble single-note runs. Chet great work is perfectly complemented by the brief but note-packed solo breaks taken by fiddler Buck Lambert and accordionist Joe Biviano. The accordion also takes the spotlight both at the beginning and the end of the recording, when Biviano plays a series of descending notes that cleverly mimic the sound of a chugging train. Each time Biviano plays this train motif, Chet answers it by mimicking a locomotive whistle on the high strings of his guitar.

"Dizzy Strings"

> **Composer:** Chet Atkins. **Producer:** Charles Grean. **Musicians:** Chet Atkins (guitar), Jim Atkins (rhythm guitar), Charles Grean (bass), Buck Lambert (fiddle), Joe Biviano (accordion). **Location and Date of Recording:** RCA Studio 1, New York City, New York, November 19, 1947. **Original Release:** RCA Victor 20-3006 (RCA Victor 78 single, 1948).

The second instrumental Chet recorded at his November 19, 1947, session at RCA Studios in New York City was an uptempo song that he himself had written called "Dizzy Strings." Like "I've Been Working on the Guitar," "Dizzy Strings" was released on a 78 single under the billing "Chet Atkins and His Colorado Mountain Boys." The song could hardly have been more aptly named, because it was so frenetic that it sounded like the musical equivalent of a multiple somersault routine.

Chet uses his Gibson L-7 electric in standard tuning on "Dizzy Strings," and he is backed by fiddle, accordion, rhythm guitar and bass. (Like all of the other songs recorded during this session, "Dizzy Strings" features rhythm guitar played by Chet's older half-brother Jim.) Playing in the key of G, Chet puts on a truly dazzling show of musicianship, zooming through the song's acrobatic melody line like a stunt pilot taking his airplane through a series of barrel rolls.

The use of a simile with the word "rolls" in it is particularly fitting here—much of the melody of "Dizzy Strings" is derived from Chet's use of banjo-style rolls that consist of multiple hammer-ons and pull-offs. The unabashedly jazzy feel of the song is a potent example of how much influence the playing of Django Reinhardt was continuing to have on Chet. Fiddler Buck Lambert and accordionist Joe Biviano pick up on this feel very nicely in the recording, turning in fast, fluid solos that mesh well with Chet's spectacular performance.

As we noted in this book's previous entry, Chet's two New York City RCA sessions in November 1947 yielded eight songs, five of them Chet-sung vocal numbers and three of them instrumentals. Given the fact that the majority of those songs featured Chet singing, it is obvious that RCA was still intent on trying to mold Chet into their own version of Merle Travis. But recordings like "Dizzy Strings" illustrated that Chet was going to end up becoming a very different kind of artist from Merle, one that was far more musically sophisticated.

"Gallopin' on the Guitar"

> **Composer:** Chet Atkins. **Producers:** Stephen H. Sholes, Charles Grean. **Musicians:** Chet Atkins (guitar), Henry "Homer" Haynes (rhythm guitar), Kenneth "Jethro" Burns (mandolin), Charles Grean (bass). **Location and Date of Recording:** Fox Theatre, Atlanta, Georgia, February 3, 1949. **Original Release:** RCA Victor 21-0021 (RCA Victor 78 single, 1949).

None of the 1947 recordings that Chet did for RCA Victor had ended up selling well, but the label continued to believe that Chet was an artist with great potential. Still, due to the 1948 American Federation of Musicians strike against the major American record companies, Chet had to wait quite a while before he could show RCA that their faith in him was warranted. After almost a year, the strike was resolved—so in early 1949, the label was finally able to give Chet another shot at making some more records for them.

At that time, RCA had set up portable recording equipment at the Fox Theatre in Atlanta, Georgia, in order to record a number of their southern-based artists, and Chet was one of the artists that they decided to record. On February 3, 1949, Chet did a session at the Fox Theatre with rhythm guitarist Henry "Homer" Haynes, mandolinist Kenneth "Jethro" Burns, and bassist Charles Grean. Chet's half-sister Billie Rose Atkins also participated in the session—she contributed vocals to two songs.

Just like Chet's two earlier RCA sessions, the Fox Theatre session yielded eight songs, five of them Chet-sung vocal numbers and three of them guitar instrumentals. And also just like Chet's two earlier RCA sessions, the songs recorded at the session that really stood out were the instrumentals that he himself had written. In fact, these particular instrumentals were by far the most potent recordings that Chet had made to date, and it wasn't difficult to figure out what made them so special. The session marked the first time that Chet had recorded with Homer and Jethro—and the

remarkable musical rapport these three men shared with one another made Chet's compositions crackle with energy. Of Chet's three instrumentals recorded at the session, unquestionably the most memorable one was the high-spirited number "Gallopin' on the Guitar."

The music that had truly brought Chet, Homer and Jethro together was the playing of jazz guitarist Django Reinhardt—all three of them admired the guitarist so much that it was very obvious that the music they created together was hugely inspired by him. "Gallopin' on the Guitar" did not sound as much like Reinhardt as some of the other instrumentals that they would record together, but its decidedly jazzy feel still echoed Reinhardt's style to at least some degree.

On "Gallopin' on the Guitar," Chet plays his Gibson L-10 acoustic in standard tuning. The guitar is recorded using Chet's removable DeArmond pickup, so it sounds much more like an electric than it does an acoustic. The song is out of the key of D, and its speedy staccato melody does indeed send Chet's fingers galloping across the L-10's fretboard. This melody includes a sections that jump to a repeated Bb-F chord pattern—in one of these sections toward the end of the song, Chet does some nimble banjo-style rolls consisting of multiple hammer-ons and pull-offs that are built around notes in the key of Bb. Evidently Chet very much liked the sound of these Bb rolls that he created, because he found a way to showcase them to even greater effect in one of his songs he recorded later in the year, "Main Street Breakdown."

"Gallopin' on the Guitar" starts out with Chet establishing the song's melody, and then Jethro takes an extended mandolin break. This break allows Chet to lay out and put a capo on the 2nd fret of the L-10. Chet then comes back in and plays just a bit of the song as a fingerstyle break in the key of C—but the capo makes it sound as if he is still playing in the key of D. Jethro takes a second mandolin break that is considerably shorter than his first one, but this break still gives Chet enough time to lay out and remove his capo. Chet then comes back in capoless, and he finishes the song out by playing its melody in unison with Jethro.

"Gallopin' on the Guitar" was first released on a 78 single by RCA Victor in early 1949 under the billing "Chet Atkins and His Guitar Pickers," and it garnered a decent amount of sales and airplay In fact, the song ended up being so well-received that its title was used to bill Chet himself for a number of years. Many of his early to mid–1950s singles were released under the billing "Chet Atkins and His Galloping Guitar." And Chet's first-ever album also tied into the "Galloping Guitar" moniker—in 1953, RCA released a collection of eight of his recordings on 10-inch record format entitled *Chet Atkins' Gallopin' Guitar*. Needless to say, "Gallopin' on the Guitar" was one of the numbers that was prominently featured on this album—the song closed out its second side.

"Centipede Boogie"

Composer: Chet Atkins. **Producer:** Stephen H. Sholes, Charles Grean. **Musicians:** Chet Atkins (guitar), Henry "Homer" Haynes (rhythm guitar), Kenneth "Jethro" Burns (mandolin), Charles Grean (bass). **Location and Date of Recording:** Fox Theatre, Atlanta, Georgia, February 3, 1949. **Original Release:** RCA Victor 21-0139 (RCA Victor 78 single, 1949), RCA Victor 48-0142 (RCA Victor 45 single, 1949).

"Centipede Boogie" was another of the Chet-penned instrumentals recorded at Chet's February 3, 1949, session for RCA Victor in Atlanta, Georgia. Like "Gallopin' on the Guitar," "Centipede Boogie" was first released on a 78 single by the label in 1949 under the billing "Chet Atkins and His Guitar Pickers." But unlike "Gallopin' on the Guitar," "Centipede Boogie" was also released on a 45 single at the same time the 78 single hit the market—by mid-1949 RCA had introduced the 45 single format to the public, so their new singles were being released both as 78s and 45s.

"Centipede Boogie" was by no means a musically complex song—it was a swing number based on a standard blues pattern out of the key of C. The song featured a busy but catchy melody played by Chet that could have been interpreted as the musical equivalent of a centipede moving as fast as its many little legs could carry it.

On the recording, Chet again plays his Gibson L-10 acoustic in standard tuning, and he is again backed up wonderfully by rhythm guitarist Henry "Homer" Haynes, mandolinist Kenneth "Jethro" Burns, and bassist Charles Grean. And the L-10 is again recorded with Chet's removable DeArmond pickup, so it sounds much more like an electric than it does an acoustic. Chet's finest moments in the song come during his solos toward the end of the recording—he unleashes a barrage of triplet notes that that are both spectacularly fast and flawlessly delivered.

Though not as well-known as "Gallopin' on the Guitar," "Centipede Boogie" still stands as a perfect example of how formidable Chet, Homer and Jethro were when they musically joined forces. And amazingly, they still had yet to record their finest work together—but that is a story we'll get to just a bit later in the book.

"The Old Buck Dance"

Composer: Chet Atkins. **Producer:** Stephen H. Sholes. **Musicians:** Chet Atkins (guitar/vocals), Henry "Homer" Haynes (rhythm guitar/vocals), Kenneth "Jethro" Burns (mandolin/vocals), Anita Carter (bass). **Location and Date of Recording:** RCA Studio A, Chicago, Illinois, October 12, 1949. **Original Release:** RCA Victor 21-0165 (RCA Victor 78 single, 1950), RCA Victor 48-0173 (RCA Victor 45 single, 1950).

In mid-1949, RCA Victor's faith in Chet had finally been rewarded when his song "Gallopin' on the Guitar" notched some sales and airplay for the label. In October 1949, RCA had Chet travel to their studios in Chicago, Illinois, in order to do several sessions. Chet took his two favorite musical collaborators with him to play on those sessions—rhythm guitarist Henry "Homer" Haynes and mandolinist Kenneth "Jethro" Burns backed him up just like they had on the February 4, 1949, session in Atlanta, Georgia, that had produced "Gallopin' on the Guitar." Two of the Carter Sisters, the group that Chet was currently working with, also made the trip to Chicago to perform with him—Helen sang, and Anita sang and played bass.

The first Chicago session was held on October 12, 1949, and it yielded four songs, all of them Chet-sung vocal numbers. RCA Victor released the songs on 78 and 45 singles in 1950 under the billing "Chet Atkins and His Guitar Pickers." None of the songs initially achieved any notable success in terms of sales or airplay, but one of them has definitely stood the test of time—that song is the Chet-penned number "The Old Buck Dance."

The song's unusual title and lyrics were likely inspired by the style of dance known as "buck dancing," a traditional Appalachian freestyle solo dance that was a forerunner of clog dancing. The biggest piece of evidence to support this conclusion is the fact that the music to "The Old Buck Dance" is similar to the music of "The Buck and Wing," a traditional instrumental tune that could well have been played for people to buck dance to over the years.

At any rate, "The Old Buck Dance" is a truly memorable slice of absurdity. It is a bluesy tune that features Chet, Homer and Jethro delivering an dazzlingly spot-on, triple unison lead vocal about the Old Buck Dance, a new dance craze that is so fun it even has Farmer Jones giving up the boogie-woogie. (Neither Helen nor Anita contributed vocals to this particular number, by the way.)

Playing in standard tuning out of the key of E, Chet serves up a number of tasty solos on electric guitar in between the song's verses—but just which of his guitars he might be playing on the song is uncertain. Chet said that used his Gibson L-10 acoustic on several of the other songs recorded during these Chicago sessions, so perhaps he used the L-10 with his removable DeArmond pickup on "The Old Buck Dance." But it seems every bit as likely that he could have used his Gibson L-7 electric on the song. We might not be able to tell if Chet is on the L-10 or the L-7 on the recording, but whichever guitar he is using, his playing is fabulous. And Jethro's mandolin breaks deserve to be singled out for praise as well—they are every bit as inspired as Chet's playing.

It should be noted that "The Old Buck Dance" is the first of Chet's vocal numbers to make this book's list of his greatest recordings. This fact should not lead you the reader to come to the conclusion that all of Chet's earlier singing efforts are completely worthless—on the contrary, a number of those efforts are actually very pleasant. But it is this author's opinion that "The Old Buck Dance" stands head-and-shoulders above all of Chet's earlier vocal numbers because it is so original and infectious. The recording shows that Homer and Jethro could bring the same kind of spark to Chet's vocal work that they had brought to his instrumental work. But unfortunately, the three would sing together on just *one* more of Chet's recordings—we'll discuss that recording, "Boogie Man Boogie," just a bit later in the book.

"Main Street Breakdown"

> **Composer:** Chet Atkins. **Producer:** Stephen H. Sholes. **Musicians:** Chet Atkins (guitar), Henry "Homer" Haynes (rhythm guitar), Kenneth "Jethro" Burns (mandolin), Anita Carter (bass). **Location and Date of Recording:** RCA Studio A, Chicago, Illinois, October 13, 1949. **Original Release:** RCA Victor 21-0329 (RCA Victor 78 single, 1950), RCA Victor 48-0329 (RCA Victor 45 single, 1950).

After doing a four-song recording session at RCA Victor's Chicago, Illinois, studios on October 12, 1949, Chet returned to RCA's Chicago studios the next day to do another session. He was backed by basically the same group as he had used the day before, with one exception. Guitarist Henry "Homer" Haynes, mandolinist Kenneth "Jethro" Burns, and bassist Anita Carter all played on Chet's songs, but the songs did not feature Helen Carter on vocals like most of the October 12 songs had.

The October 13, 1949, session was a four-song session, but unlike the previous day's session, this one was split between Chet and Homer and Jethro—in other words, Chet was the featured artist on two of its numbers, and Homer and Jethro were the featured artists on the other two. As it turned out, Chet didn't need all four of the session's songs that day to make some epic guitar history, because one of the songs he recorded would end up being universally regarded as one of his greatest works of all time. That song was the Chet-penned instrumental "Main Street Breakdown."

"Main Street Breakdown" was an uptempo number inspired by the playing of jazz guitarist Django Reinhardt. Earlier in the book, we discussed a number of Chet's recordings that were influenced by Reinhardt—but none of those recordings were influenced by the guitarist nearly as much as "Main Street Breakdown" was. The song was filled with blindingly fast, musically complex guitar lines that could have well been played by Reinhardt himself—but even *he* probably couldn't have played them as wonderfully as Chet did.

Chet wrote "Main Street Breakdown" in a key that is usually considered not that friendly for a standard-tuned guitar, the key of Bb. But Chet chose that key for a very specific reason—on his earlier song "Gallopin' on the Guitar," Chet used some banjo-style rolls consisting of multiple hammer-ons and pull-offs that were built around notes in the key of Bb. Chet evidently very much liked the sound of these Bb rolls that he created, because he used these rolls to even greater effect in "Main Street Breakdown" by building a major portion of the song's melody around them. But the melody of "Main Street Breakdown" was not comprised just of the rolls Chet first used in "Gallopin' on the Guitar"—it also featured a sprightly descending line that Chet played by hammering notes on his guitar's open G string.

Speaking of Chet's guitar, he plays his Gibson L-10 acoustic in standard tuning on "Main Street Breakdown." It is hard to come up with words to describe just how good Chet sounds on this song, but I'll give it a shot—he hits every note he plays in the recording, literally *every* note, so cleanly that his guitar almost seems to jump right out of any speaker that the recording is being played on. The quality of his performance is matched note-for-note by his backing musicians—Jethro's solos are stellar, Homer's always-driving rhythm guitar is even more powerful than usual, and Anita's bass holds everything together nicely.

"Main Street Breakdown" was first released on 78 and 45 singles by RCA Victor in 1950 under the billing "Chet Atkins and His Guitar Pickers," and it garnered a decent amount of sales and airplay just like "Gallopin' on the Guitar" had. Thanks to these records, Chet was well on his way to building a fan base that would stick with him for decades.

"Boogie Man Boogie"

Composer: Chet Atkins. **Producer:** Stephen H. Sholes. **Musicians:** Chet Atkins (guitar/vocals), Henry "Homer" Haynes (rhythm guitar/vocals), Kenneth "Jethro" Burns (rhythm guitar/vocals), Anita Carter (bass). **Location and Date of Recording:** RCA Studio A, Chicago, Illinois, October 13, 1949. **Original Release:** RCA Victor 21-0367 (RCA Victor 78 single, 1950), RCA Victor 48-0367 (RCA Victor 45 single, 1950).

Chet's recording of his classic "Main Street Breakdown" at the RCA Victor Studios in Chicago, Illinois on October 13, 1949, came with an extra added bonus. He recorded a second number at that October 13 session called "Boogie Man Boogie," and that song turned out to be very good in its own right. (As we just noted in our discussion of "Main Street Breakdown," the October 13 session was a four-song session that was split between Chet and Homer and Jethro.) "Boogie Man Boogie" was a bluesy number that was both written and sung by Chet, and it warned everyone to watch out for the "Boogie Man," because he would get anyone that didn't get out of his way fast enough.

On the recording, Chet again plays his Gibson L-10 acoustic in standard tuning, and he is again backed up splendidly by rhythm guitarist Henry "Homer" Haynes, mandolinist Kenneth "Jethro" Burns, and bassist Anita Carter. Only this time around, Jethro does not play mandolin—instead, he contributes a second rhythm guitar part. (Jethro was a very good guitarist as well as a mandolinist.) The song also features Homer and Jethro on backing vocals. Buoyed by Homer and Jethro's singing, Chet turns in one of the very best solo vocal performances of his entire career on "Boogie Man Boogie." He delivers the song's wry lyrics with just the right amount of levity in his voice, making it clear that everything you hear is all in good fun.

And when Chet stops singing and starts playing, things get even *more* fun— "Boogie Man Boogie" is in the very guitar-friendly key of E, which allows Chet to offer up a wealth of solid, blues-tinged solos throughout the song. And even though the tempo of "Boogie Man Boogie" is set at a leisurely blues pace, some of these solos are spectacularly fast, because Chet peppers them with a barrage of double-time runs.

"Boogie Man Boogie" was first released on 78 and 45 singles by RCA Victor in 1950 under the billing "Chet Atkins and His Guitar Pickers," and it did not achieve any real success in terms of sales or airplay. Still, the song deserves to be remembered in the long term by devoted Chet fans for a number of reasons—it is absurdly catchy, it features one of Chet's best-ever solo vocal performances, and it holds the distinction of being one of the precious few times that Chet, Homer and Jethro sing together on record.

"Mountain Melody"

Composer: Chet Atkins. **Producer:** Stephen H. Sholes. **Musicians:** Chet Atkins (guitar), Jack Shook (rhythm guitar), Ernie Newton (bass). **Location and Date of Recording:** Brown Radio Productions, Nashville, Tennessee, January 31, 1951. **Original Release:** RCA Victor 21-0440 (RCA Victor 78 single, 1951), RCA Victor 48-0440 (RCA Victor 45 single, 1951).

By the late 1940s, the team of the Carter Sisters, Mother Maybelle and Chet Atkins had become such a resounding success that the Nashville, Tennessee, radio station WSM invited them to become members of the Grand Ole Opry. So in mid–1950, the Carters and Chet decided to leave KWTO in Springfield, Missouri, the station where they were currently working, and move to Nashville to work for WSM. For Chet, this move to Nashville turned out to be permanent—he would call the city home for the rest of his life.

Obviously, when Chet arrived in Nashville in 1950, the city was not yet the country music recording mecca that it would eventually become—after all, Chet himself would play an integral role in transforming the city into that mecca. In fact, RCA Victor did not yet have their own permanent recording studios in Nashville—so when the label recorded any of their artists in the city, they used either portable recording equipment or local studios like Brown Radio Productions, which mainly functioned as a radio transcription service.

The first sessions that Chet recorded for RCA after returning to Nashville were held at Brown in late August 1950. These sessions produced four songs, two vocal

Chet Atkins with his D'Angelico Excel electric guitar, early 1950s.

and two instrumental, and none of them were particularly memorable. Chet's instrumental version of the well-known ballad "Indian Love Call" was probably the most noteworthy of the songs, because it marked the first time that Chet used harmonic notes on one of his records. (Guitar harmonics are the high-pitched bell-like tones that can be made to ring out on the instrument when its strings are struck, but their fundamental frequencies are dampened.) However, even this recording did not prove to have much longevity, especially for Chet himself—he would decide to record a much more polished version of the song just six years later.

Chet's next RCA recording session held in Nashville would turn out to be a more auspicious one. On January 31, 1951, he returned to Brown, and there he recorded four songs, two vocal and two instrumental. (Chet did not sing either of the session's vocal numbers—they were sung by Danny Dill.) One of the instrumentals was the uptempo Chet-penned number "Mountain Melody," which Chet remembered as being the very first song that he ever recorded using his newly purchased D'Angelico Excel electric guitar. Chet would use that guitar for recording and performing almost exclusively over the next few years, so it would be heard on some of his all-time greatest recordings.

"Mountain Melody" is one of Chet's most exuberant country numbers—it instantly gets a listener's toes tapping. On the recording, Chet plays the Excel in standard tuning out of the key of E, and he is backed by very spare rhythm guitar and bass. The unusual sound of the songs opening chords is created by Chet patting all of the guitar's strings with his open right hand instead of picking them. Chet delivers some of the song's melody in single-note lines, but much of it is delivered in bunches of notes played simultaneously on multiple strings. Chet also uses harmonics on a portion of the tune, and their great tone demonstrates how well the Excel would capture the subtleties of his playing for years to come.

"Mountain Melody" was first released on 78 and 45 singles by RCA Victor in 1951 under the billing "Chet Atkins and His Guitar Pickers." The song did not achieve any notable success in terms of sales or airplay—but still, it will always be remembered as the first recorded work to feature Chet playing one of his most legendary guitars.

"Rainbow"

Composers: Alfred Bryan, Percy Wenrich. **Producer:** Stephen H. Sholes. **Musicians:** Chet Atkins (guitar), Jim Atkins (rhythm guitar), Frank Carroll (bass). **Location and Date of Recording:** RCA Studio 1, New York City, New York, September 25, 1951. **Original Release:** RCA Victor 20-4491 (RCA Victor 78 single, 1952), RCA Victor 47-4491 (RCA Victor 45 single, 1952).

In late September 1951, Chet made another trip to RCA Victor's New York City studios in order to do several recording sessions for the label. Using his D'Angelico Excel electric guitar, he recorded two songs on September 25 and two songs on September 27—all four of these songs were instrumentals. Chet's older half-brother Jim played rhythm guitar on the sessions, just like he had done when Chet had previously recorded at RCA's New York City studios in late 1947. All of the songs recorded at these sessions turned out very well, but the one that has probably been the most fondly remembered by Chet's fans over the years is "Rainbow," which was recorded at the September 25 session. "Rainbow" was a pleasant midtempo pop number composed almost a half-century earlier by Alfred Bryan and Percy Wenrich—the song had originally been written with lyrics, and it first became a hit back in 1908.

By the time that Chet created his version of "Rainbow," he had become increasingly interested in experimenting with modern recording techniques in order to get the best and most interesting guitar sounds that he possibly could. Les Paul had been using multitrack recording technology on his recordings with Mary Ford, and the success of their work was certainly not lost on Chet—in fact, Chet had begun to overdub multiple guitar parts onto a number of his songs just like Les had done.

The first time that Chet experimented with using multitrack recording technology was during an April 23, 1951, session at RCA Studios in New York City. At that session, he recorded a version of the Fats Waller jazz instrumental "Jitterbug Waltz," and he laid down electric rhythm guitar and bass parts to accompany his main electric guitar part. This version of "Jitterbug Waltz" was released on 78 and 45 singles by RCA Victor in 1951 under the billing "Chet Atkins—Playing All Instruments." (I chose not to discuss this particular version of "Jitterbug Waltz" in detail in this book, because I feel Chet's truly definitive version of the song is the one he recorded for his classic 1959 album *Chet Atkins in Hollywood*—so we'll be examining *that* recording later in the book.)

"Rainbow" was another of Chet's early multitrack recording experiments—on the recording, Chet dubbed in a second guitar track that played a number of single-note lines that harmonized with his main guitar track. Also, he began to use heavy tape delay echo effects to expand the sound of his guitar much like Les had done—on "Rainbow," the echo effect that Chet decided to use was *so* heavy that at times the guitar sounded a bit like it was bouncing around inside of an echo chamber.

Chet plays in standard tuning out of the key of A through most of "Rainbow," and he is backed by very spare rhythm guitar (played by Jim Atkins) and bass. He renders much of the song's melody through intricate chord voicings played high on the fretboard of his guitar—these voicings put him in position to provide a bit of simultaneous fingerpicking accompaniment to his melody playing. Toward the end of the recording, he simultaneously plays the song's melody and a beautifully structured low harmony part played on the lower strings of his guitar. Chet would incorporate this kind of low harmony playing into many more of his recordings over the years.

The song migrates to the key of E three times, and during those E breaks Chet plays single-note solo lines. These lines are accompanied by Chet's dubbed-in second guitar track featuring him playing single-note lines that harmonize with his main guitar part. It has often been said that Chet could sound like two or more separate guitarists playing together when he played—but in the case of this particular song, multitrack recording allows him to actually *be* two separate guitarists. At any rate, Chet's Excel always sounds exquisite on "Rainbow," whether it is recorded straight or recorded using studio tricks.

"Rainbow" was first released on 78 and 45 singles by RCA Victor in 1952 under the billing "Chet Atkins and His Galloping Guitar," and like so many of Chet's singles released around this time, it received very little notice. Still, the song would come to be highly regarded by Chet's fans as the years went by. But it should be pointed out that it was not this version of it that those fans would become most familiar with—that version was the one that Chet recorded in 1959 for his classic album *Mister Guitar*. The *Mister Guitar* version of "Rainbow" was somewhat different from Chet's 1951 version—its most notable difference was that Chet did away with his dubbed-in second guitar track and played the song's E breaks truly as a single-guitar solo.

In truth, *both* of Chet's recordings of "Rainbow" are so wonderful that one could make an argument for either one being "definitive"—I chose to include the 1951 version in this book because it is a recording that shows how much Chet was beginning to incorporate modern recording techniques into his work. Still, I'll close my discussion of "Rainbow" by saying this—do yourself a favor and seek out both of Chet's versions of the song. You'll probably find it every bit as hard to choose between the two of them as I did.

"Good-Bye Blues"

Composers: Jimmy McHugh, Dorothy Fields, Arnold Johnson. **Producer:** Stephen H. Sholes. **Musicians:** Chet Atkins (guitar), Jerry Byrd (rhythm guitar), Ernie Newton (bass), Marvin Hughes (piano), The Beasley Singers (vocal chorus). **Location and Date of Recording:** Brown Radio Productions, Nashville, Tennessee, October 11-12, 1951. **Original Release:** RCA Victor 20-4491 (RCA Victor 78 single, 1952), RCA Victor 47-4491 (RCA Victor 45 single, 1952).

Shortly after his late September 1951 trip to RCA Victor's New York City studios, Chet was back at Brown Radio Productions in Nashville recording a new group of songs for the label. On the night of October 11, 1951, Chet recorded four songs featuring a mixed vocal group known as the Beasley Singers. Very little is known about this vocal group—there appears to be no information about just who was in the group, or what else they might have done during their career.

At any rate, the fact that a vocal group was brought in to handle all of the vocals at one of Chet's sessions was a telling sign that RCA had finally completely given up on the idea of trying to mold Chet into their own version of Merle Travis. Ever since his first session for the label back in August 1947, he had been recording songs that featured him on lead vocals—and none of those songs had ever achieved even the slightest bit of popularity. Several vocal numbers recorded at Chet's most recent previous sessions had also featured guest vocalists—so the trend to not give Chet the spotlight as a Travis-style lead singer had been established. Consequently, by the time of this October 11, 1951, session, Chet was almost exclusively a guitar soloist, *not* a vocalist. He would still step in front of the microphone to sing every now and again over the years—but his singing would be very much a novelty, not one of the main parts of his act.

The four songs that Chet and the Beasleys recorded were first released on 78 and 45 singles by RCA Victor in 1952 under the billing "Chet Atkins and His Galloping Guitar with vocal refrain by the Beasley Singers." One of these songs, "Good-Bye Blues," was issued as the flip side of the recording we examined in this book's last entry, "Rainbow." "Good-Bye Blues" was a decades-old pop vocal number written by Jimmy McHugh, Dorothy Fields, and Arnold Johnson—the most well-known version of the song had been recorded by the Mills Brothers in the early 1930s.

Chet's recording of "Good-Bye Blues" is delivered at a very fast tempo in the key of C. Playing his D'Angelico Excel electric guitar in standard tuning, Chet is backed by piano, rhythm guitar and bass. The Beasley Singers establish the song by singing on its first verse, and close it out by singing on its last verse. The group features at least one male singer on a few of the other songs recorded at this session, but only the female singers are brought on board for "Good-Bye Blues"—they deliver the song's vocal parts in a close harmony style that is very reminiscent of the work of the Andrews Sisters.

After the Beasleys sing the first verse of "Good-Bye Blues," Chet takes over for the next two verses. On the first verse he solos on, Chet uses an innovative guitar technique that he had not used on any of his previous recordings. He plays a number of passages that feature harmonics paired with regularly fretted notes, often referred to as "pure tones"—in other words, runs of harmonic notes and pure tones being played together simultaneously. Chet developed this technique in order to create a multi-note, chiming sound similar to the sound of a steel guitar—and he would go on to use it to great effect on a number of other recordings he would make over the years.

On the second verse that Chet solos on, he plays another innovative run of notes that would make its way into a number of his subsequent recordings. At 1 minute, 29 seconds, into the song, Chet plays a jarringly dissonant descending run against a G chord. The crazy jumble of notes found in this run seem to be designed to knock listeners out of their comfort zone just a bit—when Chet plays these notes, he seems to be saying, "Hang on, everybody, we're about to hit some musical turbulence here." It is unclear as to just where this dissonant descending run came from—maybe Chet picked it up from another guitarist, or maybe he made it up himself. Either way, he ended up using it to great effect many times over the years.

The session that produced "Good-Bye Blues" didn't do all that much to further Chet's career—and it certainly didn't do anything for the Beasley Singers' career either, considering that they were basically never heard from again. Even still, "Good-Bye Blues" should be considered a noteworthy recording of Chet's, because it is one that really captures him evolving into a more and more adventurous player.

"The Third Man Theme"

Composer: Anton Karas. **Producer:** Stephen H. Sholes. **Musicians:** Chet Atkins (guitar). **Location and Date of Recording:** Brown Radio Productions, Nashville, Tennessee, May 16, 1952. **Original Release:** RCA Victor 20-4925 (RCA Victor 78 single, 1952), RCA Victor 47-4925 (RCA Victor 45 single, 1952).

In the early 1950s, Chet made the decision to start recording himself playing the guitar unaccompanied by any other musicians. Of course, this decision made perfect sense—Chet's style of playing was so incredibly multi-layered that he could easily play the melody of a song and simultaneously support that melody with one or more accompanying parts of his own. However, it should be pointed out that the very first recordings that Chet had made without any other musicians could not truly be called "unaccompanied." In 1951, he had laid down several songs that featured dubbed-in tracks of him playing along with his main guitar track. So in truth, there *were* multiple musicians playing these particular songs—and all of these musicians were Chet himself.

Chet's first venture into strictly unaccompanied recording that was free of multitrack studio tricks occurred on May 16, 1952, when he laid down five songs for RCA Victor at Brown Radio Productions in Nashville. One of these songs remained unreleased for many years, but the other four of them found their way onto various RCA releases around the time that Chet first recorded them. Those releases included various 45 and 78 singles that carried the billing "Chet Atkins and His Galloping Guitar," as well as Chet's first-ever album, *Chet Atkins' Gallopin' Guitar*. That album was released by RCA in 1953, and it was a collection of eight of Chet's recordings on 10-inch record format.

One of the strongest songs recorded at this session was "The Third Man Theme," a jaunty midtempo instrumental originally written and performed by zitherist Anton Karas for the popular 1949 British film noir production *The Third Man*. Chet's memorable rendition of "The Third Man Theme" aptly demonstrated that the song could work every bit as well as a guitar piece as it had a zither piece.

On "The Third Man Theme," Chet plays his D'Angelico Excel electric guitar in standard tuning out of the key of G. He generally sticks closely to Karas's version of the song in terms of arrangement and tempo, but he does offer a number of his own well thought-out embellishments to its melody. One of Chet's most clever little flourishes occurs during the very last moments of the song, when he almost instantly jumps between a very high note, a harmonic note, and several lower notes before closing out the tune with a full G chord. And all of the self-accompanying patterns that Chet has devised to play with the song's melody are so full-sounding that the recording sounds like it is being played by at least two guitarists.

Chet's version of "The Third Man Theme" did not become a hit in terms of sales or airplay when it was first released on 78 and 45 singles in 1952. Still, it would end up holding a special place in the history of his recording career—the year after it had been released as a single, it was chosen to be the opening track on *Chet Atkins' Gallopin' Guitar*. "The Third Man Theme" also appeared on one of the versions of Chet's second album, *Stringin' Along with Chet Atkins*—that album was also released by RCA in 1953. The story behind the various versions of *Stringin'* is a confusing one—we'll get into that story in detail when we discuss another song that appeared on the album, "Oh. By Jingo, Oh. By Gee. (You're the Only Girl for Me)," later in the book.

But even though this version of "The Third Man Theme" had been prominently featured on Chet's first-ever albums, the guitarist would elect to record a new version of the song just four years later. In 1956, RCA decided to re-release *Stringin' Along with Chet Atkins* as a 12-inch record—Chet was evidently unsatisfied with the many of the original recordings found on the 1953 *Stringin'*, including "The Third Man Theme," so he recorded brand new versions of them for the 1956 *Stringin'*.

Chet's 1956 version of "The Third Man Theme" is markedly different from his 1952 version of the song in a number of ways. First and foremost, Chet tuned his guitar in a different manner for the 1956 recording—he tuned his low E string down to D. He then played the song out of the key of G like he had on the 1952 recording—but his D-tuned low E string allowed him to play low D notes on the self-accompanying patterns he had created for the song. This was something that he could *not* do when he used standard tuning on the 1952 recording.

Also, the 1956 version is played at a bit of a slower tempo than the 1952 version, and it features a percussionist lightly accompanying Chet's playing. Both of Chet's versions of "The Third Man Theme" are very well-done, but this author prefers the 1952 version because it is a bit more aggressive and playful than the 1956 version. Also, the historical significance of the 1952 version cannot be denied—it was a standout number from Chet's first-ever strictly unaccompanied recording session, and it also ended up being the first track on his first-ever album.

"Imagination"

Composer: Chet Atkins. **Producer:** Stephen H. Sholes. **Musicians:** Chet Atkins (guitar). **Location and Date of Recording:** RCA Studio 2, New York City, New York, July 29-30, 1952. **Original Release:** RCA Victor 20-4925 (RCA Victor 78 single, 1952), RCA Victor 47-4925 (RCA Victor 45 single, 1952).

Chet must have been quite pleased with his first venture into strictly unaccompanied recording that took place in Nashville on May 16, 1952, because he again recorded unaccompanied at his very next recording session about two months later. He laid down four songs for RCA Victor at their studios in New York City on the night of July 29, 1952.

Chet used his D'Angelico Excel electric guitar for all four of these songs, and the guitar was tuned in a very unusual manner—this manner will be a bit difficult to explain, but I'll give it a try here. Guitarists often use a tuning pattern that is referred to as open G—when a guitar is tuned to open G, its strings sound out a G chord when they are strummed unfretted. The most common way to tune a guitar to open G is to start with a standard-tuned guitar, tune the low E string down to D, tune the A string down to G, and then tune the high E string down to D. For this recording session, Chet's Excel was tuned in this configuration, but it was tuned up a half step from open G—so instead of his strings being tuned to D-G-D-G-B-D, they were tuned to Eb-Ab-Eb-Ab-C-Eb. This meant that when Chet played out of the key of G, it sounded as if he was playing out of the key of Ab.

Chet played all four of the session's songs in the key of G using this "open G but a half step up" tuning configuration. All of the songs turned out very well, but it should be noted that they ended up sounding very musically similar to one another since they were all played in the same key using the same manner of tuning. The four songs were released by RCA on various 45 and 78 singles that carried the billing "Chet Atkins and His Galloping Guitar" around the time that Chet first recorded them—and they also appeared on Chet's first-ever album released in 1953, *Chet Atkins' Gallopin' Guitar*.

The Chet-penned midtempo instrumental "Imagination" was definitely among the strongest of the songs recorded at this session. Its 1952 single release placed it on the flip side of the recording we examined in this book's last entry, "The Third Man Theme."

While the chord progression of "Imagination" is very basic, the song is still one of Chet's most elegant and memorable compositions. Its catchy melody moves along at an unhurried pace, and Chet supports it with just the right amount of harmony lines and rhythmic self-accompaniment. Like so much of Chet's best guitar work, "Imagination" comes off as something quite close to a musical miracle—his multi-layered, perfectly executed playing on the recording creates an aural landscape that is both infectiously happy and deeply peaceful.

It should be noted that the same session that produced "Imagination" also produced another recording that would turn out to be a landmark of Chet's illustrious career. At the session, Chet recorded his first-ever version of the well-known instrumental "Black Mountain Rag." This version of "Black Mountain Rag" was spectacularly done by Chet, and it would always be held in high esteem by his fans as the years went by. The reason that Chet's first recorded version of "Black Mountain Rag" is not given its own entry in this book is because he would eventually end up recording an even *more* spectacular and revered version of the song—that version would appear on his 1971 album *Pickin' My Way*. We'll examine Chet's 1971 version of "Black Mountain Rag" in detail later in the book.

"Chinatown, My Chinatown"

Composers: Jean Schwartz, William Jerome. **Producer:** Stephen H. Sholes. **Musicians:** Chet Atkins (guitar), Al Chernet (rhythm guitar), Marty Gold (organ), Charles Green (bass). **Location and Date of Recording:** RCA Studio 1, New York City, New York, July 30, 1952. **Original Release:** RCA Victor 20-4896 (RCA Victor 78 single, 1952), RCA Victor 47-4896 (RCA Victor 45 single, 1952).

Chet was back in RCA Victor's studios in New York City the very next night after his July 29, 1952, unaccompanied recording session that yielded "Imagination." On July 30, he recorded four songs for the label, and all of these numbers featured him playing with backing musicians. Two of the songs were instrumentals, and the other two featured lead vocals by Rosalie Allen. Far and away the most compelling of the songs Chet recorded during this session was one of the instrumentals, "Chinatown, My Chinatown."

"Chinatown, My Chinatown" was originally written by Jean Schwartz and William Jerome as an uptempo vocal number in 1910, and it eventually became a jazz/pop standard after being recorded by artists such as Al Jolson, The Mills Brothers, Tommy Dorsey, and Louis Armstrong. For his version of the song, Chet kept its tempo extremely fast—and this breakneck pace offered him the opportunity to showcase his ever more formidable guitar technique.

On "Chinatown, My Chinatown," Chet plays his D'Angelico Excel electric guitar in standard tuning out of the key of A, and he is backed by very spare rhythm guitar, organ, and bass. The Excel is often drenched in a heavy echo effect, making some of Chet's notes Chet slap right back at the listener almost immediately after they are first heard. He renders much of the song's jazzy melody through chord voicings played up and down the neck of his guitar—these voicings put him in position to provide a generous amount of simultaneous fingerpicking accompaniment to his melody playing.

Chet drives home the theme of "Chinatown, My Chinatown" by incorporating a number of innovative harmony lines that are derived from traditional Chinese music. And Chet delivers even more moments of dazzling virtuosity during the song when he plays a section of it using harmonics paired with pure tones. (Chet first used this technique on his 1951 recording of "Good-Bye Blues," which we discussed in detail earlier.)

"Chinatown, My Chinatown" was first released on 78 and 45 singles by RCA Victor in 1952 under the billing "Chet Atkins and His Galloping Guitar," and while it did not become a hit by any means, it was very well-received by Chet's growing fan base. The recording's reputation has not lessened over time—it has remained a favorite amongst Chet fans for over six decades.

"The Bells of St. Mary's"

Composers: A. Emmett Adams, Douglas Furber. **Producer:** Stephen H. Sholes. **Musicians:** Chet Atkins (guitar), Grady Martin (rhythm guitar), Jerry Byrd (steel guitar), Charles Grean (bass), Phil Kraus (drums). **Location and Date of Recording:** RCA Studio 1, New York City, New York, March 18, 1953. **Original Release:** RCA Victor 20-5300 (RCA Victor 78 single, 1953), RCA Victor 47-5300 (RCA Victor 45 single, 1953).

In March 1953, Chet made another of his periodic trips to New York City to record at RCA Victor's studios there. He recorded a total of seven songs for the label at this time, three instrumentals on March 18, and another four instrumentals on March 20. The most memorable of the songs that were laid down on March 18 was the decades-old pop standard "The Bells of St. Mary's."

"The Bells of St. Mary's" was originally written by A. Emmett Adams and Douglas Furber as a vocal number in 1917, but the most well-known version of the song was not recorded until almost three decades later—Bing Crosby sang it in the famed 1945 musical film of the same name. Chet's version of "The Bells of St. Mary's" was very far removed from Crosby's slow ballad version—he played it as a bright midtempo number.

On the recording, Chet plays his D'Angelico Excel electric guitar in standard tuning out of the key of C, and he is backed by rhythm guitar, steel guitar, bass and drums (Interestingly, the March 18, 1953 session marked the first time that Chet had ever used either a steel guitarist or a percussionist on one of his recordings.) Chet renders the uplifting melody of "The Bells of St. Mary's" in a manner that is both very ebullient and very tasteful.

We've noted Chet's innovative use of harmonics paired with regularly fretted notes in our discussions of "Good-Bye Blues" and "Chinatown, My Chinatown" just a bit earlier in this book, and "The Bells of St. Mary's" has a section near the beginning of the recording that sounds like Chet is again employing this technique. But those are not harmonics played with fretted notes that you hear in the song—rather, Chet plays the melody of the song using straight harmonics, and those harmonics are accompanied by a high-phrased harmony line played by steel guitarist Jerry Byrd.

"The Bells of St. Mary's" was first released on 78 and 45 singles by RCA Victor in 1953 under the billing "Chet Atkins and His Galloping Guitar." It should be pointed out that Chet recorded a second version of the song much later in his career—it was featured on his 1974 album *Superpickers*. The *Superpickers* version of "The Bells of St. Mary's" is a far more jazzy, uptempo version of the song, and it features a host of other musicians soloing in between Chet's guitar parts. It is definitely a very enjoyable recording—that said, however, the 1953 version of "The Bells of St. Mary's" is Chet's version of the song that his fans tend to remember the most fondly.

"Country Gentleman"

Composers: Chet Atkins, Boudleaux Bryant. **Producer:** Stephen H. Sholes. **Musicians:** Chet Atkins (guitar), Henry "Homer" Haynes (rhythm guitar), Kenneth "Jethro" Burns (mandolin), Charles Grean (bass). **Location and Date of Recording:** RCA Studio 2, New York City, New York, March 20, 1953. **Original Release:** RCA Victor 20-5300 (RCA Victor 78 single, 1953), RCA Victor 47-5300 (RCA Victor 45 single, 1953).

Two days after the March 18, 1953, recording session that had produced "The Bells of St. Mary's," Chet returned to RCA Victor's studios in New York City to do another session. This time around, he recorded four instrumentals for the label with rhythm guitarist Henry "Homer" Haynes, mandolinist Kenneth "Jethro" Burns, and bassist Charles Grean—the exact same personnel that had backed him on his landmark record "Gallopin' on the Guitar" several years earlier. At this March 20 session, Chet, Homer, Jethro and Charles recorded a song that ended up becoming every bit as much of a landmark in Chet's career as "Gallopin' on the Guitar" had been—that song was "Country Gentleman," a number that Chet had co-written with the famed songwriter Boudleaux Bryant.

We'll take a just moment here to examine the history of Chet's collaboration with Boudleaux. Boudleaux and his wife Felice wrote songs together for decades, and during that time they composed many legendary hits such as "All I Have to Do Is Dream," "Bye Bye Love" and "Rocky Top." Chet had been an admirer of the Bryants' work since the late 1940s, and this admiration led him to form an infrequent songwriting partnership with Boudleaux. A number of the songs the two men wrote together during the early 1950s ended up becoming hit records, including "Midnight" (recorded by Red Foley) and "How's the World Treating You" (recorded by Eddy Arnold.)

During his career, Chet recorded most all of the songs that he had written with Boudleaux—for example, Chet recorded his own version of "Midnight" that pre-dated Foley's version of the song. (It was recorded at the October 11-12, 1951, session that yielded "Good-Bye Blues," one of the songs we discussed earlier in the book.) But without a doubt, the Atkins/Bryant composition that would end up having the most profound impact on Chet's career was "Country Gentleman."

"Country Gentleman" is a very aptly named song, because it could certainly be considered one of the most country-sounding records that Chet ever made. It is a moderately tempoed instrumental that has an irresistibly jaunty feel to it—its syncopated melody is high-spirited and very memorable, and its rhythm bounces along like a horse at a brisk trot. Because of both its title and bright melody, the song is able to evoke images of an idyllic rural setting in the minds of many of its listeners.

On the recording, Chet plays his D'Angelico Excel electric guitar in standard tuning out of the key of A, and he renders most of the song's melody through chords that are voiced high on the guitar's fretboard. "Country Gentleman" is actually a very simple song in terms of its chord structure—but Chet's high chord voicings and syncopated picking patterns make the song a considerably more complex work than its chord structure alone would indicate.

Of course, Chet is superbly backed by Homer, Jethro, and Charles on "Country Gentleman"—Jethro delivers an easygoing but agile mandolin break, and Homer and Charles unfailingly keep the song in its rhythmic sweet spot. Chet closes out the recording by simultaneously playing the song's melody and a beautifully structured low harmony part played solely on the A string of his guitar. Incidentally, it is worth noting that the manner in which Chet plays "Country Gentleman" is obviously inspired by one of his earlier records—his 1951 recording of "Rainbow" featured the same kind of high chord voicings and low harmony parts found in "Country Gentleman." (We discussed "Rainbow" earlier in this book.)

"Country Gentleman" was first released on 78 and 45 singles by RCA Victor in 1953 under the billing "Chet Atkins and His Galloping Guitar"—its flip side was the song we discussed in this book's last entry, "The Bells of St. Mary's." This particular single sold better than many of Chet's other records that were released around the same time period. And the popularity of "Country Gentleman" would not be confined to just this single release—the song would continue to grow in stature over the years. In fact, it eventually became so popular with Chet's fans that it basically became his unofficial theme song.

The song's title actually *did* become an official moniker for Chet after he entered into his endorsement deal with the Gretsch Company. In 1957, Gretsch released a new guitar model called the Chet Atkins Country Gentleman. The Chet Atkins Country Gentleman was manufactured by Gretsch all the way up until 1981, when Chet left Gretsch to enter into an endorsement deal with the Gibson Guitar Corporation. Gibson manufactured their own version of the Chet Atkins Country Gentleman until 2005. In 2007, the Atkins family licensed Chet's name back to Gretsch, and the company again began manufacturing their original version of the Chet Atkins Country Gentleman. So as of 2014, well over 60 years after the initial release of the song "Country Gentleman," you can *still* buy a brand-new guitar bearing the song's name.

There is even *more* evidence to be offered up to illustrate the incredible staying power that "Country Gentleman" has had throughout the decades. Chet decided to title the 1974 autobiography he co-authored with Bill Neely *Country Gentleman*—so evidently Chet himself was comfortable with the fact that the song's title had basically become his second name.

Since "Country Gentleman" followed Chet so closely throughout his career, it is not surprising that he chose to re-record the song several times over the years. A new version of it was featured on Chet's classic 1959 album *Mister Guitar*—this version featured Chet being accompanied by a very spare arrangement of rhythm guitar, piano, bass, and drums. He also recorded an orchestral version of the song with Arthur Fiedler and the Boston Pops for their 1966 collaborative album *The Pops Goes Country*. These later versions of "Country Gentleman" are extremely enjoyable, but they certainly do not have the energy or the historical significance of the original 1953 version.

"City Slicker"

Composer: Chet Atkins. **Producer:** Stephen H. Sholes. **Musicians:** Chet Atkins (guitar), Louis Innis (rhythm guitar), Jerry Byrd (bass). **Location and Date of Recording:** Thomas Productions, Nashville, Tennessee, September 17, 1953. **Original Release:** RCA Victor 20-5484 (RCA Victor 78 single, 1953), RCA Victor 47-5484 (RCA Victor 45 single, 1953).

Both Chet's work as a solo artist and his work with the Carter sisters really had his career moving into high gear by the early 1950s. Things got even busier for him as Steve Sholes, RCA Victor's director of country music operations, began relying on him to contract musicians for many of the label's Nashville sessions—Chet even began producing some of these sessions if Sholes could not attend them himself.

But all of this work did not stop Chet from finding some time to arrange a session of his own for the label every so often—one of these sessions was held at Thomas Productions in Nashville on September 17, 1953. (Thomas was used for some of RCA's Nashville recording sessions until the label finally decided to build their own studio in the city—as we noted earlier in the book, RCA had also regularly used Nashville's Brown Radio Productions for the same purpose.) This September 17 session yielded four instrumentals, and arguably the most compelling of the bunch was the Chet-penned number "City Slicker."

One could speculate that when Chet wrote "City Slicker," he might well have been trying to create a song that was the polar opposite of his recently recorded number "Country Gentleman." "Country Gentleman" evoked images of an idyllic rural setting with both its title and bright melody. "City Slicker" evoked images of an unsettling urban presence with both its title and slightly foreboding, E minor-chord based melody.

On "City Slicker," Chet plays his D'Angelico Excel electric guitar in standard tuning, and he is accompanied by rhythm guitar and bass. The song features very sophisticated melody and chord patterns—so sophisticated, in fact, that could really be a question of debate as to what key the song is actually in. One could argue that it is out of the key of G—but then again, much of its melodic and chordal focus is on phrases that use E minor and E major chords as their primary starting point. Consequently, one could also argue that the song is out of the key of E every bit as much as it is out of the key of G. At any rate, Chet's playing on "City Slicker" is every bit as sophisticated as his writing—he delivers the song's melody with brilliant skill and precision.

"City Slicker" was first released on 78 and 45 singles by RCA Victor in 1953 under the billing "Chet Atkins and His Galloping Guitar," and it achieved very little success in terms of sales or airplay. Perhaps that was because the record was so musically complex that it was hard to classify just what style of music it actually was. "City Slicker" certainly wasn't country—in fact, it sounded quite a bit more like jazz.

All in all, "City Slicker" probably sounded more like rockabilly than any other style of music. Rockabilly was just starting to form into its own unique genre during the early 1950s, and Chet was certainly never considered one of its primary architects. But "City Slicker" featured Chet delivering a truly masterful rockabilly style performance—so it would seem that he somehow found a way to add rockabilly music to his bag of tricks almost before there even *was* rockabilly.

Perhaps the only firm conclusion we can reach about just what style of music "City Slicker" might be is that it is "difficult to classify"—but that's all right, because that conclusion alone offers compelling proof of how musically adventurous Chet was becoming during the 1950s.

"Kentucky Derby"

Composers: Chet Atkins, Boudleaux Bryant. **Producer:** Chet Atkins. **Musicians:** Chet Atkins (guitar), Louis Innis (rhythm guitar), Ernie Newton (bass). **Location and Date of Recording:** Thomas Productions, Nashville, Tennessee, December 24, 1953. **Original Release:** RCA Victor 20-5704 (RCA Victor 78 single, 1954), RCA Victor 47-5704 (RCA Victor 45 single, 1954).

Out of all of the Chet Atkins recordings that I chose to include in this book, "Kentucky Derby" might be the one that Chet fans will find to be my most surprising pick. The recording did not achieve any notable amount of sales or airplay when it was first released, and it never grew to be a particular favorite amongst Chet fans in the years that followed. But there are two factors that have led me to feel that "Kentucky Derby" is a very notable recording of Chet's. First, it features Chet offering up a potent combination of clever songwriting, great playing, and memorable arranging. Second, it is a perfect example of Chet's great interest in creating novelty records—an interest he would maintain throughout his entire career.

Like everyone in the music industry, Chet was very aware of the fact that vocal records were far more popular with the general public than instrumental records—and the few instrumental records that *did* become hits were often novelty numbers that used music to paint a funny, indelible picture in listener's minds. Like most all musicians, Chet was keenly interested in creating music that had a chance of being a hit record—so he wrote and recorded many novelty instrumentals over the years in the hopes that one of them might grab the public's attention and shoot to the top of the charts. Obviously, this never really happened—none of Chet's novelty numbers ever became big hits. But they now stand as a very interesting facet of his recorded work.

Before we get into discussing "Kentucky Derby," we'll quickly make note of Chet's earlier novelty record efforts. At a session on July 29-30, 1952 (the same session that produced the song "Imagination," which we discussed earlier), Chet recorded a solo guitar instrumental that he co-wrote with Boudleaux Bryant called "Hangover Blues." That number incorporated a large helping of intentionally played sour notes in order to bring to mind the splitting headache feel of a terrible hangover.

And at a session on September 17, 1953 (the same session that produced the song "City Slicker," which we just discussed), Chet recorded another instrumental he co-wrote with Boudleaux called "Peeping Tom." That number incorporated sound effects such as a woman's scream and a policeman's whistle in order to paint a musical picture of a peeping tom searching for women to leer at. ("Hangover Blues" was released by RCA Victor both as a 1952 single and as a track on Chet's first-ever album released in 1953, *Chet Atkins' Gallopin' Guitar*. "Peeping Tom" remained unreleased until it was included on the Chet Atkins CD set *Galloping Guitar: The Early Years* released by Bear Family Records in 1993.)

"Kentucky Derby" was yet *another* novelty instrumental written by Chet and Boudleaux—so one must come to the conclusion that Boudleaux must have been every bit as interested in creating a hit novelty record as Chet was. The song was a breakneck-paced number that captured the feel and the sounds of an exciting horse race, and Chet recorded it during a four-song session for RCA Victor at Thomas Productions in Nashville on December 24, 1953. (It is worth noting that this was the first of Chet's sessions that he ever produced himself—after all, he was producing sessions for other musicians, so he could certainly produce one of his own sessions from time to time.)

On "Kentucky Derby," Chet plays his D'Angelico Excel electric guitar in standard tuning out of the key of A, and he is accompanied by bass and a percussion part that brilliantly mimics the sound of hoofbeats. This hoofbeat percussion is what really drives the recording—but sadly, there is no way of knowing for sure just who might have played it, because the only musicians credited for playing on this session are Louis Innis on rhythm guitar and Ernie Newton on bass. "Kentucky Derby" does not have a rhythm guitar part, so perhaps it is Innis laying down the hoofbeat part. At any rate, whoever is playing this rock-solid percussion provides the key element that holds the entire recording together.

For years, Chet's records had been released under the billing "Chet Atkins and His Galloping Guitar"—on "Kentucky Derby," Chet is given the chance to truly live up to this billing, and he does not disappoint. His guitar gallops along with his percussionist's hoofbeat part at a furious pace, and he cleverly incorporates snippets of horse race-themed music such as "The Call to the Post" and "The Old Grey Mare" into the song. Chet even manages to throw in a few runs that capture the feel, if not the actual notes, of The *William Tell* Overture, which of course instantly conjures up images of The Lone Ranger furiously riding to the rescue on his horse Silver.

"Kentucky Derby" was first released on 78 and 45 singles by RCA Victor in 1954—and obviously, the label chose to stick with their practice of billing Chet under the phrase "Chet Atkins and His Galloping Guitar" for *this* particular record. The recording deserves to be remembered as one of Chet's earliest and finest forays into the realm of novelty records. We'll be discussing a number of his other novelty records later in the book.

"Wildwood Flower"

Composer: Traditional. **Producer:** Chet Atkins. **Musicians:** Chet Atkins (guitar), Louis Innis (rhythm guitar), Ernie Newton (bass). **Location and Date of Recording:** Thomas Productions, Nashville, Tennessee, December 24, 1953. **Original Release:** RCA Victor 20-5638 (RCA Victor 78 single, 1954), RCA Victor 47-5638 (RCA Victor 45 single, 1954).

"Kentucky Derby" may never have made that much of an impression on Chet fans after it was recorded during a four-song session for RCA Victor at Thomas Productions in Nashville on December 24, 1953—but one of the other numbers recorded at that same session certainly did. Chet's wonderful instrumental interpretation of the traditional folk song "Wildwood Flower" became a favorite amongst his fans, which led him to regularly include the number in his live shows throughout the rest of his career.

"Wildwood Flower" was based on a folk song from the 1800s called "I'll Twine 'Mid the Ringlets" written by Maud Irving and Joseph Philbrick Webster, and it first gained widespread popularity when it was recorded by the original lineup of the Carter Family in 1928. The Carters performed the song as a vocal number with its traditional lyrics, and it remained a staple of the group's repertoire throughout their entire career. Chet also had a very long history with "Wildwood Flower," one that went all the way back to the time when he was a boy—he played the song on the fiddle at his first public performance when he was just ten years old.

Chet's affectionate interpretation of "Wildwood Flower" stands as a fitting tribute to his long relationship with both the Carter Family and the song itself. On the recording, Chet plays his D'Angelico Excel electric guitar in standard tuning out of the key of C, and he is accompanied by spare rhythm guitar and bass.

For generations, "Wildwood Flower" has been one of the most rudimentary songs for a fledgling folk/country guitarist to learn. And most every guitarist plays it in standard tuning out of the key of C like Chet does on his recording of the song—this is because its melody can so easily be rendered out of standard C, F and G7 chords. One of the most striking aspects of Chet's version of "Wildwood Flower" is that he makes a point of playing through its melody pattern one time in a decidedly basic fashion—in other words, in a manner that is much like the way that a beginning guitarist would render the song. It is a testament to Chet's admirable sense of musicianship that he would want to showcase the simple beauty of "Wildwood Flower" by taking a moment to play it in its most basic form.

Of course, after Chet does this, he does offer up a number of interesting embellishments to the song's melody. These embellishments feature a substantial amount of intricate chord voicings, harmony lines, and self-accompanying fingerpicking patterns—but they never become so busy that they overwhelm the melody itself.

"Wildwood Flower" was first released on 78 and 45 singles by RCA Victor in 1954 under the billing "Chet Atkins and His Galloping Guitar," and the recording did not achieve any great success in terms of sales or airplay. But the fact that Chet's inspired version of the song continued to win over his fans for decades to come certainly proved that the recording did not need initial sales or airplay to stand the test of time.

"Downhill Drag"

Composers: Chet Atkins, Boudleaux Bryant. **Producer:** Stephen H. Sholes. **Musicians:** Chet Atkins (guitar), Henry "Homer" Haynes (rhythm guitar), Kenneth "Jethro" Burns (mandolin), Holly Swanson (bass). **Location and Date of Recording:** RCA Studios, Chicago, Illinois, March 9, 1954. **Original Release:** RCA Victor 20-5704 (RCA Victor 78 single, 1954), RCA Victor 47-5704 (RCA Victor 45 single, 1954).

In March 1954, Chet traveled to RCA Victor's studios in Chicago to do two sessions for the label with his longtime musical collaborators, rhythm guitarist Henry "Homer" Haynes and mandolinist Kenneth "Jethro" Burns. The first of these sessions was held on March 8, and the second on March 9. Though Chet, Homer and Jethro would find a number of ways to work together throughout the rest of the 1950s, the 1960s, and the early 1970s, the sessions would mark the last time that the three men would perform together on any of Chet's solo recordings.

On March 8, Chet, Homer and Jethro held a split session that yielded four songs, two of them Chet's and two of them Homer and Jethro's. One of the Chet numbers recorded that day was a curiosity that is worth taking note of here—Chet turned in a very well-sung lead vocal on a bluesy ballad entitled "Get Up and Go" written by Mac McCarthy. For some reason, RCA decided not to release the song in any form. In fact, it remained unissued for almost a half-century—it finally saw the light of day when it was included on the Chet Atkins CD set *Galloping Guitar: The Early Years* released by Bear Family Records in 1993.

As we noted earlier in the book, RCA Victor had originally signed Chet to a recording contract because they hoped they could mold him into their own version of singer/guitarist Merle Travis—but of course, Chet simply was not the kind of lead-singing frontman that Merle was. So over his first few years with the label, his records featured more and more of his guitar playing and less and less of his singing. Chet's lead-singing career had basically reached its end with his recording of "Get Up and Go"—the song would mark his last recorded attempt at being a straight-ahead singing frontman who crooned serious ballads. He was now truly a guitarist only, not a singer/guitarist. (Obviously, Chet would still step up to the microphone to sing a comedy or novelty number every now and again in the decades that followed—we'll be examining a few of those numbers later in the book.)

Chet Atkins playing his D'Angelico Excel electric guitar at a recording session with guitarist Henry "Homer" Haynes and mandolinist Kenneth "Jethro" Burns, early 1950s.

The March 9 session was all Chet's, and it yielded four instrumentals. One of the session's standouts was "Downhill Drag," a lively midtempo number co-written by Chet and Boudleaux Bryant. On the recording, Chet, Homer and Jethro were joined by Holly Swanson on bass. The song also featured a percussionist lightly playing a snare drum—but that whoever that percussionist was did not receive credit for performing on the session.

On "Downhill Drag," Chet plays his D'Angelico Excel electric guitar in standard tuning out of the key of C. His ebullient rendering of the song's bright, syncopated melody is very similar to his playing on "Country Gentleman," the Atkins-Bryant composition that he had recorded and released the year before. Some of the song's melody lines feature Chet and Jethro playing them in unison, and Jethro also turns a relaxed solo part.

"Downhill Drag" was first released on 78 and 45 singles by RCA Victor in 1954 under the billing "Chet Atkins and His Galloping Guitar" as the flip side of "Kentucky Derby," a song we discussed just a bit earlier in the book. The single releases of the songs recorded at Chet's March 1954 Chicago sessions marked the end of Homer and Jethro's direct involvement with his solo records. This was probably due to the simple fact that Homer and Jethro's career as a country comedy duo had continued to flourish, so they had to devote most of their time to their own projects. But even though Homer and Jethro did not play on any more Chet Atkins records, their wonderful contributions to his music made during the late 1940s and early 1950s would be fondly remembered by Chet fans for decades to come.

The three men were part of a loosely knit group of top session players known as the Country All-Stars—that group recorded and released a 10-inch record called *String Dustin'* on the RCA Victor label in 1953. The Country All-Stars went on to hold a 1956 recording session that Chet, Homer and Jethro all participated in.

And the three men even formed a brand-new band in the late 1960s—their group the Nashville String Band recorded and released six albums for RCA between 1969 and 1972. (Since this book is strictly about the greatest recordings that Chet made as a solo artist, none of the fine work created by the Country All-Stars or the Nashville String Band is included in its entries.) And after Homer passed away in 1971, Chet performed live with Jethro on many occasions. Chet's long and incredibly productive relationship with Homer and Jethro did not truly reach its end until Jethro passed away in 1989.

"Indiana (Back Home in Indiana)"

Composers: James Hanley, Ballard MacDonald. **Producer:** Stephen H. Sholes. **Musicians:** Chet Atkins (guitar), Bud Isaacs (steel guitar), Dale Potter (fiddle), John Gordy (piano), Bob Moore (bass), Buddy Harman (drums). **Location and Date of Recording:** Thomas Productions, Nashville, Tennessee, September 26, 1954. **Original Release:** *A Session with Chet Atkins* (RCA Victor album, 1954).

On September 26, 1954, Chet held a four-song session for RCA Victor at Thomas Productions in Nashville to record songs that would be used for his third album, *A Session with Chet Atkins*. That album was released by RCA in December 1954. *A Session with Chet Atkins* was Chet's first album to be released as a 12-inch LP record, as well as his first to feature songs that were actually recorded for a specific album project. His previous two albums *Chet Atkins' Gallopin' Guitar* and *Stringin' Along with Chet Atkins* (both released by RCA in 1953) were 10-inch records that were collections of songs that had been previously released as singles.

In order to avoid any confusion, it should be pointed out here that *Stringin' Along with Chet Atkins* was re-released as a 12-inch LP record in 1956, and this version was radically different from its 1953 incarnation. We mentioned the 1956 *Stringin'* in our discussion of Chet's 1952 recording of "The Third Man Theme" earlier in the book, and we'll examine the 1956 *Stringin'* in detail when we discuss Chet's 1956 recording of "Oh. By Jingo, Oh. By Gee. (You're the Only Girl for Me)" a bit later in the book.

A Session with Chet Atkins marked another important first in Chet's career—the recording sessions for the album were among the first sessions he ever did that featured him playing a Gretsch guitar. Throughout 1954, Gretsch and Chet worked on designing their guitars, and the instruments they would come up with would turn out to be a resounding success. The Gretsch 6120 Chet Atkins Hollow Body model and the Gretsch 6121 Chet Atkins Solid Body model were released before the end of the year, and they sold extremely well right out of the gate. The 6120 was the model that Chet was directly involved in designing, and it ended up being the more popular of the two models.

The first Gretsch guitar that Chet regularly used was a modified version of the 6120— this modified version had uncut f-holes, so it was actually much less of a true "hollow body" guitar than a standard 6120. Chet's 6120 had two output jacks that allowed the guitar's treble and bass strings to be plugged into their own separate inputs. (The instrument's pickups were wired in a manner that sent the treble strings' signal to one jack, and the bass strings' signal to the other.) This guitar was the one that Chet used on the songs recorded for *A Session with Chet Atkins*.

All of the numbers recorded for *A Session with Chet Atkins* were designed to be showcases not just for Chet's playing, but also for the excellent studio musicians who were backing him up. The album featured multiple solos performed by steel guitarist Bud Isaacs, fiddler Dale Potter, and pianist John Gordy. These musicians played spectacularly through all of the solos found on *A Session with Chet Atkins*—but it must be noted that their solos drastically limited the amount of playing time Chet got to have on his very first 12-inch album.

Since every tune on *A Session with Chet Atkins* turned out wonderfully, it is hard to choose a particular one to highlight for this book—I've chosen to discuss Chet's rendition of "Indiana (Back Home in Indiana)." The song was originally written in 1917 as a vocal number, but it truly became a hit when it was recorded as an instrumental by the Original Dixieland Jazz Band later that same year. Over the years, it became a jazz standard that was recorded by many different artists.

On "Indiana (Back Home in Indiana)," Chet plays his modified 1955 Gretsch 6120 electric guitar in standard tuning. He starts off the recording by playing the song's introduction at a leisurely tempo in the key of C, unaccompanied by any of his backing musicians. Then the band kicks in with him, and the song moves to a more brisk tempo. Chet solos for a verse, still playing in the key of C. The song then migrates to the key of F, and solos are taken by Potter, Isaacs, and Gordy. Chet closes out the recording with a final solo in the key of F, throwing in some nice octave work and a playful quote of the traditional folk tune "The Girl I Left Behind."

Chet would hold two more recording sessions with the same personnel to record the remainder of the songs found on *A Session with Chet Atkins*—these sessions were held in Nashville on September 27 and November 16, 1954. The album's release sent a clear message that Chet had truly arrived as an adventurous artist who was capable of seamlessly blending many different styles into his guitar playing.

Here is one final note regarding "Indiana (Back Home in Indiana)." Chet would record the number one more time during his career—he performed a slightly rocked-up version of the song for his 1963 album *Teen Scene*.

"Silver Bell"

> **Composers:** Percy Wenrich, Edward Madden. **Producer:** Stephen H. Sholes. **Musicians:** Chet Atkins (guitar), Hank Snow (guitar), Ernie Newton (bass), Buddy Harman (drums). **Location and Date of Recording:** Thomas Productions, Nashville, Tennessee, October 3, 1954. **Original Release:** RCA Victor 20-5995 (RCA Victor 78 single, 1955), RCA Victor 47-5995 (RCA Victor 45 single, 1955).

In early 1955, all of the hard work that Chet had been doing over the years to further his career finally jelled together to propel him to the heights of success that he had always dreamed of. He had won so many admirers that he had his own nationwide fan club actively working to promote his music, he had just signed a deal to endorse his own brand of Gretsch guitars, and perhaps best of all, for the first time he had several singles rising to the top of the record charts. The first of these singles to be recorded was "Silver Bell," an instrumental duet that Chet recorded with one of RCA Victor's biggest stars, singer/guitarist Hank Snow.

Chet and Hank recorded "Silver Bell" during a four-song session for RCA at Thomas Productions in Nashville on October 3, 1954. The song was originally written as an uptempo vocal number by Percy Wenrich and Edward Madden in 1911—but Chet and Hank used their distinctive guitar styles to make the song into a very catchy instrumental, one that would be capable of grabbing the attention of countless people throughout the United States.

We have been able to pin down exactly which of Chet's guitars he used for most all of the recordings discussed earlier in this book, but "Silver Bell" is the recording that is going to force us out of that practice. Once Chet signed his endorsement deal with Gretsch, he constantly recorded with that brand of guitar—but he did not use only one *specific* Gretsch, because over the years the company supplied him with many different guitars. There were definitely a few Gretsches that he used much more than others—but even still, there is no way of knowing just which Gretsch he might have used on many of the songs we'll be discussing throughout the rest of the book. If I have found reliable evidence about Chet using a particular guitar on a particular recording, I will be using that evidence—but if not, my discussion of Chet's choice of guitars on his recordings will be far less specific from here on out.

That said, it seems very likely that Chet used his modified 1955 Gretsch 6120 electric guitar with uncut f-holes and two output jacks to record "Silver Bell." He recorded all of the songs for his album *A Session with Chet Atkins* using this instrument, and they were recorded right around the same time "Silver Bell" was recorded.

At any rate, Chet plays an electric guitar in standard tuning out of the key of A on "Silver Bell," and he is joined by Hank playing an acoustic guitar that is also in standard tuning. The two are accompanied by very spare bass and drums. Chet and

Hank's guitar parts could hardly be more different from one another—Chet plays the song using his signature style of fingerpicked melody lines and simultaneous accompanying patterns, and Hank plays the song by flatpicking its melody in a very simple, percussive style. One might think that these two very different styles of guitar playing would conflict with one another—but just the opposite is true, they blend together so strikingly that "Silver Bell" is a joy to listen to.

"Silver Bell" was first released on 78 and 45 singles by RCA Victor in early 1955 under the billing "Chet Atkins and Hank Snow Guitar Duet." In the spring of that year, it reached the number 15 spot on the U.S. country single charts. Incidentally, "Silver Bell" was technically not Chet's first radio hit, it was his *second*—his solo record "Mister Sandman" had made it on the charts shortly before "Silver Bell." "Mister Sandman" was recorded about a month after Chet and Hank had recorded "Silver Bell," but it RCA released it shortly before the release of Chet and Hank's record. We'll discuss "Mister Sandman" in this book's next entry.

"Mister Sandman"

>**Composer:** Pat Ballard. **Producer:** Stephen H. Sholes. **Musicians:** Chet Atkins (guitar), Bud Issacs (steel guitar), Marvin Hughes (piano/celeste), Ernie Newton (bass), Buddy Harman (drums). **Location and Date of Recording:** RCA Victor Studio, Methodist Television, Radio & Film Commission, Nashville, Tennessee, November 17, 1954. **Original Release:** RCA Victor 20-5956 (RCA Victor 78 single, 1955), RCA Victor 47-5956 (RCA Victor 45 single, 1955).

"Mister Sandman" is arguably the single most historically important recording that Chet ever made during his half century-long career. It was his first-ever hit record, and to this day it still stands as a perfect blend of his greatest musical strengths. The recording showcases Chet's extraordinary ability to arrange a piece of music for the guitar, and his equally extraordinary ability to play those arrangements to perfection. "Mister Sandman" captures the formidable power of Chet's talent at a moment in time when he himself thought he was playing guitar better than he had ever played in his entire life.

In other words, if you ever meet someone who knows nothing at all about Chet Atkins, just about the only thing you will really need to introduce this person to Chet's genius is "Mister Sandman"—the recording offers a sonic portrait of his skill as an arranger, a self-accompanying fingerstyle player, and an innovative soloist that is just *that* complete.

"Mister Sandman" was both a very new and very popular number when Chet recorded his version of the song. Written by Pat Ballard, "Mister Sandman" was first recorded in 1954 by the female singing quartet the Chordettes. The Chordettes' version of the song went to number one on the U.S. pop single charts before the end of that year.

It could be said that practically no other song in history had been as well-tailored to Chet's strengths as the Chordettes' version of "Mister Sandman" was. The recording featured a bouncy tempo, a complex chord structure, jazzy melody and harmony lines, and multiple key changes. All of these elements gave Chet an embarrassment of riches to work with when he was constructing his interpretation of the song.

In 1954, after years of holding their Nashville recording sessions at independently owned studios such as Brown Radio Productions and Thomas Productions, RCA Victor finally decided to establish their own permanent recording studio in the city. The label set up this studio inside of a building owned by the Methodist Television, Radio & Film Commission. Chet recorded his version of "Mister Sandman" during a four-song session for the label at the new studio on November 17, 1954. (That session was split with fellow RCA recording artist Ruby Wells, so only two of its songs were Chet's.)

As was the case with "Silver Bell," it seems very likely that Chet used his modified 1955 Gretsch 6120 electric guitar with uncut f-holes and two output jacks to record "Mister Sandman," since he used that instrument on many of his other recordings made around the same time period.

We have not discussed any of the different guitar amplifiers that Chet used on his recordings up until this point in the book—but the amp that Chet used for his recording of "Mister Sandman" is so historically noteworthy that it deserves our attention. In the early 1950s, an Illinois musician/electronics repairman named Ray Butts designed a guitar amp that he dubbed the EchoSonic. The amp was equipped with a built-in tape loop that recorded the signal from a guitar and played it back a fraction of a second later—this gave the guitar's sound a pronounced slap-back/echo effect. In 1954, Ray traveled to Nashville to show Chet the EchoSonic, and Chet was so impressed with the amp that he immediately started using it for selected live appearances and recording sessions, including the "Mister Sandman" session.

Chet's version of "Mister Sandman" features him playing a Gretsch electric guitar through his EchoSonic amp, and he is backed by celeste, piano, bass and drums. The focus of the recording is almost solely on Chet's playing, so these backing parts are so subtle that you really have to listen for them to realize they are even there. (Incidentally, a steel guitarist is also given credit for playing on the recording, but even the most thorough listen of the song does not reveal a single note of steel guitar.)

Chet starts out "Mister Sandman" by fingerpicking the song's melody and a simultaneous accompanying pattern in the key of A. After taking the song through its intro and first chord progression in that key, he moves to the key of D and restates the intro. However, he doesn't stay in that key for long—he moves to the key of G for the song's second chord progression. It is at this point in the song when Chet's backing musicians play their most prominent supporting role—their accompaniment allows Chet to focus his playing on harmonically dense chords infused with vibrato, and some nimble single-note solo runs. Chet then moves the song to the key of C for a final intro and chord progression—he closes out the recording by again fingerpicking the song's melody and a simultaneous accompanying pattern.

Chet's version of "Mister Sandman" was first released on 78 and 45 singles by RCA Victor in January 1955 under the billing "Chet Atkins and His Galloping Guitar." His recording of the song didn't reach the very top of the charts like The Chordettes' version did, but it still became his first official radio hit—it reached the number 13 spot on the U.S. country single charts in early 1955. After all his years of hard work, Chet had finally reached a level of success that could really only be summed up through the use of one particular word—and that word was "star." Chet Atkins was now a star, and he would continue to be one for many, many years to come.

Incidentally, Chet did record one more version of "Mister Sandman" late in his career—it was created for his album *The Magic of Chet Atkins* released in 1990 by

Heartland Music. On *The Magic of Chet Atkins* "Mister Sandman," Chet was backed by strings, keyboards, bass, and drums, and he played a Gibson Chet Atkins CE guitar. (The CE was the solidbody acoustic that Chet and Gibson designed together in the early 1980s.)

This version of "Mister Sandman" was pleasant enough, but very few people ever heard it because the album it was on never received any sort of widespread release. Heartland Music was a division of CBS Special Products that specialized in the kind of direct-to-customer releases only found in mail-order catalogs. Consequently, *The Magic of Chet Atkins* ended up being a decidedly obscure album that was familiar only to the most devoted Chet fans.

"Darling, Je Vous Aime Beaucoup"

Composer: Anna Sosenko. **Producer:** Chet Atkins. **Musicians:** Chet Atkins (guitar), Jack Shook (rhythm guitar), Bob Moore (bass), Farris Coursey (drums). **Location and Date of Recording:** RCA Victor Studio, Methodist Television, Radio & Film Commission, Nashville, Tennessee, March 7, 1955. **Original Release:** *Pickin' the Hits* (RCA Victor Extended Play 45, 1955).

On March 7, 1955, Chet held a recording session for RCA Victor at the label's Nashville studio. The purpose of the four-song session was to record all of the numbers for Chet's next recording project, a four-song Extended Play 45 entitled *Pickin' the Hits*. That EP was released by RCA in mid–1955 under the billing "Chet Atkins and His Galloping Guitar."

Chet decided to record "Mister Sandman" when that song was a current radio hit—and as evidenced by *Pickin' the Hits'* title, he stuck with that song selection strategy for this new project. All four of the EP's numbers, "(The Wallflower) Dance With Me, Henry," "Tweedlee Dee," "Cherry Pink and Apple Blossom White," and "Darling, Je Vous Aime Beaucoup" had been radio hits right around the time the EP was first recorded. Chet would continue to use this strategy of interpreting current material for his own recordings for decades.

Not surprisingly, Chet's playing on all four of these songs was equally stellar—we'll examine "Darling, Je Vous Aime Beaucoup" because it is arguably the most musically sophisticated of the bunch. (Incidentally, the number's French title translated entirely into English means simply "Darling, I love you very much.") "Darling, Je Vous Aime Beaucoup" was written as a slow-tempoed vocal ballad in 1935 by Anna Sosenko, and that same year it was recorded by one of Chet's biggest musical heroes, jazz guitarist Django Reinhardt. Reinhardt's version of the song featured a lead vocal that was sung by the popular French singer/actor Jean Sablon. In 1954, the legendary singer/pianist Nat "King" Cole recorded what would become the most well-known version of the song—that recording reached #7 on the U.S. pop charts in early 1955. (Obviously, Cole's version of "Darling, Je Vous Aime Beaucoup" was the version of the song that led Chet to record the number for his EP.)

On "Darling, Je Vous Aime Beaucoup," Chet plays a Gretsch electric guitar in standard tuning out of the key of E, and he is backed by very spare rhythm guitar, bass and drums. He renders the song using far less self-accompanying patterns than he has used on many of his previous recordings—instead, he chooses to interpret the number's beautiful melody through many delicately phrased single-note solo passages.

However, there is far more to Chet's work on "Darling, Je Vous Aime Beaucoup" than just single-note solos—he infuses much of his playing with rich chords and inventive harmony lines.

All in all, there is a thoughtful artistry to Chet's interpretation of "Darling, Je Vous Aime Beaucoup" that feels very much like a quantum leap in his playing style. It could be argued that the recording seems to capture him at the very moment he was evolving into something that went far beyond him being simply a "country guitarist"—he was a world-class instrumentalist now, one that could play virtually any kind of music.

In fact, it should be pointed out that "Darling, Je Vous Aime Beaucoup" is the first of Chet's recordings we have discussed in detail in this book that could be classified as an "easy listening" record. Over the years as Chet matured as an artist, he started playing more and more music that could best be described as "sedate." Of course, he would still continue to turn out a good number of toe-tappers—but the overall relaxing nature of Chet's music would lead to him being viewed by the general public as an easy listening artist every bit as much as a country artist.

At any rate, Chet's *Pickin' the Hits* EP may not have produced any hit radio singles like "Mister Sandman" when it was first released—but even still, its wonderful quality definitely helped to bolster his ever growing reputation.

"Minute Waltz"

Composer: Frédéric Chopin (arranged by Chet Atkins). **Producer:** Chet Atkins. **Musicians:** Chet Atkins (guitar). **Location and Date of Recording:** RCA Victor Studio, Methodist Television, Radio & Film Commission, Nashville, Tennessee, October 26, 1955. **Original Release:** *Chet Atkins in Three Dimensions* (RCA Victor album, 1955).

Chet's incredible growth as a musical artist in the early to mid–1950s led him to develop a concept for his second 12-inch LP record that was far more sophisticated than any of his previous recording projects. The album would be titled *Chet Atkins in Three Dimensions*, and it would showcase him playing three distinctly styles of music—those styles were folk, pop and classical. Each style would be represented by four separate songs, bringing the total number of songs on the album to twelve. Obviously, Chet had been recording a wide variety of folk and pop numbers for years—but *Chet Atkins in Three Dimensions* would mark the first time that he seriously delved into the realm of classical music on record.

As if this concept was not ambitious enough, Chet decided to raise the stakes even higher—he would play all of the songs found on *Chet Atkins in Three Dimensions* virtually unaccompanied. Several supporting rhythm guitar and bass guitar tracks would show up on the album, but these tracks were played by Chet himself.

On October 26, 1955, Chet held the first recording session for *Chet Atkins in Three Dimensions* at RCA Victor's Nashville studio—this session yielded three songs. Out of these three, the one that probably gave the clearest indication of just how special Chet's new album was going to be was "Minute Waltz," one of the album's classical music pieces. It seems very likely that Chet himself was especially pleased with this particular recording, since it was chosen to be the album's closing track.

The official title of "Minute Waltz" was "The Waltz in D-flat major, Op. 64, No. 1," and it was composed in 1847 by the famed Polish composer/pianist Frédéric Chopin. Chopin wrote the piece as a waltz for solo piano, and was not him but his music publisher who gave the piece its "Minute Waltz" nickname. Of course, that nickname was meant to mean "small waltz," not a waltz that should be frantically played in one minute flat. But even when the waltz was played at its proper tempo, it still was a very fast-moving, exciting piece.

Chet's arrangement of "Minute Waltz" as a solo guitar piece is very complex, and it retains all of the musical acrobatics found in Chopin's original composition. On the recording, Chet plays a Gretsch electric guitar in standard tuning out of the key of D—his guitar is capoed at the 2nd fret, so it sounds as if he is playing out of the key of E. Chet's totally unaccompanied playing of "Minute Waltz" is spectacularly quick and precise, and it leaves no doubt that his initial attempts to record classical music works were going to be a resounding success.

"Arkansas Traveler"

Composer: Traditional (arranged by Roy Lanham). **Producer:** Chet Atkins. **Musicians:** Chet Atkins (guitar). **Location and Date of Recording:** RCA Victor Studio, Methodist Television, Radio & Film Commission, Nashville, Tennessee, October 27, 1955. **Original Release:** *Chet Atkins in Three Dimensions* (RCA Victor album, 1955).

Chet was back at RCA's Nashville studio on October 27, 1955, to record more songs for his *Chet Atkins in Three Dimensions* album. This time around, he recorded four numbers, including the song that would be used to open the album, the well-known folk tune "Arkansas Traveler." "Arkansas Traveler" had originally been written as a fiddle number by fiddler/storyteller Sanford C. Faulker in the mid–1800s. Over the span of many generations, the song became a well-loved and instantly recognizable part of American musical culture. (Of course, most kids knew it as the song with the lyrics "I'm bringing home a baby bumblebee"—but those silly words penned by an unknown lyricist became popular many years after the song was first written.)

The solo guitar arrangement that Chet used to record his version of "Arkansas Traveler" was credited to Roy Lanham—Lanham was himself a well-known guitarist who worked with a number of successful country music groups over the years. Lanham had been a friend of Chet's since the 1940s—in fact, he had played rhythm guitar on Chet's first-ever official record release, the 1947 Bullet single featuring the songs "Guitar Blues (Pickin' the Blues)" and "Brown Eyes Cryin' in the Rain."

On "Arkansas Traveler," Chet plays a Gretsch electric guitar in standard tuning out of the key of C. He opens the recording with a leisurely tempoed run-through of the song's chord progression—he plays much of its familiar melody through chords voiced high on the fretboard of his guitar, and some nicely placed harmonic notes. He takes a second run-through of the song's chord progression in waltz time, rendering its melody along with a simultaneously played accompanying pattern.

On the third chord progression of "Arkansas Traveler," Chet takes the tune in an entirely unexpected direction—he abruptly moves out of waltz time and shifts the song's chords and melody to the key of C minor. This once very happy-sounding number suddenly becomes decidedly dark and foreboding. But then Chet brightens things up by returning to the key of C for a final run-through of the tune—on that run-through, he plays much of the song's melody on his lower strings.

Obviously, Chet's playing throughout all of "Arkansas Traveler" is spectacular. But it could be said that the *real* star of this particular recording is Roy Lanham's marvelously inventive arrangement of the song. At any rate, both Chet and Roy shine on "Arkansas Traveler," and their combined talents make the recording one of Chet's all-time best.

"Ochi Chornya (Dark Eyes)"

> **Composer:** Traditional (arranged by Chet Atkins). **Producer:** Chet Atkins. **Musicians:** Chet Atkins (guitar). **Location and Date of Recording:** RCA Victor Studio, Methodist Television, Radio & Film Commission, Nashville, Tennessee, October 28, 1955. **Original Release:** *Chet Atkins in Three Dimensions* (RCA Victor album, 1955).

Chet was back at RCA's Nashville studio on October 28, 1955, to record more songs for his *Chet Atkins in Three Dimensions* album. This was his third straight day of recording numbers for the album—amazingly, it only took those three days to do most all of the recording for this very ambitious project. On October 28, Chet laid down another four songs—one of these numbers was the late 19th-century Russian romantic song "Ochi Chornya," which in English meant "Dark Eyes."

Chet grouped "Ochi Chornya" with his folk numbers on *Chet Atkins in Three Dimensions*, but the song really did not fit as neatly into that category as a song like "Arkansas Traveler" did. Over the years, "Ochi Chornya" had become known as more of a jazz standard after being recorded by artists such as Maxine Sullivan, Django Reinhardt and Louis Armstrong. But Chet did not render "Ochi Chornya" simply as a swinging jazz number like these artists had—he guided the song through a variety of musical mood shifts and tempo changes, much like the manner in which he had interpreted "Arkansas Traveler."

On "Ochi Chornya," Chet plays a Gretsch electric guitar in standard tuning out of the key of E minor, and he is accompanied by rhythm guitar and bass. These accompanying tracks are played by Chet himself. (As we noted in our discussion of "Minute Waltz," Chet recorded backing tracks to support his main guitar track for several of the songs featured on *Chet Atkins in Three Dimensions*.)

Chet opens the recording with a slow-tempoed run-through of the song's chord progression—he embellishes the song's haunting melody with a number of sweeping, note-packed, arpeggios. He takes a second run-through of the song's chord progression in waltz time, rendering its melody along with a simultaneously played accompanying pattern. Chet then moves the song to a moderate swing tempo for several chord progressions, and he embellishes its melody with some jazzy improvisations. For the finale of the recording, Chet ramps the song up to an extremely fast tempo and really lets his fingers fly—he delivers a barrage of blindingly quick solo runs that are loaded with hammer-ons, pull-offs, and dissonant notes. He closes the song with a final dramatic arpeggio, and a deep push-down/pull-up on his guitar's vibrato bar.

Incidentally, it should be pointed out that a number of recently released Chet compact disc anthologies have this recording on them, but all of these CDs used an imperfect master of the recording. At 1 minute, 12 seconds into the song, these CD versions skip several beats—in other words, they sound much like the way a song on record sounds when your record player's needle skips. So basically the only way to hear the recording without the skip is to go out and find yourself a decent copy of *Chet Atkins in Three Dimensions* on vinyl.

And make no mistake, there are a *lot* of vinyl copies of the album out in the world to be found. Chet's reputation as a world-class musical artist was spreading, so *Chet Atkins in Three Dimensions* sold quite well when it was first released by RCA Victor in late 1955. It is worth noting that the label chose to release the album under the billing "Chet Atkins and His Guitar"—the "Galloping" part of Chet's usual billing was dropped. Evidently, RCA had decided that Chet was well-known enough by this point that they didn't need to bolster his image by using a billing that made him sound a bit like a circus performer.

At any rate, Chet had made a very powerful artistic statement when he broadened his musical horizons for *Chet Atkins in Three Dimensions*—and it was a statement that would resonate with music fans for generations to come.

"The Poor People of Paris (Jean's Song)"

Composer: Marguerite Monnot. **Producer:** Chet Atkins. **Musicians:** Chet Atkins (guitar), Harold Bradley (rhythm guitar), Bob Moore (bass), Farris Coursey (drums). **Location and Date of Recording:** RCA Victor Studio, Methodist Television, Radio & Film Commission, Nashville, Tennessee, November 22, 1955. **Original Release:** RCA Victor 20-6366 (RCA Victor 78 single, 1956), RCA Victor 47-6366 (RCA Victor 45 single, 1956).

On November 22, 1955, less than a month after finishing up the recording of his groundbreaking album *Chet Atkins in Three Dimensions*, Chet was back at RCA's Nashville studio to record a new single for the label. The A-side of that single was a jaunty midtempo number called "The Poor People of Paris (Jean's Song)." The song was an instrumental version of "La Goualante du Pauvre Jean," a vocal number written by the French songwriter Marguerite Monnot. In 1954, "La Goualante du Pauvre Jean" was recorded by Monnot's longtime musical collaborator, the legendary French singer Édith Piaf. Piaf's version of the song became a big hit—in fact, it ended up being the first French record to ever reach number one on both the U.S. and British record charts.

In 1955, the American songwriter Jack Lawrence set about writing an English lyric for "La Goualante du Pauvre Jean," and what he came up with had nothing to do with the content of Monnot's original lyric. This was hardly surprising, because the very premise of Lawrence's lyric was based on his misinterpretation of the song's title. In English, "La Goualante du Pauvre Jean" means "The Ballad of Poor John"—but Lawrence took the words "pauvre Jean" to mean "pauvre *gens*," which in English means "poor people." So he based his lyric around the idea of "the poor people of Paris," not one unfortunate individual named John.

But when all was said and done, Lawrence's misinterpretation of Monnot's lyric ended up working out just fine for him—a number of different artists released successful instrumental versions of the song under Lawrence's "The Poor People of Paris" title. Of course, one of those artists was Chet—and Chet even tried to hint at the basic subject matter of Monnot's original lyric by adding the words "Jean's Song" to the title of his recording.

"The Poor People of Paris (Jean's Song)" • 1955

Before we get into discussing just how well "The Poor People of Paris (Jean's Song)" did for Chet in terms of sales and airplay, let's discuss the recording itself. Chet plays a Gretsch electric guitar in standard tuning on the recording, and he delivers the song in a relaxed swing tempo while accompanied by rhythm guitar, bass and drums. Farris Coursey's unique percussion work shares the spotlight with Chet's guitar throughout the recording. Farris not only plays drums, but he also often keeps rhythm by slapping his hands on his thighs—this creates a sound that is similar to the sound made by a tap dancer's feet.

Chet opens the song in the key of A, rendering its bouncy melody along with a simultaneously played accompanying pattern. The second time through the number's chord pattern, his backing musicians step in more prominently—this allows him to render the song's melody along with a continuous harmony part. The third time through the number's chord pattern, he moves to the key of D and again plays the song's melody along with a simultaneous accompanying pattern. He stays in the key of D for another chord pattern—at this point his backing musicians again step in more prominently, allowing him to again deliver the song's melody along with a continuous harmony part. This time around, he embellishes his playing with some nicely placed harmonic notes. He closes out the recording by returning to the key of A and again playing the song's melody along with a simultaneous accompanying pattern.

It should be noted that Chet actually recorded two separate versions of the single that featured "The Poor People of Paris (Jean's Song)." The first version of the single was released by RCA Victor in early 1956, and it listed the song's title simply as "Jean's Song." The second version of the single was released by the label not long after the first, and it listed the song's title as "The Poor People of Paris (Jean's Song)." Chet's first version of the song was much slower in tempo, so it was not nearly as energetic and catchy as his second version. This first version is available on several Chet CD anthologies—but Chet's second version is unquestionably recognized as his "official" release of the song.

It seems likely that the first

Chet Atkins playing his modified 1955 Gretsch 6120 Chet Atkins Hollow Body electric guitar on the NBC Television Network program *The Today Show* on April 4, 1957.

and second versions of this single were not actually recorded on the same day—which of course would indicate that the second version was recorded sometime after November 22, 1955, the single's officially listed recording date. However, no studio records appear to be in existence that could either prove or disprove this—so we will just have to stick with November 22, 1955 as the day the single was recorded. At any rate, neither Chet nor RCA Victor ever gave any insight as to just why two separate versions of this single were ever recorded and released in the first place.

That is all that can really be said about *that* little mystery—so now let's discuss just how well "The Poor People of Paris (Jean's Song)" did for Chet in terms of sales and airplay. Chet's second version of the song, the one titled "The Poor People of Paris (Jean's Song)," was released on 78 and 45 singles by RCA Victor in early 1956. The recording debuted on the U.S. pop single charts on February 25, 1956, eventually reaching the number 52 spot. "The Poor People of Paris (Jean's Song)" was the first of Chet's records to make it on to the pop charts—this success offered further evidence that his fan base was continuing to grow well beyond just country music fans.

Far and away the most successful version was not Chet's, but orchestra leader Les Baxter's. Baxter's version of the song reached the top spot on the U.S. pop single charts in March 1956, right at the time that Chet's version was also on the charts.

Here is one final note regarding "The Poor People of Paris (Jean's Song)." Chet played the number when he appeared on several television programs during the 1950s—these appearances included the ABC Television Network program *The Purina Grand Ole Opry* on April 28, 1956 and the NBC Television Network program *The Today Show* on April 4, 1957. During both of these appearances, Chet played "The Poor People of Paris (Jean's Song)" using his modified 1955 Gretsch 6120 Chet Atkins Hollow Body electric guitar with uncut f-holes and two output jacks. These television appearances offer strong evidence that many of the records he made around the time of their filming, including "The Poor People of Paris (Jean's Song)," were made using that particular instrument.

"Oh. By Jingo, Oh. By Gee. (You're the Only Girl for Me)"

Composer: Lew Brown, Albert Von Tizer. **Producer:** Chet Atkins. **Musicians:** Chet Atkins (guitar). **Location and Date of Recording:** RCA Victor Studio, Methodist Television, Radio & Film Commission, Nashville, Tennessee, June 20, 1956. **Original Release:** *Stringin' Along with Chet Atkins* (RCA Victor album, 1956).

In mid–1956, RCA Victor decided to re-release Chet's 1953 10-inch record *Stringin' Along with Chet Atkins* as a 12-inch LP record. This new version of *Stringin'* would end up being a very different album from the 1953 *Stringin'*—it is a confusing journey from the 10-inch record to the 12-inch record, but I'll do my best to explain that journey to you here.

Like many 10-inch records, the 1953 *Stringin'* only had eight songs on it. However, RCA did not release just one eight-song version of *Stringin'* that year, they actually released *three*—two were 10-inch records, and one was an Extended Play 45 set. For some reason, these three versions of *Stringin'* featured song lineups that were all slightly different from one another. So there were actually a total of *twelve* songs that appeared on the three 1953 releases that bore the title of *Stringin' Along with Chet Atkins*. Since 12-inch records had a longer playing time than 10-inch records or Extended Play 45 sets, RCA elected to include most all of those twelve numbers on their 12-inch *Stringin'.*

Now, here is where this journey *really* starts to get confusing. Chet was evidently unsatisfied with the majority of the recordings that had appeared on the 1953 versions of *Stringin'.* So on June 20, 1956, he recorded brand new versions of eight of them for the 12-inch record—all of these recordings were done at RCA's Nashville studio.

Consequently, the only recordings from the 1953 *Stringin'* releases that actually made it on to the 12-inch record were three numbers that Chet had recorded with Homer and Jethro. Those numbers were "Gallopin' on the Guitar," "Main Street Breakdown," and "Twelfth Street Rag."

It should be pointed out that the 1953 *Stringin'* was not even the first album of Chet's to feature "Gallopin' on the Guitar." That recording was originally featured on Chet's first-ever album, the 1953 10-inch record *Chet Atkins' Gallopin' Guitar*. Also, the 1956 *Stringin'* featured a new version of the well-known instrumental "Black Mountain Rag" that Chet had recorded the previous year—but his original 1952 recording of that number did not ever appear on any of the 1953 versions of *Stringin',* it had only appeared on *Chet Atkins' Gallopin' Guitar*.

So to recap—the 1956 12-inch version of *Stringin'* was essentially a newly recorded collection of instrumentals that had originally appeared on at least one of the three different 1953 *Stringin'* releases. But there were three recordings on the 1956 *Stringin'* ("Gallopin' on the Guitar," "Main Street Breakdown," and "Twelfth Street Rag") that truly *had* originally appeared on at least one of the three different 1953 *Stringin'* releases. And there was one song on the 1956 *Stringin'* ("Black Mountain Rag") that had not been featured on *any* of the three different 1953 *Stringin'* releases.

At any rate, one of the re-recorded *Stringin'* songs that Chet laid down on June 20 was the number that would be chosen to open the 1956 version of the album— that number was "Oh. By Jingo, Oh. By Gee. (You're the Only Girl for Me)." "Oh. By Jingo" was written by Lew Brown and Albert Von Tizer in 1919—it was an uptempo vocal number that ended up becoming one of the biggest pop hits of the post–World War I era.

Chet's original instrumental recording of "Oh. By Jingo" was done at a session at RCA's studios in New York City on March 18, 1953—the same session that yielded "The Bells of St. Mary's." This first version of "Oh. By Jingo" was very well-done, but it featured a steel guitar part played by Jerry Byrd that at times overpowered Chet's playing just a bit. On his 1956 version of "Oh. By Jingo," Chet kept the focus of the recording solely on his guitar by paring down his instrumental backing to just very subtle bass and percussion. (Just who played these parts is unknown, because Chet was the only musician given credit for performing on the session—perhaps Chet actually overdubbed them on his own.)

On the 1956 "Oh. By Jingo," Chet plays a Gretsch electric guitar in standard tuning out of the key of C—much of the song's ebullient melody is built around the chord of A minor, which gives the number a fun little dash of drama. On this particular recording, Chet never relies on his backing parts to support him while he plays single-note solos—rather, the entire song is delivered through his rendering of its melody along with a simultaneously played accompanying pattern. Chet's wonderful arrangement of the song is spiced up with some fast runs leading in and out of its melody, including a jarringly dissonant descending run against a G chord. (Earlier, we noted that Chet had used this same run in his version of "Good-Bye Blues.")

Here is one final note regarding the recordings that made up the majority of the 1956 *Stringin' Along with Chet Atkins* album, including "Oh. By Jingo." By the time these recordings were made, Chet had installed recording equipment in the garage of his Nashville home—so Chet could begin recording a song at RCA's Nashville studios, and then take the master tape of that recording home in order to work on it further in *his* studio. Once Chet began this practice of working on his recordings at home on his own time, there would be no way of knowing whether the majority of a particular recording was done at RCA, or at his home studio. We will continue to rely on RCA's existing studio records in our discussion of Chet's subsequent recordings for the label—but it should be pointed out that most of these recordings probably benefited from a significant amount of undocumented work that was done at Chet's home studio.

"Malagueña"

Composer: Ernesto Lecuona. **Producer:** Chet Atkins. **Musicians:** Chet Atkins (guitar). **Location and Date of Recording:** RCA Victor Studio, Methodist Television, Radio & Film Commission, Nashville, Tennessee, October 22, 1956. **Original Release:** *Finger-Style Guitar* (RCA Victor album, 1956).

Chet certainly had a lot of very productive days during the course of his incredible recording career—but it is hard to imagine that any of them could have been much more productive than the one he had on October 22, 1956. On that day, he recorded all twelve of the instrumentals that would be featured on his new album project *Finger-Style Guitar*. *Finger-Style Guitar* was released as a 12-inch LP record by RCA Victor in late 1956, and like his first few 12-inch records, it was immediately greeted with good reviews and strong sales. (Incidentally, by this point in time, the recording industry had adopted the 12-inch record as their standard format for most all new vinyl musical albums—so whenever we discuss one of Chet's new vinyl albums throughout the rest of the book, we will be referring to a 12-inch record.)

As we noted in this book's previous entry, by the mid–1950s Chet had installed recording equipment in the garage of his Nashville home—so from that point on, Chet often worked on his recordings at RCA's Nashville studios, and then took those recordings home in order to work on them further in *his* studio. Consequently, it is entirely possible that *Finger-Style Guitar*'s twelve numbers were not *really* all recorded at RCA on October 22, 1956. But even if Chet had only recorded *half* of what ended up on the album that day, it still would have been a very good day of work indeed.

At any rate, RCA's studio records show that Chet recorded the twelve *Finger-Style Guitar* instrumentals in three separate four-song sessions on October 22, 1956. And in his 2001 autobiography *Chet Atkins: Me and My Guitars*, Chet stated that he used his modified 1955 Gretsch 6120 electric guitar with uncut f-holes and two output jacks on all twelve of those songs. The first of these sessions featured no musicians other than Chet himself—two of the session's songs featured him playing completely alone, and the other two featured him playing along with his own overdubbed rhythm guitar and bass parts.

One of the numbers recorded at this first session that featured Chet playing completely alone was "Malaguea," a 1928 song written by Cuban composer Ernesto Lecuona. Lecuona originally wrote "Malagueña" as a vocal piece, and it was part of a larger musical work entitled *Suite Andalucia*. Over the years, *Suite Andalucia* never really caught on with the general public in its entirety, but "Malagueña" certainly did—it became very popular both as a vocal and an instrumental piece. (Incidentally, the word "Malagueña" refers to a style of Spanish dance similar to the fandango that originated in the Spanish port city of Málaga.)

On "Malagueña," Chet plays in standard tuning out of the key of E, and his arrangement of the song marvelously captures the drama of Lecuona's original composition. That arrangement allows Chet to showcase many different aspects of his masterful fingerpicking technique—he renders "Malagueña" through a brilliant combination of sweeping arpeggios, harmonics, alternation (the technique of plucking a string repeatedly using more than one finger) and simultaneously played melody and accompaniment lines.

Even though Chet's *Finger-Style Guitar* version of "Malagueña" was played on electric guitar, it would end up becoming an inspiration to countless classical guitarists over the decades. And Chet himself would turn to the nylon-string classical guitar more and more frequently over the years—he would end up performing and recording many different pieces, including "Malagueña," on that instrument. However, given both the quality and historical importance of Chet's *Finger-Style Guitar* version of "Malagueña," I have decided to include Chet's electric version of the piece in this book.

"Swedish Rhapsody"

Composer: Hugo Alfvén. **Producer:** Chet Atkins. **Musicians:** Chet Atkins (guitar), Buddy Harman (drums). **Location and Date of Recording:** RCA Victor Studio, Methodist Television, Radio & Film Commission, Nashville, Tennessee, October 22, 1956. **Original Release:** *Finger-Style Guitar* (RCA Victor album, 1956).

As mentioned in this book's previous entry, Chet recorded all twelve of the instrumentals that would be featured on his new album project *Finger-Style Guitar* at RCA's Nashville studio on October 22, 1956. Chet recorded those instrumentals in three separate four-song sessions on that day using his modified 1955 Gretsch 6120 electric guitar with uncut f-holes and two output jacks.

The second of those three sessions featured Chet playing with just a bit more accompaniment than he had used on the first session—this time around, he was not only accompanied by his own overdubbed rhythm guitar and bass parts, but also by Buddy Harman on drums.

One of the songs that Chet recorded during this second session, "Swedish Rhapsody," would become a perennial favorite of many Chet fans. "Swedish Rhapsody" was written in 1903 by the famed Swedish composer Hugo Alfvén, and bandleader Percy Faith adapted it into a short orchestral work that became a hit on the U.S. pop charts in 1953.

"Swedish Rhapsody" was actually a far more complex musical work than Faith's recording of it would indicate. The full title of the piece was *Swedish Rhapsody No. 1, Midsommarvaka*, and it was a roughly 13 and a half-minute symphonic rhapsody.

(In English "Midsommarvaka" means "Midsummer Vigil.") Faith's version of "Swedish Rhapsody" only incorporated musical themes taken from about the first 1 minute, 20 seconds, of *Swedish Rhapsody No. 1, Midsommarvaka*.

The reason why Faith's version of "Swedish Rhapsody" was based on this very small opening portion of *Swedish Rhapsody No. 1, Midsommarvaka* was because that was the portion of the piece that had become so well-known and loved by music listeners over the years—it featured an uptempo, instantly memorable melody that was both very delicate and very high-spirited. So it made perfect sense for Faith to adapt this part of the piece into a pop-oriented instrumental.

Chet's recording of "Swedish Rhapsody" stays very close to Percy Faith's version of the song in terms of its musical structure—in other words, it also is based solely on the first 1 minute, 20 seconds, of *Swedish Rhapsody No. 1, Midsommarvaka*. Chet captures the timeless melody of this part of the piece by investing it with some of his most inventive arranging and nimble playing.

On "Swedish Rhapsody," Chet plays in standard tuning, and he starts out playing in the key of A. Chet renders the first half of the song by rendering its melody along with a simultaneously played accompanying pattern, and he is backed by no instruments other than Buddy Harman's drums. Midway through the recording, Chet takes the song to the key of D—at this point, Chet and Buddy are joined by Chet's overdubbed rhythm guitar and bass parts. These parts allow Chet to offer up a generous amount of straightforward soloing—this soloing features a wealth of lively, inventive single-string runs.

The overdubbed parts stay with Chet and Buddy as Chet takes the song back to the key of A. He delivers some more straightforward soloing in that key, and then he ends the recording just the way he began it—he again plays the song's melody along with a simultaneous accompanying pattern.

It is very easy to see why "Swedish Rhapsody" turned out to be one of Chet's all-time greatest recordings. After all, when a musical masterwork is coupled with a legendary guitarist at the peak of his skills as an arranger and player, how could the final product be anything less than totally spectacular?

"Liza"

Composers: George Gershwin, Ira Gershwin, Gus Kahn. **Producer:** Chet Atkins. **Musicians:** Chet Atkins (guitar). **Location and Date of Recording:** RCA Victor Studio, Methodist Television, Radio & Film Commission, Nashville, Tennessee, October 22, 1956. **Original Release:** *Finger-Style Guitar* (RCA Victor album, 1956).

Like Chet's first four-song session held for his *Finger-Style Guitar* album, his third four-song session featured no musicians other than Chet himself—three of the session's songs featured him playing completely alone, and one featured him playing along with his own overdubbed rhythm guitar and bass parts. Chet recorded all twelve of the instrumentals that would be featured on his new album project *Finger-Style Guitar* at RCA's Nashville studio on October 22, 1956. Chet recorded those instrumentals in three separate four-song sessions on that day using his modified 1955 Gretsch 6120 electric guitar with uncut f-holes and two output jacks.)

The one song recorded at this third session that featured Chet playing with his own overdubbed rhythm guitar and bass parts was "Liza," a 1929 number written by

George Gershwin, Ira Gershwin, and Gus Kahn. The song was originally written as a vocal number, and its full title was "Liza (All the Clouds'll Roll Away)." It was originally introduced in the 1929 musical *Show Girl* which starred Ruby Keeler as an aspiring showgirl named Dixie Dugan. The same year that *Show Girl* premiered, Keeler's husband Al Jolson recorded a version of "Liza (All the Clouds'll Roll Away)" that became a top ten hit in the United States. In the years that followed, the song became a well-known jazz standard that was recorded by many different artists.

It is not hard to see why "Liza" became such an oft-recorded standard—it is a brilliantly composed piece of music. The song features a very memorable melody against a complex chord structure that is supported by a constantly moving bass line. Chet's arrangement and performance of "Liza" perfectly captures all of these elements—on the recording, he plays in standard tuning, and he starts out playing in the key of G. Chet opens the song with a slow-tempoed run-through of its chord progression, rendering its melody along with a simultaneously played accompanying pattern. He then brings the song up to a relaxed midtempo pace, again rendering its melody along with a simultaneous accompanying pattern.

Chet is then joined by his overdubbed rhythm guitar and bass parts, and they stay with him through the end of the recording—these parts allow Chet to offer up a generous amount jazzy single-note soloing. For the last quarter of the recording, Chet changes the key of the song to C, and his final solos contain passages that feature spectacularly played harmonics paired with regularly fretted notes.

In this author's opinion, Chet's version of "Liza" might well be one of his most astounding recordings ever—the amount of music that he is able to bring out of a single standard-tuned guitar on the recording, especially while he is playing unaccompanied, is simply a wonder to behold.

Finger-Style Guitar was released by RCA Victor in late 1956, and like Chet's previous albums, it was immediately greeted with good reviews and strong sales. It is interesting to note that Chet's recent record *Chet Atkins in Three Dimensions* made a specific point of heralding his ability to play widely different styles of music—both the record's name and structure made it clear that Chet was making a very conscious effort to move into new musical territory. *Finger-Style Guitar* was presented to the public with no such herald, but in reality it was every bit as musically adventurous as *Chet Atkins in Three Dimensions* had been—after all, just by examining three of the album's songs, we have taken in some Spanish dance music, a Swedish symphonic work, and a classic American musical theater number. Fortunately for fans of all different styles of music, Chet would continue to cross a wide variety of musical boundaries through his recordings for decades to come.

"Trambone"

Composer: Chet Atkins. **Producer:** Chet Atkins. **Musicians:** Chet Atkins (guitar), Floyd Cramer (piano), Jimmy Riddle (harmonica), Bob Moore (bass), Buddy Harman (drums). **Location and Date of Recording:** RCA Victor Studio, Methodist Television, Radio & Film Commission, Nashville, Tennessee, November 29, 1956. **Original Release:** RCA Victor 20-6796 (RCA Victor 78 single, 1957), RCA Victor 47-6796 (RCA Victor 45 single, 1957).

By the mid–1950s, rock and roll music had begun its phenomenal rise to popularity, and the style was well on its way to completely changing the landscape of popular music. Of course, Chet was keenly aware of this change—in fact, as we discussed in the first chapter of this book, he had ended up playing a part in launching the career of Elvis Presley, the performer who was at the center of the rock and roll revolution. Chet helped to organize Elvis's first session for RCA Victor after the singer had been signed to the label. That session was held at RCA's Nashville studio on January 10, 1956, and it produced "Heartbreak Hotel," Elvis's first number one hit on the U.S. pop charts. Chet played rhythm guitar on that record as well.

The incredible success of rock and roll performers such as Elvis led Chet to hold several recording sessions of his own that were designed to appeal to rock and roll fans. These sessions were done at RCA Victor's Nashville studio in late 1956 and early 1957. All of the songs recorded at these sessions were instrumentals, and most of them had a blues/rock feel to them. Several of them were even released as singles under a rock-themed billing—that billing was "The Rhythm Rockers featuring Chet Atkins." This attempt to market Chet to rock and roll fans was not particularly successful from a commercial standpoint—none of the songs recorded at these sessions, whether they were released under Chet's name or the Rhythm Rockers billing, garnered any significant sales or airplay.

That said, however, Chet's first foray into rock and roll music was very satisfying from an artistic standpoint, because several of the songs that he recorded at these sessions would go on to become favorites amongst Chet's longtime fans. The most notable of these was "Trambone," a Chet-penned number that was recorded on November 29, 1956. The song's unusual title was an informal way of referring to the slide trombone—and this title was a very appropriate one, because throughout "Trambone," Chet made notes played on the low strings of his electric guitar sound like glissando phrases being played on a slide trombone. He did this by pushing very far down on his guitar's vibrato bar right before the notes were struck, and then very quickly bringing the bar back up just as the notes rang out. (We've used quite a bit of music terminology in this book, but this is the first time we've used the word "glissando." Glissando is the term for a continuous glide between two different notes—and obviously, a slide trombone is the perfect instrument to play a glissando.)

Incidentally, "Trambone" was not the first recording of Chet's in which he used his vibrato bar to play glissando phrases. He had previously employed this technique on his October 22, 1956, recording of the big band standard "In the Mood" which appeared on his *Finger-Style Guitar* album. (That entire album was recorded on that one day, and we just finished our discussion of three of its other songs, "Malagueña," "Swedish Rhapsody," and "Liza.") Evidently Chet was so pleased with the results of this technique on his "In the Mood" recording that he decided to write an entire song that was built around it.

Chet gathered a great group of musicians together for "Trambone" and the other songs recorded on the November 29 session—he was backed by Floyd Cramer on piano, Jimmy Riddle on harmonica, Bob Moore on bass, and Buddy Harman on drums. This was the first of Chet's sessions to feature Floyd, who of course was a very successful musician in his own right. After moving to Nashville in 1955, Floyd had quickly become a highly sought-after studio pianist, and he played on many different hit records—in fact, he played with Chet on "Heartbreak Hotel." (Chet would continue to work with Floyd for the better part of four decades, so we will be discussing him many more times.)

On "Trambone," Chet plays a Gretsch electric guitar in standard tuning out of the key of C. The song's main chord progression is C-A minor-F-G—this pattern of chords is often referred to as the "'50s progression," because it was used in so many 1950s and early 1960s pop/rock hits. Chet renders the likable, slightly wistful melody of "Trambone" at a relaxed shuffle tempo, keeping his vibrato bar busy with glissando after glissando. Chet also plays a wealth of tasty licks that keep the song locked into a 50s rock feel. Jimmy Riddle's harmonica nicely adds to this feel by supporting Chet's playing without ever getting too much in his way. Chet has Floyd's piano take the spotlight for a short solo break near the end of the recording.

"Trambone" was not one of the songs from Chet's 1956–57 "rock" sessions that was released under the Rhythm Rockers billing—rather, RCA released it simply under Chet's name on 78 and 45 singles in early 1957. As previously mentioned, none of the songs from these sessions garnered any significant sales or airplay, including "Trambone." Still, the song became very popular with Chet fans over the years, and it also ended up having a big influence on several very notable rock and roll acts. For example, guitarist Duane Eddy recorded his own version of "Trambone" in 1961. Also, Paul McCartney publicly credited Chet's version of "Trambone" as the recording that specifically inspired him to create the classic 1965 Beatles song "Michelle." (We'll examine "Trambone's" influence on Paul in more detail when we discuss Chet's recording of "Michelle.")

It should be noted that Chet chose to re-record "Trambone" for his classic 1962 album *Down Home*—this new version of the song had much more of a relaxed feel than the first version, and it featured Chet being accompanied by an arrangement of rhythm guitar, piano, saxophone, bass, and drums. The *Down Home* version of "Trambone" is quite enjoyable, but it certainly does not have the high spirits or the historical significance of the original 1956 version.

"El Cumbanchero"

Composer: Rafael Hernández. **Producer:** Chet Atkins. **Musicians:** Chet Atkins (guitar), Floyd Cramer (piano), Bob Moore (bass), Buddy Harman (drums). **Location and Date of Recording:** RCA Victor Studio, Methodist Television, Radio & Film Commission, Nashville, Tennessee, June 22, 1957. **Original Release:** *Hi-Fi in Focus* (RCA Victor album, 1957).

During the summer of 1957, Chet held several sessions at RCA Victor's Nashville studio to record instrumentals for his new album *Hi-Fi in Focus*. The first of these sessions took place on June 22, 1957, and it yielded four songs. The first song recorded at the session, "El Cumbanchero," was chosen to be the album's opening track. "El Cumbanchero" was a fiery, rhythmically exciting dance number written in the 1940s by the famed Puerto Rican composer Rafael Hernández. In the years since the song's debut, it had become well-known after being performed and recorded by many different artists as a vocal piece—but a number of other artists, including Chet, chose to interpret it as an instrumental piece. (Incidentally, the song's title loosely translated into English means a "reveler" or "fun-loving person.")

On "El Cumbanchero," Chet plays a Gretsch electric guitar in standard tuning out of the key of D minor, and he is accompanied by piano, bass and drums. Most all of the songs we have discussed up to this point in this book have featured Chet offering up his trademark style of playing melody along with a simultaneous accompanying pattern at least to some degree, but that is not the case with "El Cumbanchero"—on this particular recording, he renders the song's melody almost entirely through straightforward single-string soloing. Every note of his performance is perfectly supported by his backing musicians from start to finish.

Chet's version of "El Cumbanchero" retains the aggressiveness and excitement of Hernandez's original composition—he plays the piece at breakneck speed, tearing into it with an abandon that instantly grabs the attention of the listener. Chet delivers a barrage of fast runs, octave phrases, and dissonant chord voicings, and his inspired playing makes the recording an exhilarating listening experience from start to finish.

"Tiger Rag"

> **Composers:** Tony Sbarbaro, Eddie Edwards, Henry Ragas, Larry Shields, Nick LaRocca, Harry De Costa. **Producer:** Chet Atkins. **Musicians:** Chet Atkins (guitar), Floyd Cramer (piano), Bob Moore (bass), Buddy Harman (drums). **Location and Date of Recording:** RCA Victor Studio, Methodist Television, Radio & Film Commission, Nashville, Tennessee, June 22, 1957. **Original Release:** *Hi-Fi in Focus* (RCA Victor album, 1957).

Chet turned in a very fiery performance when he recorded "El Cumbanchero" at the four-song session for *Hi-Fi in Focus* held at RCA Victor's Nashville studio on June 22, 1957—but he still had an abundance of fire left in him for another of the session's flashy, high-energy numbers, "Tiger Rag." "Tiger Rag" was among the very first jazz songs ever created—it was originally written and recorded as an uptempo instrumental by the Original Dixieland Jazz Band in 1917. In the years following the success of the Original Dixieland Jazz Band's version of the song, "Tiger Rag" was recorded by scores of artists—in fact, it eventually ended up becoming one of the most-recorded jazz songs of all time.

In 1931, "Tiger Rag" was outfitted with a set of lyrics for the first time—Harry De Costa, one of the Original Dixieland Jazz Band's members, wrote them when the vocal group the Mills Brothers decided to record the song. The Mills Brothers' version of "Tiger Rag" reached the top of the U.S. music charts that same year. From that point on, artists could choose to interpret the number either as a vocal or an instrumental piece. Chet was one of the artists who chose to render the song as an instrumental.

On "Tiger Rag," Chet plays a Gretsch electric guitar in standard tuning, and he is accompanied by piano, bass and drums. Simply put, Chet's version of the song is a real jaw-dropper—its tempo is blisteringly fast, and in its less than two-minute run time Chet hits you with a myriad of techniques pulled from his musical bag of tricks. His playing features melody lines delivered with simultaneously played accompanying patterns, ridiculously quick single-note solo runs, vibrato bar glissandos, and jarringly dissonant phrases. Plus, while all of that is going on, the song is quickly changing keys—it starts in the key of D, then it moves to the key of G, and then it moves to the key of C. In the middle of the recording, Chet steps back for a moment in order to let his bassist Bob Moore take a nice solo break.

Chet's version of "Tiger Rag" ended up being such a crowd-pleaser that he ended up periodically performing the song at concerts and television appearances throughout the rest of his career. He changed up his original arrangement of the song for many of these performances—but they all retained the brilliance and excitement of his *Hi-Fi in Focus* version.

"Walk, Don't Run"

Composer: Johnny Smith. **Producer:** Chet Atkins. **Musicians:** Chet Atkins (guitar), Floyd Cramer (piano), Bob Moore (bass), Buddy Harman (drums). **Location and Date of Recording:** RCA Victor Studio, Methodist Television, Radio & Film Commission, Nashville, Tennessee, July 14, 1957. **Original Release:** *Hi-Fi in Focus* (RCA Victor album, 1957).

Chet held a productive recording session for *Hi-Fi in Focus* at RCA Victor's Nashville studio on July 14, 1957—this particular session yielded six songs. One of the session's numbers, "Walk, Don't Run," ended up being among the most influential recordings that Chet ever made. "Walk, Don't Run" was a swing-tempo instrumental originally written and recorded by the well-known jazz guitarist Johnny Smith in 1953—after hearing Johnny's recording of the song, Chet decided to put together an arrangement of it that was suited to his own style of playing.

In reality, Johnny's "Walk, Don't Run" was not an all-original composition—the song was a melodic reworking of the jazz standard "Softly, as in a Morning Sunrise." "Softly, as in a Morning Sunrise" was originally written as a vocal piece by Sigmund Romberg and Oscar Hammerstein II for their hit 1928 operetta *The New Moon*. The song became a well-known jazz instrumental after being recorded by artists such as Artie Shaw and The Modern Jazz Quartet. Johnny took the chord structure of "Softly, as in a Morning Sunrise" and wrote his own minor scale-based melody for it—the result of this compositional effort was "Walk, Don't Run."

Chet's arrangement of "Walk, Don't Run" was substantially different from Johnny's original version of the song from its very first notes. Johnny's version opened with a memorable and dramatic guitar riff which was played against a pattern of descending notes played by his backing musicians—this riff was restated a number of times throughout the song. Chet chose to simplify his version of the song by completely cutting out this riff and solely focusing on the song's equally memorable A and B sections.

Also, Chet arranged his version of "Walk, Don't Run" primarily as a fingerstyle piece—he played its melody along with a simultaneous melodic counterpoint played primarily on the lower strings of his guitar. In order to do this, he changed the key of the song from Johnny's original version—Johnny had played it in D minor, and Chet crafted his fingerstyle arrangement of the song in the key of A minor. The last third of Chet's version of "Walk, Don't Run" featured him moving to the key of D minor and playing the song's melody in a straightforward soloing style that was very similar to Johnny's style of playing.

On "Walk, Don't Run," Chet plays a Gretsch electric guitar in standard tuning, and he is accompanied by piano, bass and drums. Through much of the fingerstyle portion of the song in the key of A minor, Chet's only accompaniment is the drums—but once the song moves to the key of D minor, all of Chet's backing musicians join in with him. Throughout the entire recording, Chet renders the melody of "Walk, Don't Run" in a jazzy style that is both very easygoing and very respectful of Johnny's original composition.

Once *Hi-Fi in Focus* was released by RCA Victor in late 1957, the album began to receive quite a bit of attention—and some of that attention would end up having a profound effect on the history of popular music. The founding members of the Washington state-based instrumental rock band The Ventures were big fans of the record, and "Walk, Don't Run" was the song on the album that captivated them the most. The band put together a simplified, rocked-up version of the song, recorded it, and released it as a single in 1959. The Ventures' version of "Walk, Don't Run" became a huge hit in terms of sales and airplay, and launched the band's incredibly successful, decades-long career. In fact, the band would go on to become the best-selling instrumental band of all time—and this success was in no small part due to the influence that Chet had on them.

Incidentally, Chet's music would serve as a direct inspiration to the Ventures several more times over the years. The band ended up recording several other songs that had been featured on *Hi-Fi in Focus*, including "El Cumbanchero" and "Lullaby of the Leaves." (We discussed Chet's June 22, 1957, recording of "El Cumbanchero" earlier, and we'll take just a moment here to make note of "Lullaby of the Leaves"—it was an excellent jazz number that Chet recorded during the same session that "Walk, Don't Run" was recorded.)

"Hidden Charm"

> **Composer:** James Rich. **Producer:** Chet Atkins. **Musicians:** Chet Atkins (guitar), Marvin Hughes (piano), Bob Moore (bass), Farris Coursey (drums). **Location and Date of Recording:** RCA Victor Studio, Methodist Television, Radio & Film Commission, Nashville, Tennessee, August 27, 1957. **Original Release:** RCA Victor 20-7048 (RCA Victor 78 single, 1957), RCA Victor 47-7048 (RCA Victor 45 single, 1957).

On August 27, 1957, Chet held a recording session at RCA Victor's Nashville studio that yielded one song, "Hidden Charm"—the session was his last at RCA's facility inside of the Methodist Television, Radio & Film Commission. The label had decided to move out of the Commission's building and construct a brand-new studio for their recording sessions on property that they could actually own outright. (We'll discuss RCA's new studio in the next entry.)

"Hidden Charm" was a catchy midtempo instrumental written by guitarist James "Spider" Rich that was very similar to Chet's 1955 recording of "The Poor People of Paris (Jean's Song)" in a number of ways. On "The Poor People of Paris (Jean's Song)," Chet started out playing the number in the key of A, and much of its melody was based around the chord change of an E chord to an A chord. Chet then moved the song to the key of D, which meant that much of its melody was then based around the chord change of an A chord to a D chord.

The chord structure of "Hidden Charm" was the much the same as the chord structure of "The Poor People of Paris (Jean's Song)"—it also started out in the key of A, and much of its melody was based around the chord change of an E chord to an A chord. The song also then moved to the key of D, which meant that much of its melody was then based around the chord change of an A chord to a D chord. The similarities between the two numbers did not end there—they both featured the same relaxed swing tempo, and both of their melodies often followed the exact same rhythmic pattern.

That said, however, the actual notes found in each song's melody were substantially different from one another—"The Poor People of Paris (Jean's Song)" featured a basically descending melody, and "Hidden Charm" featured a basically ascending melody. Also, each song went on to feature sections of melody that were *completely* different from one another. Still, their melodic structure was similar enough to one another that large chunks of the melody of "The Poor People of Paris (Jean's Song)" would have fit perfectly into the chord structure of "Hidden Charm," and vice versa.

On "Hidden Charm," Chet plays a Gretsch electric guitar in standard tuning, and he is accompanied by piano, bass and drums. The similarity between "The Poor People of Paris (Jean's Song)" and "Hidden Charm" is further reinforced by Chet's decision to have Farris Coursey, the drummer who played on his version of "The Poor People," also play on "Hidden Charm." Farris provides the same kind of unique percussion on "Hidden Charm" that he did on "Poor People"—he not only plays drums, but he also often keeps rhythm by slapping his hands on his thighs—this creates a sound that is similar to the sound made by a tap dancer's feet.

Chet delivers well over the first half of "Hidden Charm" by rendering its melody along with a simultaneously played accompanying pattern, and he is accompanied by nothing more than Farris's slapping. During the end of the song, all of Chet's backing musicians step in—this allows him to throw in just a bit of single-note soloing into his performance.

Even though the song itself is so derivative of "The Poor People of Paris (Jean's Song)," it still ranks among Chet's greatest recordings. Obviously, so much of the music that Chet recorded over the years is played with astonishing confidence and clarity, but "Hidden Charm" somehow seems to deliver these qualities in even *more* abundance than usual. As a result, the song stands as a timeless, perfectly focused sonic portrait of Chet's incredible skill as a guitarist.

"Hidden Charm" was released on 78 and 45 singles by RCA Victor in late 1957, and the song did not achieve any great success in terms of sales or airplay. But because it was such a wonderful recording, it still ended up becoming a favorite amongst Chet fans over the years.

"You're Just in Love"

Composer: Irving Berlin. **Producer:** Chet Atkins. **Musicians:** Chet Atkins (guitar), Floyd Cramer (piano), Bob Moore (bass), Buddy Harman (drums). **Location and Date of Recording:** RCA Victor Studio, Nashville, Tennessee, December 4, 1957. **Original Release:** *Chet Atkins at Home* (RCA Victor album, 1958).

The incredible success that the signing of Elvis Presley had brought to RCA Victor in the mid–1950s ended up being the catalyst for some major changes to the label's corporate structure. RCA's director of country music operations Steve Sholes had overseen Elvis's move to the label, which naturally led to Steve's prestige within the company taking a quantum leap. Consequently, on September 1, 1957, RCA promoted Steve to head of the label's pop singles division. Since Chet had been working as Steve's assistant for the past five years helping to organize and produce the label's sessions held in Nashville, he was given Steve's old job in early 1958.

Chet's tenure as the head of RCA's Nashville division would turn out to be astonishingly successful and influential. He directed many of the country artists he produced to adopt a more polished, pop style on their records, and these records sold so well that they ended up giving birth to a new style of country music known as the Nashville Sound. This blending of country and pop styles forever changed the face of country music, and helped to keep the genre commercially viable in the wake of the rock and roll revolution.

Steve and Chet's increased clout at RCA led them to be able to convince the label to build a stand-alone studio for their Nashville recording sessions in late 1957. Not surprisingly, it had become increasingly difficult over the years for RCA to maintain their Nashville studio inside of the Methodist Television, Radio & Film Commission. After all, musicians and record producers were used to working into the late hours of the night, and perhaps having an alcoholic drink or two while they worked—this was obviously not a working environment that sat well with a Methodist organization.

Chet helped RCA to design the new studio, which was located in downtown Nashville. The studio would eventually become known as RCA Studio B after RCA built a second Nashville studio in 1964—but during the first years of its existence, it was simply known as RCA Studios. Chet would oversee the production of countless records made by his RCA artists at the studio—and a *lot* of these records turned out to be big hits. Incidentally, more than a few of these records featured Chet playing supporting guitar parts. But luckily for those people who were fans of Chet's work as a solo act, he would still continue to make his own music at RCA Studios as well.

Chet's first session at RCA's new Nashville studio was held on December 4, 1957. Four instrumentals were recorded, three of which ended up on his 1958 album *Chet Atkins at Home*. "You're Just in Love" was the song that was chosen to be the album's final track. "You're Just in Love" was a vocal number written by Irving Berlin for his 1950 musical *Call Me Madam* starring Ethel Merman. The song was composed as a counterpoint piece—in other words, the number had a main melody and a secondary melody that ran at the same time, and each of these melodies featured lyrics and rhythmic patterns that were independent of one another. Merman starred in the 1953 film version of the musical, and in it she performed "You're Just in Love" with her co-star Donald O'Connor.

The counterpoint found in "You're Just in Love" provides a dazzling showcase for Chet's fingerstyle guitar-playing talents. On the recording, Chet plays a Gretsch electric guitar in standard tuning, and he is accompanied by piano, bass and drums. Delivering the song at a relaxed swing tempo, he starts out playing its main melody in a straightforward soloing style out of the key of E. He then moves to the key of A and renders the song's secondary melody along with a simultaneously played accompanying pattern. Staying in the key of A, he brings "You're Just in Love" to a jaw-dropping finale—he flawlessly plays both of the song's melodies at the same time, rendering the main melody on his lower strings and the secondary melody on his higher strings.

So many of Chet's recordings feature him playing some spectacularly executed sequence of notes that leaves most any guitarist who hears them wondering to themselves, "How in the world did Chet just do that?" The finale of "You're Just in Love" is definitely one of those sequences.

"Nagasaki"

Composer: Mort Dixon, Harry Warren. **Producer:** Chet Atkins. **Musicians:** Chet Atkins (guitar), Floyd Cramer (piano), Bob Moore (bass), Buddy Harman (drums). **Location and Date of Recording:** RCA Victor Studio, Nashville, Tennessee, January 9, 1958. **Original Release:** *Chet Atkins at Home* (RCA Victor album, 1958).

On January 9, 1958, Chet returned to RCA Studios in Nashville to hold another recording session for his *Chet Atkins at Home* album. The session yielded five instrumentals, four of which ended up on the album. One of the standout numbers from the session was Chet's version of "Nagasaki," a 1928 song written by Mort Dixon and Harry Warren. "Nagasaki" was originally written as a novelty vocal number that featured very silly lyrics, but over the years it had become equally well-known as a jazz instrumental. Most all of the artists who recorded versions of "Nagasaki," whether vocal or instrumental, chose to play the song at breakneck speed—but Chet slowed his version of the song down to a more relaxed swing tempo.

On "Nagasaki," Chet plays a Gretsch electric guitar in standard tuning out of the key of G, and he is accompanied by piano, bass and drums. He opens the recording by playing the song's melody along with a simultaneously played accompanying pattern, but he quickly moves to rendering the song through more straightforward soloing—this soloing features a wealth of smooth, inventive single-note runs. "Nagasaki" is definitely one of Chet's recordings that capture him completely leaving his country roots behind—every last note he plays in the song is delivered with the seasoned touch of a masterful jazz player.

"Yankee Doodle Dixie"

Composer: Chet Atkins. **Producer:** Chet Atkins. **Musicians:** Chet Atkins (guitar), Floyd Cramer (piano), Horace "Aychie" Burns (bass), Buddy Harman (drums). **Location and Date of Recording:** RCA Victor Studio, Nashville, Tennessee, January 30, 1958. **Original Release:** *Chet Atkins at Home* (RCA Victor album, 1958).

On January 30, 1958, Chet held another recording session for his *Chet Atkins at Home* album at RCA Studios in Nashville. This session yielded four instrumentals, all of which ended up on the album. Just a bit earlier in the book, we discussed his version of "You're Just in Love" that he recorded for *Chet Atkins at Home* on December 4, 1957, and how he played both of that song's counterpoint melodies at the same time. It turned out that Chet wasn't quite done with pushing himself to play two separate melodies at once for the album—at the January 30 session he recorded his original composition "Yankee Doodle Dixie," a number which featured him playing two entirely different *songs* at the same time.

In "Yankee Doodle Dixie," Chet found a way to weave melodic strains from the classic American songs "Yankee Doodle" and "Dixie" into counterpoint melodies for one another. The song's counterpoint passages were connected by passages that featured Chet soloing over chord patterns pulled from either "Yankee Doodle" or "Dixie."

Before we discuss just how Chet accomplished this almost miraculous mix of music, let's take a moment to discuss the two songs he used to create the mix in the first place. "Yankee Doodle" was a song that originated in the 1750s—the first version of the song featured lyrics made up by officers of the British Army in order to make fun of American troops during the French and Indian War. Ironically, Americans ended up liking the song so much that they made up their own words to it during the Revolutionary War era—in the years that followed, that American version of "Yankee Doodle" went on to become one of the United States' most beloved patriotic songs.

"Dixie" was an 1850s song that was credited to the Ohio-born songwriter Daniel Decatur Emmett. The song was originally performed in blackface minstrel shows, and its lyrics told the story of a freed black slave longing for the plantation of his birth. "Dixie" became the unofficial anthem of the Confederacy during the American Civil War, and after the war it remained a powerful symbol of Southern U.S. ideology.

Chet first decided to combine "Yankee Doodle" with "Dixie" some time before his *Chet Atkins at Home* sessions—in fact, he had recorded a very short unaccompanied version of "Yankee Doodle Dixie" for *Country and Western Caravan*, a 1954 live album featuring a number of RCA Victor country recording artists. That recording opened with Chet delivering a brief, humorous monologue about his decision to take on the task of learning to play two separate songs at once. The *Country and Western Caravan* version of the song turned out to be a preliminary sketch of the fully formed "Yankee Doodle Dixie" that he put together for *Chet Atkins at Home.*

On the *Chet Atkins at Home* "Yankee Doodle Dixie," Chet plays Chet plays a Gretsch electric guitar in standard tuning out of the key of A, and he is accompanied by piano, bass and drums. He starts out the recording by playing the opening melodies of "Yankee Doodle" and "Dixie" in counterpoint to one another—"Yankee Doodle" is played on his lower strings, and "Dixie" is played on his higher strings. It is a challenge just trying to follow each melody while listening to them being played simultaneously—so one can imagine how bewilderingly difficult it must have been for Chet to figure out a way to actually *play* them in that manner.

The song then moves to a relaxed swing tempo. Chet delivers some jazzy solo work over the chords to the B section of "Dixie," and after that he plays the opening melody of "Yankee Doodle" using harmonics. He then offers up just a bit more jazzy solo work over the chords to the B section of "Yankee Doodle" before closing out the recording by restating his "Yankee Doodle" and "Dixie" counterpoint.

"Yankee Doodle Dixie" was such an astonishing piece of music that it was always a huge crowd-pleaser whenever Chet played it live over the years. And its brilliance has kept it a source of fascination for guitarists right up until the present day. In fact, it is hard to imagine that "Yankee Doodle Dixie" will *ever* go out of style just as long as there are people on this earth who enjoy playing the guitar and listening to guitar music.

Chet Atkins at Home was released by RCA in mid–1958, and the album's cover featured a photo of Chet sitting in his private recording studio located in the garage of his Nashville home. Chet would soon have a new, even more elaborate home studio—in early 1958, he and his family moved to a new home in Nashville, and Chet equipped the basement of that home with all of his guitar and recording gear. Chet lived in this home for the rest of his life, and he would work there for the rest of his as well. In other words, he would continue his recording routine that had begun with the construction of his first home studio. He would record songs at studios either owned or contracted by his record label (RCA until the early 1980s, and then Columbia Records for the rest of his career)—then he would take the master tapes of those recordings home in order to work on them further in *his* studio.

As we noted in our discussion of "Oh. By Jingo, Oh. By Gee. (You're the Only Girl for Me)," once Chet began this practice of working on his recordings at home on his own time, there would be no way of knowing whether the majority of a particular RCA Chet recording was done at RCA Studios, or at his home studio. This would continue to be the case once Chet's second and final home studio was up and running.

Here are a few final thoughts regarding the *Chet Atkins at Home* album. It seemed to capture Chet consciously moving toward a much more mellow, jazzy vibe that was decidedly "easy listening" in nature. All of his earlier albums contained a number of tracks that were real showstoppers—that is, fast, musically aggressive numbers with a lot of lightning-quick playing. *Chet Atkins at Home* did not really have those kinds of numbers—even though it featured some of Chet's most technically dazzling playing, it still was made up of tracks that were on the whole quiet and reflective. The album seemed to be one that was specifically designed to be listened to during a peaceful night at home in front of a fire in the fireplace.

Chet's decision to move toward easy listening music on *Chet Atkins at Home* definitely resonated with the record-buying public—the record climbed to number 21 on the U.S. album charts, giving him his first-ever charting LP. But even though Chet's move toward a more mellow musical style on this particular record had brought him great success, he certainly did not move there to stay. In fact, the very first recording session he did after the album's completion would produce one of the best rock and roll songs that he ever created. We'll discuss that song, "Slinkey," in the next entry.

"Slinkey"

Composer: Chet Atkins. **Producer:** Chet Atkins. **Musicians:** Chet Atkins (guitar), Buddy Harman (drums). **Location and Date of Recording:** RCA Victor Studio, Nashville, Tennessee, May 3, 1958. **Original Release:** *Mister Guitar* (RCA Victor album, 1959).

On May 3, 1958, Chet held a recording session at RCA Studios in Nashville that yielded two songs, "Jessie" and "Slinkey"—both were instrumentals that would end up being featured on his 1959 album *Mister Guitar*. "Slinkey" was a Chet-penned, straight-up rock and roll number laced with just a bit of novelty sensibility. (As we noted in our discussion of "Kentucky Derby," Chet always had a great interest in creating novelty records, because just about the only instrumental records that ever became hits were novelty numbers that used music to paint a funny, indelible picture in listener's minds.) "Slinkey" could be classified as a novelty song because it was named after the popular children's toy—and on the recording, Chet played an electric guitar through a Fender amplifier outfitted with a slow, heavy tremolo setting in order to create pulsating music that brought to mind the image of a toy Slinky flipping end over end.

Incidentally, it seems that Chet might have been worried about running into copyright trouble with the owners of the Slinky brand name, because he spelled the name of his song differently from the spelling of the actual toy. The "e" he added to the name of his song certainly did not change the song's implied meaning, but it very likely could have helped him to avoid a potential lawsuit.

At any rate, on "Slinkey," Chet plays his tremolo-laced Gretsch electric guitar in standard tuning out of the key of E, and he is accompanied by nothing more than Buddy Harman's drums. Playing in midtempo 4/4 time, Chet delivers the song's catchy, blues-based melody along with a simultaneous accompanying pattern played on the low strings of his guitar—this pattern walks up and down the fretboard, filling the sonic space that would usually be covered by a bass. He embellishes his playing with a wide array of bluesy riffs that rock as hard as many of the riffs found on Chuck Berry's classic 1950s recordings. Buddy's drums enhance the recording's strong rock and roll vibe by solidly locking in with every tremolo-driven note that Chet plays.

Even though "Slinkey" was such a memorable number, it took a while for it to actually get to Chet's fans after it was recorded—as we just noted, it was laid down on May 3, 1958, but RCA Victor did not release it until it appeared on Chet's late 1959 album *Mister Guitar*. The song was originally supposed to be featured on an RCA Chet album entitled *My Brother Sings*—that album was supposed to be released in early 1959, but for some unknown reason it ended up being canceled by the label. (We'll discuss the unusual and unfortunate fate of *My Brother Sings* in detail in the next entry.) Unfortunately, "Slinkey" never did become a big hit in terms of sales or airplay once it finally made its way out into the world—but over time, Chet's fans still came to regard it as one of *Mister Guitar*'s standout tracks.

"Swanee River"

Composer: Stephen Foster. **Producer:** Chet Atkins. **Musicians:** Chet Atkins (guitar), Jim Atkins (rhythm guitar, vocal), Floyd Cramer (piano), Bob Moore (bass), Buddy Harman (drums). **Location and Date of Recording:** RCA Victor Studio, Nashville, Tennessee, July 24, 1958. **Original Release:** *The Guitar Genius* (RCA Camden album, 1963).

Chet held three recording sessions for himself on July 24, 1958, at RCA Studios in Nashville, and these sessions were very notable ones for several different reasons. First, the sessions were the first of Chet's to be recorded in stereo—RCA Victor installed stereo recording equipment in their Nashville facility in summer 1958, and Chet's July 24 sessions marked the very first time that this new equipment was put into service.

Second, over half of the songs recorded at these sessions featured Chet's older half-brother Jim on lead vocals and rhythm guitar. Jim had enjoyed a successful career as a singer/guitarist in his own right, and he had played rhythm guitar on a number of Chet's early recordings (we discussed a few of those recordings earlier)—but Jim had never sang on any of his half-brother's recorded work. After so many years of being close both personally and musically, Chet and Jim had decided to officially team up and share the spotlight with one another for an RCA album—and that album was to be titled *My Brother Sings*. Incidentally, the July 24 sessions were not only the *first* time that Jim sang on any of Chet's recordings, they were also the *last*—Jim would never again provide vocals for songs recorded by his half-brother.

Third, these sessions featured Chet playing two of his most iconic electric guitars. For most of the session's songs, he used a Gretsch Chet Atkins Country Gentleman. The model was named after his landmark 1953 song, and it featured a mahogany finish and uncut f-holes. Gretsch first released the Country Gentleman in 1958, and the model quickly became a big seller for the company. It just as quickly became Chet's instrument of choice—his July 24 session marked one of the first documented occasions that he recorded with one.

At the sessions, he also used his modified 1955 Gretsch 6120 Chet Atkins Hollow Body with uncut f-holes and two output jacks to record several songs. These output jacks allowed the guitar's treble and bass strings to be plugged into their own separate inputs, because the instrument's pickups were wired in a manner that sent the treble strings' signal to one jack, and the bass strings' signal to the other. Obviously, this guitar was an ideal instrument for a stereo recording session—the guitar's treble strings (G, B, and high E) could be sent to one channel, and its bass strings (low E, A, and D) could be sent to the other. When played back in stereo, this "split guitar" effect created a highly unusual listening experience—the notes Chet played on the 6120 bounced back and forth between the left and right speakers like some sort of sonic ping pong ball.

Chet's first two sessions on July 24 yielded six songs, all of them featuring Jim on lead vocals. The two men were backed by piano, bass and drums on the numbers, which were all very pleasant jazz/pop fare. By far the most compelling song of the bunch was "Swanee River," the well-known 1851 song written by one of America's most important early composers, Stephen Foster. The song was originally performed in blackface minstrel shows, and its lyrics told the story of a black slave longing for his home plantation. Thankfully, over the years, most artists who performed or recorded the song toned down the racist elements of its lyrics—Chet and Jim included.

On "Swanee River," Chet plays his 6120 in standard tuning out of the key of Bb—that key is usually considered not particularly friendly for a standard-tuned guitar, but Chet had a very specific reason why he chose to use it for this recording. Earlier in the book, we discussed the banjo-style rolls consisting of multiple hammer-ons and pull-offs that were built around notes in the key of Bb that Chet used on his classic compositions "Gallopin' on the Guitar" and "Main Street Breakdown." Chet decided to again use those rolls on his recording of "Swanee River," because they would provide a perfect showcase for the 6120's "split guitar" stereo effect. The rolls are played on his G and D strings—and since the 6120's channel split occurs between these two strings, half of a roll comes out on the left side, and the other half comes out on the right. So the moments in the song when Chet plays these rolls are the moments when the 6120 truly becomes that "sonic ping pong ball."

It is truly a pleasure to hear Chet revisit some of his all-time greatest riffs with a stereo twist in "Swanee River," and every bit as much of a pleasure to hear him working with so closely with his extremely talented half-brother—Jim's smooth vocals mesh perfectly with Chet's great playing.

Unfortunately, the world would not get a chance to hear how wonderfully Chet and Jim worked together at the July 24 session for a number of years. RCA Victor planned on releasing *My Brother Sings* in early 1959—the album was to include the six songs featuring Jim on lead vocals that were recorded at the first two July 24 sessions, and five more songs recorded at the third July 24 session that were Chet instrumentals. (We'll discuss those instrumentals in the next entry.) The last track that was supposed to be featured on the album was "Slinkey," the Chet-penned instrumental recorded on May 3, 1958. (We just discussed "Slinkey" in the previous entry.)

My Brother Sings was sent into final production, and thousands of copies of it were pressed by the label's record plants. But for reasons still unknown, RCA suddenly canceled the album—most of its instrumentals then ended up being included on Chet's late 1959 RCA album *Mister Guitar*, but its songs featuring Jim remained unreleased. Five out of the six Jim lead vocal numbers, including "Swanee River," would finally see the light of day when they were included on Chet's 1963 album *The Guitar Genius*. That album was released by RCA Camden, which was a budget record label created by RCA Victor. Why this strong material featuring Chet and Jim was completely shelved for five years and then consigned to such a low-profile album is a mystery that will likely never be solved—but at least the material was finally made available to Chet fans in *some* form.

"I'm Forever Blowing Bubbles"

Composer: Jaan Kenbrovin, John Kellette. **Producer:** Chet Atkins. **Musicians:** Chet Atkins (guitar), Floyd Cramer (piano), Bob Moore (bass), Buddy Harman (drums). **Location and Date of Recording:** RCA Victor Studio, Nashville, Tennessee, July 24, 1958. **Original Release:** *Mister Guitar* (RCA Victor album, 1959).

As we just noted in our discussion of "Swanee River," Chet held three sessions for his *My Brother Sings* album at RCA Studios in Nashville on July 24, 1958—the third session yielded five songs, all of them Chet instrumentals. One of the most interesting of these songs was Chet's version of "I'm Forever Blowing Bubbles." "I'm Forever Blowing Bubbles" was originally written as a vocal number in waltz time for the Broadway musical *The Passing Show of 1918*. The song was credited to Jaan Kenbrovin and John Kellette, but "Jaan Kenbrovin" was actually a clever collective pseudonym for three separate writers, James Kendis, James Brockman and Nat Vincent. The number remained popular long after the musical it was written for had faded from the scene, and it was recorded by a variety of different artists over the years.

Unlike most of the artists who had previously covered "I'm Forever Blowing Bubbles," Chet chose not to interpret the song in waltz time—he instead delivered the song in a relaxed shuffle tempo. And just as he had done on his recording of "Swanee River" made at one of his earlier July 24 sessions, he recorded "I'm Forever Blowing Bubbles" using his modified 1955 Gretsch 6120 Chet Atkins Hollow Body electric guitar with uncut f-holes and two output jacks. These output jacks allowed the guitar's treble and bass strings to be plugged into their own separate inputs, because the instrument's pickups were wired in a manner that sent the treble strings' signal to one jack, and the bass strings' signal to the other.

As we also noted in our discussion of "Swanee River," the July 24, 1958, sessions were the first of Chet's to be recorded in stereo—and the modified 6120 was an ideal instrument for a stereo recording session. The guitar's treble strings (G, B, and high E) could be sent to one channel, and its bass strings (low E, A, and D) could be sent to the other. When played back in stereo, this "split guitar" effect created a highly unusual listening experience—the notes Chet played on the 6120 moved back and forth between the left and right speakers like some sort of sonic ping pong ball.

On "I'm Forever Blowing Bubbles," Chet plays his 6120 in standard tuning out of the key of A, and he is backed by a very spare arrangement of piano, bass and drums. Like Chet's arrangement of "Swanee River," Chet's arrangement of "I'm Forever Blowing Bubbles" provides a perfect showcase for the 6120's "split guitar" stereo effect. He opens the recording by rendering the song's breezy melody along with a simultaneously played accompanying pattern. The melody is delivered on the 6120's treble strings, and the accompanying pattern is delivered on the 6120's bass strings—so in stereo it sounds as if two separate guitarists are playing together, one mixed completely to the left channel, and the other mixed completely to the right channel.

Chet then moves to rendering the song through more straightforward soloing, and he makes a point of dividing the phrases found in this soloing between the 6120's treble and bass strings. Consequently, these phrases move between the left and right channels, making it sound as if the guitar is engaging in a kind of call and response game with itself.

Since RCA inexplicably decided to cancel *My Brother Sings* (we examined this album's unfortunate fate in our discussion of "Swanee River"), most of the instrumentals that Chet recorded on July 24, 1958, ended up being featured on his late 1959 RCA album *Mister Guitar*. "I'm Forever Blowing Bubbles" was one of those instrumentals, and it ended up being recognized as one of *Mister Guitar*'s standout tracks. (Incidentally, that record contained a few other songs that we have already discussed in this book—Chet recorded brand-new versions of his classic numbers "Rainbow" and "Country Gentleman" for the album, and his May 3, 1958, recording of "Slinkey" was also part of its track list.)

Even though the "split guitar" stereo effect created by the 6120's two output jacks had proven to be capable of delivering a very novel listening experience, Chet obviously decided that he did not much care for chopping his guitar sound into two separate halves—in fact, he would almost *never* use this effect again throughout the rest of his recording career. Frankly, it *is* a bit distracting to hear Chet's playing divided into two wholly separate sound groupings—but even still, the few "split guitar" recordings that Chet made with his 6120 are very memorable, and they stand as a fascinating little chapter in the history of recording technology.

"Theme from a Dream"

Composer: Boudleaux Bryant. **Producer:** R.H. Peirce. **Musicians:** Chet Atkins (guitar), Dennis Farnon (leader), Howard Mancel Roberts (guitar), Red Callender (bass), Larry Bunker, Jack Sperling (drums), Geoffrey Clarkson (piano), John W. Cave (French horn), Victor Gottlieb, Ed Lustgarten (cellos), Kathryn Julye (harp), Joseph DeFlore, Cecil Figelski, Alexander Neiman, Milton Thomas (violas), Leonard Atkins, Jacques Gasselin, James Getzoff, Murray Kellner, Carl LaMagna, Marvin Limonick, Alfred Lustgarten, Eudice Shapiro, Jack Shulman, Henry Sugar, Robert J. Sushel, Gerald Vinci (violins). **Location and Date of Recording:** Radio Recorders Annex Studios, Hollywood, California, October 23, 1958. **Original Release:** *Chet Atkins in Hollywood* (RCA Victor album, 1959).

By late 1958, Chet had enjoyed triumph after triumph as a recording artist—and his star was still very much on the rise. In October of that year, he traveled to Hollywood, California to hold recording sessions for himself that exceeded the size and scope of any previous recording session he had ever done. On October 23, 1958, his entire *Chet Atkins in Hollywood* album was recorded in two six-song sessions at Radio Recorders Annex Studios in Hollywood. All of the numbers recorded at these sessions were instrumentals, and every one of them featured Chet playing electric guitar accompanied by a full orchestra. The noted Canadian musician Dennis Farnon arranged and conducted this orchestra, which was made up of some of Hollywood's finest studio musicians. The Radio Recorders Annex Studios sessions marked the first time that Chet had ever recorded with such a large instrumental ensemble.

Two of the songs that Chet chose to record at these sessions, "Let It Be Me" and "The Three Bells," would eventually become big hits due to the fact that Chet had brought attention to them—but it would not be *his* versions of those songs that ended up topping the charts. The Everly Brothers had become close friends with Chet when they first came to Nashville in the mid–1950s—Chet was instrumental in helping the duo to secure a recording contract with Cadence Records, and he played guitar on some of their biggest early hits, including "Bye Bye Love," "Wake Up Little Susie," and "All I Have to do Is Dream." When the Everlys heard Chet's recording of "Let It Be Me," they decided to record their own vocal version of the song, which became a top ten hit in 1960.

In 1959, Chet was producing another family act, a vocal trio known as the Browns, for RCA Victor—he convinced the trio to record "The Three Bells," which went to number one on the country, pop and R&B charts. The Browns' vocal version of "The Three Bells" would end up being remembered as a classic Nashville Sound recording, as well as one of Chet's greatest triumphs as a producer.

One of the songs that Chet recorded at the second Radio Recorders Annex Studios session, "Theme from a Dream," turned out to be one of the most hauntingly beautiful works that he ever created. "Theme from a Dream" was written by Chet's close friend and occasional songwriting collaborator Boudleaux Bryant.

When Boudleaux wrote "Theme from a Dream," he had given Chet a truly magnificent piece of music to work with. The song was a slow-tempoed, minor-key based work, and it featured an unforgettable melody that was drenched in melancholy. "Theme from a Dream" would have been a perfect showcase for Chet's talent at most any time in his career—but since the song was so emotionally powerful, it was *doubly* perfect piece for him to have access to just as he was holding his first-ever recording session with a full orchestra.

On "Theme from a Dream," Chet plays a Gretsch electric guitar in standard tuning out of the key of D minor, and he renders the song's sorrowful melody mainly through straightforward single-note soloing. However, there are points in the recording when he embellishes his playing with inventive harmony lines, simultaneously played accompanying patterns, and harmonics—and every note he plays in the song is delivered with the contemplative touch of a true musical master. The lush sounds of Dennis Farnon's orchestra heard on the recording provide a perfect musical backdrop for Chet's playing.

Chet Atkins in Hollywood was very well-received when RCA Victor first released the record in the summer of 1959. The album definitely solidified his standing as a world-class instrumentalist who could play virtually any kind of music. But interestingly, there was at least one person who felt that the album was not as good as it should have been—and that person was Chet himself. Chet decided to re-record all of his *Chet Atkins in Hollywood* guitar tracks at his home studio when the album was re-released in 1961. (The album's orchestra tracks were not modified in any way for this 1961 re-release.)

It could definitely be said that Chet's new guitar tracks for *Chet Atkins in Hollywood* were played with a bit more finesse and subtlety than his original tracks—but that does not mean that those original tracks are by *any* means bad. In fact, over the years, both versions of *Chet Atkins in Hollywood* have been made available to the public through various CD releases, and the average listener would probably not even notice that the two are actually very different from one another. Of course, all of us devoted Chet fans can quickly tell one version from another. For example, the long harmonic passage that Chet played at the end of his 1958 recording of "Theme From a Dream" is not played on his 1961 recording of the song—he replaced it with more single-note soloing.

In the final analysis, both versions of *Chet Atkins in Hollywood* are so beautifully done that it is impossible for one to make a convincing argument that one is substantially better than the other. So take this author's advice—do yourself a favor and make sure you have copies of both versions of *Chet Atkins in Hollywood* in your music collection.

"Jitterbug Waltz"

Composer: Fats Waller. **Producer:** R.H. Peirce. **Musicians:** Chet Atkins (guitar), Dennis Farnon (leader), Howard Mancel Roberts (guitar), Red Callender (bass), Larry Bunker, Jack Sperling (drums), Geoffrey Clarkson (piano), John W. Cave (French horn), Victor Gottlieb, Ed Lustgarten (cellos), Kathryn Julye (harp), Joseph DeFlore, Cecil Figelski, Alexander Neiman, Milton Thomas (violas), Leonard Atkins, Jacques Gasselin, James Getzoff, Murray Kellner, Carl LaMagna, Marvin Limonick, Alfred Lustgarten, Eudice Shapiro, Jack Shulman, Henry Sugar, Robert J. Sushel, Gerald Vinci (violins). **Location and Date of Recording:** Radio Recorders Annex Studios, Hollywood, California, October 23, 1958. **Original Release:** *Chet Atkins in Hollywood* (RCA Victor album, 1959).

As we just noted in this book's previous entry, Chet recorded his entire *Chet Atkins in Hollywood* album during two six-song sessions held at Radio Recorders Annex Studios in Hollywood, California on October 23, 1958. All of the numbers recorded at these sessions were instrumentals, and every one of them featured Chet playing electric guitar accompanied by a full orchestra. The noted Canadian musician Dennis Farnon arranged and conducted this orchestra, which was made up of some of Hollywood's finest studio musicians. The Radio Recorders Annex Studios sessions marked the first time that Chet had ever recorded with such a large instrumental ensemble.

The last song recorded at these sessions was "Jitterbug Waltz," and it ended up being perhaps the most well-known of all the tracks on *Chet Atkins in Hollywood*. "Jitterbug Waltz" was an instrumental number in waltz time composed and recorded in 1942 by the legendary jazz pianist/organist Fats Waller. The song featured a descending melody that was both very nimble and very memorable.

Chet had already recorded two different versions of "Jitterbug Waltz" earlier in his career. The first time he laid down the song was on April 23, 1951, during a session at RCA Studios in New York City. This recording marked the first time that Chet had experimented with using multitrack recording technology—he recorded electric rhythm guitar and bass parts to accompany his main electric guitar part. This version of "Jitterbug Waltz" was released on 78 and 45 singles by RCA Victor in 1951 under the billing "Chet Atkins—Playing All Instruments."

Chet again recorded the song during a four-song session for his album *Hi-Fi in*

Focus that was held at RCA's Nashville studio on June 22, 1957. (That session also yielded his classic recordings of "El Cumbanchero" and "Tiger Rag," which we discussed earlier.) This version of "Jitterbug Waltz" featured Chet on electric guitar accompanied by piano, bass and drums, and while it was very well-done, it was not chosen for inclusion on *Hi-Fi in Focus*. (It finally saw the light of day when it was included on the Chet Atkins CD set *Mister Guitar: The Complete Recordings 1955–1960* released by Bear Family Records in 2004.)

On the *Chet Atkins in Hollywood* version of "Jitterbug Waltz," Chet plays a Gretsch electric guitar in standard tuning out of the key of D, and he delivers the number in very slow waltz time. Chet renders most of the song's sprightly descending melody through straightforward single-note soloing on his high strings. Toward the end of the recording, he uses an abundance of hammer-ons and pull-offs in his playing to give the song's melody an extra lightweight quality, making it sound as if the notes he is playing are floating through the air like dandelion seeds being carried off by a sudden breeze. Dennis Farnon's orchestra perfectly supports Chet's playing by offering up inventive and occasionally unexpected musical phrases that give the recording an added depth.

As we also noted, *Chet Atkins in Hollywood* was very well-received when RCA Victor first released the record in the summer of 1959. But interestingly, there was at least one person who felt that the album was not as good as it should have been—and that person was Chet himself. Chet decided to re-record all of his *Chet Atkins in Hollywood* guitar tracks at his home studio when the album was re-released in 1961. (The album's orchestra tracks were not modified in any way for this 1961 re-release.)

It could definitely be said that Chet's new guitar tracks for *Chet Atkins in Hollywood* were played with a bit more finesse and subtlety than his original tracks—but that does not mean that those original tracks are by *any* means bad. In fact, over the years, both versions of *Chet Atkins in Hollywood* have been made available to the public through various CD releases, and the average listener would probably not even notice that the two are actually very different from one another. Of course, all of us devoted Chet fans can quickly tell one version from another—for example, the 1958 version of "Jitterbug Waltz" opens with Chet playing a few introductory measures along with the orchestra, and the 1961 version of the song opens with only the orchestra playing those introductory measures. Also, on the 1961 version of the song, Chet embellishes a portion of his melody playing with simultaneously played harmony notes—he does not do this on the 1958 version.

In the final analysis, both versions of *Chet Atkins in Hollywood* are so beautifully done that it is impossible for one to make a convincing argument that one is substantially better than the other. So I'll give you the same advice that I gave you gave you in this book's last entry—do yourself a favor and make sure you have copies of both versions of *Chet Atkins in Hollywood* in your music collection.

"Django's Castle"

Composer: Django Reinhardt. **Producer:** Chet Atkins. **Musicians:** Chet Atkins (guitar), Hank Garland (guitar), James Rich (rhythm guitar), Floyd Cramer (piano), Boots Randolph (saxophone), Bob Moore (bass), Buddy Harman (drums). **Location and Date of Recording:** RCA Victor Studio, Nashville, Tennessee, July 1,

1959. **Original Release:** RCA Victor 47-7589 (RCA Victor 45 single, 1959), *Teensville* (RCA Victor album, 1960).

Early 1959 found Chet at work on a new record project that was designed to tap into the late 1950s success of *Sing-Along with Mitch*, conductor Mitch Miller's series of sing-along albums recorded for the Columbia label. Chet's attempt to emulate Mitch's popularity was entitled *Hum and Strum Along with Chet Atkins*, and it was released by RCA Victor in the summer of 1959. Not surprisingly, Chet's playing was really not the main focus of *Hum and Strum Along with Chet Atkins*—the album was a collection of twelve standards that prominently featured the singing of a rousing, Mitch Miller-style vocal chorus. Chet managed to get in some nice guitar licks between all of the sing-along fun found on the record—but on the whole, *Hum and Strum Along with Chet Atkins* turned out to be one of his lesser efforts since his playing was not truly at the front and center of the whole affair like it had been on all of his earlier albums.

The summer of 1959 found Chet finishing up work on another new album project—this one was entitled *Mister Guitar*. Of course, the name of that record was inspired by the very appropriate nickname for him that had been growing in popularity over the past few years—his incredible skill as a guitarist had led to countless people around the world referring to him as "Mister Guitar."

Chet held a session for *Mister Guitar* on June 19, 1959, at Nashville's RCA Studios that yielded new versions of his classic numbers "Rainbow" and "Country Gentleman." The album would also end up containing a number of tracks that Chet had recorded the previous year for his canceled album *My Brother Sings*. (Earlier, we discussed the original versions of "Rainbow" and "Country Gentleman," as well as two *Mister Guitar* songs originally slated for inclusion on *My Brother Sings*, "Slinkey" and "I'm Forever Blowing Bubbles.") *Mister Guitar* was released by RCA in the fall of 1959, and it would go on to be remembered as one of Chet's all-time best albums. The record would also be instrumental in helping to further cement Chet's nickname for decades to come.

The original vinyl release of the album featured a cover with a photo of a mahogany-finished Gretsch Chet Atkins Country Gentleman electric guitar outfitted with a hat, string tie and shoes. This cover choice turned out to be particularly fitting, because in 1959 Chet received a new Country Gentleman from Gretsch, and this guitar became the instrument that he used on more of his recordings than any other guitar. Chet's 1959 Country Gentleman was equipped with a slightly wider neck than the neck of a standard Country Gentleman—the wider neck model of the guitar was eventually put into regular production by Gretsch. Chet would regularly use his 1959 Country Gentleman for recordings and personal appearances all the way up until 1980. (Incidentally, a photo of a Gretsch Chet Atkins Country Gentleman was also featured on the cover of the original 1959 vinyl release of *Chet Atkins in Hollywood*.)

Once *Hum and Strum Along with Chet Atkins* and *Mister Guitar* were finished up, Chet turned his attention toward yet another new album project, one that was aimed at the young adult market. As we noted earlier in the book, the huge popularity of rock and roll music in the mid to late 1950s led Chet to hold a number of recording sessions of his own that were designed to appeal to rock and roll fans. This time around, Chet decided to devote an entire album to songs that featured a rock and roll sensibility—that album would end up being titled *Teensville*.

The first session that Chet held for tracks that would appear on *Teensville* took place at RCA Studios in Nashville on July 1, 1959. The session was a two-song affair that was split with saxophonist Boots Randolph—Boots played on the Chet number recorded at the session as well. This session would mark the first time that Boots would play on one of Chet's records, and the two men would go on to work together musically for the better part of four decades. In fact, they would eventually forge a formal musical partnership with another of the musicians who played on this particular session, pianist Floyd Cramer. (We discussed Floyd's first session with Chet in our examination of the song "Trambone"—and we'll be discussing many of Chet's subsequent musical ventures with Floyd and/or Boots later in the book.)

The Chet number that was recorded at the July 1 session was "Django's Castle," Chet's version of guitarist Django Reinhardt's instrumental composition "Manoir de Mes Reves." Of course, "Django's Castle" was by no means Chet's first foray into musical territory covered by Django—as we noted several times earlier in the book, Chet was a huge fan of the guitarist, and some of Chet's most well-known early recordings were very Django-inspired.

Django first recorded "Manoir de Mes Reves" in 1942—the slow tempoed number featured a memorably dreamy melody, and a wealth of nimble, improvisational solo work. "Manoir de Mes Reves" ended up being so well-received that Django recorded it many more times before his death in 1953. Translated into English from French, the song's title means "Mansion of My Dreams"—likely as a tribute to the guitarist who was one of his primary musical heroes, Chet decided to insert Django's actual name into his re-title of the number.

"Django's Castle" featured an important milestone not only in the history of Chet's career, but also in the overall history of the electric guitar. Chet used a modified DeArmond foot-operated pedal on the recording that ended up being the forerunner of the modern wah-wah pedal. Chet adapted a DeArmond volume pedal by replacing the pedal's volume potentiometer that controlled loudness with a tone pot

Chet Atkins playing his 1959 Gretsch Chet Atkins Country Gentleman electric guitar, circa 1959.

that moved from extreme bass to extreme treble. When the pedal was moved, it gave Chet's guitar a crying sound similar to that of a trumpet note being muted and then unmuted. Chet's modified pedal was the first of its kind ever used with an electric guitar—because it gave his guitar such a distinctive wah-wah effect, he decided to use it on many of the songs he recorded for *Teensville*, including "Django's Castle."

On "Django's Castle," Chet plays a Gretsch electric guitar in standard tuning out of the key of D, and he is backed by rhythm guitar, piano, saxophone, bass, and drums. He beautifully renders the song's soothing melody using both his modified DeArmond pedal and an amplifier outfitted with a subtle tremolo setting. Chet does not offer up nearly as much improvisational soloing on the recording as Django did on his recordings of "Manoir de Mes Reves"—rather, Chet steps back a bit in order to make room for Boots's saxophone. Boots delivers some tasteful solo work on "Django's Castle" that perfectly complements Chet's innovative playing. Boots also states the song's melody in unison with Chet a number of times during the recording.

The combination of Django's wonderful songwriting and Chet's groundbreaking guitar sound led to "Django's Castle" being released as a 45 single by RCA Victor in late 1959. (The other side of that single was "Boo Boo Stick Beat," which is the subject of this book's next entry.) "Django's Castle" also came to be regarded as one of *Teensville*'s standout tracks when RCA released the album in early 1960. The overall high quality of *all* of the songs on found *Teensville* would propel the album to great success—it climbed to number 16 on the U.S. album charts, giving Chet his second charting LP.

"Boo Boo Stick Beat"

> **Composer:** Buddy Harman, John D. Loudermilk. **Producer:** Chet Atkins. **Musicians:** Chet Atkins (guitar), Bob Moore (bass), Buddy Harman (percussion). **Location and Date of Recording:** RCA Victor Studio, Nashville, Tennessee, July 25, 1959. **Original Release:** RCA Victor 47-7589 (RCA Victor 45 single, 1959), *Teensville* (RCA Victor album, 1960).

Chet's longtime interest in creating novelty records served him well as he was preparing *Teensville*, his album that was aimed at the young adult market. While working on the record, Chet and his musical associates had come across an informal percussion instrument sometimes referred to as a "boo boo stick," which was a section of heavy cardboard tubing that could be struck on any hard surface. Since the tubing was hollow, boo boo sticks could be cut to different lengths in order to have them create different tones when they were struck—shorter sticks created higher tones, and longer sticks created lower tones. Two of Chet's close musical associates, Buddy Harman (his regular studio drummer) and John D. Loudermilk (a singer/songwriter who was one of Chet's RCA Victor artists) decided to write a rock and roll-based novelty instrumental for Chet that was built around the unusual sound of boo boo sticks—they titled this instrumental "Boo Boo Stick Beat."

The song itself really *did* consist of little more than just the beat of boo boo sticks—it was in the key of B, but just about the only musical structure it featured was bassist Bob Moore slapping some riffs built around a B note on his instrument, and Chet vamping on some key of B-based chords on his electric guitar. Chet used his modified DeArmond pedal on the song in order to give his guitar a wah-wah effect—that unusual sound meshed very well with the multi-toned beat of the boo boo sticks. (Chet first used that pedal on his recording of "Django's Castle," the subject of this book's previous entry.)

Chet made a preliminary attempt at recording "Boo Boo Stick Beat" during a session held at Nashville's RCA Studios on July 21, 1959. The recording featured Chet on electric guitar, Bob on bass, and Buddy on boo boo stick-based percussion. This version of the song turned out to be very much a work in progress—its tempo sounded rushed, and Chet's guitar part was overly simplistic. (The July 21, 1959, version of "Boo Boo Stick Beat" remained unreleased until it appeared on the Chet Atkins CD set *Mister Guitar: The Complete Recordings 1955–1960* released by Bear Family Records in 2004.)

On July 25, 1959, Chet, Bob and Buddy returned to Nashville's RCA Studios and recorded the final, release-quality version of "Boo Boo Stick Beat." Chet played his 1959 Gretsch Chet Atkins Country Gentleman through his DeArmond pedal at this session. The July 25 version of the song was superior to the July 21 version in every way—it was musically inventive, rhythmically powerful, and infectiously high-spirited.

Chet Atkins playing his 1959 Gretsch Chet Atkins Country Gentleman electric guitar at a 1959 recording session.

As previously mentioned, there really is not all that much to Chet's guitar work in "Boo Boo Stick Beat." But his loose, improvisational playing laden with wah-wah effect makes for a good deal of raucous fun, especially when it is coupled with the beat of Buddy's boo boo sticks. In other words, Chet rocks out on this number just about as much as he would ever rock out during his entire career.

Incidentally, it should be noted that Buddy recalled that he was not the only one to play boo boo sticks on "Boo Boo Stick Beat," even though he was the only percussionist credited on the recording. Buddy stated that John D. Loudermilk (Buddy's "Boo Boo Stick Beat" co-composer) and Floyd Cramer played boo boo sticks along with him on the song.

Music fans definitely responded to the distinctive sound of "Boo Boo Stick Beat." The recording made the U.S. pop single charts when it was released as a 45 single by RCA Victor in late 1959, reaching the number 49 position. (The other side of that single was "Django's Castle.") And "Boo Boo Stick Beat" also came to be regarded as one of *Teensville*'s standout tracks when RCA released the album in early 1960. The overall high quality of *all* of the songs on found *Teensville* would propel the album to great success—it climbed to number 16 on the U.S. album charts.

"One Mint Julep"

Composer: Rudolph Toombs. **Producer:** Chet Atkins. **Musicians:** Chet Atkins (guitar), Velma Williams Smith (guitar), Floyd Cramer (piano), Boots Randolph (saxophone), Bob Moore (bass), Buddy Harman (drums), Anita Kerr, Dottie Dillard, Louis Dean Nunley, William Guilford Wright, Jr. (vocal chorus). **Location and Date of Recording:** RCA Victor Studio, Nashville, Tennessee, October 9, 1959. **Original Release:** *Teensville* (RCA Victor album, 1960), RCA Victor 47-7684 (RCA Victor 45 mono single, 1960), RCA Victor 61-7684 (RCA Victor 45 stereo single, 1960).

On October 9, 1959, Chet held a six-song session at RCA Studios in Nashville for his *Teensville* album project. All of the songs recorded at the session were basically instrumental numbers, but they did feature some supporting vocal parts provided by the well-known vocal group the Anita Kerr Singers. Anita's group had already worked with Chet a number of times over the past several years—in fact, in 1955 they had even teamed up to record a full album together.

Incidentally, that album was one of Chet's more unusual projects—it consisted entirely of little-known songs owned by the performance rights organization known as the Society of European Stage Authors and Composers (usually referred to as SESAC). All of the songs on the album featured equal parts of Chet's playing and the Anita Kerr Singers' singing. The album was given a very limited release by SESAC under several different titles—these titles included *The Amazing Chet Atkins*, *The Best Chet Yet*, and *Mr. Atkins If You Please*. Because the quality of the material on this album was decidedly pedestrian, it was certainly one of Chet's less memorable recording projects. At any rate, the Anita Kerr Singers were on board for Chet's October 9, 1959, session, and they would work with Chet many more times over the next few years. (We'll be discussing some of Chet's subsequent recordings featuring the Anita Kerr Singers later.)

One of the strongest songs recorded at the October 9 session was Chet's version of "One Mint Julep." "One Mint Julep" was a humorous blues vocal number written by Rudolph Toombs that was first recorded by the rhythm and blues vocal group the Clovers in late 1951. The Clovers' version of the song reached the number 2 position on the U.S. rhythm and blues charts the following year. The slow, swinging tempo and low-down blues melody of "One Mint Julep" perfectly lent itself to Chet's fingerstyle guitar-playing talents.

On "One Mint Julep," Chet plays a Gretsch electric guitar in standard tuning out of the key of A. His guitar is capoed at the 1st fret, so it sounds as if he is playing out of the key of Bb. On the recording, he is backed by guitar, piano, saxophone, bass, drums, and Anita's vocal chorus. Chet uses his modified DeArmond pedal on the song in order to give his guitar a wah-wah effect. (We discussed that pedal in detail in our examination of Chet's recording of "Django's Castle.")

Chet opens "One Mint Julep" by playing through two of the song's verse progressions, expressively rendering its melody along with a simultaneously played accompanying pattern. During the number's B section, he takes a step back in order to let Boots Randolph take a nice extended solo break—Boot's continues this solo break over one of the song's verse progressions. At the end of the recording, Chet steps back in for one last verse progression, again playing the song's melody along with a simultaneous accompanying pattern.

Since "One Mint Julep" had proven to be one of *Teensville*'s strongest tracks when the album was released in early 1960, RCA Victor decided to release the recording as a 45 single that same year. (The other side of that single was "Teensville," which is the subject of this book's next entry.) "One Mint Julep" ended up reaching the number 82 position on the U.S. pop single charts. And as mentioned in this book's past two entries, the overall high quality of *all* of the songs on found *Teensville* would propel the album to great success—it climbed to number 16 on the U.S. album charts.

"Teensville"

Composer: Wayne Cogswell. **Producer:** Chet Atkins. **Musicians:** Chet Atkins (guitar), Velma Williams Smith (guitar), Floyd Cramer (piano), Bob Moore (bass), Buddy Harman (drums), Anita Kerr, Dottie Dillard, Louis Dean Nunley, William Guilford Wright, Jr. (vocal chorus). **Location and Date of Recording:** RCA Victor Studio, Nashville, Tennessee, October 13, 1959. **Original Release:** *Teensville* (RCA Victor album, 1960), RCA Victor 47-7684 (RCA Victor 45 mono single, 1960), RCA Victor 61-7684 (RCA Victor 45 stereo single, 1960).

On October 13, 1959, Chet held one last recording session for his *Teensville* album at RCA Studios in Nashville. The session yielded three instrumentals, all of which featured supporting vocal parts provided by The Anita Kerr Singers. One of these instrumentals was the number written by singer/songwriter Wayne Cogswell that gave the album its title, "Teensville."

"Teensville" was a high-energy, swing-tempo rock song that was musically built on a three-chord blues pattern in the key of E. However, it also featured a clever little secondary chord pattern that was used both at the beginning and in the middle of the number—this chord pattern moved from E to C, then from A to A minor, and then resolved by returning to E. The pattern gave "Teensville" a bit of unexpected musical depth, especially when it was topped with an inventive melody line played by Chet.

Speaking of Chet's playing, he uses a Gretsch electric guitar in standard tuning on "Teensville," and he is backed by guitar, piano, bass, drums, and Anita's vocal chorus. Chet uses his modified DeArmond pedal on the song in order to give his guitar a wah-wah effect. (Chet obviously knew that he was really on to something when he first created that pedal during the making of *Teensville*—after all, he used it on most every one of the numbers found on the album, including the last three recordings we have discussed.)

During the recording, Chet delivers a potent combination of straightforward single-note soloing (played over top of the song's secondary chord pattern sections), power-packed chords, and walking blues lines that are fretted on his lower strings—and much of this great guitar work is drenched in hard-edged wah-wah sound. As

Chet Atkins with his 1959 Gretsch Chet Atkins Country Gentleman electric guitar, preparing for an informal performance with an unidentified group of backing musicians, circa 1960. Note that he is playing the guitar through his Standel amplifier.

Chet rocks out on "Teensville," he is nicely supported by Floyd Cramer's bluesy piano soloing, and the Anita Kerr Singers' "oohs" and yelping "whoos."

Not surprisingly, RCA Victor chose to issue *Teensville*'s very memorable title track as a single when the album was first released in early 1960. (The other side of that single was "One Mint Julep," which was the subject of the previous entry.) "Teensville" ended up reaching the number 73 position on the U.S. pop single charts. And as mentioned in this book's past three entries, the overall high quality of *all* of the songs on found *Teensville* would propel the album to great success—it climbed to number 16 on the U.S. album charts, giving Chet his second charting LP.

In other words, Chet's first full-length foray into rock-based music aimed at the young adult market had turned out to be a substantial success. But Chet chose not to simply try to re-create that success with his next album project—instead, he put down his electric guitar, and went to work on a new album that would feature him playing only nylon-string acoustic guitar. We'll discuss that album entitled *The Other Chet Atkins* and one of its standout tracks, "Peanut Vendor," in the next entry.

"The Peanut Vendor"

Composer: Moisés Simóns, L. Wolfe Gilbert, Marion Sunshine. **Producer:** Chet Atkins. **Musicians:** Chet Atkins (guitar), Ray Edenton, Hank Garland (guitars),

Bob Moore (bass), Buddy Harman, Douglas Kirkham (drums). **Location and Date of Recording:** RCA Victor Studio, Nashville, Tennessee, December 8, 1959. **Original Release:** *The Other Chet Atkins* (RCA Victor album, 1960).

By the time that Chet had first gained widespread fame as a guitarist, he was primarily known as an electric player—however, he had always maintained a keen interest in the acoustic guitar as well. That interest led him to want to learn more and more about the nylon-string acoustic guitar, an instrument commonly referred to as a "classical guitar" since it was often used for the playing of classical music works.

Since Chet had always been a fingerstyle guitarist, his playing translated extremely well to the fingerpicking techniques normally used by classical guitar players. Consequently, he began devoting an increasing amount of his playing time to the classical guitar. Chet first recorded with one in 1955 when he made his initial excursion into the realm of classical music for his landmark album *Chet Atkins in Three Dimensions*. He used the instrument for one of that album's four classical selections—the particular selection he used it for was a stately medley of "Minuet—from French Harpsichord Suite" and "Prelude—from Six Short Preludes," two compositions by Johan Sebastian Bach. (We discussed several other tracks from *Chet Atkins in Three Dimensions* earlier in the book, but this is the first time we've mentioned Chet's recording of "Minuet" and "Prelude.")

In late 1959, Chet decided to take his love for the classical guitar to a whole new level—he began work on an entire album of songs that featured him playing the instrument. He chose to title the album *The Other Chet Atkins* since it showcased an aspect of his playing that was markedly different from his electric work. Interestingly, the classical guitars Chet would have used to record the album were not the finest of instruments—the first classical guitars that he bought for himself in the 1950s were ones that were built by relatively undistinguished guitar makers. In the years to come, he would end up playing classical guitar every bit as much as he played electric—and of course, this change in his playing focus would lead him to acquire a number of extremely high-quality classical guitars. But his first full-length foray into classical guitar playing was accomplished with decidedly ordinary guitars.

Even though *The Other Chet Atkins* was devoted to Chet's playing of the classical guitar, the album was definitely *not* a classical music outing. Rather, Chet picked a selection of pop, flamenco and Latin selections to record for the album. One of these selections was a song that Chet had already shown affection for—"The Peanut Vendor" was a catchy dance number written by Cuban composer Moisés Simóns in the 1920s. The original Spanish-language title of the song was "El Manisero" (the Spanish word for "peanut vendor"), and it featured lyrics written in Spanish. Over the years, "The Peanut Vendor" ended up becoming very popular not just in Cuba, but also in the United States—English-language lyrics for the song were written by L. Wolfe Gilbert and Marion Sunshine.

Chet decided to cover "The Peanut Vendor" as an instrumental—he first recorded it on November 29, 1956, at the same session that yielded "Trambone," a number we discussed in detail earlier in this book. Chet played that version of "The Peanut Vendor" on electric guitar, and it appeared on one of the handful of singles issued by RCA Victor under the billing "The Rhythm Rockers featuring Chet Atkins." Chet's initial version of the song was agreeable enough, but it did not achieve any real success in terms of sales or airplay. And of course, "The Peanut Vendor" was really far better-suited to be played as a flamenco-style acoustic guitar piece than as an electric guitar number—so Chet wisely decided to create a brand-new instrumental version of the song for *The Other Chet Atkins*. He recorded that version during a four-song session held at RCA Studios in Nashville on December 8, 1959. (That particular session was the first one held for *The Other Chet Atkins*.)

On *The Other Chet Atkins* version of "The Peanut Vendor," Chet plays his classical guitar in standard tuning out of the key of A, and he is backed by guitar, bass, and percussion. There is also a whistling part on the recording that mimics the sound of a peanut vendor calling out "peanuts." In terms of musical structure, "The Peanut Vendor" is a ridiculously simple song, consisting of nothing more than a high-spirited melody played against a two-chord pattern that is repeated over and over again. For all of you guitarists who would like to play along with Chet on this recording, the two chords in that pattern are A and E. (In fact, if you are *not* a guitarist but you would still like to play along with Chet, this is just the recording for you—just take a few minutes to learn those two rudimentary chords, and then you can strum along with Chet to your heart's content.)

"The Peanut Vendor" allows Chet to showcase his relatively newfound, but already considerable, skill as a nylon-string acoustic guitarist. He renders the song using a wide variety of different guitar techniques—he plays its melody along with simultaneously played accompanying patterns, he delivers a wealth of nimble single-note solo passages, and he strums full chords in dramatic flamenco style.

Once *The Other Chet Atkins* was released by RCA Victor in late 1960, Chet fans began to realize that their musical hero was an artist of even more depth than they had previously given him credit for. And of course, his distinguished tenure as a nylon-string acoustic guitarist had only just begun with this particular album—throughout the rest of this book, we will be discussing many more recordings that feature Chet playing the nylon-string acoustic guitar.

"Hot Mocking Bird"

Composer: Traditional (arranged by Bud Isaacs). **Producer:** Chet Atkins. **Musicians:** Chet Atkins (guitar), Velma Williams Smith (guitar), Floyd Cramer (piano), Bob Moore (bass), Buddy Harman (drums). **Location and Date of Recording:** RCA Victor Studio, Nashville, Tennessee, February 23, 1960. **Original Release:** *Chet Atkins' Workshop* (RCA Victor album, 1961), RCA Victor 47-7847 (RCA Victor 45 mono single, 1961), RCA Victor 37-7847 (RCA Victor Compact 33 single, 1961).

Early 1960 found Chet beginning to work on another new album project—this album would end up being entitled *Chet Atkins' Workshop* in honor of his elaborate home recording studio. In fact, the album's liner notes would be devoted to a discussion of how Chet's sense of perfectionism had led him to record many of his final guitar tracks at his home studio instead of at RCA Studios in Nashville. In the notes, Chet explained his decision to record in this manner. He said that due to his label's financial interests, he felt that he couldn't spend nearly as much time on his guitar tracks as he wanted while he was working in their studio—but when he was working by himself in his home studio, he felt free to take all the time he needed in order to get his guitar tracks just right.

Chet might have finished up many of his recording projects at his home studio, but most all of these projects still had to begin at RCA's recording facilities where Chet and his group of backing musicians could comfortably work together. So on February 23, 1960, Chet recorded five songs for *Chet Atkins' Workshop* at RCA Studios in Nashville. One of the most memorable numbers from that session was "Hot Mocking Bird," a jazzy, uptempo instrumental arrangement of the well-known mid–19th century ballad "Listen to the Mocking Bird" written by Septimus Winner and Richard Milburn. The arrangement of "Hot Mocking Bird" was credited to Bud Isaacs, a steel guitarist who had worked with Chet a number of times over the years. (Isaacs was prominently featured on Chet's 1954 album *A Session with Chet Atkins*.)

On "Hot Mocking Bird," Chet plays a Gretsch electric guitar in standard tuning out of the key of A, and he is backed by rhythm guitar, piano, bass, and drums. He starts off by rendering the happy melody of "Listen to the Mocking Bird" in a fairly straightforward manner, but then he starts taking the song through many unexpected twists and turns. He delivers a combination of single-note solos and chord patterns that could probably be best described as "impressionistic"—in fact, his playing ends up moving so far beyond the song's traditional melody that "Hot Mocking Bird" at times becomes an excursion into dissonant bebop jazz territory. In other words, "Hot Mocking Bird" is a particularly adventurous musical outing for Chet—especially when one considers the fact that most all of the other songs found on *Chet Atkins' Workshop* are far more sedate and easy listening in nature.

Chet Atkins' Workshop was released by RCA Victor in February 1961, and it was hailed as yet another musical triumph for Chet—in fact, it quickly became one of the most commercially successful albums of his entire career. It climbed to number 7 on the U.S. album charts, making it his highest-charting album of all time, and only one to ever break the top ten. And since "Hot Mocking Bird" was one of *Chet Atkins' Workshop*'s standout tracks, RCA Victor decided to release the song as a single in early 1961. The single was released both as a standard mono 45 and as a Compact 33. "Hot Mocking Bird" never made the charts as a single, but it undoubtedly helped to promote the *Chet Atkins' Workshop* album as a whole.

I should probably take just a moment to explain just what a Compact 33 single actually was—the Compact 33 was a short-lived record format introduced by RCA in the early 1960s. A Compact 33 single included two songs just like a standard single, but it featured two separate versions of those songs—one version was mixed in mono, and the other was mixed in stereo.

Incidentally, there are two *completely* different versions of "Hot Mocking Bird" in existence that were obviously both recorded during the time *Chet Atkins' Workshop* was first being made. Both of these versions have been released on various Chet CD anthologies and CD pressings of *Chet Atkins' Workshop*, so it is hard to conclude just which of them should be considered the "definitive" one. The version that first appeared on the 1961 vinyl release of the album featured a Chet guitar track that was laden with effects—for instance, certain single-note phrases that he played were thickened with very heavy delay.

Considering the subject matter of the *Chet Atkins' Workshop* liner notes, it seems likely that the version of "Hot Mocking Bird" that appeared on the original release of the album featured a guitar track that Chet recorded while working alone at his home studio—and the other version that found its way onto later releases likely featured a preliminary guitar track that Chet recorded with his backing musicians while working at RCA Studios. This version featured far less effects on Chet's guitar, so it is relatively easy to tell the two versions apart from one another. At any rate, both of these versions of "Hot Mocking Bird" are spectacularly played, and they are generally very similar to one another in terms of their musical structure—so a Chet fan really can't go wrong with either version.

"Theme from *The Dark at the Top of the Stairs*"

Composer: Max Steiner. **Producer:** Neely Plumb, Dick Peirce. **Musicians:** Chet Atkins (guitar), Bob Thompson (leader), Al Hendrickson, Alfred Viola (guitars), Joe Mondragon (bass), Dick Shanahan (drums), Larry Bunker (vibes), Ernie Freeman (piano), Arthur Gleghorn (flute), Arthur Briegleb, Vincent DeRosa, Arthur Maebe, Richard Perissi (French horns), Ted Nash (saxophone), Jesse Ehrlich, Ed Lustgarten, George Neikrug, Emmet Sargeant, Eleanor Aller Slatkin, Olga Zundell (cellos), Israel Baker, Bobby Bruce, Herman Clebanoff, Eliott Fisher, James Getzoff, Benny Gill, Leonard Malarsky, Erno Neufeld, Louis Raderman, Nathan Ross, Ambrose Russo, Ralph Schaefer, Sidney Sharp, Darrell Terwillinger (violins). **Location and Date of Recording:** RCA Victor Studio 1, Hollywood, California, September 6, 1960. **Original Release:** RCA Victor 47-7796 (RCA Victor 45 mono single, 1960), RCA Victor 61-7796 (RCA Victor 45 stereo single, 1960).

On September 6, 1960, Chet held a recording session with a full orchestra at RCA Studios in Hollywood, California—the session was very similar to the orchestra sessions he had held in Hollywood on October 23, 1958, for his 1959 album *Chet Atkins in Hollywood*. But this time around, his California trip yielded only one instrumental song instead of an entire album. Working with an ensemble of top-flight studio musicians led by the well-known composer/conductor Bob Thompson, Chet recorded "Theme from *The Dark at the Top of the Stairs*." The song was a movie theme that had just recently been written by the legendary film composer Max Steiner for the 1960 motion picture drama *The Dark at the Top of the Stairs* starring Robert Preston and Dorothy McGuire.

Despite its foreboding title, "Theme from *The Dark at the Top of the Stairs*" was actually a very happy-sounding piece of orchestral pop music. The song's cheerful melody ambled along at a relaxed swing tempo, sounding far more like a selection from a romantic comedy than from a serious drama.

On "Theme from *The Dark at the Top of the Stairs*," Chet plays a Gretsch electric guitar in standard tuning. He starts out playing in the key of C, but midway through the recording the song moves to the key of A. Chet renders the song's easygoing melody mainly through straightforward single-note soloing. He also offers up some octave work and simultaneously played harmony lines to adorn that melody. Chet plays his guitar through an amplifier outfitted with a slow, heavy tremolo setting—the pulsating guitar sound he creates serves as an interesting contrast to the lush musical backdrop provided by Bob Thompson's orchestra.

RCA Victor released "Theme from *The Dark at the Top of the Stairs*" as a single in late 1960. The recording did end up charting, but its success was decidedly modest—it reached the number 103 position on the U.S. pop single charts in October of that same year.

Ironically, even though "Theme from *The Dark at the Top of the Stairs*" ended up being one of Chet's relatively few charting singles, it quickly became one of his more inaccessible records. After it was released as a single, it was featured on a four-song Compact 33 Double EP called *Chet Atkins Plays Great Movie Themes*—the other three tracks on that EP were movie-related numbers pulled from the *Chet Atkins in Hollywood* album, "Theme from *Picnic*," "Limelight," and "Meet Mr. Callaghan." (We briefly discussed RCA's short-lived Compact 33 format in this book's previous entry—but in that entry, we only went over what a Compact 33 *single* was. A Compact 33 Double featured four separate songs just like a standard EP release.)

"Theme from *The Dark at the Top of the Stairs*" never appeared on any other vinyl collection of Chet material other than *Chet Atkins Plays Great Movie Themes*—and since that collection was released on such a peculiar format, the song undeservedly fell into obscurity. Well over four decades after its initial release, "Theme from *The Dark at the Top of the Stairs*" finally made its way onto another Chet anthology collection—the recording was included on the Chet Atkins CD set *Mister Guitar: The Complete Recordings 1955–1960* released by Bear Family Records in 2004.

"It Ain't Necessarily So"

Composers: George Gershwin, Ira Gershwin. **Producer:** Chet Atkins. **Musicians:** Chet Atkins (guitar), Floyd Cramer (piano), Bob Moore (bass), Buddy Harman (drums), Karl Garvin (trumpet), Dorothy Walker, Brenton Banks, Howard Carpenter, Vernal Richardson, Lillian Hunt, Solie Fott, Harry Nides (violins), Mildred Oonk (viola), Byron Bach (cello). **Location and Date of Recording:** RCA Victor Studio, Nashville, Tennessee, March 16, 1961. **Original Release:** *The Most Popular Guitar* (RCA Victor album, 1961).

On March 16, 1961, Chet recorded eight instrumentals for his new album *The Most Popular Guitar* in two four-song sessions at RCA Studios in Nashville. The record would end up being stylistically very similar to his 1959 album *Chet Atkins in Hollywood*, because most all of its songs featured him being accompanied by a large string section. One of the numbers recorded at the first March 16 session, "It Ain't Necessarily So," was chosen to open the album.

"It Ain't Necessarily So" was originally written as a slow-tempoed, bluesy vocal piece by George and Ira Gershwin for their classic 1935 opera *Porgy and Bess*. Over the years, the song gained fame not only as a part of the opera, but also as a stand-alone number that was recorded by many different artists. The mournful, minor-key based melody of "It Ain't Necessarily So" made it equally powerful as either a vocal or instrumental work—so naturally, it served as a perfect showcase for Chet's contemplative guitar soloing.

On "It Ain't Necessarily So," Chet plays a Gretsch electric guitar out of the key of E minor. His guitar is capoed at the 3rd fret, so it sounds as if he is playing out of the key of G minor. On the recording, he is backed by an ensemble that includes strings and a trumpet soloist. He renders much of the song's haunting melody through chords voiced up and down the neck of his guitar, but he also delivers some expressive single-note soloing laced with bluesy string bends. Chet's masterful playing is perfectly supported both by the musical backdrop provided by his string section and Karl Garvin's soulful, muted trumpet work.

The Most Popular Guitar was released by RCA Victor in mid–1961. Strangely, even though it was an excellent record, every bit as good as Chet's previous album *Chet Atkins' Workshop*, it did not end up enjoying anywhere near the same level of commercial success that *Workshop* had. In fact, *The Most Popular Guitar* only reached number 119 on the U.S. albums chart. Fortunately, this commercial slump would prove to be very temporary—Chet's next record, *Christmas with Chet Atkins*, would take Chet back up the charts. We'll discuss one of the numbers from that album, "Jingle Bell Rock."

"Jingle Bell Rock"

Composer: Joe Beal, Jim Boothe. **Producer:** Chet Atkins. **Musicians:** Chet Atkins (guitar), Velma Smith (guitar), Floyd Cramer (piano), Bob Moore (bass), Buddy Harman (drums), Anita Kerr, Dorothy Dillard, Gil Wright, Louis Nunley (vocal chorus). **Location and Date of Recording:** RCA Victor Studio, Nashville, Tennessee, May 24, 1961. **Original Release:** *Christmas with Chet Atkins* (RCA Victor album, 1961), RCA Victor 47-7971 (RCA Victor 45 single, 1961).

Chet found himself thinking about Christmas in the spring of 1961, even though the holiday was still about a half of a year away. He had decided to record a Christmas album entitled *Christmas with Chet Atkins* that would be released right before the 1961 holiday season—so on May 23 and 24 of that year, he held four separate recording sessions for the album at RCA Studios in Nashville. Those sessions yielded fourteen songs, all of which ended up being featured on the record.

Chet's longtime recording engineer at RCA Bill Porter recalled that he brought Christmas decorations into the studio for the sessions in order to try to get everyone into the holiday spirit, even though the weather was warm and summer-like right outside of the studio door. It would seem that Bill's strategy must have worked at least to some degree, because Chet and company ended up creating a Christmas album that would long be remembered as a true holiday classic.

It should be noted that *Christmas with Chet Atkins* did not mark the first time that Chet recorded a selection of Christmas music. In October 1955, he laid down a version of "Jingle Bells" and a medley of traditional holiday songs at RCA Studios in Nashville. Those recordings were released as a single by RCA Victor during the 1955 holiday season, but they did not achieve any notable sales or airplay. (RCA issued that single in both 45 and 78 formats.)

While *Christmas with Chet Atkins* was basically an instrumental album, Chet chose to adorn many of its numbers with supporting vocal parts provided by the Anita Kerr Singers—their singing brought an extra dimension to the record that made it even more warm and festive. Chet divided the album's songs into two distinctly separate sections—all of its first-side songs featured him playing electric guitar, and all of its second-side songs featured him playing acoustic guitar. Most all of the Christmas songs that Chet decided to use for the album, both the electric and the acoustic ones, were traditional works. However, he did include a few recently created holiday numbers on the record as well. One of these newer numbers was "Jingle Bell Rock"—Chet recorded it with electric guitar, and it was picked to open the album.

"Jingle Bell Rock" was a midtempo, rockabilly flavored Christmas vocal number written by Joe Beal and Jim Boothe, and it was recorded by country singer Bobby Helms in 1957. Helms' version of the song became a top ten-selling single the following year, and it remained a perennial holiday favorite from that point on. Chet recorded his version of "Jingle Bell Rock" at one of the *Christmas with Chet Atkins* sessions held on May 24, 1961.

On "Jingle Bell Rock," Chet plays a Gretsch electric guitar in standard tuning out of the key of C. He is backed by piano, bass, drums, and Anita's vocal chorus—and of course, there are a few jingle bells that ring out on the recording as well. Chet ramps up the tempo of the song, playing it quite a bit faster than the tempo used in Helms' original version—this change gives Chet's "Jingle Bell Rock" less of a rockabilly feel and more of a swing feel.

Chet renders much of the song's catchy melody through straightforward single-note soloing on his high strings. That said, however, his playing does go beyond just this single-note soloing—he often throws in simultaneously played harmony lines to accompany his melody playing. Chet's tasteful blend of melody and harmony in "Jingle Bell Rock" make the recording a high-spirited affair from beginning to end. Midway through the recording, Chet steps back in order to let Anita's vocal chorus sing just a few lines from the song's opening verse.

When RCA Victor released *Christmas with Chet Atkins* in late 1961, they also chose to release "Jingle Bell Rock" as a 45 single. It was very fittingly backed with another of the album's wonderful electric guitar numbers, "Jingle Bells." "Jingle Bell Rock" ended up not making much of an impression as a single (it couldn't quite crack the top 100 on the U.S. pop single charts), but the *Christmas with Chet Atkins* record as a whole turned out to be very successful—it reached the number 12 spot on the U.S. album charts, making it Chet's second-highest charting album ever. Even better, the album just seemed to get better and better as the years went by—each Christmas, both Chet fans and holiday music fans looked forward to it being a part of their holiday celebration.

Well over two decades after the release of *Christmas with Chet Atkins*, Chet decided to record a new Christmas album. He had left RCA and signed with Columbia Records, and one of his first projects for his new label was his 1983 album *East Tennessee Christmas*. Just like he had done on *Christmas with Chet Atkins*, Chet chose to open *East Tennessee Christmas* with his cover of "Jingle Bell Rock." In keeping with the old adage "if it ain't broke, don't fix it," Chet's 1983 version of the song was very similar in style and arrangement to his 1961 version of the song.

"Salty Dog Rag"

Composer: "Papa" John Gordy. **Producer:** Chet Atkins. **Musicians:** Chet Atkins (guitar), Velma Smith (guitar), Floyd Cramer (piano), Boots Randolph (saxophone), Charlie McCoy (harmonica), Henry Strzelecki (bass), Morris Palmer (drums). **Location and Date of Recording:** RCA Victor Studio, Nashville, Tennessee, October 3, 1961. **Original Release:** *Down Home* (RCA Victor album, 1962).

Even though Chet's initial fame had come from him being recognized mainly as a country music guitarist, by the early 1960s he had made a string of excellent albums that were far more cosmopolitan and easy listening in nature than they were country. Chet decided to return to a more informal, country music-based setting for his next album project. That album would be entitled *Down Home*, and it would feature a selection of music that was a bit more, well, *down home* than the music found on his recent albums.

This does not mean that *Down Home* was strictly a country music record—it still featured Chet covering songs that he had chosen from a wide range of musical styles. That said, however, the album as a whole just felt very laid-back, much like a relaxed jam session amongst a group of good friends. For example, gone were the lush string sections found on Chet's albums such as *Chet Atkins in Hollywood* and *The Most Popular Guitar*, and in their place were foot-tapping solo breaks played by harmonicist Charlie McCoy and saxophonist Boots Randolph.

In fact, it is really no exaggeration to say that the lineup of musicians that Chet used for *Down Home* played a major role in making the album a true classic. In addition to Charlie and Boots, pianist Floyd Cramer also played on the record. Charlie, Boots and Floyd were not only among Chet's closest musical collaborators, but they were also star performers in their own right—so naturally, their combined contributions to *Down Home* were invaluable in helping to make the album one of Chet's all-time finest.

Incidentally, we've discussed both Floyd and Boots earlier in this book, but this is the first time we've mentioned Charlie McCoy. Charlie's spectacular harmonica work would be featured on a number of Chet's recordings in the coming years. (We'll be examining a few of those recordings a bit later.)

On October 3, 1961, eight instrumentals were recorded for the *Down Home* album in two four-song sessions held at RCA Studios in Nashville. One of those numbers was a likable remake of Chet's classic 1956 composition "Trambone." (We discussed Chet's original recording of "Trambone" earlier.) Another number from the sessions, "Salty Dog Rag," was chosen to be the album's opening track. The song was a midtempo vocal number written by "Papa" John Gordy about a dance known as the "Salty Dog Rag." The most well-known version of "Salty Dog Rag" was recorded by the legendary country singer Red Foley in 1951—it became a top ten country hit the following year. Chet's version of "Salty Dog Rag" was musically quite different from Foley's, because he sped up the tempo of the song and slightly altered its chord progression.

On "Salty Dog Rag," Chet plays a Gretsch electric guitar in standard tuning out of the key of C, and he is accompanied by piano, saxophone, harmonica, bass, and drums. Chet starts out the recording by rendering the song's melody along with a simultaneously played accompanying pattern, and after one time through the song's chord progression, he offers up some relaxed single-note soloing. He then steps back in order to let Boots and Charlie take solo breaks. After their solos, Chet steps back in for some more single-note soloing, and he closes out the recording by again playing the song's melody along with a simultaneous accompanying pattern.

Chet put in a very good day of work for *Down Home* on October 3, 1961, but he still had yet to record the song that would unquestionably turn out to be the album's most-remembered number. We'll discuss that song, "Windy and Warm," next.

"Windy and Warm"

Composer: John D. Loudermilk. **Producer:** Chet Atkins. **Musicians:** Chet Atkins (guitar), Velma Smith (guitar), Floyd Cramer (piano), Henry Strzelecki (bass), Morris Palmer (drums). **Location and Date of Recording:** RCA Victor Studio, Nashville, Tennessee, October 5, 1961. **Original Release:** *Down Home* (RCA Victor album, 1962).

On October 5, 1961, Chet held a session at RCA Studios in Nashville to record one more song for his *Down Home* album. The song he recorded at this session, "Windy and Warm," would come to be as well-known and loved as any song he ever recorded in his entire career. "Windy and Warm" was an instrumental composed by John D. Loudermilk, a singer/songwriter who was one of Chet's RCA Victor artists. The song featured a minor key-based melody so that was so absurdly catchy, most listeners only needed to hear it one time to have it burned into their memory.

On "Windy and Warm," Chet plays a Gretsch electric guitar out of the key of A minor. His guitar is capoed at the 3rd fret, so it sounds as if he is playing out of the key of C minor. On the recording, he is backed by guitar, piano, bass and drums. The song also features some great supporting vocal parts that are built around Chet's singing—he subtly scats along with his playing several times in the recording, and he is the lead voice in a vocal chorus that sings a few well-placed, almost spooky-sounding "aahs."

On "Windy and Warm," Chet never relies on his backing parts to support him while he plays single-note solos—rather, the entire song is delivered through his playing of its melody along with a simultaneously played accompanying pattern. Simply put, "Windy and Warm" is quintessential Chet—the recording is self-reliant, low-key and very soulful, just like the man himself.

Down Home was released by RCA Victor in 1962, and Chet's decision to move back toward more country-based music on the album definitely resonated with the record-buying public—the record climbed to number 31 on the U.S. album charts. And of course, "Windy and Warm" was instantly recognized as one of the album's standout tracks.

In fact, Chet's *Down Home* version of "Windy and Warm" would end up becoming one of the recordings that Chet would be most identified with for the rest of his life—the number became a regular feature in both his concert and television appearances, and he only had to play the first few notes of the song to draw enthusiastic applause from most any audience he might be in front of.

Incidentally, Chet had already taken a stab at recording "Windy and Warm" before he laid down the version of the song that would appear on *Down Home*—he had previously recorded the number during a session at RCA Studios in Nashville on April 5, 1961. That version was released as a single in 1961, but it did not achieve any notable amount of sales or airplay. Chet's single version of "Windy and Warm" was markedly different from his *Down Home* version in terms of instrumentation and arrangement—for example, Chet used a nylon-string acoustic guitar on the recording, and he played the song at a noticeably slower tempo.

Finally, there is a third Chet recording of "Windy and Warm" that we should take note of before we move on. On June 10, 1965, he recorded a very enjoyable orchestral version of the song with Arthur Fiedler and the Boston Pops for their 1966 collaborative album *The Pops Goes Country*.

"Mayan Dance"

Composer: Antonio Lauro. **Producer:** Chet Atkins. **Musicians:** Chet Atkins (guitar), Ray Edenton (guitar), Tupper Saussy (piano), Henry Strzelecki (bass), John Greubel (drums), Cecil Brower, Brenton Banks, Lillian Hunt, Vernal Richardson (violins). **Location and Date of Recording:** RCA Victor Studio, Nashville, Tennessee, February 21, 1962. **Original Release:** *Caribbean Guitar* (RCA Victor album, 1962).

On February 14, 15, and 16, 1962, Chet held recording sessions for his new album *Caribbean Guitar* at RCA Studios in Nashville. Of course, the title of the record perfectly summed up its focus—Chet had chosen a variety of calypso, Latin and Caribbean-flavored songs to record for the album. All of the numbers that Chet recorded for *Caribbean Guitar* were instrumentals.

Most of the album was completed at the February 14, 15, and 16 sessions—but on February 21, Chet held a session at RCA Studios in Nashville to record "Mayan Dance," another song that was slated for inclusion on the album. "Mayan Dance" was a waltz piece written for classical guitar with an incredibly fiery and complex musical structure, and it was chosen to open *Caribbean Guitar*. (Incidentally, that February 21 session yielded another especially noteworthy Chet recording entitled "Scare Crow." "Scare Crow" was not at all Caribbean-themed, so it was held for release on a later Chet album. We'll discuss that recording in detail in the next entry.)

Interestingly, "Mayan Dance" was not really the official title of the musical piece that Chet recorded and released under that name. The piece was written in the 1930s by the well-known South American composer for the guitar Antonio Lauro. When it was recorded by the legendary classical guitarist Andrés Segovia, Segovia titled it "Vals Criollo." ("Vals Criollo" is a Spanish title, which in English means "Creole Waltz"—in this context, "Creole" refers to native Argentineans.)

Chet renamed the piece "Mayan Dance" when he recorded his version of it for *Caribbean Guitar*, but the piece soon had two *more* titles bestowed on it. It was called simply "Waltz Number 3" when Lauro grouped it with three of his other waltzes into a four-piece work entitled *Four Venezuelan Waltzes*. Then Lauro decided to name three of the waltzes in that work after three of his loved ones—so the piece that had been known as "Vals Criollo," "Mayan Dance," and "Waltz Number 3" was given the title "Natalia" in honor of Lauro's daughter.

Now that we've got all of that confusing title business sorted out, let's discuss Chet's recording of "Mayan Dance." On the recording, Chet plays a Gretsch electric guitar in standard tuning out of the key of E minor, and he is accompanied by guitar, piano, bass, drums and a violin section. The song contains one section that changes to the key of E major, but then it returns to E minor.

"Mayan Dance" is simply one of Chet's most virtuosic recorded performances of all time. The piece was originally written as a traditional classical guitar work, and a tremendously challenging one at that—somehow Chet brings the same level of musical mastery and intensity to it through his own unique style of playing. One might think that such a complex piece would not hold up very well when played by a guitarist using a thumbpick and an electric guitar. But in Chet's hands, the piece does far more than just "hold up"—it is shaped into a truly magnificent listening experience.

Caribbean Guitar ended up being very well-received when it was released by RCA Victor in the summer of 1962, reaching number 33 on the U.S. albums chart. Perhaps even more importantly, songs on the album such as "Mayan Dance" offered further evidence to show just how driven Chet was to continually broaden his musical horizons.

"Scare Crow"

Composer: Jerry Reed. **Producer:** Chet Atkins. **Musicians:** Chet Atkins (guitar), Ray Edenton (guitar), Tupper Saussy (piano), Henry Strzelecki (bass), John Greubel (drums), Cecil Brower, Brenton Banks, Lillian Hunt, Vernal Richardson (violins). **Location and Date of Recording:** RCA Victor Studio, Nashville, Tennessee, February 21, 1962. **Original Release:** *Our Man in Nashville* (RCA Victor album, 1963).

As we discussed in this book's previous entry, Chet's February 21, 1962, session at RCA Studios in Nashville yielded one of Chet's all-time greatest recorded performances, "Mayan Dance." Another instrumental song was recorded at that particular session that would turn out to be very noteworthy in its own right. That song was called "Scare Crow," and it was the first number Chet ever recorded that was written by Jerry Reed Hubbard.

Jerry was a singer/songwriter/guitarist who was known professionally simply as Jerry Reed, and he was an artist whose career was very much on the rise. His song "Misery Loves Company" was recorded by Porter Wagoner, and that recording became a number one country hit in 1962. That same year, Jerry was signed to a contract by Columbia Records—he wrote and recorded for the label for a little over a year, parting ways with them in mid-1963. Jerry's skill as a guitarist was every bit as great as his skill as a singer/songwriter—in fact, he was an *incredibly* gifted fingerstyle player, very much on the same level with Chet.

During this early stage of his career, Jerry recorded a demo of "Scare Crow" and sent it to Chet. Chet liked the song so much that he decided to record his own version of it for his album project *Our Man in Nashville*. The song was a midtempo blues-based number that was loaded with a wide variety of inventive, nimbly played guitar riffs.

On "Scare Crow," Chet plays a Gretsch electric guitar in standard tuning out of the key of A, and he is accompanied by guitar, piano, bass, drums and a violin section. He brings a loose, soulful feel to Jerry's composition that shows just how musically in synch the two men were with one another from the very first moment they joined forces.

And *man*, did they ever join forces. Chet and Jerry forged an incredibly successful musical partnership with one another that would end up lasting all the way from the early 1960s through the late 1990s. After signing Jerry to RCA Victor in 1964, Chet produced a number of Jerry's recordings that became chart-topping hits. And Chet recorded dozens of Jerry's compositions for his own albums. The two men also recorded several very successful collaborative albums—we'll be discussing those albums and some of their standout tracks later.

It should be noted that the relationship between Chet and Jerry went beyond being just a mutually beneficial musical partnership—they also became very close personal friends, and both men would cherish that friendship for the rest of their lives.

Incidentally, after recording "Scare Crow" for *Our Man in Nashville* on February 21, 1962, Chet decided to feature a second Jerry-penned instrumental on the album. That song was called "Down Home," and it was recorded during a session held at RCA Studios in Nashville on March 8, 1962. *Our Man in Nashville* was released by RCA Victor in early 1963, and "Scare Crow" was chosen to be the album's opening track. While *Our Man in Nashville* did not end up enjoying anywhere near the same level of commercial success that many of Chet's recent albums had, it still came to be highly regarded by many of Chet's longtime fans.

"The Old Rugged Cross"

Composer: George Bennard. **Producer:** Chet Atkins. **Musicians:** Chet Atkins (guitar), Velma Smith (guitar), Bill Pursell (organ), Henry Strzelecki (bass). **Location and Date of Recording:** RCA Victor Studio, Nashville, Tennessee, June 5, 1962. **Original Release:** *Chet Atkins Plays Back Home Hymns* (RCA Victor album, 1962).

In mid–1962, Chet decided to record an album of well-known hymns entitled *Chet Atkins Plays Back Home Hymns*. He hardly could have ever come up with a more appropriate musical theme for himself, given the fact that his playing style could be so beautifully smooth and peaceful. All of the hymns he recorded for the album were rendered as instrumentals.

On May 23 and June 5, 1962, Chet held recording sessions for *Chet Atkins Plays Back Home Hymns* at RCA Studios in Nashville. One of the songs he recorded at the June 5 session was "The Old Rugged Cross," a hymn composed in 1912 by George Bennard. Over the years, "The Old Rugged Cross" had become so well-loved by the public that it was not only sung in churches, but it was also performed and recorded by a wide variety of secular artists.

On "The Old Rugged Cross," Chet plays a Gretsch electric guitar in standard tuning out of the key of E, and he is accompanied by guitar, organ, and bass. Throughout the recording, he gently renders the hymn's beautiful melody along with simultaneously played harmony lines. Chet's delicate, thoughtful treatment of "The Old Rugged Cross" captures his playing at its most contemplative—in fact, the same thing could really be said of every one of the selections found on *Chet Atkins Plays Back Home Hymns*.

"Wheels"

Composer: Norman Petty. **Producer:** Chet Atkins. **Musicians:** Chet Atkins (guitar), Hank Garland (guitar), Floyd Cramer (organ), Bill Pursell (piano), Henry Strzelecki (bass), William Ackerman (drums). **Location and Date of Recording:** RCA Victor Studio, Nashville, Tennessee, December 10, 1962. **Original Release:** *Travelin'* (RCA Victor album, 1963).

In late 1962, Chet decided to embark on an album project that would be inspired by all of the traveling around the world he had done while on his musical tours. This album was appropriately titled *Travelin',* and its liner notes were mainly devoted to a discussion of Chet's recent South African concert performance in Johannesburg, South Africa, with fellow RCA artists Floyd Cramer and Jim Reeves. The album featured a variety of songs from around the world, including several that he had performed on his recent tours. All of these songs were performed as instrumentals.

On December 10, 1962, Chet recorded four songs for *Travelin'* during a session held at RCA Studios in Nashville. One of those numbers was "Wheels," a bright midtempo song written by Norman Petty. Petty was a musician/record producer best known for his studio production work for the legendary rock and roll singer/guitarist

Buddy Holly. "Wheels" was chosen to be the opening track for *Travelin'* when the album was released by RCA Victor in 1963.

On "Wheels," Chet plays a Gretsch electric guitar in standard tuning mainly out of the key of A. The song briefly moves to the key of D in the middle of the recording, but then it returns to A. Backed by guitar, organ, piano, bass and drums, Chet renders much of the song's happy melody along with a simultaneously played accompanying pattern—but he also renders quite a bit of the song's melody through more straightforward soloing. Some of these solo lines are played using chord voicings that move up and down the neck of his guitar, and some of them are played as single-note phrases.

Incidentally, Chet would record two more excellent versions of "Wheels" during his career. He and singer/guitarist Hank Snow performed an instrumental duet of the song for their 1969 collaborative album *C.B. Atkins and C.E. Snow by Special Request*. And Chet recorded a live performance of the song for his 1980 live album *The Best of Chet on the Road ... Live*. On both of these recordings, Chet played "Wheels" on a nylon-string acoustic guitar instead of an electric.

"Alley Cat"

Composer: Frank Bjorn. **Producer:** Chet Atkins. **Musicians:** Chet Atkins (guitar), Hargus "Pig" Robbins (piano), Henry Strzelecki (bass), William Ackerman, Ken Buttrey (drums). **Location and Date of Recording:** RCA Victor Studio, Nashville, Tennessee, March 1, 1963. **Original Release:** *Teen Scene* (RCA Victor album, 1963).

In early 1963, Chet decided record a new album that was aimed at the young adult market, much like his 1960 album *Teensville* had been. This new album's connection to *Teensville* was made very apparent by its title—it was named *Teen Scene*. On March 1, 1963, Chet recorded eight instrumentals for *Teen Scene* during two four-song sessions held at RCA Studios in Nashville. One of the most enjoyable songs that Chet recorded at these sessions was "Alley Cat," a catchy midtempo number written by the Danish pianist/composer Bent Fabric under the pseudonym of Frank Bjorn. Fabric's instrumental recording of "Alley Cat" was a worldwide hit when it was released in 1962, and it won the 1963 Grammy Award for Best Rock and Roll Recording.

Incidentally, it should be pointed out that by today's standards, there is not the slightest bit of "rock and roll" found in Fabric's "Alley Cat"—but one must remember that in those years right before The Beatles took the musical world by storm, rock and roll was a very different (and much more docile) animal.

Chet's version of "Alley Cat" is very similar to Fabric's in terms of style, arrangement and tempo—in other words, in this day and age the recording sounds far more like easy listening music than it does teen-oriented pop. On "Alley Cat," Chet plays Chet plays a Gretsch electric guitar in standard tuning out of the key of C, and he is accompanied by piano, bass, and drums. Chet renders much of the song's easygoing melody through straightforward single-note soloing on his high strings. That said, however, his playing does go beyond just this single-note soloing—he often throws in simultaneously played harmony lines to accompany his melody playing.

Teen Scene was moderately successful when it was first released by RCA Victor in 1963, climbing to number 93 on the U.S. album charts. Chet returned to the realm of country music after recording this project—he began work on a new album called *Guitar Country*, which would turn out to one of his all-time best country records. We'll discuss two songs from that record, "Freight Train" and "A Little Bit of Blues," in this book's next two entries.

"Freight Train"

Composer: Charles Albertine. **Producer:** Bob Ferguson. **Musicians:** Chet Atkins (guitar), Ray Edenton (rhythm guitar), Floyd Cramer (piano/electric piano), Henry Strzelecki (bass), Buddy Harman (drums). **Location and Date of Recording:** RCA Victor Studio, Nashville, Tennessee, October 1, 1963. **Original Release:** *Guitar Country* (RCA Victor album, 1964), RCA Victor 47-8342 (RCA Victor 45 single, 1964).

In the autumn of 1963, Chet began work on a new country music album that would be given the very fitting title of *Guitar Country*. The album was basically an all-instrumental work, though the Anita Kerr Singers did provide supporting vocals on several of its songs. Chet held a three-song recording session for *Guitar Country* at RCA Studios in Nashville on October 1, 1963. His cover of the early twentieth century American folk song "Freight Train" was one of the songs recorded at the session, and it was chosen to open up the album.

When RCA Victor released *Guitar Country* it in 1964, they also chose to release "Freight Train" as a 45 single that same year. For some reason, the credits of the album and single listed Charles Albertine as the composer of "Freight Train," but Albertine did not actually write the song—"Freight Train" was originally written as a vocal number by the legendary folksinger/guitarist Elizabeth Cotten.

Cotten's style of playing guitar was very unusual. She was left-handed, so she held her guitar the opposite way from right-handed players—in other words, she picked with her left hand and fretted with her right. But she did not re-string her guitar in the opposite direction like most left-handed players do, so her strings went from high to low down her guitar instead of the standard configuration of low to high. This led her to develop her own style of fingerpicking that was almost completely backwards from the way most anyone else would fingerpick a guitar. "Freight Train" was born out of Cotten's unique playing style, and in the 1950s and 1960s the song became a staple of the folk music boom—it was covered by many folk artists such as Mike Seeger, Pete Seeger, Joan Baez and Peter, Paul and Mary.

When Chet found "Freight Train," he had truly found one of his signature pieces—after his version of the song appeared on *Guitar Country* and was released as a single, it became a regular feature in both his concert and television appearances. "Freight Train" did not end up charting as a single, but the song definitely helped to make *Guitar Country* a very successful album—it reached the number one spot on the U.S. country music album charts, and the number 64 spot on the U.S. album charts. (1964 was the first year that a separate genre chart was established for country music—so after that point, many of Chet's albums appeared on both the country and the overall albums charts.) In fact, "Freight Train" would end up becoming one of the songs that Chet would be most identified with for the rest of his life—Chet only had to play the first few notes of the song to draw enthusiastic applause from most any audience he might be in front of.

It is no surprise that Chet's version of "Freight Train" became so well-loved—it still stands as one of his most vibrant, sunny-sounding recordings. The song's chug-along style, coupled with Chet's perfectly syncopated fingerpicking, instantly evokes an image of a freight train smartly rolling down a long railroad track.

On "Freight Train," Chet plays a Gretsch electric guitar in standard tuning, and he is backed by electric piano, piano, rhythm guitar, bass and drums. Interestingly, Chet's guitar track on the recording actually consists of two rather separate sections. The first section occurs during the song's opening two chord progressions in the key of F—in this first section, Chet's guitar is capoed at the 5th fret. He renders the song's melody and a simultaneously played accompanying pattern in the key of C, but the capo makes it sound as if he is playing out of the key of F.

The second section of Chet's guitar track begins when the song switches to the key of C, and it continues all the way through to the end of the song. In this section, Chet has removed the capo from his guitar, and most of his playing consists of single-note solo melody lines or melody lines paired with harmony parts. He takes the song through its first chord progression in C, and then lays out for a moment during a second C chord progression in order to make room for a brief electric piano interlude played by Floyd Cramer. The song then returns to the key of F, and there he takes it through one final chord progression.

Chet does not musically or rhythmically vary the basic melody of "Freight Train" at all throughout his version of the song—instead, he unwaveringly keeps his focus on the beauty of the song's simple tune. All in all, Chet's steady interpretation of "Freight Train" could not be more fitting, because it is every bit as precise and effective as the workings of a well-run railroad.

Incidentally, Chet would record one more version of "Freight Train" during his career. He and the noted French guitarist Marcel Dadi recorded a live duet performance of the song for Chet's 1980 live album *The Best of Chet on the Road ... Live*. On this recording, "Freight Train" was incorporated into a medley with another railroad-themed song, "Chattanooga Train." Chet played a Gretsch electric guitar on "Freight Train/ Chattanooga Train," and his playing of "Freight Train" in this medley featured a number of jazzy chord changes not found in his original 1963 version of the song.

"A Little Bit of Blues"

Composer: Jerry Reed. **Producer:** Bob Ferguson. **Musicians:** Chet Atkins (guitar), Ray Edenton (rhythm guitar), Floyd Cramer (electric piano), Henry Strzelecki (bass), Buddy Harman (drums). **Location and Date of Recording:** RCA Victor Studio, Nashville, Tennessee, October 1, 1963. **Original Release:** *Guitar Country* (RCA Victor album, 1964).

As discussed earlier, the first Jerry Reed-penned instrumental that Chet covered was "Scare Crow," which appeared on Chet's 1963 album *Our Man in Nashville*. From that point on Reed's work would have a profound influence on Chet's career, and Chet would end up recording many more of Reed's compositions. "A Little Bit of Blues" is another one of the earliest Reed instrumentals that Chet covered, and it is also one of the very best. Like "Freight Train," "A Little Bit of Blues" was recorded was recorded at RCA Studios in Nashville on October 1, 1963, and it was featured on Chet's classic 1964 album *Guitar Country*.

"A Little Bit of Blues" is essentially just what its title implies—it is a soulful, basic blues song with a memorable guitar hook and a relaxed tempo. The tune may be based on basic blues patterns, but its composition is incredibly complex, featuring a barrage of syncopated guitar lines that run in tandem with its melody.

Chet plays this formidable piece masterfully on a Gretsch electric guitar, accompanied by electric piano, rhythm guitar, bass and drums. The electric piano is played by Floyd Cramer, who takes a short, relaxed solo break near the end of the recording. Chet employs a little tuning trick on "A Little Bit of Blues" that makes learning the song just a bit more difficult for any guitarist brave enough to try to take it on. Chet plays the song out of the key of D, but his guitar is tuned down a whole step so that his strings are tuned D-G-C-F-A-D from low to high. Consequently, Chet sounds as if he is playing the song out of the key of C, not D.

"Satan's Doll"

> **Composer:** Johnny Smith. **Producer:** Bob Ferguson. **Musicians:** Chet Atkins (guitar), Bill Pursell (piano), Henry Strzelecki (bass), Buddy Harman (drums). **Location and Date of Recording:** RCA Victor Studio, Nashville, Tennessee, February 12, 1964. **Original Release:** *Progressive Pickin'* (RCA Victor album, 1964).

In early 1964, Chet decided to undertake one of his most musically ambitious album projects to date. The album would be entitled *Progressive Pickin',* and it could not have been more aptly titled. Chet chose a selection of very musically sophisticated songs, many of them straight-up jazz compositions, to record for the album. All of the numbers featured on *Progressive Pickin'* were instrumentals.

With the release of *Progressive Pickin',* Chet was going to challenge his audience in a way that he had not challenged them before. The album was not simply going to include a few jazzy-sounding numbers the way that several of his previous albums had—rather, it was going to be very much a jazz album from beginning to end.

On February 11 and 12, 1964, Chet held recording sessions for *Progressive Pickin'* at RCA Studios in Nashville—these sessions yielded five songs. One of the numbers recorded at the February 12 session, "Satan's Doll," was chosen to open the album. "Satan's Doll" was a minor key-based, swing-tempo instrumental written by the well-known jazz guitarist Johnny Smith. Johnny originally recorded "Satan's Doll" with jazz accordionist Art Van Damme for their 1962 collaborative album *A Perfect Match.*

Of course, it was no surprise that Chet turned to Johnny for the number that would set the tone for *Progressive Pickin'.* Johnny was the composer of the instrumental "Walk Don't Run," which Chet had recorded for his 1957 album *Hi-Fi in Focus.* Chet's version of that song had ended up being among the most influential and admired jazz-based recordings that he ever made. (We discussed Chet's version of "Walk Don't Run" earlier.) Johnny even wrote the liner notes for *Progressive Pickin',* and in them he praised Chet's sense of musical perfectionism.

On "Satan's Doll," Chet plays a Gretsch electric guitar in standard tuning out of the key of B minor, and he is backed by piano, bass and drums. The song is a very challenging piece of music—its chord structure, melody, and harmony lines all take many unexpected and often dissonant turns. Chet's playing brilliantly covers all of these bases, and one really needs to listen to the recording multiple times in order to appreciate everything he is doing in it. He delivers melody lines delivered with simultaneous accompanying patterns, tasteful single-note solo runs, inventive chord voicings, and smooth string bends. About halfway through the recording, Chet briefly steps back in order to make room for a great piano solo played by Bill Pursell.

We definitely need to make note of one thing in particular that Chet plays in "Satan's Doll." At 3 minutes, 16 seconds, into the recording, he plays a blindingly fast, up-and-down arpeggio pattern. Over the years, this memorably acrobatic pattern became known by Chet fans as the "superlick." Chet would go on to use his superlick to great effect in many more of his recordings throughout the rest of his career.

Incidentally, "Satan's Doll" did not mark the first time that Chet had used the superlick in one of his recordings. He publicly stated that he remembered first using it in "Copper Kettle," a number that appeared on his 1964 album *Guitar Country*. ("Copper Kettle" was recorded on October 3, 1963, at RCA Studios in Nashville, right around the time the two *Guitar Country* tracks we discussed in this book, "Freight Train" and "A Little Bit of Blues," were recorded.)

But in truth, Chet had started using the superlick even *before* "Copper Kettle." For example, it can be heard in "Maria Elena," a number that appeared on his 1960 album *The Other Chet Atkins*. ("Maria Elena" was recorded on December 8, 1959, at RCA Studios in Nashville. Earlier in this book, we discussed another song from *The Other Chet Atkins* recorded on that same day, "The Peanut Vendor.")

Let's get back to *Progressive Pickin'.* The album was released by RCA Victor in 1964, and perhaps because it was a far more musically challenging record than many of his recent releases, it did not end up making the charts. Still, the album deserves to be remembered as one of Chet's particularly adventurous artistic endeavors.

One final note about *Progressive Pickin'*—it was outfitted with a decidedly ironic album cover. The graphics on that cover consisted of little more than a photograph of Chet that was cut into the shape of a guitar flatpick. Of course, Chet *never* used a flatpick when he played—being the fingerstyle guitarist that he was, he always used a thumbpick.

"Kicky"

Composer: Jerry Reed. **Producer:** Bob Ferguson. **Musicians:** Chet Atkins (guitar), Bill Pursell (piano), Henry Strzelecki (bass), Buddy Harman (drums). **Location and Date of Recording:** RCA Victor Studio, Nashville, Tennessee, February 19, 1964. **Original Release:** *Progressive Pickin'* (RCA Victor album, 1964).

Although the majority of Chet's *Progressive Pickin'* album was devoted to instrumentals with a jazz sensibility, he still included a few numbers on the album that leaned more toward his home base of country music. One of these numbers was "Kicky," a fast-tempoed guitar instrumental written by Jerry Reed. "Kicky" made for a truly exhilarating listening experience, mainly because of its blues-based melody that moved at a high speed through most every measure of the song. Chet recorded "Kicky" during a three-song session held for *Progressive Pickin'* at RCA Studios in Nashville on February 19, 1964.

On "Kicky," Chet plays a Gretsch electric guitar in standard tuning out of the key of E, and he is accompanied by piano, bass, and drums. Chet renders most all of the song's jackrabbit-quick melody through single-note soloing, but there are passages in the song where he embellishes that melody with chord voicings and simultaneously played accompanying patterns. Toward the end of the recording, Chet briefly steps back in order to make room for an energetic piano solo played by Bill Pursell.

As mentioned in this book's previous entry, *Progressive Pickin'* did not end up enjoying anywhere near the same level of commercial success that many of Chet's recent albums had—this might have been because it was a far more musically challenging record than many of those other albums. But even still, a number of tracks from *Progressive Pickin'* have continued to be favorites of longtime Chet fans right up until this day—and "Kicky" is definitely one of those tracks.

"Wimoweh"

Composer: Paul Campbell. **Producer:** Bob Ferguson. **Musicians:** Chet Atkins (guitar), Ray Edenton (guitar), Floyd Cramer (piano), Boots Randolph (vibes), Henry Strzelecki (bass), Buddy Harman (drums). **Location and Date of Recording:** RCA Victor Studio, Nashville, Tennessee, June 1, 1964. **Original Release:** *My Favorite Guitars* (RCA Victor album, 1964).

On June 1, 1964, Chet held a recording session at RCA Studios in Nashville for a new album project. The album would end up consisting entirely of instrumentals, and it would be given the title of *My Favorite Guitars* in honor of the favorite guitars that Chet owned. In fact, the album's liner notes were written by Chet himself, and in them he discussed the three guitars that he considered to be his absolute favorites at that time.

Not surprisingly, the first was a Gretsch Chet Atkins Country Gentleman, the guitar model that he played on more of his recordings than any other instrument. In his *My Favorite Guitars* liner notes, Chet did not specifically state that his regularly used 1959 Country Gentleman was the Country Gentleman he was referring to—in fact, the cover of the album featured a photo of him with a different, later model Gent.

The other two guitars were among Chet's more recent acquisitions. One was a Del Vecchio Dinamico resonator guitar Chet had received from Nato Lima. Nato was a guitarist from Ceará, Brazil, who played in a well-known guitar duo known as Los Indios Tabajaras—the other half of that duo was Nato's brother Antenor. The success of Los Indios Tabajaras reached all the way to the U.S. in late 1963, when their recording of the popular Mexican song "Maria Elena" became a top ten hit. (Incidentally, Chet had recorded that same song a few years earlier—it appeared on his 1960 album *The Other Chet Atkins*.)

Chet loved the sound of the Del Vecchio that Nato had played on that song, so he asked Nato if he could get him one—Nato responded to Chet's request by selling him that actual guitar. In his *My Favorite Guitars* liner notes, Chet did not refer to this guitar as a Del Vecchio—instead, he called it his "Los Indios Tabajaras guitar."

We should take just a moment to discuss just what kind of guitar a resonator is. A resonator is an acoustic guitar that has one or more spun metal cones built into the guitar's sound board. These cones produce a resonator's sound, which is considerably louder than the sound produced by a standard acoustic guitar with a single, completely hollow soundhole.

The other recently acquired guitar that Chet listed as his favorite in his *My Favorite Guitars* liner notes was a Juan Estruch classical guitar. Chet would use his Juan Estruch on the majority of his classical guitar recordings over the next few years.

In the *My Favorite Guitars* liner notes, Chet even went on to state just which of his three favorite guitars were used for each song that appeared on the album.

At the June 1 session, Chet recorded two songs that would be featured on *My Favorite Guitars*—and on both of these songs, he played a Country Gentleman. One of the numbers was "Wimoweh," a South African song with a long and interesting history. The song was written in the 1920s by the Zulu composer Solomon Linda, who titled it simply "Mbube," which in English means "lion." "Mbube" was basically a chant song with a wordless improvised melody, and it became very popular in South Africa when it was recorded by Linda's group The Evening Birds.

In the late 1940s, "Mbube" was brought to the attention of the U.S. folksinger Pete Seeger, who began performing it with his folk group the Weavers. The Weavers gave the song a new title, "Wimoweh," which basically did not mean anything in *any* language—the word was simply a mishearing of the Zulu phrase "uyimbube," which in English means "he is a lion." At any rate, it turned out that "Wimoweh" didn't really need to mean anything in order to be a big success—the Weavers' recording of the song became a U.S. top ten hit in the early 1950s.

In 1961, the song was reworked yet again—this time around, it was fashioned into "The Lion Sleeps Tonight," a number with English lyrics penned by songwriters George David Weiss, Hugo Peretti, and Luigi Creatore. That same year, "The Lion Sleeps Tonight" was recorded by the U.S. vocal group The Tokens. The Tokens' version of "The Lion Sleeps Tonight" reached the top spot on the U.S. pop single charts, becoming an even bigger hit than the Weavers' version of "Wimoweh."

When Chet recorded his version of the song for *My Favorite Guitars*, he decided not to use its most recent, and probably most-recognized, title of "The Lion Sleeps Tonight"—instead, he titled it "Wimoweh." Like most all recorded versions of "Wimoweh," Chet's "Wimoweh" was listed as being written by "Paul Campbell"—but that name was simply a pseudonym used by the members of the Weavers.

On "Wimoweh," Chet plays his Country Gentleman in standard tuning out of the key of E, and he is accompanied by guitar, piano, vibes, bass, and drums. He opens the recording by simultaneously playing both the song's chant part and melody

Chet Atkins with a Gretsch Chet Atkins Country Gentleman electric guitar, early 1960s.

part. After that, he offers up a number of different playing techniques—he delivers single-note solos, solos played with accompanying harmony lines, and boldly strummed chord patterns. In fact, Chet's chording in parts of "Wimoweh" is so forceful that the number would have fit very well on one of his rock-based albums.

After the June 1 session, Chet briefly stepped away from his *My Favorite Guitars* project to work on another new album project—he held a number of sessions for *Reminiscing*, his album of guitar duets with fellow RCA Victor artist Hank Snow. We'll discuss one of the tracks from that album, "Brahms' Lullaby," in the next entry of this book.

"Brahms' Lullaby"

Composer: Johannes Brahms. **Producers:** Chet Atkins, Bob Ferguson. **Musicians:** Chet Atkins (guitar), Hank Snow (guitar), Velma Smith (guitar), Hargus "Pig" Robbins (piano), Henry Strzelecki (bass), Buddy Harman (drums), Brenton Banks, Howard Carpenter, Solie Fott, Lillian Hunt, Martin Katahn (violins). **Location and Date of Recording:** RCA "Nashville Sound" Studio, Nashville, Tennessee, July 14, 1964. **Original Release:** *Reminiscing* (RCA Victor album with Hank Snow, 1964).

In July 1964, Chet decided to undertake making the first collaborative album of his career, and he chose a particularly fitting performer to make it with—that performer was singer/guitarist and fellow RCA artist Hank Snow. Chet's 1954 recording of "Silver Bell" was a guitar duet with Hank, and that record ended up becoming Chet's first-ever hit single—so the performer who shared the spotlight with him on his first hit record would now share the spotlight with him on his first collaborative album.

It should be pointed out that Chet had previously participated in collaborative recordings that had been released as albums. For example, he worked with rhythm guitarist Henry "Homer" Haynes and mandolinist Kenneth "Jethro" Burns in a loosely knit group of top session players known as The Country All-Stars—that group recorded and released a 10-inch record called *String Dustin'* on the RCA Victor label in 1953. But since Chet had truly become a star solo performer in his own right, he had never made a collaborative album with another star performer who shared top billing with him.

The album that Chet and Hank ended up making together was entitled *Reminiscing*—that title was taken from a song called "Reminiscing" that the two men had recorded together in 1956. (The song was released as a single by RCA Victor that same year.) Interestingly, the liner notes for *Reminiscing* discussed the fact that the song "Reminiscing" was the inspiration for the album's title, but the song itself was not featured the album. At any rate, the *Reminiscing* album solely consisted of instrumental guitar duets by Chet and Hank.

On July 14, 1964, Chet and Hank held a four-song session for the album at RCA Studios in Nashville. One of the songs they recorded at the session was "Brahms' Lullaby," the 1868 lullaby written by the famed German composer Johannes Brahms. The original title of Brahms' piece was "Wiegenleid: Guten Abend, gute Nacht," which translated into English means "lullaby: good evening, good night." The song originally featured lyrics pulled from German folk poems—but of course, as the song's popularity grew around the world, many different sets of lyrics in most every language imaginable were created for it.

Chet plays a Gretsch electric guitar in standard tuning on "Brahms' Lullaby," and he is joined by Hank playing an acoustic guitar that is also in standard tuning. The two are accompanied by very spare piano, bass and drums, as well as a violin section. The recording opens with Chet and Hank playing a verse of the song together out of the key of A, and then Hank solos on a verse of the song played out of the key of D. The song returns to the key of A, and Chet closes out the recording by soloing over one final verse.

As was the case with "Silver Bell," Chet and Hank's guitar parts are noticeably different from one another in "Brahms' Lullaby"—Chet's touch is subtle and gentle, and Hank's touch is straightforward and percussive. These two very different styles of guitar playing blend together nicely on the recording, especially during the song's first verse, when Hank plays a nice harmony part along with Chet's tender single-note melody playing.

Reminiscing was released by RCA Victor in the summer of 1964—it did not achieve any notable chart success, but it was widely admired by fans of both Chet and Hank. The two men would team up for another album before the decade was out—that album was released in 1969, and it was called *C.B. Atkins and C.E. Snow by Special Request*. We'll discuss one of the numbers from that album, "Poison Love," later.

"Chopin Waltz No. 10 in B Minor"

Composer: Frédéric Chopin. **Producer:** Bob Ferguson. **Musicians:** Chet Atkins (guitar). **Location and Date of Recording:** RCA Victor Studio, Nashville, Tennessee, November 11, 1964. **Original Release:** *My Favorite Guitars* (RCA Victor album, 1964).

After recording the *Reminiscing* album with Hank Snow in July 1964, Chet went back into the studio in order to record songs for several other album projects he had in the works. One of these albums was *My Favorite Guitars*, which he had first started recording songs for back on June 1 of that year. His November 11, 1964, recording session at RCA Studios in Nashville yielded six numbers, five of which ended up on *My Favorite Guitars*. One of these *My Favorite Guitars* songs was a beautiful solo guitar rendition of "Chopin Waltz No. 10 in B Minor."

The original title of "Chopin Waltz No. 10 in B Minor" was "Waltz Op. 69, No. 2," and it was composed in 1829 by the famed Polish composer/pianist Frédéric Chopin. Chopin wrote the piece as a waltz for solo piano in the key of B minor. The piece was not published until 1852, several years after Chopin's death—it was at that time it was assigned its series number of "10." Though "Waltz Op. 69, No. 2" was by no means one of Chopin's more technically demanding pieces, its lovely, haunting melody had made it a favorite amongst music lovers for generations.

Interestingly, Chet's version of "Chopin Waltz No. 10 in B Minor" was not really in the key of B minor. When Chet arranged the waltz as a solo guitar piece, he changed it to the more guitar-friendly key of A minor. When discussing the piece in the liner notes he wrote for *My Favorite Guitars*, Chet pointed this out this fact—he also stated that he used one of his favorite guitars, his Juan Estruch classical, to record the piece.

(We discussed the *My Favorite Guitars* liner notes earlier when we examined "Wimoweh," one of the songs recorded for the album on June 1.)

Chet's affinity for the classical guitar had continued to grow over the years, and his recording of "Chopin Waltz No. 10 in B Minor" offered strong evidence of that trend. The piece clearly showed that while Chet was not a classical guitar player in the strictest sense of the word, by the 1960s the instrument had become every bit as vital to his musical endeavors as the electric guitar had ever been.

Chet's arrangement and performance of "Chopin Waltz No. 10 in B Minor" is magnificent—he plays his Juan Estruch in standard tuning on the recording, and he treats Chopin's masterful composition with the respect and care that it deserves. There are probably some classical purists who would question Chet's decision to change the piece from the key of B minor to the key of A minor. But playing the waltz in the key of A minor allows Chet to use his open A and low E strings as root notes during many of the passages in the piece. He often strikes these strings while simultaneously playing melody and harmony phrases—and because these strings are played completely open, they ring out with greater sustain, bringing added fullness to his overall guitar sound.

My Favorite Guitars was released by RCA Victor in 1964, and it was the first of Chet's albums to feature a basically equal balance of electric and acoustic guitar numbers. And it would be far from the last, because throughout the rest of his recording career, Chet would consider himself every bit as much of an acoustic guitarist as he was an electric guitarist.

"Yakety Axe"

Composer: Boots Randolph, James Rich. **Producer:** Bob Ferguson. **Musicians:** Chet Atkins (guitar), Ray Edenton (guitar), Jerry Smith (piano), Charlie McCoy (harmonica), Henry Strzelecki (bass), Buddy Harman (drums). **Location and Date of Recording:** RCA Studios, Nashville, Tennessee, April 23, 1965. **Original Release:** *More of That Guitar Country* (RCA Victor album, 1965), RCA Victor 47-8590 (RCA Victor 45 single, 1965).

In late April 1965, Chet began work on a new country music album entitled *More of That Guitar Country*—obviously, the album was given that title in order to bill it as a sequel to his hit 1964 country music album *Guitar Country*. The majority of *More of That Guitar Country* was recorded during sessions held at RCA Studios in Nashville on April 21, 23 and 26—four songs were recorded on April 21, another four songs were recorded on April 23, and three songs were recorded on April 26. Like *Guitar Country*, *More of That Guitar Country* was basically an all-instrumental work, though the Anita Kerr Singers did provide supporting vocals on several of its songs.

Far and away the most memorable song recorded at these *More of That Guitar Country* sessions was a number recorded on April 23 called "Yakety Axe." "Yakety Axe" was Chet's guitar interpretation of "Yakety Sax," an uptempo saxophone instrumental written by two of Chet's close musical collaborators, Boots Randolph and James "Spider" Rich. (Of course, Boots had played sax on a number of Chet's records since the late 1950s—and Spider had composed several guitar instrumentals that Chet ended up recording, including the 1957 song "Hidden Charm.") Chet's decision to change the title of his version of the song from "Yakety Sax" to "Yakety Axe" was a clever play on words, since "axe" is a slang term for a guitar.

Boots first recorded "Yakety Sax" in 1958 when he was signed with RCA Victor, but that version of the song did not achieve any notable success in terms of sales or airplay. Boots left RCA and signed with Monument Records, and he re-recorded "Yakety Sax" for Monument in 1963. That version of the song became a hit, reaching the number 35 spot on the U.S. pop single charts.

It was certainly no surprise that "Yakety Sax" ended up finding a wide audience, since it featured such a memorable, joyfully raucous melody. That melody worked in phrases from "Entrance of the Gladiators," the well-known 1897 military march written by the Czech composer Julius Fučík. (For those of you who don't recognize that title, just think of the crazy-sounding music that is often played while circus clowns are performing—*that* music is "Entrance of the Gladiators.") Boots belted out "Yakety Sax" with a level of excitement that matched the excitement found in the composition itself, which made his recording of the song a truly exhilarating listening experience.

In fact, Boots' version of the song is still winning over listeners to this day, because many people find it by watching old episodes of the long-running British comedy television show *The Benny Hill Show*. From the late 1960s through the late 1980s, Boots' recording of "Yakety Sax" was played during many of that show's zany routines.

Chet's "Yakety Axe" certainly matches both the high spirits and the great musical quality of Boots' "Yakety Sax." On the recording, Chet plays a Gretsch electric guitar in standard tuning out of the key of G, and he is backed by guitar, piano, harmonica, bass and drums. The song moves to the key of C during its "Entrance of the Gladiators" section, but then it returns to the key of G. There is something about "Yakety Axe" that is markedly different from most every other song that Chet ever recorded—*every* note he plays in the song is played using the technique of single-note soloing. In other words, he never renders the song's melody along with a simultaneously played accompanying pattern, or delivers simultaneously played harmony lines to accompany his melody playing. Of course, Chet's decision to play "Yakety Axe" in this manner is right on target—the song comes across wonderfully as a rapid-fire, staccato guitar-picking affair. (Incidentally, Chet does completely lay out for a moment in the middle of the recording in order to make room for a nice harmonica solo played by Charlie McCoy.)

Chet's recording of "Yakety Axe" was chosen to open up of *More of That Guitar Country* when RCA Victor released the album in 1965. The label also chose to release the song as a single that same year. Both the album and the single turned out to be very successful—the album climbed to number 4 on the U.S. country music album charts, and the single reached that same position on the U.S. country music single charts. "Yakety Axe" even cracked the top 100 on the U.S. pop single charts, reaching the number 98 position.

Here is one final note regarding "Yakety Axe"—Chet ended up recording another version of the song late in his career that was very different from his original version. A vocal version of "Yakety Axe" featuring lyrics written by Merle Travis was recorded by Chet and Mark Knopfler for their 1990 collaborative album *Neck and Neck*. Merle's lyrics for the song told the story of a down-on-his-luck guitar picker who was happy to stick with his "yakety axe" in spite of all of his troubles. The *Neck and Neck* "Yakety Axe" featured Chet delivering Merle's wordy, humorous lyrics in a talking blues style—

and after Chet's vocal part was done, Chet and Mark spent the rest of the recording trading guitar licks with one another.

"Alabama Jubilee"

Composer: Jack Yellen, George L. Cobb. **Producer:** Peter Delheim. **Musicians:** Chet Atkins (guitar), Arthur Fiedler and the Boston Pops (orchestra), Henry Strzelecki (bass), John Greubel (drums). **Location and Date of Recording:** Symphony Hall, Boston, Massachusetts, June 10, 1965. **Original Release:** *The Pops Goes Country* (RCA Victor album with Arthur Fiedler and the Boston Pops, 1966).

In June 1965, Chet traveled to Boston, Massachusetts to take part in two orchestral recording sessions that were perhaps even more ambitious and prestigious than his classic 1958 Hollywood orchestral recording sessions. These Boston sessions were held at Symphony Hall on June 10 and 11, and they featured Chet performing with the famed orchestra the Boston Pops, who were led by the legendary conductor Arthur Fiedler. Two of Chet's regular studio musicians were brought in to play with Chet and the orchestra on the sessions—those musicians were bassist Henry Strzelecki and drummer John Greubel. Twelve instrumentals were recorded at the sessions, six on June 10 and six on June 11, and all of them were featured on the 1966 Boston Pops/Chet collaborative album *The Pops Goes Country*.

Two of the songs recorded on June 10 were orchestral remakes of classic Chet recordings from years past—those numbers were "Country Gentleman," which Chet had previously recorded in 1953 and 1959, and "Windy and Warm," which Chet had previously recorded in 1961. (We discussed Chet's original versions of both of these numbers earlier.)

Another of the numbers recorded at the June 10 session "Alabama Jubilee," was also a song that Chet had previously recorded. "Alabama Jubilee" was originally written as an uptempo vocal number by Jack Yellen and George L. Cobb in 1915, and over the years it became a standard that was recorded by many different artists. Chet's first recorded version of the song was a lightning-fast instrumental workout done for his classic 1954 album *A Session with Chet Atkins*. Chet's 1965 version of "Alabama Jubilee" was not played at quite the same breakneck speed that his 1954 version of the number was—but because Chet was paired with the fabulous Boston Pops on the recording, it still was every bit as exciting as Chet's earlier take on the song.

On Chet's 1965 version of "Alabama Jubilee," he plays a Gretsch electric guitar in standard tuning, and he starts the song out in the key of A. He renders the song's high-spirited melody along with a simultaneously played accompanying pattern, and he is superbly backed by the Boston Pops, Henry and John from his very first note. In the middle of the recording, the key of the song moves to C, and its tempo briefly shifts to a surprisingly funky 4/4 rock tempo—at this point, Chet throws in some bluesy solo licks over top of the orchestra. The song then moves to the key of F, and returns to its usual double-time quick tempo—it is here that Chet and the orchestra close out the proceedings with a loud, showstopping finish.

The Pops Goes Country was released by RCA Victor in 1966, and it ended up being so well-received that Chet and the Boston Pops would decide to record another full album together just a few years later. That album was entitled *Chet Atkins Picks on the Pops*, and it was released in 1969. We'll discuss one of the tracks off of the album, "Medley: The Battle of New Orleans/Sugarfoot Rag," a bit later in the book.

"From Nashville with Love"

> **Composer:** John D. Loudermilk. **Producers:** Chet Atkins, Bob Ferguson. **Musicians:** Chet Atkins (guitar), Ray Edenton (rhythm guitar), Bob Moore (bass), John Greubel (drums) Kenneth Goldsmith, Solie Fott, George Binkley, Dorothy Walker, Roby Story, Martin Katahn (violins), Byron Bach, Harvey Wolfe (cellos). **Location and Date of Recording:** RCA "Nashville Sound" Studio, Nashville, Tennessee, December 29, 1965. **Original Release:** *From Nashville with Love* (RCA Victor album, 1966), RCA Victor 47-8781 (RCA Victor 45 single, 1966).

Even for devoted Chet fans who have taken it upon themselves to carefully study the details of his career, it is hard to comprehend just how much work he was actually able to complete during those years that he was both a very successful recording artist and a very powerful RCA Victor executive. His recording of the song "From Nashville with Love" offers us a good chance to try to take in just how many projects he was capable of being involved in at one particular point in time.

So here's a snapshot of Chet's career at the time he was recording "From Nashville with Love"—the number was recorded during a session at RCA Studios in Nashville on December 29, 1965, and it would end up being the title track of the new album that he was just beginning to work on. At that same session, Chet also recorded an instrumental version of the Beatles' song "Michelle" which would be featured on his 1966 album *Chet Atkins Picks on the Beatles*. Chet had been at work at RCA's Nashville studios recording songs for *that* album since late October 1965. (We'll discuss Chet's recording of "Michelle" in the next entry.)

Also at this time, Chet was anticipating the upcoming release of *The Pops Goes Country*, his collaborative album with Arthur Fiedler and The Boston Pops that he had recorded in Boston, Massachusetts in June 1965. And of course, while he was in the midst of working on all of these projects for his own career as a guitarist, as an RCA executive he was overseeing the work of many of the label's other artists. In later years, Chet would discuss the fact that all of this work both as an artist and an executive was really wearing him down—but through this work, Chet certainly left an incredible musical legacy for countless people all around the world to enjoy.

Now, on to our discussion of "From Nashville with Love"—the song was an instrumental number composed by John D. Loudermilk, a singer/songwriter who was one of Chet's RCA Victor artists. Chet had already recorded several of John's compositions, most notably the 1961 classic "Windy and Warm." "From Nashville with Love" was a relaxed midtempo song that featured a melody that was both very cheerful and very catchy.

On "From Nashville with Love," Chet plays a classical guitar in the key of G using open G tuning. He is using the most common form of that particular style of tuning on the recording—his low E string is tuned down to D, his A string is tuned down to G, his D, G and B strings are unchanged, and his high E string is tuned down to D. This tuning allows Chet to render much of the song's melody on his higher strings while simultaneously playing accompanying notes on his open lower strings. Chet is backed by guitar, bass, drums, and a string section comprised of violins and cellos on "From Nashville with Love"—the string section plays a wealth of musical phrases that harmonize nicely with Chet's guitar work.

There is probably no way of knowing for sure just which of his classical guitars Chet used to record "From Nashville with Love"—but since he had used his Juan Estruch classical to record a number of the songs found on his recently released *My Favorite Guitars* album, it seems likely that he would have used that particular guitar on the recording. (As we noted just a bit earlier in this book, Chet himself wrote the liner notes for *My Favorite Guitars*, and in those notes he discussed just which of his guitars he used to record that album's songs—the Juan Estruch was one of those guitars.) At any rate, whatever classical guitar Chet might be using on "From Nashville with Love," he plays the song with a wonderful blend of precision and enthusiasm.

All of the other songs that Chet ended up recording for his *From Nashville with Love* album were similar in style and spirit to "From Nashville with Love"—in other words, they were all instrumentals with a decidedly easy listening feel to them. When the album was released by RCA Victor in 1966, the label also chose to release its title track as a 45 single. "From Nashville with Love" ended up not making much of an impression as a single (it only reached number 132 on the U.S. pop single charts), but the *From Nashville with Love* album as a whole turned out to be fairly successful—it reached the number 26 spot on the U.S. country album charts.

"Michelle"

> **Composers:** John Lennon, Paul McCartney. **Producers:** Chet Atkins, Bob Ferguson. **Musicians:** Chet Atkins (guitar), Ray Edenton (rhythm guitar), Bob Moore (bass), John Greubel (drums) Kenneth Goldsmith, Solie Fott, George Binkley, Dorothy Walker, Roby Story, Martin Katahn (violins), Byron Bach, Harvey Wolfe (cellos). **Location and Date of Recording:** RCA "Nashville Sound" Studio, Nashville, Tennessee, December 29, 1965. **Original Release:** *Chet Atkins Picks on the Beatles* (RCA Victor album, 1966).

This discussion of Chet's rendition of The Beatles' song "Michelle" composed by John Lennon and Paul McCartney offers us the perfect opportunity to examine the many interesting connections that developed between Chet and The Beatles over the years. The members of the Beatles had been fans of Chet's even before the band was first formed, and he would end up having a very direct influence on them in a number of ways—for example, McCartney publicly credited Chet's fingerpicking style that incorporated a melody line and a simultaneous accompanying pattern as the major inspiration for the music of "Michelle." According to McCartney, the Chet recording that specifically inspired him to create "Michelle" was "Trambone." (We discussed Chet's 1956 recording of "Trambone" earlier.)

Incidentally, it should be pointed out that even though "Michelle" was officially credited to the songwriting team of Lennon and McCartney, in reality the song was almost solely composed by McCartney. Lennon and McCartney composed many Beatles songs in tandem during the band's early years, but eventually most of the team's Beatles songs were primarily composed by just one of the team, with limited assistance from the other.

Before we examine the song "Michelle" any further, let's go over some of the other ways that Chet influenced the Beatles. The band's lead guitarist George Harrison had actually been inspired by Chet even more so than McCartney—Harrison publicly credited Chet as being one of the guitarists he admired the most when he was a young man.

This admiration ended up manifesting itself in Harrison's choice of guitars. In early 1963, right as the Beatles began to achieve their spectacular success, Harrison decided to make a major upgrade to his guitar arsenal—he purchased a Gretsch Chet Atkins Country Gentleman, and he favored using this model through much of 1964. But the Country Gentleman was not the only Chet Gretsch model that Harrison ended up becoming attached to—in late 1963 he purchased a Gretsch Chet Atkins Tennessean, and he frequently used this model throughout 1964 and 1965.

Of course, this meant that untold numbers of guitarists all over the world were seeing Harrison playing Gretsch guitars bearing Chet's name, so sales of Chet Atkins Gretsch models exploded in the mid–1960s. Harrison and the Beatles never ended up officially endorsing Chet Gretsches, but they really didn't have to—their use of those guitars turned out to be a huge unofficial advertisement for both the Gretsch Company and Chet himself.

In late 1965, Chet returned this favor by recording an entire album of Beatles songs entitled *Chet Atkins Picks on the Beatles.* The record featured Chet performing 12 instrumental versions of numbers written by Lennon and McCartney. Chet did not elect to perform any Harrison-written Beatle songs on this particular album, but Harrison still ended up having a connection to the project—he penned liner notes, in which he highly praised Chet's talent and the manner in which Chet had interpreted some of his band's songs.

One of the songs on the album was "Michelle," which the Beatles had released on their late 1965 album *Rubber Soul.* There is probably no way of knowing if Chet actually had any idea that "Michelle" was inspired by his playing at the time he recorded his version of the song—but whether he knew this fact or not, his version of "Michelle" turned out to be a masterful performance, undoubtedly one of the album's high points.

Chet recorded his version of "Michelle" at RCA Studios in Nashville, Tennessee on December 29, 1965. (This was the same session that yielded the song "From Nashville with Love," the subject of the previous entry.) This recording was made well after all of the other songs on *Chet Atkins Picks on the Beatles* were recorded—they were all laid down at RCA's Nashville studios in late October and early November 1965.

"Michelle" was markedly different from all of those other songs found on *Chet Atkins Picks on the Beatles.* Almost every one of them had rather heavy-handed bass and drum accompaniment, and extended harmonica solo breaks played by Charlie McCoy. This gave the album an overall instrumental rock/rockabilly feel—and while this feel was certainly pleasant enough, it came across as a decidedly obvious attempt to infuse Chet's sensibilities with the sensibilities of The Beatles' early recordings. In other words, one could argue that perhaps most of the songs on the album worked just a bit too hard to capture a "Beatle vibe," and not quite hard enough to capture a "Chet vibe." (Even Chet's version of The Beatles' classic acoustic ballad "Yesterday" was slightly rocked up—the recording featured Chet on electric guitar, and he was accompanied by bass and drums.)

But exactly the opposite is true of Chet's version of "Michelle." On the recording, he is accompanied by guitar, bass, drums, and a string section comprised of violins and cellos—this expansive, elegant accompaniment offers Chet the perfect setting to interpret the song's unforgettable melody. On "Michelle," Chet plays a Gretsch electric guitar in the key of D, and his low E string is tuned down to D. (This form of tuning is often referred to as "drop D.")

Playing at a smoothly swinging tempo, Chet first establishes the melody of the song by rendering it with a simultaneously played accompanying pattern. As the song goes on, he plays much of its melody through single-note soloing that features a wealth of tasteful, jazz-tinged embellishments. Chet's embellishments perfectly compliment the song, and never come close to cluttering up its timeless tune—in the case of "Michelle," this is a particularly appropriate thing, considering that Chet himself had a hand in the creation of that tune.

Chet Atkins Picks on the Beatles was quite successful when it was released by RCA Victor in early 1966, climbing to the number 6 spot on the U.S. country album charts. But in spite of this success, Chet would never again record an entire album devoted to Beatles songs. However, he would end up covering a number of other songs by the band over the years. And Chet would even end up working with the Beatle who composed "Michelle"—in 1974, while Paul McCartney was in Nashville to record an album with his group Wings, he and Chet recorded a song written by McCartney's father Jim entitled "Walking in the Park with Eloise." The song, which also featured Floyd Cramer on piano, was given a very limited release on a single. Incidentally, that single gave no hint to the fact that it had been created by some truly legendary musicians—McCartney decided to bill his collaboration with Chet and Floyd as "The Country Hams."

"A Taste of Honey"

Composer: Ric Marlow, Bobby Scott. **Producers:** Chet Atkins, Bob Ferguson. **Musicians:** Chet Atkins (guitar), Ray Edenton (guitar), Henry Strzelecki (bass), John Greubel (drums). **Location and Date of Recording:** RCA Studios, Nashville, Tennessee, March 23, 1966. **Original Release:** *It's a Guitar World* (RCA Victor album, 1967).

Keeping up his usual incredibly fast working pace, Chet had begun work on several new album projects for himself by early 1966. One of these projects was *It's a Guitar World*, an internationally flavored instrumental album that was similar in spirit to his 1964 album *My Favorite Guitars*. Not only did the album contain songs from around the world, but it also featured Chet engaging in some unusual multinational musical experimentation—several of the album's selections would feature him playing with Indian sitarist Harihar Rao. Still, many of the numbers found on *It's a Guitar World* did not stray all *that* far from Chet's tried-and-true musical style, including his jazzy cover of the song "A Taste of Honey." Chet recorded "A Taste of Honey" for *It's a Guitar World* at RCA Studios in Nashville, Tennessee on March 23, 1966.

"A Taste of Honey" was not that old of a song at the time Chet recorded it, but it already had a unique and distinguished history. It was originally written by Ric Marlow and Bobby Scott as an instrumental piece for the 1960 Broadway version of the 1958 British play *A Taste of Honey*. In 1962, pop singer Lenny Wright recorded a vocal version of the song—the Beatles heard Wright's version, and they liked it so much that they added it to their own repertoire. The band recorded their version of "A Taste of Honey" for their classic 1963 debut album *Please Please Me*.

In 1965, trumpeter Herb Alpert recorded an instrumental version of the song with his group the Tijuana Brass—this version of the song was released as a single, and it became a top ten hit in the U.S. All of the previous versions of "A Taste of Honey" had been played in a waltz time that occasionally switched to midtempo swing time, but Alpert chose to play the song as an out-and-out swing number. When Chet recorded his version of "A Taste of Honey," he followed Alpert's lead and played it entirely in swing tempo.

On "A Taste of Honey," Chet plays a Gretsch electric guitar in standard tuning out of the key of A minor, and he is accompanied by guitar, bass, and drums. He opens the recording by simultaneously playing—well, by simultaneously playing *everything*. Let's put it this way—if one were compiling a list of Chet's very finest moments on record, the mind-boggling first minute of "A Taste of Honey" would certainly have to be considered for inclusion on that list.

During that minute, Chet first establishes a walking bass line on the lower strings of his guitar, and then he adds in the song's melody over top of that. The melody and the bass line move quite independently of one another, so one would think that playing those two parts together would be about as much as any mortal guitarist would want to take on—but then Chet finds a way to add in a separate *third* part into his playing as well. He works in a number of rich chord voicings while he is still playing his melody and bass parts—so in effect, he is playing melody, bass and rhythm all at the same time.

Incidentally, drummer John Greubel is lightly playing his snare while Chet is doing all of this. But it would have been fun to have had Chet play that snare drum part with his feet just to prove that he could have taken on *four* separate parts if he had really wanted to. At any rate, after that first minute Chet moves to rendering the song's melody through some jazzy single-note soloing. He then closes out the recording by returning to his simultaneously played melody, bass and rhythm parts. Amazingly, even with everything that Chet has going on musically in "A Taste of Honey," his playing throughout the recording is perfectly relaxed and silky-smooth.

Chet would continue recording songs for *It's a Guitar World* all the way up through the end of 1966. During the time he was laying down songs for that album, he was also recording songs for his other album projects he was simultaneously working on, such as *From Nashville with Love* and *Music From Nashville, My Home Town*. (We discussed the title track of *From Nashville with Love* just a bit earlier in this book, and we'll discuss a song from *Music From Nashville, My Home Town* called "Prancin' Filly" next.) So it was early 1967 before *It's a Guitar World* was finally ready to be released by RCA Victor. The record was quite successful when it came out, climbing to number 19 on the U.S. country album charts and to number 148 on the U.S. pop album charts.

"Prancin' Filly"

Composer: James Atkins. **Producer:** Chet Atkins. **Musicians:** Chet Atkins (guitar), Ray Edenton (guitar), Bill Pursell (piano), Henry Strzelecki (bass), John

Greubel (drums). **Location and Date of Recording:** RCA Studios, Tennessee, March 25, 1966. **Original Release:** *Music From Nashville, My Home Town* (RCA Camden album, 1966).

As we just noted in this book's previous entry, Chet spent most of 1966 recording songs for a number of his different album projects. One of these projects was *Music From Nashville, My Home Town*, an instrumental album released by RCA Victor's budget label RCA Camden that same year. On March 25, 1966, Chet recorded a very special number called "Prancin' Filly" for the album at RCA Studios in Nashville, Tennessee. The reason that "Prancin' Filly" was so special was because it was written by Chet's father James, who of course was a very talented musician in his own right. "Prancin' Filly" was a uptempo, minor key-based song that sounded as if it had been pulled from the playlist of a traditional bluegrass band. The title of the song could not have been more appropriate, because its speedy staccato melody definitely brought to mind the image of a prancing filly.

On "Prancin' Filly," Chet played his Del Vecchio Dinamico resonator guitar that he had received from the Brazilian guitarist Nato Lima several years earlier. (We discussed Chet's Del Vecchio in some detail earlier in this book when we examined the liner notes that Chet wrote for his 1964 album *My Favorite Guitars*—and that examination can be found in this book's entry covering Chet's recording of "Wimoweh.") Chet normally played this guitar with its strings tuned up a half step from standard tuning, so from low to high its tuning was F-Bb-Eb-Ab-C-F.

On "Prancin' Filly," Chet plays his half step up-tuned Del Vecchio out of the key of A minor—because of his tuning, it sounds as if he is playing the song out of the key of B flat minor. At one point during the recording, the song briefly changes to the key of D minor, which of course sounds like the key of E flat minor given the guitar's tuning. Backed by guitar, piano, bass and drums, Chet renders the song's rapid-fire melody mainly through single-note soloing, and the metallic sound of the Del Vecchio perfectly accentuates his exciting, percussive performance.

As we have noted a number of times earlier in this book, Chet would be known primarily as a country guitarist throughout his career. Obviously, our journey through Chet's history as a recording artist has shown (and will continue to show) that Chet was certainly much *more* than simply a "country guitarist." But "Prancin' Filly" proves beyond the shadow of

Chet Atkins playing his Del Vecchio Dinamico resonator guitar, and Jerry Reed playing a nylon-string acoustic guitar, 1967.

a doubt that while Chet might have played many different styles of music, he could still play country music as well or better than any guitarist that ever lived.

"Prissy"

Composer: Priscilla Hubbard. **Producer:** Bob Ferguson. **Musicians:** Chet Atkins (guitar), Jerry Reed (guitar), Ray Edenton (guitar), Jerry Smith (piano), Boots Randolph (saxophone), Roy Huskey (bass), Wayne Moss (electric bass), Jerry Carrigan (drums). **Location and Date of Recording:** RCA Studios, Nashville, Tennessee, July 22, 1966. **Original Release:** RCA Victor 47-8927 (RCA Victor 45 single, 1966).

On July 22, 1966, Chet held a three-song recording session at RCA Studios in Nashville—one of the songs recorded at this session was a number called "Prissy." The song's title was actually the nickname of its composer—"Prissy" was written by Jerry Reed's wife Priscilla Hubbard. Priscilla was herself a successful country music singer and musician—under the name Priscilla Mitchell, she had recorded a number of hit singles in the mid–1960s. (Her most well-known records were duets with country singer Roy Drusky.) Priscilla's "Prissy" was a pleasant midtempo instrumental that had an old-time, almost Tin Pan Alley feel to it.

On "Prissy," Chet plays a Gretsch electric guitar in standard tuning out of the key of C, and he is backed by guitar, piano, saxophone, bass and drums. Chet renders the song's happy-sounding melody mainly through a combination of single-note soloing and melodic passages embellished with harmony notes. However, there is one point in the recording when he renders the song's melody along with a simultaneously played accompanying pattern. Boots Randolph plays a nice saxophone part throughout "Prissy" that reinforces the song's old-time atmosphere.

"Prissy" was released as a 45 single by RCA Victor in 1966 and it ended up being rather successful, reaching the number 30 spot on the U.S. country single charts late that same year. But ironically, even though "Prissy" ended up being one of Chet's relatively few charting singles, it quickly became one of his more inaccessible records. After it was released as a single, it was never included on any of Chet's albums, including the many Chet compilation albums that were released over the years. To this day, "Prissy" remains a very hard Chet recording to find—but any Chet fan who takes the time to track it down will undoubtedly feel that his effort was well worth it.

"Tears"

Composers: Django Reinhardt, Stephane Grappelli. **Producers:** Chet Atkins, Bob Ferguson. **Musicians:** Chet Atkins (guitar), Wayne Moss (guitar), Jerry Smith (piano), Bobby Dyson (bass), Richard Morris (marimbas/scraper), John Greubel (drums). **Location and Date of Recording:** RCA "Nashville Sound" Studio, Nashville, Tennessee, February 27, 1967. **Original Release:** *Chet Atkins Picks the Best* (RCA Victor album, 1967).

In early 1967, Chet began holding recording sessions at RCA Studios in Nashville to lay down songs for a new instrumental album that would be entitled *Chet Atkins Picks the Best*. At a session on February 27 of that year, he recorded a version of the song "Tears" for the album. "Tears" was a number co-written in 1937 by one of his main musical heroes, jazz guitarist Django Reinhardt. Django had composed the song with his close musical collaborator, the legendary jazz violinist Stephane Grappelli.

"Tears" was a moody, midtempo piece that featured an unforgettably beautiful minor key-based melody. However, the song did not stay in its minor key from beginning to end—it switched in and out of major key several times, which made its musical structure even more interesting and complex. For his version of "Tears," Chet generally stuck very close to the version that its composers had recorded in 1937—but he did slow down the tempo of the song from Django and Stephane's original recording, which made the number even more brooding.

On "Tears," Chet plays a Gretsch electric guitar out of the key of A minor. His guitar is capoed at the 3rd fret, so it sounds as if he is playing out of the key of C minor. On the recording, he is backed by guitar, bass and drums. (The studio credits for the session when "Tears" was recorded also list musicians playing piano and percussion, but these instruments are not audible on this particular song.) Chet renders much of the song's inventive, timeless melody through richly voiced chords, but he also employs just a bit of expressive single-note soloing as well. Simply put, "Tears" is unquestionably one of Chet's finest moments as a jazz player—every last aspect of his playing is exquisitely tasteful, including his overall guitar tone, his chord choices, and his tempo.

Chet Atkins Picks the Best was released by RCA Victor in 1967, and was very much an easy listening album in terms of its song selection. Even though the album did not make the charts, it ended up becoming a very important milestone in Chet's recording career when it won him his first-ever Grammy Award. At the Grammy Awards of 1968, *Chet Atkins Picks the Best* won the Grammy Award for Best Pop Instrumental Performance.

Here is one final note regarding "Tears"—Chet ended up recording another excellent version of the song late in his career. That version was a guitar duet with Mark Knopfler that appeared their 1990 collaborative album *Neck and Neck*. Chet used a classical guitar for that recording, and he again played the song in the key of A minor—but this time around he did not use a capo on his guitar.

"Yellow Bird"

Composers: Alan Bergman, Michael Keith, Norman Luboff. **Producers:** Chet Atkins, Bob Ferguson. **Musicians:** Chet Atkins (guitar). **Location and Date of Recording:** RCA Studios, Nashville, Tennessee, July 18, 1967. **Original Release:** *Class Guitar* (RCA Victor album, 1967).

Throughout the 1960s, Chet had been playing acoustic guitar more and more frequently on his recordings, but he had not made a strictly acoustic guitar album since his 1960 classical guitar outing *The Other Chet Atkins*. In July 1967, Chet decided to record a second all-classical guitar album, and that album would end up being entitled *Class Guitar*. All of the songs on *Class Guitar* were recorded during sessions held at RCA Studios in Nashville on July 14, 17 and 18. Most of the songs featured Chet playing unaccompanied, though he was joined by Jerry Reed and Bunyan Webb on classical guitar on several numbers.

One of the songs recorded at the July 18 session, "Yellow Bird," was chosen to open the album. "Yellow Bird" was an Americanized version of a 19th century Haitian vocal song "Choucoune" written by Oswald Durand and Michel Mauleart Monton. "Choucoune" began life as a lyrical poem about a beautiful Haitian woman written by Durand, and Monton wrote music to accompany that poem some years after it was first published.

In the late 1950s, the song was rewritten into a midtempo ballad with English lyrics called "Yellow Bird" by songwriter Alan Bergman. Over the next few years, "Yellow Bird" was recorded by a number of well-known artists. The most successful recording of the song was a Hawaiian music-style instrumental version performed by the Arthur Lyman Group—it was released as a single in 1961, and it became a top ten hit in the U.S. that same year.

In fact, one of the artists who had recorded "Yellow Bird" was Chet himself—he included a version of the song on his 1962 album *Caribbean Guitar*. Chet's *Caribbean Guitar* recording of "Yellow Bird" was an instrumental, and he used an electric guitar on it. It was an excellent recording, but his unaccompanied classical guitar rendition of it recorded for *Class Guitar* was arguably even *more* memorable because it was so delicate and intimate. (Incidentally, Chet's *Class Guitar* recording of "Yellow Bird" was arranged by the noted Argentine classical guitarist Jorge Morel.)

On the *Class Guitar* "Yellow Bird," Chet plays a classical guitar in the key of G. His low E string is tuned down to D, his A string is tuned down to G, and his D, G, B and high E strings are unchanged from standard tuning. This tuning allows Chet to render much of the song's melody on his higher strings while simultaneously playing accompanying notes on his open lower strings. He also works many open harmonic notes played on the 12th fret of his guitar into his performance.

Chet Atkins playing a classical guitar during a concert performance in Amsterdam, North Holland, March 7, 1969.

There is probably no way of knowing for sure just which of his classical guitars Chet used to record all of the songs found on *Class Guitar*, including "Yellow Bird"—but since his most regularly played classical at the time was his Juan Estruch classical, it seems likely that he would have used that particular guitar for these recordings. At any rate, whatever classical guitar Chet might be using on "Yellow Bird," his quietly thoughtful rendition of the song makes a listener feel as if they are sitting right next to Chet while he is playing. (This feeling is reinforced by the fact that you can clearly hear Chet's foot tapping along with his playing during the recording.)

Class Guitar was released by RCA Victor in 1967, and its song selection very much reflected the overall theme of the album—many of its songs were pieces that had originally been written for classical guitar, or pieces that had been regularly played by various classical guitarists over the years. The record was quite successful when it came out, climbing to the number 26 spot on the U.S. country album charts, and it was also warmly received by longtime Chet fans.

"Foggy Mountain Top"

Composer: A.P. Carter. **Producer:** Chet Atkins. **Musicians:** Chet Atkins (guitar), Jerry Reed (guitar), Wayne Moss (guitar), Sonny Osborne (banjo), Charlie McCoy (harmonica) Henry Strzelecki (bass), Jerry Carrigan (drums). **Location and Date of Recording:** RCA "Nashville Sound" Studio, Nashville, Tennessee, August 31, 1967. **Original Release:** *Chet* (RCA Camden album, 1967).

On August 31, 1967, Chet held a five-song session at RCA Studios in Nashville to record numbers for *Chet*, a new instrumental album that would be released by RCA Victor's budget label RCA Camden later that same year. Chet obviously intended for *Chet* to be a country music album, pure and simple, because many of its songs were covers of well-known country numbers. Plus, a few of the songs on the album featured foot-tapping banjo and harmonica solos played by two of Nashville's very best country musicians—the banjo was played by Sonny Osborne, and the harmonica was played by Charlie McCoy.

One of the songs recorded at the August 31 session, "Foggy Mountain Top," was chosen to open *Chet*. "Foggy Mountain Top" was a vocal number written in the 1920s by A.P. Carter, one of the founding members of the Carter Family—the Carters recorded and performed the song many times throughout their long career. Another well-known version of the song was recorded in 1961 by bluegrass legends Lester Flatt and Earl Scruggs. (Incidentally, Mother Maybelle Carter performed with Flatt and Scruggs on this recording.)

On "Foggy Mountain Top," Chet plays a Gretsch electric guitar in standard tuning, and he is backed by guitar, banjo, harmonica, bass and drums. Playing at a fast tempo, Chet renders the song's melody along with a simultaneously played accompanying pattern out of the key of C. The song then changes to the key of G, and Chet offers up some straightforward solo playing that features both melody and harmony lines. After this solo work, he lays out in order to make room for some nice lead breaks played by Charlie on the harmonica and Sonny on the banjo. The song returns to the key of C, and Chet finishes the song out by again rendering the song's melody along with a simultaneous accompanying pattern. His final notes on "Foggy Mountain Top" offer up one last musical flourish as he plays the superlick several times. (We discussed Chet's superlick in detail in our examination of Chet's recording of "Satan's Doll" earlier in this book.)

Songs off of *Chet* like "Foggy Mountain Top" showed that while Chet certainly had long since moved beyond playing primarily country music, he still very much enjoyed playing the style whenever the opportunity arose.

"Drive In"

Composer: Jerry Reed. **Producer:** Bob Ferguson. **Musicians:** Chet Atkins (guitar), Henry Strzelecki (bass), Jerry Carrigan (drums). **Location and Date of Recording:** RCA Studios, Nashville, Tennessee, November 28, 1967. **Original Release:** *Solo Flights* (RCA Victor album, 1968).

In late 1967, Chet decided to begin work on an album of instrumental songs with stripped-down arrangements—this new album was given the not-quite accurate title of *Solo Flights*. Of course, the reason that this title was not really accurate was because on the album Chet might have been playing with less musicians than usual, but he really wasn't playing *solo*.

At any rate, not only would *Solo Flights* feature less backing musicians than many of Chet's other albums, it would also feature Chet playing a very unusual guitar. This guitar was a Gretsch electric that had its low E and A strings replaced with bass guitar E and A strings—so these strings were an octave lower than a regular guitar's low E and A strings. Consequently, when this instrument was played by a fingerstyle guitarist like Chet, it had the potential of sounding very much like a guitarist and a bassist playing together. This instrument was dubbed the "octabass guitar," and Chet used it on all of the songs featured on side one of the album. (All of the songs on side two of the album featured Chet playing acoustic guitar.)

On November 28, Chet recorded three songs for the *Solo Flights* album during a session at RCA Studios in Nashville—he used the octabass on all three of these numbers. Arguably the most memorable song recorded at this session was "Drive In," a slow, bluesy tune written by Jerry Reed.

Interestingly, the studio credits for the session when "Drive In" was recorded really weren't very clear as to just which musicians were actually playing on the song. These credits did not list a musician playing organ, even though that instrument was clearly audible on "Drive In." Plus, the credits *did* list Henry Strzelecki as playing bass, even though the only bass part that was audible in "Drive In" was Chet's octabass strings.

Anyway, Chet plays the octabass on "Drive In," and he is accompanied by organ and drums. He plays the song out of the key of E, but he has tuned the strings on the octabass tuned up a half step from standard tuning—so from low to high its tuning is F-Bb-Eb-Ab-C-F. Consequently, it sounds as if he is playing the song out of the key of F, not E. He renders all of the number's blues-based melody with a simultaneously played accompanying pattern. This pattern features lots of notes played on the bass strings of his octabass, so his playing really *does* sound far more like a guitarist and a bassist playing together than it does just a single guitarist.

Even though the octabass ended up creating such a distinctive, full sound on *Solo Flights*, Chet chose not to record with the instrument again after the album was released by RCA Victor in 1968. Of course, this decision really made perfect sense—

after all, the heavier bass strings on the octabass could never have allowed Chet to play with the kind of subtlety and speed that he was accustomed to.

"Blue Angel"

Composer: Natalicio Moreyra Lima. **Producer:** Bob Ferguson. **Musicians:** Chet Atkins (guitar), Jerry Reed (guitar), Earl Porter (guitar), Boyce Hawkins (organ), Bobby Byson (bass), Buddy Harman (drums). **Location and Date of Recording:** RCA Studios, Nashville, Tennessee, May 24, 1968. **Original Release:** *Hometown Guitar* (RCA Victor album, 1968), RCA Victor 47-9578 (RCA Victor 45 single, 1968).

In April and May of 1968, Chet held recording sessions at RCA Studios in Nashville for a new album that would be entitled *Hometown Guitar*. The album was basically an all-instrumental work, though a group of background singers did provide supporting vocals on several of its songs. Interestingly, this vocal chorus was basically the original Anita Kerr Singers without Anita. By the time *Hometown Guitar* was being made, Anita had moved to Los Angeles to continue her musical career there— so the chorus that performed on the album was comprised of Anita's longtime Nashville-based singers paired with the well-known country singer (and Jerry Reed's wife) Priscilla Hubbard.

All in all, *Hometown Guitar* was very much a country music album in the vein of Chet's earlier albums *Guitar Country* and *More of That Guitar Country*—but ironically, its most well-remembered number, "Blue Angel," was not a country song at all. "Blue Angel" was recorded during a session held for *Hometown Guitar* on May 24, and the song quickly became recognized as one of Chet's finest-ever moments on record.

"Blue Angel" was a piece written for classical guitar by Chet's friend Nato Lima— Nato was a guitarist from Ceará, Brazil, who played in a well-known guitar duo known as Los Indios Tabajaras—the other half of that duo was Nato's brother Antenor. As we noted earlier, Nato had sold Chet his Del Vecchio Dinamico resonator guitar in the early 1960s, and that guitar had quickly become one of Chet's favorite instruments.

By writing "Blue Angel," Nato had given Chet one *more* thing that would greatly enrich his musical legacy. The song was an exciting, fast-tempoed number that featured a spectacularly acrobatic melody, and it offered Chet a golden opportunity to showcase his incredible talent. Needless to say, Chet definitely made the most of this opportunity—*man*, did he ever make the most of it.

On "Blue Angel," Chet plays his Juan Estruch classical guitar, and he is backed by guitar, organ, bass and drums. Interestingly, he does not play the Juan Estruch strictly as an acoustic instrument on the recording. Rather, the guitar is recorded through a Baldwin Prismatone pickup that Chet had decided to install on it sometime during the 1960s.

The song's wonderfully inventive melody repeatedly changes between the key of A minor and the key of A major throughout the song. Chet plays "Blue Angel" out of these keys, but he has tuned the strings on his guitar tuned up a half step from standard tuning—so from low to high its tuning is F-Bb-Eb-Ab-C-F. Consequently, it sounds as if he is playing the song out of the keys of B flat minor and B flat major, not A minor and A major.

Chet renders most all of the melody of "Blue Angel" through single-note soloing, and his playing is simply breathtaking. The notes that he plays in the recording race up and down his fretboard, and across all of his strings, and they do not slow up from the first moment of the song until the last.

When RCA Victor released *Hometown Guitar* in late 1968, they also chose to release "Blue Angel" as a 45 single. That single did not end up charting, but the *Hometown Guitar* album as a whole turned out to be quite successful—it reached the number 17 spot on the U.S. country album charts. And over the years, "Blue Angel" grew to be so well-loved by Chet's longtime fans that it became a regular feature in both his concert and television appearances. In fact, Chet would record a live version of "Blue Angel" later in his career—that recording would be featured on his 1980 live album *The Best of Chet on the Road ... Live*. Like Chet's original 1968 version of the song, this live version featured him playing a classical guitar.

"Theme from *Zorba the Greek*"

Composer: Mikis Theodorakis. **Producer:** Bob Ferguson. **Musicians:** Chet Atkins (guitar), Jerry Reed (guitar), Richard Morris (vibes/bells), William Sanders (bass), Byron Williams, Solie Fott, Lillian Hunt, George Binkley, Brenton Banks, Pierre Menard, Akira Nagai (violins), Marvin Chantry, Gary Van Osdale (violas), Harold Cruthirds, Sadao Harada (cellos). **Location and Date of Recording:** RCA Studios, Nashville, Tennessee, November 20, 1968. **Original Release:** *Lover's Guitar* (RCA Victor album, 1969), RCA Victor 47-9725 (RCA Victor 45 single, 1969).

The second half of 1968 found Chet at RCA Studios in Nashville, starting work on a new album project that would become the first in a series of several albums—the album was called *Solid Gold '68*, and it featured Chet playing instrumental versions of current radio hits. He followed up this album with two more *Solid Gold* albums over the next two years, *Solid Gold '69* and *Solid Gold '70*. These albums were pleasant enough, but both their material and their expansive arrangements certainly did not showcase Chet's talent in its best light.

Chet began work on another album project in late 1968 that could not really be called "new." He recorded several songs for an album called *Relaxin' with Chet*, which was in large part a reworked version of his 1958 album *Chet Atkins at Home*—eight of the ten songs found on *Relaxin' with Chet* were originally on *Chet Atkins at Home*.

In November 1968, Chet began work on another album that *could* truly be called "new." *Lover's Guitar* was the name of this album, and it was a collection of intimate acoustic guitar performances that featured Chet either on his classical or his Del Vecchio. During a four-song session for *Lover's Guitar* held at RCA Studios in Nashville on November 20, Chet recorded a memorable version of "Theme from *Zorba the Greek*." "Theme from *Zorba the Greek*" was a rousing dance piece written by the well-known composer Mikis Theodorakis for the 1964 film *Zorba the Greek*.

On "Theme from *Zorba the Greek*," Chet plays a classical guitar in the key of G. His low E string is tuned down to D, his A string is tuned down to G, and his D, G, B and high E strings are unchanged from standard tuning. This tuning allows Chet to render much of the song's melody on his higher strings while simultaneously playing accompanying notes on his open lower strings. On the recording, he is accompanied by guitar, bass, percussion and a large string section comprised of violins, violas and cellos. "Theme from *Zorba the Greek*" starts out slow and pensive—but as the song goes on, its tempo gets faster and faster, and its melody gets more and more ebullient. By the end of the recording, the song has become so infectiously high-spirited that most any listener will be tapping their toes to it.

(As was the case with some of the earlier Chet classical guitar recordings we discussed in this book, there is probably no way of knowing for sure just which of his classical guitars Chet used to record "Theme from *Zorba the Greek*"—but since his most regularly played classical at the time was his Juan Estruch classical, it seems likely that he would have used that particular guitar for this recording.)

When RCA Victor released *Lover's Guitar* in 1969, they also chose to release "Theme from *Zorba the Greek*" as a 45 single. Neither the album nor the single ended up charting—but even still, over the years *Lover's Guitar* and its standout selection "Theme from *Zorba the Greek*" came to be highly regarded by Chet's longtime fans.

"Medley: The Battle of New Orleans/Sugarfoot Rag"

> **Composers:** Jimmy Driftwood ("The Battle of New Orleans"), Hank Garland, George Vaughn ("Sugarfoot Rag"). **Producer:** Peter Delheim. **Musicians:** Chet Atkins (guitar), Arthur Fiedler and the Boston Pops (orchestra), Robert Moore (bass), Jerry Carrigan (drums). **Location and Date of Recording:** Symphony Hall, Boston, Massachusetts, June 6, 1969. **Original Release:** *Chet Atkins Picks on the Pops* (RCA Victor album with Arthur Fiedler and the Boston Pops, 1969).

In June 1969, Chet traveled to Boston, Massachusetts, to record the album *Chet Atkins Picks on the Pops* with the legendary conductor Arthur Fielder and his orchestra the Boston Pops. This was Chet's second collaborative album with Fiedler and the Pops, the first being *The Pops Goes Country*. (That album was released by RCA Victor in 1966—earlier in the book, we discussed one of its numbers, "Alabama Jubilee.") Like the recording sessions held for *The Pops Goes Country*, the sessions for *Chet Atkins Picks on the Pops* were held at Boston's Symphony Hall. Unfortunately, the only paperwork documenting these sessions that is in existence is incomplete—it shows that Chet and the Pops recorded at least part of the album on June 6, but it is unclear if that was the only day that sessions for the album were held.

At any rate, all of the songs that Chet and the Pops recorded for *Chet Atkins Picks on the Pops* were instrumentals. Their rousing recording of a medley of two songs, "The Battle of New Orleans" and "Sugarfoot Rag," was chosen to close the album. "The Battle of New Orleans" was a well-known 1950s folk song with music and lyrics written by Jimmy Driftwood. The most successful version of song was recorded by country singer Johnny Horton—it reached the top spot on the U.S. pop and country single charts in 1959, and won the 1960 Grammy Award for Best Song of the Year. "Sugarfoot Rag" was an uptempo country number written by the legendary country guitarist Hank Garland and George Vaughn. Hank's instrumental recording of "Sugarfoot Rag" was a hit when it was released as a single in 1949, and the song was then covered as a vocal number by country singer Red Foley the following year.

Interestingly, "Sugarfoot Rag" was a number that Chet had previously recorded not too long before his 1969 session with the Pops—he had featured an excellent version of the song on his classic 1964 album *Guitar Country*. But obviously the Chet/Pops rendition of "Sugarfoot Rag" mixed in with "The Battle of New Orleans" made for a version of the song that was completely different from Chet's *Guitar Country* version.

On "Medley: The Battle of New Orleans/Sugarfoot Rag," Chet plays a Gretsch electric guitar in standard tuning backed by the mighty sound of the Boston Pops. He starts the recording by rendering the melody of "The Battle of New Orleans" in the key of G. All of his playing in this part of the song consists of single-note soloing. The number then switches to the key of A for its "Sugarfoot Rag" section—Chet renders the melody of that song both through single-note soloing, and playing melody notes along with a simultaneously played accompanying pattern. Staying in the key of A, the number returns to "The Battle of New Orleans," and Chet wraps up the proceedings by again rendering that song's melody through single-note soloing. Chet's playing throughout "Medley: The Battle of New Orleans/Sugarfoot Rag" is wonderfully crisp, and he is perfectly supported by the Pops' powerful musical volleys.

Chet Atkins Picks on the Pops was released by RCA Victor in 1969, and though the album did not achieve any substantial chart success, it became well-loved both by Chet fans and Boston Pops fans. Chet would never again record another album with the Pops, but he would perform live with the orchestra on occasion—in fact, he even appeared with them on their long-running PBS Television Network show *Evening at Pops* several times during the 1970s.

"Poison Love"

> **Composer:** Elmer Laird. **Producers:** Chet Atkins, Rony Light. **Musicians:** Chet Atkins (guitar/vocals), Hank Snow (guitar/vocals), Pete Wade (guitar), Larry Butler (piano), Bob Moore (bass), Bill Walker (vibes), Jimmy Isbell (drums). **Location and Dates of Recording:** RCA Studios, Nashville, Tennessee, July 29, 1969, and October 27, 1969. **Original Release:** *C.B. Atkins and C.E. Snow by Special Request* (RCA Victor album with Hank Snow, 1969).

In July 1969, Chet and singer/guitarist Hank Snow began holding recording sessions at RCA Studios in Nashville for their collaborative album that would end up being entitled *C.B. Atkins and C.E. Snow by Special Request*. This was Chet's second collaborative album with Hank, the first being *Reminiscing*. (That album was released by RCA Victor in 1964—earlier, we discussed one of its songs, "Brahms' Lullaby.")

During a three-song session held for *C.B. Atkins and C.E. Snow by Special Request* on July 29, Chet and Hank recorded the musical tracks for a song they planned to sing as a duet called "Poison Love." They would lay down their final vocal tracks for the song at a separate session held on October 27. "Poison Love" was a midtempo ballad about a love affair gone wrong written by Elmer Laird, and it was first recorded by Hank back in 1956—Chet and Hank's decision to record a new version of the song for *C.B. Atkins and C.E. Snow by Special Request* was a certainly a good one, because their performance together on the recording turned out to be one of the album's high points.

Chet plays a Gretsch electric guitar in standard tuning on "Poison Love," and he is joined by Hank playing an acoustic guitar that is also in standard tuning. The two are accompanied by guitar, piano, bass, vibes, and drums. The recording opens with Hank and Chet trading solo guitar lines back and forth in the key of A. The song then modulates to the key of D, and Hank sings its first verse by himself. Chet joins Hank for the song's first chorus, singing in beautifully close harmony with Hank's melody

Chet Atkins playing a Chet Atkins Nashville electric guitar, late 1960s.

singing. The song then modulates to the key of G for another guitar solo break, and the two men repeat on guitar what they just did vocally—Hank plays melody, and Chet plays a harmony part along with that melody. The song stays in the key of G, and Chet ably takes over lead vocal duties for its second verse—he stays on melody for the song's second chorus, and Hank nicely supports him by singing a low harmony part.

As "Poison Love" fades out, Chet and Hank engage in a bit of good-natured ribbing of one another. Hank tells Chet that he had better stick to the guitar, and Chet responds to him by saying that Hank had better stick to singing. Of course, there is not a shred of truth to be found in this ribbing—the excellent playing and singing of both men on "Poison Love" proves this point beyond the shadow of a doubt.

In fact, this seems like a good spot in the book to address the popularly held notion that throughout Chet's long career, he was always a very poor vocalist. This notion is really not accurate at all—Chet was by no means a spectacularly gifted singer, but he was more than capable of turning in very likable vocal performances, especially on songs that had a bit of wry humor to them. In fact, we discussed two of his all-time best recorded vocal performances earlier in the book, "The Old Buck Dance" and "Boogie Man Boogie." And we are by no means done with Chet's singing yet—later in the book, we'll be discussing some excellent Chet vocal numbers recorded in the 1970s, 1980s and 1990s.

Of course, it always made for a good joke that this man who delivered such an angelic guitar sound could only croak like a frog when he sang—so over the years, Chet often played this joke up for all it was worth when he was in front of an audience. But the truth was that he *could* sing quite well, and he would leave behind some wonderful recorded vocal performances to offer proof of that fact—"Poison Love" was definitely one of those performances.

C.B. Atkins and C.E. Snow by Special Request was released by RCA Victor in 1969, and though the album did not achieve any substantial chart success, it was well-received by both Chet and Hank's fans. Chet did not end up collaborating with Hank on any more records after the two men made *C.B. Atkins and C.E. Snow by Special Request*—but Hank's great contributions to Chet's music made during the 1950s and 1960s would be fondly remembered by Chet fans for decades to come.

"Steeplechase Lane"

Composer: Jerry Reed Hubbard. **Producer:** Bob Ferguson. **Musicians:** Chet Atkins (guitar), Jerry Reed (guitar), Pete Wade (guitar), James Crawford (guitar), Jerry Smith (piano), Kossie Gardner (organ/vibes), Norbert Putnam (bass), Larrie Londin (drums). **Location and Date of Recording:** RCA Studios, Nashville, Tennessee, January 26, 1970. **Original Release:** *Yestergroovin'* (RCA Victor album, 1970), RCA Victor 47-9827 (RCA Victor 45 single, 1970).

The latter half of 1969 found Chet at RCA Studios in Nashville working on *Solid Gold '69*, an album that featured him playing instrumental versions of current radio hits. Right at the end of that year, he began work on a new instrumental album that was definitely more "Chet style" in nature than a self-consciously topical album like *Solid Gold '69*—this new album would be entitled *Yestergroovin'.* The album's title was particularly appropriate, because Chet invested the record with a nostalgic, low-key feel that was very refreshing.

During a session for *Yestergroovin'* held at RCA Studios in Nashville on January 26, 1970, Chet recorded the song that would be chosen to open the album, "Steeplechase Lane." "Steeplechase Lane" was a catchy midtempo number written by Jerry Reed—and Jerry played guitar on Chet's recording of the song as well.

On "Steeplechase Lane," Chet plays a Gretsch electric guitar out of the key of A. His guitar is capoed at the 3rd fret, so it sounds as if he is playing out of the key of C. On the recording, Chet is backed by guitar, organ, bass and drums, and he renders the much of the song's easygoing melody along with a simultaneously played accompanying pattern. Even though the song is very low-key, there are times during the recording when it is actually hard to tell just which guitar parts are being played by Chet, and which are being played by his supporting guitarists—this is because the song features a number of different guitar tracks that are constantly overlapping one another. All of these guitar tracks give "Steeplechase Lane" a musical thickness that is very sonically satisfying.

When RCA Victor released *Yestergroovin'* in 1970, they also chose to release "Steeplechase Lane" as a 45 single. Neither the album nor the single ended up achieving any significant chart success—but even still, over the years *Yestergroovin'* and its standout selection "Steeplechase Lane" came to be highly regarded by Chet's longtime fans.

Incidentally, Chet would record one more version of "Steeplechase Lane" later in his career—that recording appeared on his 1974 album of Jerry Reed-penned instrumentals entitled *Chet Atkins Picks on Jerry Reed*. The *Chet Atkins Picks on Jerry Reed* version of "Steeplechase Lane" was very enjoyable, but it did not end up becoming as well-remembered as Chet's first recorded version of the song.

"Tennessee Stud"

Composer: Jimmy Driftwood. **Producers:** Chet Atkins, Bob Ferguson. **Musicians:** Chet Atkins (guitar), Jerry Reed (guitar), Henry Strzelecki (bass), Jerry Carrigan (drums), Larrie London (drums), Farrell Morris (congas/percussion). **Location and Date of Recording:** RCA Studios, Nashville, Tennessee, May 7, 1970. **Original Release:** *Me and Jerry* (RCA Victor album with Jerry Reed, 1970), RCA Victor 47–9890 (RCA Victor 45 single with Jerry Reed, 1970).

In early 1970, Chet and Jerry Reed recorded ten instrumentals for their first-ever collaborative album entitled *Me and Jerry*. The manner in which the album was recorded was quite a departure from Chet's usual recording routine. As we have discussed a number of times earlier in this book, Chet would often lay down backing tracks for his records at RCA Studios in Nashville, and then perfect his guitar tracks for those songs at his home studio at a later date. For *Me and Jerry*, Chet and Jerry basically turned this routine upside-down—they first recorded their guitar tracks at Chet's home studio unaccompanied by any other musicians, and then they took those finished tracks to RCA's Nashville studio to add backing tracks to them! Consequently, RCA's studio logs ended up indicating that all of *Me and Jerry* was recorded in one day, on May 7, 1970. But in reality, only the backing tracks for the album were recorded on that day, not Chet and Jerry's guitar tracks.

At any rate, the number that was chosen to open *Me and Jerry* was "Tennessee Stud." "Tennessee Stud" was a well-known 1950s folk song with music and lyrics written by Jimmy Driftwood. Over the years, the song was covered by a number of different artists, including Eddy Arnold and Doc Watson. Chet and Jerry chose to interpret "Tennessee Stud" as a hard-driving midtempo instrumental—but they still sung a line or two of the song's lyrics together in a winningly off-the-cuff manner.

On "Tennessee Stud," Chet plays his Del Vecchio Dinamico resonator guitar, and Jerry plays a classical guitar. The two are accompanied by bass, drums and percussion. Chet and Jerry play the song out of the key of D, and they are in standard tuning with the exception of their low E strings—those strings are tuned down to D. (This form of tuning is often referred to as "drop D.") On this number and every other number found on the album, Chet's guitar is mixed hard to the right, and Jerry's guitar is mixed hard to the left—so it is very easy to distinguish one man's playing from the other when listening to the song.

Chet opens the recording by playing the song's melody through some powerful single-note soloing, and then Jerry takes over for a round of straight-up improvisational soloing that is at times accompanied note-for-note by his fabulous scat singing. Chet jumps back in to play the song's melody through single-note soloing—and as the song fades out, Chet throws in a few improvisational licks of his own.

When RCA Victor released *Me and Jerry* in 1970, they also chose to release "Tennessee Stud" as a 45 single—that single did not end up charting. (The flip side of that single was "Cannonball Rag," the subject of this book's next entry.) Still, the album as a whole ended up being quite successful, reaching the number 13 spot on the U.S. country album charts. But its biggest success came in the form of a very prestigious award—at the Grammy Awards of 1970, *Me and Jerry* won the Grammy Award for Best Country Instrumental Performance. This marked the second time that Chet had won a Grammy—his first Grammy win was for his 1968 album *Chet Atkins Picks the Best*. (Earlier in the book, we discussed a song off of that album, "Tears.")

"Cannonball Rag"

Composer: Merle Travis. **Producers:** Chet Atkins, Bob Ferguson. **Musicians:** Chet Atkins (guitar), Jerry Reed (guitar), Henry Strzelecki (bass), Jerry Carrigan (drums), Larrie London (drums) Farrell Morris (congas/percussion). **Location and Date of Recording:** RCA Studios, Nashville, Tennessee, May 7, 1970. **Original Release:** *Me and Jerry* (RCA Victor album with Jerry Reed, 1970), RCA Victor 47–9890 (RCA Victor 45 single with Jerry Reed, 1970).

As noted in our discussion of "Tennessee Stud," Chet and Jerry Reed recorded all ten of the instrumentals that would be featured on their first-ever collaborative album *Me and Jerry* at Chet's home studio and at RCA's Nashville studio during the first half of 1970.

Along with "Tennessee Stud," another of the standout numbers Chet and Jerry recorded for *Me and Jerry* was their version of the well-known guitar instrumental "Cannonball Rag." "Cannonball Rag" was a fast-tempoed number written and recorded in the 1940s by Chet and Jerry's longtime musical hero, singer/guitarist Merle Travis.

Chet plays a Gretsch electric guitar in standard tuning on "Cannonball Rag," and he is joined by Jerry playing a classical guitar that is also in standard tuning. Playing in the key of G, the two are accompanied by bass, drums and percussion. Like all of the other numbers found on *Me and Jerry*, Chet's guitar is mixed hard to the right and Jerry's guitar is mixed hard to the left on "Cannonball Rag"—so it is very easy to distinguish one man's playing from the other when listening to the song.

The recording opens with Chet and Jerry doing Merle's fingerpicking style proud as Chet renders the song's speedy melody along with a simultaneously played accompanying pattern, and Jerry renders a harmony part to that melody along with a simultaneously played accompanying pattern. The two men then swap extended solo breaks, Chet taking the first one and Jerry taking the second. Chet's break has a decidedly jazzy feel to it, with a nice run of harmonic notes thrown in. Jerry's unleashes a barrage of furiously picked notes during his break that do not let up from start to finish. Chet and Jerry close out the recording by restating the song's melody together.

When RCA Victor released *Me and Jerry* in 1970, they also chose to release "Cannonball Rag" as a 45 single. (The flip side of that single was "Tennessee Stud," the subject of our last entry.) The single did not end up charting. But as we also noted in our discussion of "Tennessee Stud," the *Me and Jerry* album as a whole ended up being quite successful, reaching the number 13 spot on the U.S. country album charts and winning a Grammy Award for Best Country Instrumental Performance.

Incidentally, Chet would record one more version of "Cannonball Rag" later in his career—he and the song's composer Merle Travis performed an instrumental duet of the song for their 1974 collaborative album *The Atkins-Travis Traveling Show*. But in truth, that version of "Cannonball Rag" barely even featured Chet—it was a short, rather offhand affair that primarily consisted of Merle soloing at a ridiculously fast tempo.

Since *Me and Jerry* turned out to be so well-received, it was no surprise that Chet and Jerry would decide to record another album together not even two years later. We'll discuss that album entitled *Me and Chet* a bit later when we examine two of its standout tracks, "The Mad Russian" and "Nashtown Ville."

"El Condor Pasa"

Composers: Jorge Milchberg, Paul Simon. **Producer:** Bob Ferguson. **Musicians:** Chet Atkins (guitar), Jerry Shook (guitar), Johnny Gimble (mandolin), Jerry Smith (piano), Roy Huskey (bass), Farrell Morris (marimba/vibes/shaker), Larrie London (drums). **Location and Date of Recording:** RCA Studios, Nashville, Tennessee, November 23, 1970. **Original Release:** *For the Good Times and Other Country Moods* (RCA Victor album, 1971).

In late 1970, Chet was definitely on a very potent artistic roll—he had just finished work on *Me and Jerry*, his first-ever collaborative album with Jerry Reed, and that album had turned out to be a truly spectacular musical showcase for both guitarists. In November of that year, he headed into RCA Studios in Nashville to begin work on a new album that would be entitled *For the Good Times and Other Country Moods*. The album would be given that title because one of the numbers Chet recorded for it was a cover of the song "For the Good Times" written by Kris Kristofferson. (The most successful version of that song was recorded by country singer Ray Price—it reached the top spot on the U.S. country single charts in mid–1970.) *For the Good Times and Other Country Moods* was basically an all-instrumental work, though a group of background singers did provide supporting vocals on several of its songs.

The material that Chet picked for the album reflected his continuous, almost otherworldly growth as a musical artist. *For the Good Times and Other Country Moods* obviously featured the word "country" in its title—and this title was very appropriate, because there was certainly a lot of country music to be found on the album. But Chet also infused the record with healthy doses of pop, jazz, world music, and even opera. You might be thinking to yourself, "*opera?*" Why, yes—he recorded a jazz-tinged version of "Vesti la Giubba," the most famous aria from Ruggero Leoncavallo's 1892 Italian opera *Pagliacci*, for the album. Obviously, Chet had long maintained an interest in recording albums that featured a wide range of musical styles—but the variety of music that he seamlessly brought together for *For the Good Times and Other Country Moods* was nothing short of astounding.

One of the album's standout tracks, "El Condor Pasa," was recorded on November 23, 1970. "El Condor Pasa" was a South American song with a long and interesting history. It was originally written as an orchestral piece by Peruvian composer Daniel Alomia Robles for his 1913 musical play of the same name. (Translated into English from Spanish, "El Condor Pasa" means "The Condor Passes.")

In the mid–1960s, Paul Simon of the famed vocal duo Simon and Garfunkel heard a musician named Jorge Milchberg perform the song with Los Incas, his group of musicians from Argentina and Uruguay. Simon liked the piece so much that he wrote a set of English lyrics for the song—and then he and Garfunkel recorded this new version of "El Condor Pasa" using the Los Incas instrumental recording of the song as their backing track. Simon and Garfunkel's version of "El Condor Pasa" was featured on their classic 1970 album *Bridge Over Troubled Water*—it was also released as a single that same year, eventually becoming a top 20 hit in the United States.

On the *For the Good Times and Other Country Moods* version of "El Condor Pasa," Chet plays a classical guitar with its low E string tuned down to D. (This form of tuning is often referred to as "drop D.") He is accompanied by guitar, mandolin, piano, bass, drums and percussion. Chet opens the recording by rendering the song's beautiful melody along with a simultaneously played accompanying pattern out of the key of B minor. The song then modulates to the key of D flat minor, and Chet switches to playing melody mainly through single-note soloing.

Much of his playing at this point in the recording is adorned with a lovely, very heavy delay effect—this effect is created not through an actual delay unit, but through a tape recording machine that is set to repeatedly play back the notes he is playing. Chet would use this tape-generated delay effect on his guitar for a number of the other songs found on *For the Good Times and Other Country Moods*, including "Snowbird," the subject of our next entry.

For the Good Times and Other Country Moods was released by RCA Victor in 1971. The record ended up being quite successful, reaching the number 17 spot on the U.S. country album charts. And the album was every bit as much of an artistic success as it was a commercial success—it proved beyond the shadow of a doubt that Chet could make music that was still every bit as adventurous as the groundbreaking records he had made almost a quarter of a century earlier.

Interestingly, the liner notes written for the record offered a perfect little summation of Chet's first quarter-century in the music business. They discussed his ongoing friendship with his longtime musical hero singer/guitarist Merle Travis and the belief that RCA Victor executive Stephen H. Sholes had in Chet's talent when he first signed Chet to the label. They also discussed Chet's incredible success as an RCA producer, and his musical collaborations with renowned artists such as Floyd Cramer, Boots Randolph, and Arthur Fiedler and the Boston Pops. The first 25 years of Chet's career had truly been amazing—and even more amazingly, that career still had another 25 years to go before it was done.

"Snowbird"

> **Composer:** Gene MacLellan. **Producer:** Bob Ferguson. **Musicians:** Chet Atkins (guitar), Jerry Shook (guitar), Jerry Smith (piano), Henry Strzelecki (bass), Farrell Morris (bongos/percussion), William Ackerman (drums), Larrie London (drums), Albert Coleman, William Fitzpatrick, Laurence Harvin, Marianne Harvin, Jo Parker (violins), Gary Van Osdale, Bobby Becker (violas), Byron Bach (cello). **Location and Dates of Recording:** RCA "Nashville Sound" Studio, Nashville, Tennessee, December 11, 1970, and December 18, 1970. **Original Release:** *For the Good Times and Other Country Moods* (RCA Victor album, 1971), RCA Victor 47–9956 (RCA Victor 45 single, 1971).

As we just noted in our discussion of "El Condor Pasa," Chet made a very powerful artistic statement with the wide range of music that he brought together for his classic 1971 instrumental album *For the Good Times and Other Country Moods*. Probably the one single song on *For the Good Times and Other Country Moods* that best captured just how great that album turned out to be was Chet's cover of "Snowbird."

"Snowbird" was a vocal number composed by Canadian songwriter Gene MacLellan. The most well-known version of song was recorded by the country/pop singer (and fellow Canadian) Anne Murray—in 1970, it reached the top five on the Canadian pop single charts, and the top ten on the U.S. pop and country single charts. Even though "Snowbird" was very much a melancholy number about a love affair gone wrong, it featured both a happy-sounding melody and a fast tempo.

Chet recorded his version of "Snowbird" at RCA Studios in Nashville on December 11, 1970, during a three-song session held for *For the Good Times and Other Country Moods*. String tracks for the number were recorded at a separate session held on December 18, 1970.

On "Snowbird," Chet plays a Gretsch electric guitar in standard tuning. He is accompanied by guitar, bass, drums, percussion, and a string section comprised of violins, violas and cellos. Chet opens the recording by playing the song's gently descending melody through single-note soloing out of the key of A. His soloing quickly becomes ever more complex as he adds a wealth of tasteful, jazz-tinged embellishments to that melody.

In fact, his playing quickly becomes downright spectacular—for example, at just about a half-minute into the recording, Chet uses a beautifully inverted version of his famed superlick. Chet would normally play the superlick as a blindingly fast, up-and-down arpeggio pattern—in "Snowbird," he plays the superlick as a blindingly fast, *down-and-up* arpeggio pattern.

And Chet just keeps on playing at that same jaw-dropping level throughout the rest of the recording. He delivers note after note with a combination of silky smoothness and unbelievable speed, and many of these notes are adorned with a lovely, very heavy delay effect. (As we discussed in our examination of "El Condor Pasa," this delay effect found in a number of the songs on *For the Good Times and Other Country Moods* is created not through an actual delay unit, but through a tape recording machine that is set to repeatedly play back the notes he is playing.) About midway through "Snowbird," the song changes to the key of D—Chet continues to play its melody through single-note soloing from this point until the end of the recording. However, he does occasionally throw in simultaneously played harmony lines to accompany his melody playing.

Simply put, "Snowbird" is quintessential Chet. The recording is country, it is jazz, it is pop—but above all, it is simply *Chet*. One of the most remarkable aspects of his playing was that somehow, he could consistently find a way to make his playing both tremendously exciting and deeply peaceful at the same time—and "Snowbird" is a shining example of this phenomenon.

When *For the Good Times and Other Country Moods* was released by RCA Victor in 1971, "Snowbird" was chosen to be the album's opening track. The record ended up being quite successful, reaching the number 17 spot on the U.S. country album charts. The label also chose to release "Snowbird" as a 45 single that same year. The song did not end up charting, but it still received a richly deserved honor from the music industry—at the 1972 Grammy Awards, it won the Grammy Award for Best Country Instrumental Performance. Chet had now won three Grammys during his career—and he still had many more Grammy wins to come.

"Lover Come Back to Me"

Composers: Sigmund Romberg, Oscar Hammerstein II. **Producers:** Chet Atkins, Jerry Reed. **Musicians:** Chet Atkins (guitar), Pete Wade (guitar), Henry Strzelecki (bass), Larrie London (drums). **Location and Date of Recording:** RCA Studios, Nashville, Tennessee, June 9, 1971. **Original Release:** *Pickin' My Way* (RCA Victor album, 1971).

In the summer of 1971, Chet began work on a new instrumental album at RCA Studios in Nashville that would be entitled *Pickin' My Way*. He reached far back into his musical past for this particular record—two of its songs were new versions of numbers that had originally appeared on his first-ever album, *Chet Atkins' Gallopin' Guitar*. That album was released by RCA Victor in 1953, and it was a collection of eight of Chet's recordings on 10-inch record format. The two songs from the album that Chet chose to revisit for *Pickin' My Way* were "Lover Come Back to Me" and "Black Mountain Rag." On *Chet Atkins' Gallopin' Guitar*, both numbers had been recorded with Chet playing electric guitar unaccompanied by any other musicians. For *Pickin' My Way*, both numbers were recorded with Chet playing a classical guitar, and he was accompanied by backing musicians.

"Lover Come Back to Me" was a vocal ballad written by Sigmund Romberg and Oscar Hammerstein II for their hit 1928 operetta *The New Moon*. The success of the operetta spawned two film versions of the same name, one in 1930 and one in 1940. And over the years, "Lover Come Back to Me" became a standard that was recorded by scores of different artists. Many of these artists, including Chet, chose to interpret the song as an uptempo number, even though the song was originally written as a ballad.

Chet's recording of "Lover Come Back to Me" that appeared on *Chet Atkins' Gallopin' Guitar* was recorded on May 16, 1952, when he laid down five songs for RCA Victor at Brown Radio Productions in Nashville. That session marked the first time that Chet had ever recorded strictly unaccompanied. (Incidentally, the session also yielded Chet's first recording of "The Third Man Theme," which we discussed in detail earlier in this book.) Chet's recording of "Lover Come Back to Me" for *Pickin' My Way* was recorded at RCA Studios in Nashville on June 9, 1971.

On both the *Chet Atkins' Gallopin' Guitar* and *Pickin' My Way* versions of "Lover Come Back to Me," Chet played the song in standard tuning in the key of C. And as just mentioned, he played it as an uptempo number, though the *Pickin' My Way* version was played considerably faster than the *Chet Atkins' Gallopin' Guitar* version. The *Chet Atkins' Gallopin' Guitar* version of "Lover Come Back to Me" was very enjoyable—that said, however, the *Pickin' My Way* version was a much more impressive recording because it provided such a perfect showcase for Chet's incredible talent both as an acoustic player and a jazz player.

On the *Pickin' My Way* "Lover Come Back to Me," Chet's classical guitar is accompanied by guitar, bass, drums and percussion. Chet opens the recording by rendering the song's melody along with a simultaneously played accompanying pattern, and after about a minute, he switches to playing melody mainly through single-note soloing. This soloing is loaded with jazzy embellishments to the song's melody that are fabulously nimble and inventive—he throws in multiple hammer-ons and pull-offs, jarringly dissonant phrases, and even a few superlicks.

"Lover Come Back to Me" was chosen to be the opening track for *Pickin' My Way* when the album was released by RCA Victor in 1971. The record turned out to be quite successful, reaching the number 30 spot on the U.S. country album charts—and of course, it was also warmly received by longtime Chet fans. Incidentally, Chet would record one more excellent version of "Lover Come Back to Me" just a few years after the release of *Pickin' My Way*—he and guitarist Les Paul performed an instrumental duet of the song for their 1976 collaborative album *Chester and Lester*.

"Black Mountain Rag"

Composer: Tommy Magness. **Producers:** Chet Atkins, Jerry Reed. **Musicians:** Chet Atkins (guitar), Henry Strzelecki (bass), Larrie London (drums). **Location and Date of Recording:** RCA Studios, Nashville, Tennessee, July 14, 1971. **Original Release:** *Pickin' My Way* (RCA Victor album, 1971), RCA Victor 74–0536 (RCA Victor 45 single, 1971).

In this book's previous entry examining "Lover Come Back to Me," we began our discussion of Chet's decision to reach far back into his musical past for his 1971 instrumental album *Pickin' My Way*. For that album, Chet recorded new versions of two songs that had originally appeared on his first-ever album, the 1953 RCA Victor release *Chet Atkins' Gallopin' Guitar*. Those songs were "Lover Come Back to Me" and "Black Mountain Rag." We're done with "Lover Come Back to Me," so now we'll discuss "Black Mountain Rag."

"Black Mountain Rag" was a well-known instrumental song with a decidedly obscure history. In the late 1930s, it gained popularity as an uptempo fiddle number under the title "Black Mountain Blues." Fiddler Leslie Keith claimed to have written it by putting together bits and pieces of several traditional tunes. In 1947, fiddler Curly Fox recorded a version of the song under the title of "Black Mountain Rag," and that recording became a big seller. However, Chet did not credit either of these fiddlers for bringing "Black Mountain Rag" to his attention—he said that he learned it from hearing fiddler Tommy Magness play it, and he gave Tommy the songwriting credit for the number.

Chet recorded his first version of "Black Mountain Rag" during a session at RCA Victor's New York City studios on July 29, 1952—that version featured him playing electric guitar unaccompanied by any other musicians, and it was the one that appeared on *Chet Atkins' Gallopin' Guitar*. (Incidentally, that session also yielded the Chet-penned song "Imagination," a number we discussed earlier.)

However, this was not the only version of "Black Mountain Rag" that Chet recorded during this time period. He laid down a second version of the number during a session at RCA's Nashville studio on April 8, 1955—this version was played at a much faster tempo than the first version, and it featured Chet playing electric guitar accompanied by a lone percussionist. It was included on the 1956 version of Chet's album *Stringin' Along with Chet Atkins*.

Both of these electric guitar versions of "Black Mountain Rag" were spectacularly done by Chet, and they would always be held in high esteem by his fans as the years went by. But Chet decided that he wanted to record the song as an acoustic guitar number—so the version he did for *Pickin' My Way* was played on one of his classical guitars. This version of "Black Mountain Rag" was so musically epic that that it would turn out to be hands-down his *most* spectacular and revered version of the song. It was recorded during a session held for the album at RCA Studios in Nashville on July 14, 1971.

On the *Pickin' My Way* "Black Mountain Rag," Chet plays a classical guitar in the key of G using open G tuning. He is using the most common form of that particular style of tuning on the recording—his low E string is tuned down to D, his A string is tuned down to G, his D, G and B strings are unchanged, and his high E string is tuned down to D.

Incidentally, Chet used this same tuning configuration for his two earlier versions of "Black Mountain Rag"—but it should be pointed out that on each of these versions, he used it with a twist. On the 1952 recording of the song, Chet's guitar was tuned in this configuration, but it was tuned up a half step from open G—so instead of its strings being tuned to D-G-D-G-B-D, they were tuned to Eb-Ab-Eb-Ab-C-Eb. This meant that when Chet played out of the key of G, it sounded as if he was playing out of the key of Ab.

And for the 1955 recording of the song, his guitar was tuned in this configuration, but it was tuned up a *whole* step from open G—so instead of its strings being tuned to D-G-D-G-B-D, they were tuned to E-A-E-A-Db-E. This meant that when Chet played out of the key of G, it sounded as if he was playing out of the key of A. But for the *Pickin' My Way* "Black Mountain Rag," there was no twist on his open G tuning—it really was in the key of G.

On the *Pickin' My Way* "Black Mountain Rag," Chet is accompanied by guitar, bass, drums and percussion. The amount of music that he is able to bring out of a single guitar throughout the song is simply a wonder to behold—and he fingerpicks the number at such a blazing fast tempo that one really needs to listen to it multiple times in order to take in everything he is doing in it. His open G tuning allows him to work up an arrangement for the song that features melody lines, self-accompanying patterns, bold chord voicings, harmonics, and a whirlwind of ingenious musical phrases that connect all the different aspects of his playing together. In fact, some of these phrases are *so* ingenious that it is very hard to pick out the individual notes he is playing in them—consequently, a number of times during the song, his guitar almost sounds like it is a human voice animatedly rising and falling in conversation.

When RCA Victor released *Pickin' My Way* in 1971, they also chose to release "Black Mountain Rag" as a 45 single. That single did not end up charting, but the *Pickin' My Way* album as a whole turned out to be quite successful—it reached the number 30 spot on the U.S. country album charts. And during the years following the release of the album and single, "Black Mountain Rag" grew to be so well-loved by Chet's longtime fans that it became a regular feature in both his concert and television appearances.

"When You Wish Upon a Star"

Composers: Leigh Harline, Ned Washington. **Producers:** Chet Atkins, Jerry Reed. **Musicians:** Chet Atkins (guitar). **Location and Date of Recording:** RCA Studios, Nashville, Tennessee, July 14, 1971. **Original Release:** *Pickin' My Way* (RCA Victor album, 1971).

If the only song that Chet had recorded during the July 14, 1971, session held for his *Pickin' My Way* album at RCA Studios in Nashville had been his epic interpretation of "Black Mountain Rag," it would have been a spectacular day of work. But Chet ended up making that day twice as spectacular when he made another recording at the session that was every bit as momentous as "Black Mountain Rag." At that session, he laid down an unaccompanied classical guitar rendition of "When You Wish Upon a Star" that truly pushed the sonic boundaries of solo guitar music.

But before we get into the particulars of Chet's playing on the recording, let's go over the distinguished history of "When You Wish Upon a Star." The song was a slow-tempoed, inspirational vocal ballad written by Leigh Harline and Ned Washington for the 1940 Walt Disney animated musical film *Pinocchio*. In the film, "When You Wish Upon a Star" was sung by Cliff Edwards, playing the character of Jiminy Cricket. The number won the 1940 Academy Award for Best Original Song, and in the following years it became one of The Walt Disney Company's most iconic musical works. In fact, it was used on so many Disney television programs, and at so many Disney theme park attractions, that it essentially became the unofficial theme song of the company.

And the song's great success was not confined just to Disney works. "When You Wish Upon a Star" became a standard that was recorded by scores of artists, both as a vocal piece and as an instrumental. In fact, Chet himself had recorded an instrumental version of the song for one of his albums just a few years before he recorded it for *Pickin' My Way*—that version was featured on Chet's 1968 release *Solo Flights*.

Interestingly, Chet's *Solo Flights* version of "When You Wish Upon a Star" was *very* similar to his *Pickin' My Way* version of the song. For example, both were instrumentals that featured Chet playing a classical guitar in standard tuning out of the key of C. Also, both versions featured him using his trademark technique of playing harmonic notes paired with pure tones. (Chet first used this technique on his 1951 recording of "Good-Bye Blues," which we discussed in detail a bit earlier in this book.) Finally, in both versions he was basically unaccompanied by any other musicians. (I'm using the words "basically unaccompanied" here because on the *Solo Flights* version of the song, Chet's guitar was accompanied by a very subtle bell part.)

It might seem strange that Chet would choose to re-record a song that he had so recently featured on an album, especially when that re-recording was so similar to his earlier version—but in the case of "When You Wish Upon a Star," Chet had refined his arrangement of the number to such a high degree that he just couldn't wait to tackle it in the studio again. Most of that refinement involved using far more harmonic notes paired with pure tones.

As we just mentioned, on the *Pickin' My Way* version of "When You Wish Upon a Star," Chet plays a classical guitar in standard tuning out of the key of C, and he is unaccompanied by any other musicians. Chet delivers the entire song at a very slow, almost free time tempo. He starts off the recording by playing a series of gorgeous harmonic notes and pure tones that quickly and gracefully cascade after one another like notes being played on a harp. Then he renders the melody of the song, and a harmony part to that melody, using harmonic notes paired with pure tones.

At a little over a minute into the recording, Chet briefly switches to playing strictly regularly fretted notes, rendering the song's melody with simultaneously played accompanying patterns. And throughout the rest of the recording, Chet plays the song through a combination of regularly fretted and harmonic notes that is simply magical. The incredibly sophisticated musical phrases that he is able to create by playing harmonic notes paired with pure tones still stands as one of the greatest demonstrations of this technique ever recorded—because of this fact, the recording remains a great inspiration to many guitarists to this day.

As mentioned in this book's previous two entries, *Pickin' My Way* was quite successful when it was released by RCA Victor in 1971, reaching number the 30 spot on the U.S. country album charts—and of course, it was also warmly received by longtime Chet fans. Incidentally, Chet would record one more excellent version of "When You Wish Upon a Star" later in his career—a live performance of the song was featured on his 1980 live album *The Best of Chet on the Road ... Live*. That version generally adhered very closely to the *Pickin' My Way* version—however, it did include a number of tempo shifts and jazzy chord voicings that were not found in either of Chet's two earlier recorded versions of the song.

"The Mad Russian"

> **Composers:** Paul Yandell, Jerry Reed. **Producers:** Chet Atkins, Jerry Reed. **Musicians:** Chet Atkins (guitar), Jerry Reed (guitar), Paul Yandell (guitar), Stephen Schaffer (bass), Larrie Londin (drums). **Location and Date of Recording:** RCA Studios, Nashville, Tennessee, November 9, 1971. **Original Release:** *Me and Chet* (RCA Victor album with Jerry Reed, 1972).

In late 1971, Chet and Jerry Reed began holding sessions at RCA Studios in Nashville to record instrumentals for their second collaborative album entitled *Me and Chet*. The record was a follow-up to their 1970 Grammy Award–winning collaborative album *Me and Jerry*. *Me and Chet* was recorded during a number of different sessions held between November 1971 and March 1972.

The first session for the record was held on November 9, 1971, and it yielded just one song. That song was "The Mad Russian," a number written by Jerry Reed and guitarist Paul Yandell. Paul also played rhythm guitar on Chet and Jerry's recording of the song as well. Paul had been regularly working with Jerry since 1970, and Chet quickly became every bit as impressed by Paul's talent as Jerry had been. In fact, Paul would begin regularly working with *Chet* from the recording of "The Mad Russian" all the way up until the end of Chet's career. Simply put, Paul became Chet's right-hand man—not only did he provide steady accompaniment for Chet at countless recording sessions and live appearances for more than two decades, but he also became one of Chet's closest personal friends.

Jerry and Paul's "The Mad Russian" is a fast-paced number with an equally fast-paced, minor-key based melody, and it does have a sound to it that brings to mind a furiously paced Russian dance. On the recording, Chet plays a Gretsch electric guitar, and Jerry plays a classical guitar. The two are accompanied by guitar, bass, and drums. Chet and Jerry play the song out of the key of E minor in standard tuning—a number of times the song moves to the key of G, which considerably lightens its overall mood. On this number and every other number found on the album, Chet's guitar is mixed hard to the right, and Jerry's guitar is mixed hard to the left—so it is very easy to distinguish one man's playing from the other when listening to the song.

Jerry opens the recording by playing the song's melody through some furiously fingerpicked single-note soloing, and then Chet takes over for a round of soloing that features single-note playing paired with a wealth of harmony lines. On the whole, Chet's soloing is more relaxed and improvisational than Jerry's tricky, note-packed melody playing. The recording closes out with Jerry restating that melody one final time.

Me and Chet was released by RCA Victor in 1972—and thanks to its excellent tracks like "The Mad Russian," it ended up being quite successful, reaching the number 24 spot on the U.S. country album charts. We'll discuss one more song from the album, "Nashtown Ville," in the next entry.

"Nashtown Ville"

> **Composer:** Chet Atkins. **Producers:** Chet Atkins, Jerry Reed. **Musicians:** Chet Atkins (guitar), Jerry Reed (guitar), Paul Yandell (guitar), Henry Strzelecki (bass), Larrie Londin (drums). **Location and Date of Recording:** RCA Studios, Nashville, Tennessee, March 2, 1972. **Original Release:** *Me and Chet* (RCA Victor album with Jerry Reed, 1972).

As we just noted in our discussion of "The Mad Russian," Chet and Jerry Reed's second collaborative album *Me and Chet* was recorded during a number of different sessions held at RCA Studios in Nashville between November 1971 and March 1972. The Chet-penned instrumental "Nashtown Ville" was laid down during a four-song session for the album held on March 2, 1972.

Chet's "Nashtown Ville" is a relaxed midtempo number that features a simple but very catchy melody. Chet plays a steel-stringed acoustic guitar in standard tuning on the recording, and he is joined by Jerry playing a classical guitar that is also in standard tuning. Playing in the key of A, the two are accompanied by guitar, bass, and drums. Like all of the other numbers found on *Me and Chet*, Chet's guitar is mixed hard to the right and Jerry's guitar is mixed hard to the left on "Nashtown Ville"—so it is very easy to distinguish one man's playing from the other when listening to the song.

The recording opens with Chet rendering the song's likable melody along with a simultaneously played accompanying pattern. Jerry then adds some nice harmony lines to Chet's melody, as well as a few relaxed solo lines of his own. The recording closes with Jerry throwing in some rhythmic chord voicings that perfectly complement Chet's melody playing.

As we also noted in our discussion of "The Mad Russian," *Me and Chet* was quite successful when it was released by RCA Victor in 1972, reaching the number 24 spot on the U.S. country album charts. The next record that featured Chet teaming with Jerry would not be a collaborative album in the strictest sense of the word—the 1974 album *Chet Atkins Picks on Jerry Reed* would feature Chet covering ten Jerry-penned instrumentals, but Jerry himself would only appear on two of those ten. We'll discuss a number off of that album, "Baby's Coming Home," a bit later in this book.

"The Masterpiece"

> **Composer:** Jean-Joseph Mouret, Paul Parnes. **Producers:** Chet Atkins (Nashville), Ethel Gabriel (New York). **Musicians:** Chet Atkins (guitar), Jerry Shook (guitar), Pete Wade (guitar), Steve Schaffer (bass), Larrie Londin (drums), Farrell Morris (percussion), Louis Stone, Louis Haber, Harry Lookofsky, Elliott Rosoff, Max Hallander, Michael Comins, Aaron Rosand (violins), Seymour Berman, David Sackson

(violas), Seymour Barab, Maurice Bialkin (cellos). **Locations and Dates of Recording:** RCA Studios, Nashville, Tennessee, June 22, 1972, RCA Studios, New York City, New York, July 7, 1972. **Original Release:** *Chet Atkins Picks on the Hits* (RCA Victor album, 1973).

In May 1972, Chet began work on a new album that would be entitled *Chet Atkins Picks on the Hits*. This album was similar to the three albums in his *Solid Gold* album series in the sense that it featured expansively arranged instrumental versions of current radio hits—but obviously, it was not really a continuation of that series in the sense that it was not named *Solid Gold*, or branded with a certain year. (The individual *Solid Gold* albums were named *Solid Gold '68*, *Solid Gold '69*, and *Solid Gold '70*.) *Chet Atkins Picks on the Hits* marked a bit of a departure from Chet's normal recording routine—Chet started recording the album's songs at RCA Studios in Nashville with his backing musicians, and then those Nashville recordings were sent to RCA's New York City Studios to have string tracks added to them.

Chet laid down his tracks for "The Masterpiece," the song that would be chosen to open *Chet Atkins Picks on the Hits*, during a five-song Nashville session for the album held on June 22, 1972. String tracks for the number were recorded at a New York session held on July 7, 1972. "The Masterpiece" was a modernized version of the Rondeau from *Symphonies and Fanfares for the King's Supper* written in 1729 by the French composer Jean-Joseph Mouret. The reason that Chet's version of the song was named "The Masterpiece" was because a 1950s orchestral version of Mouret's Rondeau had recently been used as the theme music for a new PBS television series called *Masterpiece Theatre*. (That series premiered on the network in early 1971.)

On "The Masterpiece," Chet plays a classical guitar out of the key of D, and he is in standard tuning with the exception of his low E string—that string is tuned down to D. (This form of tuning is often referred to as "drop D.") Chet is backed by guitar, bass, drums, and a string section comprised of violins, violas and cellos on the recording. "The Masterpiece" opens with Chet playing unaccompanied—he renders Mouret's timeless melody through crisp single-note soloing adorned with harmony lines and rich chord voicings. Then Chet's backing musicians join in with his playing—surprisingly, Chet and company deliver the piece in a powerful, almost rocking 4/4 tempo, which makes its stately melody come across as infectiously joyful. Chet's guitar is perfectly supported by his string section's grand, exciting musical phrases from the moment they start playing with him until the very last note of the recording.

Chet Atkins Picks on the Hits was released by RCA Victor in late 1972. The record turned out to be fairly successful, reaching the number 38 spot on the U.S. country album charts. After Chet finished up this album that featured such expansive musical arrangements, he decided to revisit his passion of recording unaccompanied by any other musicians—the end result of these recordings would be his 1973 album appropriately entitled *Alone*. We'll discuss three songs off of that album in the next three entries of this book.

"The Claw"

Composer: Jerry Reed. **Producer:** Chet Atkins. **Musicians:** Chet Atkins (guitar). **Location and Date of Recording:** RCA Studios, Nashville, Tennessee, February 27, 1973. **Original Release:** *Alone* (RCA Victor album, 1973).

On February 27, 1973, Chet held a session at RCA Studios in Nashville to record songs for his new instrumental album project *Alone*. Twelve songs were recorded for the album on that day, but three of them were never released in any way, shape, or form. Another four songs were recorded for the album on March 5, 1973, but one of them was never released—consequently, just those two days of recording ended up yielding a full twelve-song album. Obviously, *Alone* was billed as an album that featured Chet playing unaccompanied by any other musicians. But in truth, Chet was not really completely alone on the record—guitarist Paul Yandell and drummer Larrie London provided very spare accompaniment on several of its numbers.

However, Chet *was* very much alone for "The Claw," an *Alone* number written by Jerry Reed. "The Claw" was a quintessential Jerry composition—it was an exhilarating fingerstyle guitar workout in the key of A that was built around a soulful, blues-based melody. Much of that melody consisted of fast hammer-ons and pull-offs played on the lower strings of the guitar that alternated with bold chord voicings.

On "The Claw," Chet plays a classical guitar in standard tuning out of the key of A, and he delivers every last note of Jerry's great song with power and excitement. Playing at a quick but solid tempo, he nails the hammer-on/pull-off-based melody of the number, and he also throws in some spectacularly fast licks consisting of multiple triplet notes.

Chet's long day of recording songs for *Alone* on February 27, 1973, was a productive day of work, to say the least—in fact, we'll be discussing two more classic numbers he recorded on that day in the next two entries of this book. And before we move on, it should be pointed out that Chet would record one more excellent version of "The Claw" late in his career. That version was recorded with the song's composer—Chet and Jerry laid down a duet of "The Claw" for their 1991 collaborative album *Sneakin' Around*.

"Take Five"

Composer: Paul Desmond. **Producer:** Chet Atkins. **Musicians:** Chet Atkins (guitar), Paul Yandell (guitar), Larrie Londin (percussion). **Location and Date of Recording:** RCA Studios, Nashville, Tennessee, February 27, 1973. **Original Release:** *Alone* (RCA Victor album, 1973).

It would be a difficult task to pick just which of the dozen instrumentals that Chet recorded for his classic 1973 album *Alone* ended up being the best-remembered of the bunch—but Chet's masterful version of "Take Five" would certainly have to be near the top of that list. Like "The Claw" (the subject of our previous entry), "Take Five" was recorded during a twelve-song session held for the album at RCA Studios in Nashville on February 27, 1973. (As we mentioned in our discussion of "The Claw," three of the songs recorded on that day were never released—the last three songs featured on the album were recorded during a session at RCA Studios in Nashville on March 5, 1973.)

"Take Five" was a jazz instrumental written by alto saxophonist Paul Desmond that was in the unusual time signature of 5/4. The song featured a hauntingly memorable, minor key-based melody crafted around that time signature. Desmond was a member of the jazz group The Dave Brubeck Quartet, and in 1959 he recorded a version of "Take Five" with them. The distinctive meter and the unforgettable melody of the song helped that recording to receive far more attention from the general public than most any other jazz song had ever received. In fact, the Dave Brubeck Quartet's version of "Take Five" eventually became the best-selling jazz single of all time. (Ironically, that single did not become a hit when it was first released in 1959—it became a hit when it was re-released in 1961.)

Chet's *Alone* version of "Take Five" is an arrangement of the song created by the noted Argentine classical guitarist Jorge Morel. On the recording, Chet plays a Gretsch electric guitar in standard tuning out of the key of E minor. Even though Chet recorded "Take Five" for an album called *Alone*, he is not really alone at all on the recording—guitarist Paul Yandell and drummer Larrie Londin provide him with some very spare percussion accompaniment. You might think it is a bit strange for me to state that Paul provides Chet with percussion accompaniment on "Take Five"— after all, Paul is credited with playing *guitar* on the song. But Paul's sole contribution to the recording is to play his electric guitar much like one would play a drum—using his hand, Paul taps out a simple beat for the song on his guitar's pickup and strings.

Chet may not be playing completely alone on "Take Five," but most all of the music found in his rendition of the song his delivered through his fabulous guitar work. He renders the song through a potent combination of expressive single-note melody playing and rich chord voicings. In other words, "Take Five" is one of those incredible Chet recordings where you know it is just him playing solo, but you still cannot help but think that you are hearing two or more guitarists playing together.

"Londonderry Air"

Composer: Traditional (arranged by Chet Atkins). **Producer:** Chet Atkins. **Musicians:** Chet Atkins (guitar). **Location and Date of Recording:** RCA Studios, Nashville, Tennessee, February 27, 1973. **Original Release:** *Alone* (RCA Victor album, 1973).

What an incredible day of recording Chet had on February 27, 1973, when he laid down a bunch of songs for his new album project *Alone*—we've already examined two of the classic songs he recorded on that day, and we're about to examine a third. The last song he laid down on that day was an achingly beautiful, unaccompanied version of "Londonderry Air." "Londonderry Air" was an Irish air written by an unknown composer sometime in the first half of the 19th century. In the early 1900s, the English songwriter Frederic Weatherly wrote a set of lyrics to accompany the air's beautiful, melancholy melody—of course, those lyrics were entitled "Danny Boy," and over the decades the air became known to far more people as "Danny Boy" than as "Londonderry Air."

Incidentally, Chet had recorded a version of "Londonderry Air" much earlier in his career—that recording was featured in the folk section of his landmark 1955 album *Chet Atkins in Three Dimensions*. Chet's 1955 version of "Londonderry Air" was very enjoyable, but it certainly did not have the kind of emotional power or musical complexity that his 1973 version had.

On "Londonderry Air," Chet plays a Gretsch electric guitar out of the key of D, and he is in standard tuning with the exception of his low E string—that string is tuned down to D. (This form of tuning is often referred to as "drop D.") Playing at a slow, almost free time tempo, he is unaccompanied by any other musicians throughout the entire song. Chet opens the recording by playing much of the song's melody through rich, imaginative chords voiced on the higher strings of his guitar. Later in the recording, he plays the song's melody along with simultaneously played accompanying patterns that prominently feature his open D-tuned low E string and his open A string—and because these strings are played completely open, they ring out with greater sustain, bringing added fullness to his overall guitar sound. Chet's playing on "Londonderry Air" also features a number of harmony lines played on the lower strings of his guitar that nicely complement his melody lines.

Alone was released by RCA Victor in 1973, and the record ended up being fairly successful, reaching the number 42 spot on the U.S. country album charts. But it could be argued that the album really turned out to be much more of an artistic success than a commercial success—after all, it offered truly compelling proof of just how amazing Chet's playing could be when it was stripped down to nothing more than the man himself and his guitar.

Incidentally, Chet would record one more excellent version of "Londonderry Air" later in his career—that recording would be featured on his 1979 album *The First Nashville Guitar Quartet*. *The First Nashville Guitar Quartet* version of "Londonderry Air" featured Chet playing classical guitar with three other classical guitarists, Liona Boyd, John Knowles, and John Pell.

"Fiddlin' Around"

Composer: Johnny Gimble. **Producers:** Bob Ferguson, Jerry Reed. **Musicians:** Chet Atkins (guitar/vocals), Johnny Gimble (fiddle/vocals), Charlie McCoy (harmonica/vocals), Paul Yandell (guitar), Jerry Shook (guitar), Weldon Myrick (steel guitar), Bobby Thompson (banjo), Hargus "Pig" Robbins (piano), Henry Strzelecki (bass), Larrie Londin (drums). **Location and Date of Recording:** RCA Studios, Nashville, Tennessee, July 30, 1973. **Original Release:** *Superpickers* (RCA Victor album, 1973), RCA Victor APBO-0146 (RCA Victor 45 single, 1973).

In the summer of 1973, Chet began work on a new instrumental album called *Superpickers*. The concept of this album was a simple one. Chet had gathered some of the finest studio musicians in Nashville to record a collection of country songs—and these songs would give Chet's group of musicians a chance to really show off their respective talents. The musicians who most prominently shared the spotlight with Chet on *Superpickers* were fiddler Johnny Gimble, harmonicist Charlie McCoy, and steel guitarist Weldon Myrick. Incidentally, this was by no means the first time that Chet had based an album around this concept of trading solos with multiple session players—in fact, he had done the exact same thing on his 1954 album *A Session with Chet Atkins*, one of his first-ever LP projects.

Recording sessions for *Superpickers* were held at RCA Studios in Nashville during June and July of 1973. Far and away the album's best-remembered song, "Fiddlin' Around," was recorded during a four-song session for the album held on July 30, 1973. "Fiddlin' Around" was a midtempo country swing number written by Johnny Gimble. The song was basically a fiddle-driven instrumental, but it also featured Johnny, Chet and Charlie trading humorous dialogue with one another in between their solo breaks. This dialogue was spoken, not sung, and it extolled the virtues of idly passing the time by playing their beloved instruments—in other words, just "fiddling around."

On "Fiddlin' Around," Chet plays a Gretsch electric guitar in standard tuning out of the key of G. He, Johnny and Charlie are accompanied by Weldon's steel guitar, as well as banjo, bass and drums. (Incidentally, guitarists Paul Yandell and Jerry Shook and pianist Hargus "Pig" Robbins are also given credit for playing on the recording—but even the most thorough listen of the song does not reveal a single note from their instruments.) Johnny solos first on "Fiddlin' Around," followed by Chet, and then Charlie. Weldon also gets the chance to offer up a short lead break, but he is never part of the song's wordplay. Both the dialogue and the great solos featured in "Fiddlin' Around" convey just how much fun Chet and company are having while making this recording.

When RCA Victor released *Superpickers* in 1973, they also chose to release "Fiddlin' Around" as a 45 single. The album itself did not end up charting, but "Fiddlin' Around" did—it reached the number 75 spot on the U.S. country single charts. And over the years, the song became fondly remembered by Chet fans as one of his most lighthearted recordings.

"I'll See You in My Dreams"

> **Composers:** Isham Jones, Gus Kahn. **Producer:** Jerry Reed, Chet Atkins. **Musicians:** Chet Atkins (guitar), Merle Travis (guitar), Jerry Reed (guitar). **Location and Date of Recording:** RCA Studios, Hollywood, California, January 16, 1974. **Original Release:** *The Atkins-Travis Traveling Show* (RCA Victor album with Merle Travis, 1974).

In January 1974, Chet traveled to RCA Studios in Hollywood, California, to hold a recording sessions for what would turn out to be one of the most historic collaborative albums he ever made throughout his entire career. At these sessions held on January 15 and 16, he and his longtime musical hero singer/guitarist Merle Travis recorded songs for their album that would be entitled *The Atkins-Travis Traveling Show*. Even though Merle had been one of Chet's primary musical inspirations for decades, the two had never recorded together before.

The Atkins-Travis Traveling Show was co-produced by Jerry Reed, who also played rhythm guitar on several of its songs. All of the guitar tracks that Chet, Merle and Jerry recorded for the album were played on acoustic guitars. Interestingly, Chet's longtime guitar sideman Paul Yandell remembered that Chet had used a Martin D-45 for all of the numbers on *The Atkins-Travis Traveling Show*—but this particular guitar was not one that Chet ever owned or played regularly, so it is a bit of a mystery as to just why he decided to record this album with it.

At any rate, nine songs were recorded for the album at the January Hollywood sessions, but four of them were never released in any way, shape, or form. Another six songs were recorded for the album back at RCA Studios in Nashville on January 23—consequently, those two days of recording on opposite sides of the country ended up yielding a full eleven-song album.

One of the numbers recorded at the January 16 Hollywood session, "I'll See You in My Dreams," was chosen to be the closing track of *The Atkins-Travis Traveling Show*. "I'll See You in My Dreams" was a midtempo pop vocal ballad written in 1924 by Isham Jones and Gus Kahn. Jones recorded a version of the song with the Ray Miller Orchestra that became a number one hit in the U.S. the following year. In the ensuing decades, the song became a standard that was recorded by many different artists, both as a vocal number and as an instrumental.

One of the artists who recorded "I'll See You in My Dreams" as an instrumental was another of Chet's longtime musical heroes, jazz guitarist Django Reinhardt—Django's first recorded version of the song was released in 1939. Django's wonderful rendition of "I'll See You in My Dreams" led Merle to start performing the song as an instrumental in the 1950s, and in 1968 he recorded a version of it for his 1968 album *Strictly Guitar*. Chet and Merle also decided to cover the song as an instrumental for *The Atkins-Travis Traveling Show*.

On "I'll See You in My Dreams," both Chet and Merle play their acoustic guitars in standard tuning out of the key of C, and they are backed by Jerry on acoustic guitar. Chet and Merle's guitars are capoed at the 2nd fret, so it sounds as if they are playing out of the key of D. On this number and every other number found on the album, Chet's guitar is mixed hard to the left, and Merle's guitar is mixed hard to the right—so it is very easy to distinguish one man's playing from the other when listening to the song.

Merle kicks off the recording by rendering the song's unforgettable melody along with a simultaneously played accompanying pattern, and then Chet steps in to take a straightforward single-note solo. After his solo, Chet hands the song back to Merle, who offers up a straightforward solo of his own. Chet then takes one more solo, and the two close out the recording by Merle restating the song's melody and Chet playing a harmony part along with that melody. Needless to say, both Chet and Merle play "I'll See You in My Dreams" beautifully—but what really makes the recording so special is that it perfectly captures the marvelous musical rapport these two legendary guitarists have with one another.

Incidentally, on *The Atkins-Travis Traveling Show*, "I'll See You in My Dreams" opened with a funny little song fragment that featured Chet and Merle singing about their "Atkins-Travis Traveling Show"—in the song, they said that it was time for them to close their act because they were out of songs. When "I'll See You in My Dreams" appeared on various compilation albums over the years, this "traveling show" bit was cut from the recording. (Actually, the "traveling show" bit was by no means the only singing on *The Atkins-Travis Traveling Show*—the album featured several enjoyable novelty vocal numbers sung by Chet and Merle.)

The Atkins-Travis Traveling Show was released by RCA Victor in 1974, and the record ended up being quite successful, reaching number the 30 spot on the U.S. country album charts. But its biggest success came in the form of a very prestigious award—at the Grammy Awards of 1974, *The Atkins-Travis Traveling Show* won the Grammy Award for Best Country Instrumental Performance. Unfortunately, even though Chet and Merle's album had been so well-received, the two would never record together again.

Here is one final note regarding "I'll See You in My Dreams"—Chet ended up recording another excellent version of the song late in his career. That version was a guitar duet with Mark Knopfler that appeared their 1990 collaborative album *Neck and Neck*. Chet used a Gibson electric guitar for that recording, and he again played the song in the key of C—but this time around he did not use a capo on his guitar.

"Baby's Coming Home"

Composer: Jerry Reed. **Producers:** Chet Atkins, Jerry Reed, Bob Ferguson. **Musicians:** Chet Atkins (guitar), Paul Yandell (guitar), Henry Strzelecki (bass), Larrie Londin (drums). **Location and Date of Recording:** RCA Studios, Nashville, Tennessee, March 7, 1974. **Original Release:** *Chet Atkins Picks on Jerry Reed* (RCA Victor album, 1974).

Not long after finishing up recording *The Atkins-Travis Traveling Show* with Merle Travis, Chet turned his attention to a new album project—this new record would be entitled *Chet Atkins Picks on Jerry Reed*, and it was an album consisting entirely of Jerry Reed-penned instrumentals. Recording sessions for *Chet Atkins Picks on Jerry Reed* were held at RCA Studios in Nashville during February and March of 1974.

Incidentally, Jerry might have written all of the songs on *Chet Atkins Picks on Jerry Reed*, but he only played on a few of them—he appeared on the numbers "Mister Lucky" and "Squirrelly." Another number that Chet laid down for the album, "Steeplechase Lane," was a remake—Chet had originally recorded that song for his 1970 album *Yestergroovin'.*

Probably the best-remembered song Chet recorded for *Chet Atkins Picks on Jerry Reed* was "Baby's Coming Home"—it was laid down during a three-song session for the album held on March 7, 1974. "Baby's Coming Home" was a bright midtempo number that featured a melody that was both very catchy and very happy-sounding.

On "Baby's Coming Home," Chet plays a Gretsch electric guitar in standard tuning out of the key of C—his guitar is capoed at the 2nd fret, so it sounds as if he is playing out of the key of D. On the recording, he is accompanied by guitar, bass, and drums. He opens the recording by rendering the song's memorable melody along with a simultaneously played accompanying pattern—and after about a minute, he switches to playing its melody through soloing that features a lovely combination of harmonic and regularly fretted notes. Chet closes out the song by again rendering the song's melody along with a simultaneous accompanying pattern. Like so much of Chet's best guitar work, his multi-layered playing on "Baby's Coming Home" creates an aural landscape that is both infectiously happy and deeply peaceful.

Chet Atkins Picks on Jerry Reed was released by RCA Victor in 1974. Jerry wrote some warm, humorous liner notes for the album that discussed his long-held admiration for Chet's playing. The album did not end up charting, but it still ended up being highly regarded by both fans of Chet and Jerry.

"The Entertainer"

Composer: Scott Joplin. **Producers:** Chet Atkins, Bob Ferguson. **Musicians:** Chet Atkins (guitar). **Location and Date of Recording:** RCA Studios, Nashville, Tennessee, July 24, 1974. **Original Release:** RCA Victor PB-10046 (RCA Victor 45 single, 1974), *Chet Atkins Goes to the Movies* (RCA Victor album, 1976).

During a single-song session held at RCA Studios in Nashville on July 24, 1974, Chet recorded an unaccompanied version of "The Entertainer" that would end up being the focal point of his album *Chet Atkins Goes to the Movies*. "The Entertainer" was a piano rag written by the famed ragtime composer Scott Joplin in 1902. Throughout the years, the song became widely regarded as one of the greatest ragtime musical works ever created, and it became even more well-known when it was used as the theme music for the 1973 Oscar-winning film *The Sting* starring Paul Newman and Robert Redford.

The arrangement for Chet's version of "The Entertainer" was created by John Knowles, a talented fingerstyle guitarist/arranger who would become one of Chet's closest musical collaborators over the next two decades. John's guitar arrangement of "The Entertainer" was played in the key of D, with the instrument's low E string tuned down to D. (This form of tuning is often referred to as "drop D.") On Chet's recording of "The Entertainer," he plays a classical guitar, and his thoughtful rendering of John's richly layered arrangement makes the song sound every bit as timeless as a guitar piece as it had a piano piece.

RCA Victor released "The Entertainer" as a 45 single in 1974, but the recording would make far more of an impression when it was included on Chet's album *Chet Atkins Goes to the Movies* released by the label in 1976. At the Grammy Awards of 1976, "The Entertainer" won the Grammy Award for Best Country Instrumental Performance. (Incidentally, the rest of the *Chet Atkins Goes to the Movies* album was recorded during sessions held at RCA Studios in Nashville in late 1974, and it achieved a fair amount of success in its own right, reaching the number 43 spot on the U.S. country album charts.)

Incidentally, Chet did record one more version of "The Entertainer" late in his career—it was created for his album *The Magic of Chet Atkins* released in 1990 by Heartland Music. On *The Magic of Chet Atkins* "The Entertainer," Chet was backed by strings, keyboards, bass, and drums, and he played a Gibson Chet Atkins CE guitar. (The CE was the solidbody acoustic that Chet and Gibson designed together in the early 1980s—we discussed it in detail in the second chapter of this book.)

This version of "The Entertainer" was pleasant enough, but very few people ever heard it because the album it was on never received any sort of widespread release. Heartland Music was a division of CBS Special Products that specialized in the kind of direct-to-customer releases only found in mail-order catalogs. Consequently, *The Magic of Chet Atkins* ended up being a decidedly obscure album that was familiar only to the most devoted Chet fans.

"The Night Atlanta Burned"

Composer: John D. Loudermilk. **Producers:** Chet Atkins, Bob Ferguson. **Musicians:** Chet Atkins (guitar), Paul Yandell (guitar), Lisa Silver (violin), Robert Taylor (mandolin). **Location and Date of Recording:** RCA Studios, Nashville, Tennessee, April 23, 1975. **Original Release:** *The Night Atlanta Burned* (RCA Victor album with The Atkins String Company, 1975), RCA Victor PB-10346 (RCA Victor 45 single with the Atkins String Company, 1975).

By the mid–1970s, Chet's recording career had been going on for almost three decades, and his long list of achievements was so impressive that he had inarguably reached "legend" status. That status was certainly confirmed by the fact that he had recently had received one of the highest honors he would ever receive—in 1973, he was inducted into the Country Music Hall of Fame. But all of this good work certainly came at a price—in fact, over the years Chet had been working so hard as both a recording executive and a performing artist that he had been feeling more and more burnt-out. Consequently, he felt it was time for him to step away from the power position he had maintained at RCA Victor, and to focus more on his own musical pursuits.

Some of these pursuits were definitely far more artistically driven than commercially driven—this was certainly the case with his 1975 album *The Night Atlanta Burned*. This album was not even released under his own name—instead, it was released under the billing "The Atkins String Company." The premise of the album was to blend country, folk and bluegrass music with the sensibilities of a classical string quartet. The nucleus of musicians that Chet used for this project were himself and Paul Yandell on guitar, Lisa Silver on violin and viola, and Johnny Gimble on mandolin.

The first session for *The Night Atlanta Burned* was held at RCA Studios in Nashville on April 23, 1975—it yielded two songs, one of them being the album's fast-tempoed title track written by John D. Loudermilk. (Of course, the title "The Night Atlanta Burned" referred to the Union Army's burning of the city of Atlanta during the American Civil War.) Loudermilk actually wrote a total of four songs for the album—like most all of the songs featured on the record, his compositions were rooted in country, folk and bluegrass.

Chet, Paul and Lisa all played on the April 23 session, but apparently Johnny did not—instead, its mandolin parts were credited to a mandolinist named Robert Taylor. At any rate, like all of the songs found on *The Night Atlanta Burned*, its title track very much did maintain the sensibilities of a classical string quartet. None of the song's instrumental parts stood out from one another—instead, they locked in together to create a larger, richly detailed musical portrait.

Given the nature of this musical project, it is rather hard to discuss Chet's guitar part on "The Night Atlanta Burned" separate from the rest of the recording. However, it can be pointed out that Chet plays a classical guitar in the key of D, and his low E string is tuned to D. (This form of tuning is often referred to as "drop D.") He renders much of the song's buoyant melody along with Lisa and Robert—and Robert incorporates brief strains of the Civil War-related songs "The Battle Hymn of the Republic" and "Dixie" into his part.

When RCA Victor released *The Night Atlanta Burned* in 1975, they also chose to release "The Night Atlanta Burned" as a 45 single. Ironically, even though this album project was not created with commercial interests in mind, both the album and its single ended up being fairly successful— *The Night Atlanta Burned* reached the number 30 spot on the U.S. country album charts, and its title track reached the number 77 spot on the U.S. country single charts. Perhaps even more importantly, *The Night Atlanta Burned* helped to set the tone for the remainder of Chet's recording career—the majority of his album projects would be more collaborative in nature, and they would reflect his own musical interests far more than commercial interests.

"Caravan"

Composer: Duke Ellington, Irving Mills, Juan Tizol. **Producer:** Chet Atkins. **Musicians:** Chet Atkins (guitar), Les Paul (guitar), Paul Yandell (guitar), Ray Edenton (guitar), Bobby Thompson (guitar), Randy Goodrum (piano), Henry Strzelecki (bass), Bob Moore (bass), Larrie Londin (drums). **Location and Date of Recording:** RCA Studios, Nashville, Tennessee, May 6, 1975. **Original Release:** *Chester and Lester* (RCA Victor album with Les Paul, 1976).

In the spring of 1975, Chet and the legendary guitarist Les Paul teamed up to make their first collaborative album. Needless to say, this was a truly historic pairing, because these two giants of the guitar world had never recorded together. And it didn't take anything more than just listing the given names of the two men to give their album a very catchy title—the record was dubbed *Chester and Lester*.

Chet and Les held recording sessions for *Chester and Lester* at RCA Studios in Nashville on May 6 and 7, 1975—working with some of Chet's top studio musicians, they laid down six instrumentals on May 6 and seven instrumentals on May 7. Out of these thirteen songs, ten were included on the album.

Chet's longtime guitar sideman Paul Yandell participated in the *Chester and Lester* sessions, and he remembered that they were surprisingly informal. Chet and Les would work out basic arrangements for the songs they were going to record, quickly run through them, and then commit them to tape. Paul also recalled that both Chet and Les did almost no re-recording or overdubbing of their guitar parts—consequently, most everything the two played on the record was worked out spontaneously. As it turned out, Chet and Les definitely did not need to put one more bit of preparation into *Chester and Lester* than they did—the album would end up being a truly remarkable work, one that perfectly captured the musical meeting of two undisputed geniuses of the guitar.

One of the particularly memorable numbers that Chet and Les recorded on May 6 was their version of "Caravan." "Caravan" was a 1936 jazz number written by Duke Ellington, Irving Mills, and Juan Tizol. Ellington began regularly performing the song with his orchestra that same year, and its exotic, chromatic note-based melody quickly made it a favorite among audiences. Ellington's 1937 recording of "Caravan" became a top five hit in the U.S.—and in the years that followed, the song became a jazz standard that was recorded by scores of artists. The song was usually played as an instrumental, just like Ellington's hit recording of it had been played. However, "Caravan" had initially been composed with lyrics, so quite a few vocal versions of the song were recorded as well.

Both Chet and Les had recorded instrumental versions of "Caravan" earlier in their careers, and those versions were recorded around roughly the same time. Les's first version of the song was released in 1950, and it was one of his groundbreaking multitrack recording experiments—it featured multiple sped-up guitar tracks that sounded like eerie music coming from a distant alien planet. Chet's first recorded version of the song was done for his classic 1954 album *A Session with Chet Atkins*—that recording was a jazzy, slightly dreamy affair that featured Chet sharing his soloing time with celeste and steel guitar.

On the *Chester and Lester* version of "Caravan," Chet plays his 1959 Gretsch Chet Atkins Country Gentleman electric guitar in standard tuning, and Les plays a Gibson Les Paul, which is also in standard tuning. They play the song at a very fast tempo out of the key of D minor, and they are accompanied by guitar, piano, bass, and drums. (Incidentally, the credits for the May 6 session list multiple rhythm guitarists and bassists, so it is impossible to know for sure just which musicians played on which songs—but at least a few of these players are present on "Caravan.")

Chet opens the recording by rendering the song's melody along with a simultaneously played accompanying pattern, and Les answers Chet's playing with bursts of dramatic, dissonant chord voicings. Les then steps in to take a straightforward single-note solo that is packed with volleys of blindingly fast flatpicking. After his solo, Les hands the song back to Chet, who offers up some single-note soloing of his own. During this soloing, Chet matches Les's fast playing by throwing in a few superlicks. Chet and Les then close out the recording by joining forces and playing the song's melody in unison. The number fades out with Les getting a few last improvisational licks in.

It is just amazing to hear two such incredibly talented, and incredibly different, guitar legends play together on "Caravan" and the rest of *Chester and Lester*. The music they create is decidedly jazz-based, but even more so, it is simply *Chet* and *Les*. Chet's playing is silky smooth, and Les's playing is jagged and biting—but their contrasting guitar styles join together to create a musical experience that is a for-the-ages masterpiece.

Chester and Lester was released by RCA Victor in 1976, and the record ended up being very successful, reaching number the 11 spot on the U.S. country album charts. And *Chester and Lester* would go on to reach even greater heights of success—at the Grammy Awards of 1976, the album won the Grammy Award for Best Country Instrumental Performance. We'll discuss one more number from *Chester and Lester*, "Avalon," in the next entry of this book.

"Avalon"

Composer: Buddy DeSylva, Al Jolson, Vincent Rose. **Producer:** Chet Atkins. **Musicians:** Chet Atkins (guitar), Les Paul (guitar), Paul Yandell (guitar), Ray Edenton (guitar), Bobby Thompson (guitar), Randy Goodrum (piano), Henry Strzelecki (bass), Bob Moore (bass), Larrie Londin (drums). **Location and Date of Recording:** RCA Studios, Nashville, Tennessee, May 7, 1975. **Original Release:** *Chester and Lester* (RCA Victor album with Les Paul, 1976).

As we just noted in our discussion of "Caravan," Chet and Les Paul held recording sessions for their legendary 1976 album *Chester and Lester* at RCA Studios in Nashville on May 6 and 7, 1975—working with some of Chet's top studio musicians, they laid down six instrumentals on May 6 and seven instrumentals on May 7. Out of these thirteen songs, ten were included on the album.

As we also noted in our discussion of "Caravan," *Chester and Lester* was a true masterwork because it was such a perfect blend of Chet and Les's contrasting guitar styles. That said, however, Chet and Les didn't let the pressure of creating a momentous album stop them from having a lot of fun during the recording of that album. Nowhere was this fact more apparent than on their version of "Avalon," which was laid down on May 7.

"Avalon" was a 1920 pop vocal number written by Buddy DeSylva, Al Jolson, and Vincent Rose. Jolson recorded the song the following year, and that recording became a top five hit in the United States. In the years that followed, "Avalon" became a jazz standard that was recorded by many different artists, both as a vocal number and an instrumental.

Chet had recorded an excellent instrumental version of "Avalon" earlier in his career. That version was laid down on March 9, 1954, during a session held at RCA Victor's studios in Chicago with Chet's longtime musical collaborators, rhythm guitarist Henry "Homer" Haynes and mandolinist Kenneth "Jethro" Burns. (Incidentally, that session also yielded "Downhill Drag," a Chet/Boudleaux Bryant instrumental we discussed in detail earlier.) Chet's first version of "Avalon" was included on an Extended Play 45 entitled *Chet Atkins and His Guitar* released by RCA Victor in 1955.

Of course, for *Chester and Lester* Chet and Les also chose to cover "Avalon" as an instrumental—that said, however, their version of number did contain a good amount of memorably funny dialogue. (We'll discuss that dialogue in detail in just a moment.)

On "Avalon," Chet plays his 1959 Gretsch Chet Atkins Country Gentleman electric guitar in standard tuning, and Les plays a Gibson Les Paul, which is also in standard tuning. They play the song in the key of F, and they are accompanied by guitar, piano, bass, and drums. (Incidentally, the credits for the May 7 session list multiple rhythm guitarists and bassists, so it is impossible to know for sure just which musicians played on which songs—but at least a few of these players are present on "Avalon.")

The recording opens with Chet, Les and their backing musicians playing the song at a relaxed tempo. Les renders the song's melody through single-note soloing, and Chet supports that soloing by offering up a variety of chord voicings, accompanying patterns, and harmony lines. Les then steps back in order to let Chet take a nice solo of his own. After Chet's lead break, Les and Chet trade some fast, nimbly played solo lines with one another, and then Les closes out the song by restating the song's melody through single-note soloing.

But as it turns out, the recording is far from over. Chet starts bantering with Les, telling him that they need to play the song at a faster tempo—then playing at breakneck speed, Chet kicks off the song a second time. Les and the backing musicians join in with him, and everyone tears through the song with abandon. Chet and Les lay out midway through this second version of the tune, and they start up a conversation. Chet tells Les about a particular live performance he had done with a symphony—at that performance, he forgot to zip up the pants of his tuxedo. After much laughter, the two close out the recording with a bit more great playing.

When *Chester and Lester* was released by RCA Victor in 1976, and the record ended up being very successful, reaching number the 11 spot on the U.S. country album charts and winning the 1976 Grammy Award for Best Country Instrumental Performance. Since *Chester and Lester* turned out to be so well-received, it was no surprise that Chet and Les would decide to record another album together two years later. We'll discuss that album entitled *Guitar Monsters* a bit later in the book when we examine one of its standout tracks, "It Don't Mean a Thing (If It Ain't Got That Swing)."

"Frog Kissin'"

Composer: Buddy Kalb. **Producer:** Chet Atkins. **Musicians:** Chet Atkins (guitar/vocals), Ray Stevens (keyboards/vocals), Jack Williams (bass), Jerry Carrigan (drums), The Nashville Sounds (vocal accompaniment). **Location and Date of Recording:** RCA Studios, Nashville, Tennessee, March 25, 1976. **Original Release:** *The Best of Chet Atkins and Friends* (RCA Victor album, 1976), RCA Victor PB-10614 (RCA Victor 45 single, 1976).

In early 1976, Chet began work on a new album project that would be entitled *The Best of Chet Atkins and Friends.* As evidenced by its title, this record was billed as a "greatest hits" collection of Chet's collaborative work with other artists over the years—but in reality, the record was far more than just a compilation of previously released songs. About half of its numbers were ones that were pulled from Chet's catalog of past releases, and the other half of its numbers were new songs that Chet recorded specifically for the album.

One of these new songs was the novelty vocal ballad "Frog Kissin'" written by Buddy Kalb, a songwriter who regularly worked with the renowned country/comedy singer Ray Stevens. Chet and Ray decided to team up and record a version of Buddy's song for Chet's new album—so they laid down "Frog Kissin'" during a session held at RCA Studios in Nashville on March 25, 1976.

In the liner notes Chet penned for *The Best of Chet Atkins and Friends*, he stated that Ray not only arranged and produced "Frog Kissin'," but also sang and played keyboards on the number. But even though Ray was so involved in the creation of "Frog Kissin'," the recording itself was definitely a showcase for Chet—and it did not spotlight his guitar work, it spotlighted his vocal work. Chet sang lead on the number, turning in a charming, low-key vocal performance that fit perfectly with the song's feel-good theme.

That theme was inspired by the age-old fairy tale plot device of a princess kissing a frog, and that frog turning into a handsome prince. In other words, every last person in the world, even some pour soul who was totally down on their luck, could find happiness if they could find someone who would just love them for who they were.

This is the first Chet song we've discussed in this book that doesn't prominently feature his guitar playing—in fact, even though the studio credits for "Frog Kissin'" list him as playing guitar, there really isn't a note of guitar to be heard in the number. So we'll have to look at this song a bit differently from the way we've looked at all of the other songs found in this book.

As mentioned above, Chet delivers a very likable lead vocal on "Frog Kissin'," and his cheery singing heightens the overall lighthearted feel of the recording. Ray sings in perfect harmony with Chet on the song's choruses, and he offers up a wealth of croaky-sounding electric keyboard parts that keep the number's "frog" theme at the front and center of the recording. Incidentally, "Frog Kissin'" sounds as if it is being played in front of a live audience, but it isn't—all of the applause and laughter heard during the recording has been dubbed in, much like a laugh track that has been added to the episode of a sitcom.

When RCA Victor released *The Best of Chet Atkins and Friends* in late 1976, they also chose to release "Frog Kissin'" as a 45 single. Both the album and its single ended up being quite successful—*The Best of Chet Atkins and Friends* reached the number 25 spot on the U.S. country album charts, and "Frog Kissin'" reached the number 40 spot on the U.S. country single charts. This marked the first time that one of Chet's vocal numbers had charted as a single—so after three decades of recording, Chet was now officially a singing star.

"Frog Kissin'" was not the only new song Chet recorded for *The Best of Chet Atkins and Friends* that would turn out to be among his all-time best—in fact, we'll be discussing three more classic numbers recorded for the album just a bit later in this book.

"Cascade"

Composer: Gene Slone. **Producer:** Bob Ferguson. **Musicians:** Chet Atkins (guitar), Paul Yandell (guitar), Mark Casstevens (guitar), Randy Goodrum (clavinet), Hargus "Pig" Robbins (piano), Bob Moore (bass), Larrie Londin (drums). **Location and Date of Recording:** RCA Studios, Nashville, Tennessee, July 23, 1976. **Original Release:** *Me and My Guitar* (RCA Victor album, 1977) RCA Victor PB-11071 (RCA Victor 45 single, 1977).

On July 23, 1976, Chet held a recording session at RCA Studios in Nashville. One of the instrumentals laid down at this session, "Terry on the Turnpike," would end up being one of the duet numbers featured on Chet's album *The Best of Chet Atkins and Friends*. (We'll discuss that song in detail in the next entry of this book.) But another one of the instrumentals recorded at this session, "Cascade," would not be featured on that album because it was definitely an "all Chet" number. Chet's version of "Cascade" was chosen to be the opening track for his 1977 album *Me and My Guitar*. The number was a fast-tempoed guitar workout composed by songwriter/guitarist Gene Slone. "Cascade" sounded for all the world like it could had been written by the master guitar composer (and Chet's close friend) Jerry Reed—the song featured an inventive, note-packed melody that flew up, down, and across all the strings of the guitar.

Of course, Chet does Gene Slone proud on his rendition of "Cascade." On the recording, Chet plays a classical guitar that sounds as if it being recorded through a pickup, and he is accompanied by guitar, clavinet, piano, bass, and drums. Playing in the key of C, Chet's renders the song's jackrabbit-quick melody mainly through single-string soloing—however, that soloing is embellished with some harmonic passages and some simultaneously played harmony lines. About midway through the recording, Chet briefly moves the song to the key of G, and then he returns it to C. The melody of "Cascade" is so spectacularly quick that one might think it would have to be played in more of a hard-hitting, percussive style, much like Jerry Reed's playing—but amazingly, Chet's delivery of that lightning-quick melody is just as smooth as silk.

There is probably no way of knowing just what guitar Chet used to record the songs he laid down at his July 23 session, including "Cascade"—but his guitar sound on the songs he recorded that day is so similar to the guitar sound that he got on his May 24, 1968 recording of "Blue Angel" that one might guess he used the same guitar for both recording sessions. It is a known fact that Chet used his Juan Estruch classical outfitted with a Baldwin Prismatone pickup for "Blue Angel"—so maybe he used that same guitar/pickup combination for the July 23 session that produced "Cascade."

When RCA Victor released *Me and My Guitar* in 1977, they also chose to release a 45 single from the album that featured both its title track and "Cascade." (Incidentally, the song "Me and My Guitar" was written by James Taylor, and it was a bluesy vocal number sung by Chet about the kinship that can develop between a guitar player and their instrument.) Neither song from that single ended up charting, but the *Me and My Guitar* album as a whole ended up being fairly successful—it reached the number 50 spot on the U.S. country album charts.

"Terry on the Turnpike"

Composer: Chet Atkins. **Producer:** Chet Atkins. **Musicians:** Chet Atkins (guitar), Boots Randolph (saxophone), Paul Yandell (guitar), Mark Casstevens (guitar),

Randy Goodrum (clavinet), Hargus "Pig" Robbins (piano), Bob Moore (bass), Larrie Londin (drums). **Location and Dates of Recording:** RCA Studios, Nashville, Tennessee, July 23, 1976 and September 3, 1976. **Original Release:** *The Best of Chet Atkins and Friends* (RCA Victor album, 1976).

As we just noted in our discussion of "Cascade," Chet's July 23, 1976, recording session at RCA Studios in Nashville yielded not only that instrumental, but also the instrumental "Terry on the Turnpike." Chet chose to hold off on releasing "Cascade" for about a year (it was included on his 1977 album *Me and My Guitar*), but "Terry on the Turnpike" was slated for inclusion on his 1976 album *The Best of Chet Atkins and Friends.* This was because "Terry on the Turnpike" was crafted to be a duet with Chet and his longtime musical collaborator, saxophonist Boots Randolph. Chet and Boots had been playing together since the late 1950s, and they even regularly toured with one another—during the 1960s and 1970s, Chet, Boots and pianist Floyd Cramer hit the road together to perform a series of concerts known as *The Music Masters.*

"Terry on the Turnpike" was a Chet composition based on the centuries-old traditional tune "Paddy on the Turnpike," and it was a fast-tempoed number that featured a driving, high-spirited melody. In other words, it was the perfect number to showcase the exciting musical rapport between Chet and Boots. The song was recorded during two separate sessions—Chet and his backing musicians laid down tracks for the num-

Chet Atkins with a Gretsch Chet Atkins Country Gentleman electric guitar during a concert performance with saxophonist Boots Randolph (middle) and pianist Floyd Cramer (right), circa 1970.

ber at the July 23 session, and Boots added his parts for the song at a session held on September 3.

On "Terry on the Turnpike," Chet plays a classical guitar that sounds as if it being recorded through a pickup, and he is accompanied by Boots's sax, guitar, clavinet, piano, bass, and drums. (As we noted in our discussion of "Cascade," it seems like a good possibility that Chet might have been using his Juan Estruch classical outfitted with a Baldwin Prismatone pickup for the songs he recorded on July 23—and that includes "Terry on the Turnpike.") Playing in the key of G, Chet opens the recording by rendering the song's rapid-fire melody through crisp single-string soloing. About midway through the number, Chet steps back in order to let Boots take a rousing solo break. The two close out the recording by Boots playing the song's melody, and Chet playing nice high harmony part along with that melody.

RCA Victor released *The Best of Chet Atkins and Friends* in late 1976, and the record ended up being quite successful, reaching the number 25 spot on the U.S. country album charts. We'll be discussing two more classic numbers recorded for that album in the next two entries of this book.

"Sweet Georgia Brown"

Composers: Ben Bernie, Maceo Pinkard, Kenneth Casey. **Producer:** Chet Atkins. **Musicians:** Chet Atkins (guitar), Lenny Breau (guitar). **Location and Date of Recording:** RCA Studios, Nashville, Tennessee, September 3, 1976. **Original Release:** *The Best of Chet Atkins and Friends* (RCA Victor album, 1976).

As we just noted in this book's previous entry, Chet held a recording session with Boots Randolph at RCA Studios in Nashville on September 3, 1976, to lay down tracks for their instrumental duet "Terry on the Turnpike" that was featured on Chet's album *The Best of Chet Atkins and Friends*. That day would turn out to be a particularly memorable one in the history of Chet's recording career, because in addition to working with Boots, Chet laid down two other duets with two separate artists for *The Best of Chet Atkins and Friends*—and these duets would go on to be remembered as two of Chet's all-time best recordings. The first of these duets was an instrumental version of "Sweet Georgia Brown" that Chet recorded with jazz guitarist Lenny Breau.

As we have made our way through the history of Chet's recording career, we have discussed the legendary guitarists that greatly influenced his playing style—these guitarists include Merle Travis, Django Reinhardt, Les Paul and Jerry Reed. Lenny Breau was inarguably a guitarist who influenced Chet every bit as much as these renowned players. Lenny was born into a musically gifted family in 1951—his parents were professional musicians, and he followed in their footsteps by taking up the guitar at a young age. Lenny gravitated toward fingerstyle guitar playing, and Chet's music became one of his main musical inspirations.

As the years went by, Lenny evolved into one of the true geniuses of the guitar—his playing blended jazz, country, classical and flamenco styles, and his abilities were so extraordinary that he could simultaneously play a number of complex guitar parts that were almost wholly independent of one another. Lenny expanded Chet's use of artificial harmonics by playing them using pull-offs, which allowed him to construct spectacularly fast harmonic patterns.

Chet was so impressed by Lenny's talent that he signed Lenny to an RCA Victor recording contract in the late 1960s, but unfortunately Lenny developed drug and alcohol problems that prevented him from ever reaching his full potential as a recording artist. He did still manage to create a precious few incredible guitar albums, and he also occasionally recorded with Chet. One of the first songs that Chet and Lenny recorded together was "Sweet Georgia Brown."

"Sweet Georgia Brown" was a jazz/pop vocal number written in 1925 by Ben Bernie, Maceo Pinkard, and Kenneth Casey. That same year, Ben Bernie and his orchestra recorded an instrumental version of the song, and that recording became a number one hit in the U.S. In the years that followed, the song became a jazz standard that was recorded by scores of artists. The song was usually played as an instrumental, just like Bernie's hit recording of it had been played. (Incidentally, Chet had recorded an instrumental version of the song a number of years before he recorded it with Lenny—that version was featured on his 1968 album *Hometown Guitar*.)

On "Sweet Georgia Brown," Chet plays a Gretsch electric guitar in standard tuning, and Lenny plays an electric guitar which is also in standard tuning. They play the song at a relaxed tempo in the key of G, and they are not accompanied by any other musicians. On the number, Chet's guitar is mixed hard to the left, and Lenny's guitar is mixed hard to the right—so it is very easy to distinguish one man's playing from the other when listening to the song.

Chet and Lenny open the recording by Chet rendering the song's melody along with a simultaneously played accompanying pattern, and Lenny playing answering phrases to that melody. The two then play some chiming harmonic patterns together, and after these harmonics, Chet turns the song almost completely over to Lenny. Lenny delivers the song's melody along with an incredible array of simultaneously played, musically sophisticated backing patterns. All that Chet does to accompany Lenny's lead break is to play his own guitar much like one would play a drum—using his hand, he taps out a simple beat for the song on his guitar's pickup and strings.

Lenny then turns the song over to Chet, who turns in a smooth, inventive solo break of his own. Unlike Lenny's lead break, Chet's lead break features a wealth of single-note soloing—so Lenny keeps playing along with Chet, providing chord-based accompaniment for him. The two then close out the recording by Chet again rendering the song's melody along with a simultaneously played accompanying pattern, and Lenny playing answering phrases to that melody.

The musical bond that Chet and Lenny shared was nothing short of astounding, and "Sweet Georgia Brown" is perfect evidence of that bond. Throughout the recording, the two players move as one, and they end up creating a sonic portrait that is a timeless masterwork. Chet and Lenny would eventually record an entire album together called *Standard Brands*—we'll discuss a song from that album, "Polka Dots and Moonbeams," later.

"Do I Ever Cross Your Mind"

Composer: Dolly Parton. **Producer:** Chet Atkins. **Musicians:** Chet Atkins (guitar/vocals), Dolly Parton (guitar/vocals). **Location and Date of Recording:** RCA Studios, Nashville, Tennessee, September 3, 1976. **Original Release:** *The Best of Chet Atkins and Friends* (RCA Victor album, 1976).

Chet's day of work at RCA Studios in Nashville on September 3, 1976, for his album project *The Best of Chet Atkins and Friends* was a very productive one. In addition to recording duets with Boots Randolph and Lenny Breau on that day, he also recorded a duet with country superstar Dolly Parton. Chet had known Dolly since she had first moved to Nashville in the mid–1960s, and over the years they had become close friends. The two of them decided to record a song that Dolly had written called "Do I Ever Cross Your Mind" for inclusion on Chet's new album. Dolly had written the song in 1973, but she had not recorded or released it in any form before she and Chet took it into the studio.

"Do I Ever Cross Your Mind" was a sweet, simple country vocal ballad that sounded for all the world as if it could have been a traditional folk song that had been around for generations. In keeping with the song's unpretentious nature, Chet and Dolly chose to record it with nothing more than just the two of them singing and playing classical guitars.

For this recording, Chet used a new classical guitar that he had recently acquired. In the early 1970s, Chet had met a Kentucky luthier named Hascal Haile, and Hascal ended up building a number of classical guitars for him. In 1975, Hascal built one for Chet that featured ornate inlay work created by DiAnne Patrick—this instrument was the one that Chet played on "Do I Ever Cross Your Mind."

On "Do I Ever Cross Your Mind," Chet plays his Hascal Haile with its low E string tuned down to D. (This form of tuning is often referred to as "drop D.") Dolly plays a classical guitar in standard tuning that is capoed at the second fret. The two perform the song at a moderately fast tempo out of the key of D. (Technically, Dolly plays out of the key of C, but since her guitar is capoed, it sounds as if she is playing in D.)

On the number, Chet's guitar and vocals are mixed hard to the left, and Dolly's guitar and vocals are mixed hard to the right—so it is very easy to distinguish Chet's playing from Dolly's when listening to the song. (Of course, their vocal parts would have been easy to distinguish from one another no matter how they had been mixed.)

Chet and Dolly open the recording with a little guitar intro—Chet renders the song's melody along with a simultaneously played accompanying pattern, and Dolly fingerpicks along with him. Dolly sings lead on the song, and she beautifully delivers its heartfelt lyrics about someone lamenting over a lost love. Chet occasionally chimes in with some nicely sung low harmony parts—charmingly, he flubs the lyrics of his very first part, and he chides himself with an "aha," much to Dolly's amusement.

In between the song's verses, Chet and Dolly offer up some informal, toe-tapping country guitar playing. During this playing, Chet casually throws in some licks that are both spectacularly fast and very tasteful. The two sound so comfortable playing and singing together on "Do I Ever Cross Your Mind" that if one didn't know any better, one would assume they had been regularly performing as a duo for years and years.

As mentioned a bit earlier in this book, RCA Victor released *The Best of Chet Atkins and Friends* in late 1976, and the record ended up being quite successful, reaching the number 25 spot on the U.S. country album charts. In the years following the release of that album, "Do I Ever Cross Your Mind" became an increasingly noteworthy number in Dolly's repertoire. She recorded a solo version of the song that appeared on her 1982 album *Heartbreak Express*—that version was also released as a single that same year, and it became a number one country hit in the United States. Also, she and

Chet recorded a second version of "Do I Ever Cross Your Mind" later in their careers—the two of them teamed with country singer Randy Travis to record an excellent version of the song for Randy's 1990 album *Heroes & Friends*.

"It Don't Mean a Thing (If It Ain't Got That Swing)"

Composers: Duke Ellington, Irving Mills. **Producer:** Bob Ferguson. **Musicians:** Chet Atkins (guitar), Les Paul (guitar), Paul Yandell (guitar), Randy Goodrum (piano), Joe Osborne (bass), Randy Hauser (drums). **Location and Date of Recording:** RCA Studios, Nashville, Tennessee, November 16, 1977. **Original Release:** *Guitar Monsters* (RCA Victor album with Les Paul, 1978).

In November 1977, Chet and Les Paul began holding sessions at RCA Studios in Nashville to record songs for their second collaborative album entitled *Guitar Monsters*. The record was a follow-up to their 1976 Grammy Award-winning collaborative album *Chester and Lester*. Like *Chester and Lester*, *Guitar Monsters* was recorded in its entirety at RCA Studios in Nashville within the span of just a few days. Working with some of Chet's top studio musicians, Chet and Les laid down numbers for the album on November 15 (two songs), 16 (four songs) and 18 (six songs). Out of these twelve songs, all but one were included on the album. The majority of the numbers on *Guitar Monsters* were instrumentals, but the album did contain a few novelty vocal numbers sung by Chet and Les.

Generally speaking, Chet and Les used the same winning formula to create *Guitar Monsters* that they had used to create *Chester and Lester*. The two would work out basic arrangements for the songs they were going to record, quickly run through them, and then commit them to tape. Chet and Les did very little re-recording or overdubbing of their guitar parts—consequently, most everything the two played on the record was worked out spontaneously.

One of the standout tracks on *Guitar Monsters* was Chet and Les's rendition of "It Don't Mean a Thing (If It Ain't Got That Swing)," which was recorded on November 16. "It Don't Mean a Thing (If It Ain't Got That Swing)" was a jazz vocal number written by Duke Ellington and Irving Mills in 1931. Ellington began regularly performing the song with his orchestra the following year, and its wonderfully catchy music and lyrics quickly made it a favorite among audiences. In the years that followed, the song became a jazz standard that was recorded by scores of artists. The song was usually played as a vocal number, just like Ellington's orchestra played it. However, there were still quite a few artists who chose to render "It Don't Mean a Thing (If It Ain't Got That Swing)" as an instrumental.

One of those artists was Chet—he had recorded an excellent instrumental version of the song that was included on his 1964 album *My Favorite Guitars*. On that version of "It Don't Mean a Thing (If It Ain't Got That Swing)," Chet played a Gretsch electric guitar, and he was backed by guitar, piano, vibes, bass and drums. For *Guitar Monsters*, Chet and Les also chose to cover the song as an instrumental.

On the *Guitar Monsters* "It Don't Mean a Thing (If It Ain't Got That Swing)," Chet plays his 1959 Gretsch Chet Atkins Country Gentleman electric guitar in standard tuning, and Les plays a Gibson Les Paul, which is also in standard tuning. They play the song in the key of E, and they are accompanied by guitar, piano, bass, and drums. Actually, the marvelously inventive melody of "It Don't Mean a Thing (If It

Ain't Got That Swing)," makes it a bit difficult to pin down just what key the song really is in—the number continually jumps between E minor and E major, and part of its chord progression is structured around the key of G. At any rate, on this number and every other number found on the album, Chet's guitar is mixed hard to the left, and Les's guitar is mixed hard to the right—so it is very easy to distinguish one man's playing from the other when listening to the song.

The recording opens with Les playing some slow, bluesy licks. Then Chet launches into playing the song's melody at a relaxed swing tempo, rendering it along with a simultaneously played accompanying pattern. After this intro, the two then spend the rest of the recording trading exquisitely played solo lines with one another. "It Don't Mean a Thing (If It Ain't Got That Swing)" is an informal, decidedly jazzy outing, just like all of the numbers found on *Guitar Monsters*. The album really allows Chet and Les to just relax and play their guitars as only they know how—and as a result, it is a wonderful, highly listenable record.

Guitar Monsters was released by RCA Victor in 1978, and the record ended up being quite successful, reaching number the 27 spot on the U.S. country album charts. Unfortunately, Chet and Les would never record together again after doing this album—but the two collaborative albums they did make together would continually be held in high esteem by music critics, music historians, and most importantly, their devoted fans.

"Love Song of Pepe Sanchez"

Composer: John Pell. **Producer:** Chet Atkins. **Musicians:** Chet Atkins, Liona Boyd, John Knowles, John Pell (guitars). **Location and Dates of Recording:** C.A. Workshop, Nashville, Tennessee, November 10, 1978, and November 24, 1978. **Original Release:** *The First Nashville Guitar Quartet* (RCA Victor album with the First Nashville Guitar Quartet, 1979), RCA Victor PB-11523 (RCA Victor 45 single with the First Nashville Guitar Quartet, 1979).

As we noted in our discussion of "The Night Atlanta Burned," Chet's recording projects became both more artistically driven and collaborative in nature as he ramped down his relationship with RCA Victor during the mid to late 1970s. A perfect example of this change in his musical focus was his 1979 instrumental album *The First Nashville Guitar Quartet*. The premise of the record was very similar to the premise of his 1975 record *The Night Atlanta Burned*—it blended country, folk and bluegrass music with the sensibilities of a classical string quartet.

But *The First Nashville Guitar Quartet* was different from *The Night Atlanta Burned* in that it did not incorporate any other instruments besides guitar into its quartet format. In other words, *The First Nashville Guitar Quartet* was not just the name of the album, it was the name of the *group* that made the album. The First Nashville Guitar Quartet consisted of Chet, Liona Boyd, John Knowles and John Pell.

We've discussed John Knowles earlier in the book—he was the fingerstyle guitarist/arranger that arranged Chet's Grammy-winning version of "The Entertainer." However, this is the first time we've mentioned Liona Boyd and John Pell. Liona Boyd was a well-known Canadian classical guitarist who had studied with some of the world's finest classical guitarists, including Andrés Segovia and Julian Bream. John

Pell was a guitarist who had recorded and toured with Chet's close friend Dolly Parton in the mid-1970s.

Chet brought this talented group of guitarists together to form The First Nashville Guitar Quartet, and they recorded their album project at Music City Music Hall in Nashville and at Chet's Nashville home studio. By this point, Chet's studio had been given an official name—the credits for *The First Nashville Guitar Quartet* listed the studio as "C.A. Workshop." Working either at Music City Music Hall or C.A. Workshop, Chet and the rest of the Quartet recorded all of the songs for the album during sessions held between September and November 1978. These songs took in a wide variety of musical styles, but the majority of them reflected the group's country, folk and classical origins.

One of the songs, "Love Song of Pepe Sanchez," was recorded at C.A. Workshop on November 10 and 24. When RCA Victor released *The First Nashville Guitar Quartet* in 1979, they also chose to release "Love Song of Pepe Sanchez" as a 45 single that same year. The number was written by quartet member John Pell, and it was an uptempo Latin-flavored piece featuring a bright, memorably inventive melody. Interestingly, while the *The First Nashville Guitar Quartet* album was officially billed as a Chet Atkins work, the "Love Song of Pepe Sanchez" single did not feature Chet's name anywhere in its billing—instead, it was released under the billing of "The First Nashville Guitar Quartet."

Given the nature of this musical project, it is rather hard to discuss Chet's guitar part on "Love Song of Pepe Sanchez" separate from the rest of the recording. However, it can be pointed out that Chet plays a classical guitar in the key of C. Also, one of the guitars heard on the recording has its low E string tuned to C, and its A string tuned to G. (This form of tuning is often referred to as "drop C.") Since the song is played in the key of C, this tuning allows the guitar's low strings to be played openly throughout much of the song and fill the sonic space that would usually be covered by a bass.

Neither the "Love Song of Pepe Sanchez" single nor the *The First Nashville Guitar Quartet* album ended up charting when they were released. But even still, the wonderful music that Chet made with The First Nashville Guitar Quartet stands as a fascinating little chapter in his recording history.

"The Stars and Stripes Forever"

Composer: John Phillip Sousa. **Producer:** Chet Atkins. **Musicians:** Chet Atkins (guitar), Randy Hauser (drums). **Location and Date of Recording:** Music City Music Hall, Nashville, Tennessee, September 12, 1979. **Original Release:** *The Best of Chet on the Road ... Live* (RCA Victor album, 1980).

By the mid-1970s, Chet's recording career had been going on for over three decades, and he still had yet to issue a full live album. In late 1977, he began work on such an album, but it would take quite a bit of time before it was seen through to completion. Two of Chet's concert performances in Paris, France were recorded—these concerts were held at Paris's Olympia Theatre on December 10 and 11, 1977. Over 20 songs were recorded at these shows, all of them of very high quality, but Chet chose not to release them until he had compiled even more live material.

And he did not get around to doing this until almost two years after the Paris shows had been recorded. On September 12, 1979, he recorded four songs during a live performance at Music City Music Hall in Nashville. Two of these songs featured him being accompanied by the musicians from his touring band, and two of them featured him playing with little or no accompaniment. One of the numbers that he recorded without his band was an amazing solo guitar arrangement of John Phillip Sousa's famed American patriotic march "The Stars and Stripes Forever."

Sousa had composed "The Stars and Stripes Forever" on Christmas Day 1896. The march received its premiere the following year, and it was immediately hailed as one of the composer's finest works. Throughout the years, "The Stars and Stripes Forever" became one of the U.S.'s most beloved patriotic songs, and it was heard at countless Independence Day celebrations and fireworks displays. While the march was usually recorded or performed by a large brass band, it was occasionally arranged for other forms of instrumentation. For example, in the 1940s the legendary Russian-born classical pianist Vladimir Horowitz arranged the march as a solo piano piece to celebrate his becoming an American citizen.

In the 1970s, the talented fingerstyle guitarist/arranger Guy Van Duser arranged "The Stars and Stripes Forever" as a solo guitar piece. This arrangement incorporated an incredible amount of the musical parts found in Sousa's original composition—so obviously, it was very challenging to play, even for the most skilled fingerstyle guitarist. Chet learned Guy's arrangement of the song, and he started performing it at many of his concert appearances—audiences loved it so much that it soon became one of the major highlights of his show.

On his September 12, 1979, live recording of "The Stars and Stripes Forever," Chet plays a classical guitar in standard tuning, and his only accompaniment is some occasional, and very spare, drumming by Randy Hauser. Playing at a brisk march tempo, Chet opens the recording playing in the key of E. The song then modulates to the key of A for its famed melodic section that features a counterpoint melody played by a piccolo. Toward the end of the recording, Chet plays the piccolo's part on his high strings—and as he does this, he simultaneously plays the song's main melody on the lower strings of his guitar.

Obviously, Chet's performance of Guy's mind-boggling arrangement of "The Stars and Stripes Forever" is spectacular—and since Chet can't be shooting off fireworks in Music City Music Hall to bring the piece to the grandiose finish that it deserves, he finds an altogether different, and wonderfully funny, way to wrap things up. After all of the masterful playing he has done, he sings these words along with the song's melody—"You may think that this is the end ... well, it is." And with that pithy line, his playing just stops dead in its tracks.

Once Chet had both his 1977 Paris live recordings and his 1979 Nashville live recordings to work with, he finally decided to put a live album together. The end result of his efforts was *The Best of Chet on the Road ... Live*, released by RCA Victor in 1980. The album's title was certainly a bit misleading, because it was not a "best of" collection at all—in fact, none of its recordings had ever been released in any form. *The Best of Chet on the Road ... Live* featured the 1979 Nashville-recorded songs (including "The Stars and Stripes Forever"), as well some of the 1977 Paris-recorded songs. But because this record was only a single album, relatively few of the Paris-recorded numbers could be included on it. (Incidentally, all of Chet's December 1977 Paris recordings were released by RCA, just not in the U.S.—they were included on a 1979 album released only in France entitled *And Then Came ... Chet Atkins*.)

In truth, *The Best of Chet on the Road ... Live* was a rather hodgepodge affair because its song selection lacked any sense of continuity. Since the album bounced back and forth between numbers recorded in Paris and numbers recorded in Nashville, it literally had an "all over the map" feel to it. And the album's jumbled nature was further heightened by its inclusion of one song that was not from either the Paris or Nashville live recordings—in fact, it wasn't even a live recording at all.

That song was called "Blind Willie," and it had been recorded during the March 25, 1976, session at RCA Studios in Nashville that had produced "Frog Kissin'" (discussed earlier). Like "Frog Kissin'," "Blind Willie" was written by Buddy Kalb, produced by Ray Stevens, sung by Chet, and outfitted with an applause track to make it sound like a live recording. Unlike "Frog Kissin'," the song was not an out-and-out humorous novelty number—it was a story song about the legendary blues singer/guitarist Blind Willie McTell.

Blind Willie" was a pleasant enough diversion, but mixing it with two sets of live recordings done years apart on different continents made for an album that certainly did not capture the experience of actually seeing Chet in concert. That said, however, *The Best of Chet on the Road ... Live* still enjoyed a decent amount of success when it was released, reaching the number 43 spot on the U.S. album charts. And it should be pointed out that "Blind Willie" achieved a modest amount of chart success when RCA released it as a single in 1980, reaching the number 83 spot on the U.S. country single charts. But over the years, what Chet fans would remember the most about *The Best of Chet on the Road ... Live* was not "Blind Willie"—rather, it was the great guitar performances that Chet delivered on songs such as "The Stars and Stripes Forever."

"On My Way to Caanan's Land"

Composer: Chet Atkins. **Producers:** Chet Atkins, John D. Loudermilk. **Musicians:** Chet Atkins (guitar/vocals), Doc Watson (guitar/vocals), Jerry Shook (rhythm guitar), Michael Coleman (bass), Terry McMillan (percussion). **Location and Date of Recording:** Music City Music Hall, Nashville, Tennessee, September 25, 1979. **Original Release:** *Reflections* (RCA Victor album with Doc Watson, 1980), RCA Victor PB-12138 (RCA Victor 45 single with Doc Watson, 1980).

By the late 1970s, Chet's track record of making collaborative albums with other artists was a truly stellar one. In a span of about 15 years, he had recorded a number of well-received albums with a list of legendary guitarists that read like some sort of six-string hall of fame. Just to recap, that list included Hank Snow, Jerry Reed, Merle Travis and Les Paul. And Chet was about to add another legend to that list—in late 1979, he embarked on an album project with the famed singer/guitarist Doc Watson.

Like Chet, Doc was born and raised in the Depression-era rural south, and his musical heritage was firmly rooted in country music. Unlike Chet, Doc was a traditional flatpicking guitarist who had stayed very close to his country, bluegrass and folk roots throughout his entire career. As a matter of fact, Doc's flatpicking was regarded as some of the best playing to be found in his genre. The pairing of one of the world's greatest country flatpicking guitarists with one of the world's greatest country fingerpicking guitarists certainly had the potential of being an historic musical summit.

Needless to say, this pairing resoundingly lived up to its potential. Chet and Doc recorded their album entitled *Reflections* at Music City Music Hall in Nashville on September 25, 26 and 27, 1979, and it turned out to be a wonderfully down-to-earth collection of old-time country songs. Since Doc was every bit as much of a singer as he was a guitarist, four of the ten songs he and Chet laid down for the album were vocal numbers. Chet sang on these vocal numbers as well—consequently, *Reflections* featured more of his singing than just about any other album he had ever made.

One of the vocal numbers that Chet and Doc recorded for *Reflections* on September 25 was "On My Way to Caanan's Land," and it was chosen to the album's closing track. For some reason Chet was listed as the song's composer on the original album, but in reality "On My Way to Caanan's Land" was a very old traditional tune. The song, described by Doc in the album's liner notes as "an old-time foot stomping spiritual," was a perfect number to close out this historic, wonderfully informal session pairing two true giants of country guitar. In those same liner notes, Chet added that he first heard "On My Way to Caanan's Land" while attending the Copper Ridge Holiness Church in Lutrell, Tennessee when he was about 10 years old. Chet went on to mention that he thought it was "kind of traditional" to mention the names of friends while singing the song.

And that is just what Chet and Doc do in their version of the song. In Chet's solo verse, he sings that he is on their way to Canaan's Land even if friends of his such as Minnie Pearl, Porter Wagoner and Dolly Parton won't go with him. In between Chet and Doc's great singing, the two lay down a wealth of fabulous guitar solos while playing in the key of E. Backed by rhythm guitar, bass and just a bit of percussion, Chet plays his Hascal Haile classical guitar in standard tuning and Doc plays his Gallagher steel-string acoustic guitar, also in standard tuning. These legends trade lick after lick, always offering perfect support of one another and never getting in each other's way. Chet and Doc may say that they are only on their way to Canaan's land in this recording, but their tremendous performances offer up a slice of Heaven right here on earth for anyone who is a fan of great guitar playing.

When RCA Victor released *Reflections* in 1980, they also chose to release "On My Way to Caanan's Land" on a 45 single—that single was paired with "Tennessee Rag/Beaumont Rag," the subject of this book's next entry. Curiously, even though both the album and the single were of exceptionally high quality, neither of them made the charts at all. But in the long run, the pairing of Chet and Doc on *Reflections* came to be recognized as a true high-water mark in the careers of both men.

"Tennessee Rag/Beaumont Rag"

Composers: Chet Atkins ("Tennessee Rag"), Doc Watson ("Beaumont Rag"). **Producers:** Chet Atkins, John D. Loudermilk. **Musicians:** Chet Atkins (guitar), Doc Watson (guitar), Jerry Shook (rhythm guitar), Michael Coleman (bass), Terry McMillan (percussion). **Location and Date of Recording:** Music City Music Hall, Nashville, Tennessee, September 26, 1979. **Original Release:** *Reflections* (RCA Victor album with Doc Watson, 1980), RCA Victor PB-12138 (RCA Victor 45 single with Doc Watson, 1980).

One of the standout instrumentals that Chet and Doc Watson recorded for their 1980 album *Reflections* was their lively medley of "Tennessee Rag/Beaumont Rag." As noted in this book's previous entry discussing "On My Way to Caanan's Land," Chet and Doc recorded *Reflections* at Music City Music Hall in Nashville on September 25, 26 and 27, 1979—and "Tennessee Rag/Beaumont Rag" was recorded on September 26. For some reason, on the original album Chet was listed as the composer of "Tennessee Rag," and Doc was listed as the composer of Beaumont Rag." But in reality, both songs were very old traditional tunes that had been performed by scores of artists.

On "Tennessee Rag/Beaumont Rag," Chet plays his Hascal Haile classical guitar in standard tuning and Doc plays his Gallagher steel-string acoustic guitar, also in standard tuning. The two are backed by rhythm guitar, bass and just a bit of percussion Playing in the key of C at a fast tempo, Doc opens the recording by playing the melody of "Tennessee Rag," and then he steps back to allow Chet to do some melody playing on the song. About midway through the recording, Doc goes into "Beaumont Rag"—staying in the key of C, the two then trade some melody playing on that song.

When RCA Victor released *Reflections* in 1980, they also chose to release "Tennessee Rag/Beaumont Rag" on a 45 single—that single was paired with "On My Way to Caanan's Land." Neither the album nor the single charted when they were first released—but over the years, the pairing of Chet and Doc on *Reflections* came to be remembered as an historic meeting of two legends of country guitar.

"Orange Blossom Special"

Composer: Ervin T. Rouse. **Producer:** Chet Atkins. **Musicians:** Chet Atkins (guitar), Paul Yandell (guitar), Randy Goodrum (keyboards), Terry McMillan (harmonica/percussion), Steve Wariner (bass), Randy Hauser (drums). **Location and Date of Recording:** C.A. Workshop, Nashville, Tennessee, March 23, 1981. **Original Release:** *Country After All These Years* (RCA Victor album, 1981).

Early 1981 found Chet at work on a new instrumental country album for RCA Victor appropriately entitled *Country After All These Years*. Like several of Chet's recent recording projects for the label, this new album was not recorded at RCA's Nashville studio—rather, it was recorded at C.A. Workshop, his home studio. On March 23, 1981, Chet laid down five songs for *Country After All These Years*—one of these songs, "Orange Blossom Special," was chosen to open the album.

"Orange Blossom Special" was a fast-tempoed 1938 fiddle tune written by Ervin T. Rouse. Rouse wrote the song in honor of the Seaboard Air Line Railroad passenger train of the same name that ran between New York City, New York and Miami, Florida. "Orange Blossom Special" was originally written with lyrics, but over the years it became more widely known as an instrumental. In fact, the popularity of the song earned it the nickname "the fiddler player's national anthem," and it was performed and recorded by scores of country and bluegrass artists.

Chet himself had recorded an excellent instrumental version of "Orange Blossom Special" earlier in his career. That version was performed with Arthur Fiedler and the Boston Pops for their 1966 collaborative album *The Pops Goes Country*. Of course, for *Country After All These Years* Chet again chose to cover "Orange Blossom Special" as an instrumental.

On the *Country After All These Years* "Orange Blossom Special," Chet plays a Gretsch electric guitar in standard tuning out of the key of A, and he is accompanied by guitar, keyboards, harmonica, percussion, bass and drums. Chet's lineup of backing musicians on this particular recording are all players that had figured very prominently in his career—so prominently, in fact, that they really should be mentioned individually. Chet's longtime guitar sideman Paul Yandell not only backs up Chet on the number, but he also helped Chet to write its arrangement. This arrangement includes an extra melodic section that is played over some jazz-based chords.

The song's keyboards are played by Randy Goodrum, a keyboardist/songwriter who had recently composed a number of hit songs for various artists. Randy would continue to write, record and perform music with Chet right up until the end of Chet's career. The harmonica and percussion parts on "Orange Blossom Special" are performed by Terry McMillan, another talented musician who would regularly record and perform with Chet for a number of years. The bassist for the song is Steve Wariner—Steve had been working as one of Chet's backing musicians since 1977, and he would eventually leave Chet's employment in order to have a hugely successful career of his own as a country singer/songwriter/guitarist. And the drummer for "Orange Blossom Special" is Randy Hauser, and excellent percussionist who had played on many of Chet's recent recordings.

Chet and company deliver "Orange Blossom Special" at a very quick tempo, sounding very much like a train speeding down the tracks. Chet renders most of the song's fly by melody through crisp single-note soloing. Quite a bit of that soloing is accompanied with equally crisp single-note harmony soloing—this harmony soloing is also played by Chet, on a second guitar track. Chet delivers some of the melody of the number by using the technique of tapping—that is, fretting a note solely by pushing it into the fretboard instead of fretting the note with one hand and picking it with the other. In the middle of the recording, Chet steps back in order to let Randy take a jazzy keyboard break.

Country After All These Years was released by RCA Victor in 1981. Even though the album did not make the charts, it ended up becoming yet another important milestone in Chet's recording career when it won him his sixth Grammy. At the Grammy Awards of 1982, *Country After All These Years* won the Grammy Award for Best Country Instrumental Performance.

"Polka Dots and Moonbeams"

Composers: Jimmy Van Heusen, Johnny Burke. **Producer:** Chet Atkins. **Musicians:** Chet Atkins (guitar), Lenny Breau (guitar). **Original Release:** *Standard Brands* (RCA Victor album with Lenny Breau, 1981).

As we noted earlier in this book, Chet had been ramping down his executive involvement with RCA Victor since the mid–1970s. And by the early 1980s, he had decided that it was time to completely sever his ties with the label. This could not have been an easy decision for Chet—after all, he had been with RCA as an artist for about 35 years, and his staggeringly successful executive tenure with the label had led to the creation of country music's world-famous "Nashville sound." In other words, Chet had revolutionized country music both as an artist and a producer of other artists while he was with RCA—so it must have been hard for him to walk away from the company that he had shared so many musical triumphs with.

But walk away he did. Simply put, Chet felt that RCA had grown to be less supportive of his eclectic musical projects than they had used to be. So he decided to find a new label, one that he felt would truly get behind his work.

One of the projects that had led Chet to feel this way about RCA was the collaborative instrumental album he recorded with jazz guitarist Lenny Breau entitled *Standard Brands*. Over the years, Chet had been one of Lenny's biggest supporters—Chet signed Lenny to RCA, produced several of his albums, and recorded with him from time to time. (We discussed the number that they laid down for Chet's 1976 album *The Best of Chet Atkins and Friends*, "Sweet Georgia Brown," earlier in this book.) Chet and Lenny had been sporadically working on *Standard Brands* for several years—in the liner notes Chet penned for the album, he stated that its songs had been recorded in 1979, 1980 and 1981. What Chet could not say in those liner notes was that Lenny's tremendous drug and alcohol problems were the reason that it took them so long to finish the album.

Still, Chet and Lenny did manage to get the album done, and it was released by RCA Victor in late 1981. But the label did very little to promote the record, so the album basically went unnoticed by everyone but Chet and Lenny's most ardent fans. Chet's disappointment over the way RCA handled *Standard Brands* was long-lasting—he even brought the subject up in his 2001 autobiography *Chet Atkins: Me and My Guitars*.

At any rate, the song that was picked to close *Standard Brands* was Chet and Lenny's version of "Polka Dots and Moonbeams." "Polka Dots and Moonbeams" was a slow-tempoed pop vocal number written in 1940 by Jimmy Van Heusen and Johnny Burke. Frank Sinatra recorded the song with The Tommy Dorsey Orchestra that same year, and it became one of his first hits. In the years that followed, the number became a big band/jazz standard that was recorded by scores of artists.

On "Polka Dots and Moonbeams," Chet and Lenny use classical guitars in standard tuning, and they are not accompanied by any other musicians. Chet starts out the recording by playing completely alone. Playing in the key of C at an easygoing tempo, he renders the song's melody along with simultaneously played harmony lines and accompanying patterns. He then lays out in order to let Lenny take a pass at the song completely on *his* own—after moving the song to the key of D, Lenny gently renders the song's melody through a combination of harmonic notes and single-note soloing. Lenny then moves to delivering the song's melody along with an incredible array of musically sophisticated backing patterns. Staying in the key of D, Chet and Lenny then close out the recording by restating the song's melody together.

Hearing Chet and Lenny play together on "Polka Dots and Moonbeams" and the rest of *Standard Brands* is a truly extraordinary musical experience. The musical bond between the two was so strong that their combined playing took on a peaceful, almost meditative quality. They just seemed to move as one, and this allowed them to create music was so beautiful that it was almost otherworldly.

Tragically, all of the beautiful music that Lenny made during his life never brought him peace. After struggling with his addictions for so many years, he was found strangled to death in his Los Angeles apartment swimming pool in 1984. His death was ruled a homicide, and the case remains unsolved. Chet was deeply grieved by the loss of his incredibly talented friend, and he mourned that loss for the rest of his life.

Not long after the release of *Standard Brands*, Chet decided which label he would sign with after leaving RCA. Chet was headed to Columbia Records, and his RCA years were officially over. On the whole, Chet's years with Columbia would certainly not be as prolific or groundbreaking as his long tenure with RCA had been. But as we will see throughout the rest of this book, Chet's time at Columbia would still produce a number of recordings that were every bit as wonderful as his best RCA recordings.

"East Tennessee Christmas"

Composers: John Knowles, Chet Atkins. **Producer:** Chet Atkins. **Locations of Recording:** C.A. Workshop, Nashville, Tennessee, Sound Emporium, Nashville, Tennessee. **Original Release:** *East Tennessee Christmas* (Columbia album, 1983).

In the early 1980s, Chet's career was very much in the throes of change. First off, he had left RCA Victor for Columbia Records, because Columbia was much more receptive to the eclectic new musical projects that he wanted to undertake. Also, Chet had decided to end his quarter-century relationship with the Gretsch Company and sign an endorsement deal with the Gibson Guitar Corporation.

Generally speaking, Chet's transition between Gretsch and Gibson was a smooth one—but his transition between RCA Victor and Columbia was a bit bumpy. His last album for RCA entitled *Great Hits of the Past* was released in 1983, and it featured Chet performing instrumental versions of hit songs that he had produced for other artists during his years at the label. *Great Hits of the Past* was an enjoyable record, but apparently RCA didn't care to give it even the slightest bit of promotion since Chet had decided to leave them—consequently, the album basically went unnoticed by everyone but the most devoted Chet fans.

Chet's first album for Columbia was every bit as underwhelming as his last album for RCA. This album was entitled *Work It Out with Chet Atkins C.G.P.*, and it was released in 1983. *Work It Out with Chet Atkins C.G.P.* was a collection of songs that were meant to be used as background music for exercising. In keeping with the album's workout theme, many of its numbers were synced up with metronome-like percussion tracks, and they ran together with no break between them. Truthfully, this record had the same kind of overly gimmicky feel that Chet's 1959 sing-along album *Hum and Strum Along with Chet Atkins* had—so it definitely turned out to be one of his lesser efforts.

We should take just a moment to make note of the "C.G.P." moniker that was a part of the *Work It Out with Chet Atkins C.G.P.* title. Chet had regretted never having any formal higher education, so in the early 1980s he lightheartedly created a "C.G.P." degree for himself, which he said stood for "Certified Guitar Player." While the C.G.P. designation might have started as a bit of an in-joke, it stuck with Chet for the rest of his career—he was billed as "Chet Atkins C.G.P." on most all of his Columbia albums, and toward the end of his life he even awarded C.G.P. degrees to several of his guitarist friends.

Chet made a wonderful return to form for Columbia by revisiting a theme that had produced one of his all-time best albums—that theme was holiday music. He had not recorded a Christmas album since his classic 1961 release *Christmas with Chet Atkins*, so it made perfect sense for him to make a brand-new Christmas album for his new label. Most all of the songs that Chet decided to record for this album were well-known standards—in fact, more than a few of them were remakes of numbers that had been featured on *Christmas with Chet Atkins*. However, he did write one new song for the record with guitarist John Knowles—that song was entitled "East Tennessee Christmas," and it would end up being the album's title track. (Incidentally, John was such a good friend and close musical collaborator of Chet's that he was the first guitarist that Chet ever awarded a C.G.P. degree to—that is, the first guitarist other than Chet himself.)

"East Tennessee Christmas" was an easygoing midtempo vocal number that featured a catchy melody and nostalgic lyrics about someone who was ready to head back to their east Tennessee home for the holidays. Obviously, this was one of Chet's most autobiographical compositions, so it was no surprise at all that he decided to sing lead on it. By the way, it should be pointed out that while *East Tennessee Christmas* was basically an instrumental album, Chet chose to adorn many of its numbers with supporting vocal parts provided by a variety of singers, including himself—this singing brought an extra dimension to the record that made it even more warm and festive.

Before we examine "East Tennessee Christmas" any further, this author should take just a moment to comment on the records that document Chet's studio work for Columbia. These records are nowhere near as detailed as the records documenting Chet's RCA studio work—so for the rest of this book, we will have to get by with less information regarding when and where specific songs were recorded, and who performed the backing tracks on those recordings. However, we *do* know that Chet continued his practice of working on his own recordings on his own time at his home studio.

Now that we have *that* disclaimer out of the way, let's get back to "East Tennessee Christmas." On the recording, Chet plays a Gibson electric guitar in the key of G, and he is accompanied by keyboards, bass, and drums. Chet opens the song by rendering its likable melody along with simultaneously played harmony lines, and then he takes a brief break from guitar playing in order to sing the song's first verse. After that verse, he offers up a bit more melody playing, and then he sings the song's second verse. Chet closes out the recording with a bit of melody playing that is accompanied by a simultaneously played accompanying pattern.

Chet's low-key playing and singing on "East Tennessee Christmas" brings to mind a wonderful Christmas Day shared with cherished friends and loved ones. And the song's lyrics may specifically discuss east Tennessee, but the number as a whole is so inviting that it captures the feel of a great Christmas no matter *where* one might live. (Incidentally, Chet is joined by other singers during his vocal parts—but as we just discussed, Columbia's studio records are not detailed enough to list just who those singers might be.)

East Tennessee Christmas was released by Columbia in late 1983, and the album did not end up charting. That said, however, the record's overall high quality made it a perennial holiday favorite amongst Chet fans over the years.

"Sunrise"

Composers: George Benson, Randy Goodrum. **Producers:** Chet Atkins, George Benson. **Musicians:** Chet Atkins (guitar), George Benson (guitar), Randy Goodrum (keyboards), David Hungate (bass), Larrie Londin (drums), Terry McMillan (percussion), Connie McCallister and the "A" Strings (strings). **Locations of Recording:** Larry Carlton Studios, Los Angeles, California; C.A. Workshop, Nashville, Tennessee; Sound Shop Studios, Nashville, Tennessee. **Original Release:** *Stay Tuned* (Columbia album, 1985), Columbia 38–04859 (Columbia 45 single, 1985).

Chet had been very interested in recording a new jazz album during the last few years he was with RCA Victor, but the label's lack of enthusiasm for his more musically ambitious projects kept that album from ever being made. Once Chet moved from RCA to Columbia, a label that was excited to support his new musical ventures, he was given the freedom to put his jazz album back at the top of his "to do" list. So throughout a good part of 1984 Chet worked on recording his jazz album for his new label—it was an all-instrumental record, and it was given the title of *Stay Tuned*.

When *Stay Tuned* was released in 1985, Columbia chose to bill it as something of an "event" album. What made *Stay Tuned* an event was the fact that it was essentially a musical summit meeting between Chet and a number of the 1980s' most prominent jazz and rock guitarists—it featured him performing duets with players such as George Benson, Earl Klugh, and Mark Knopfler. In fact, *Stay Tuned* would very much end up being a blueprint for many of the albums that Chet recorded for Columbia—on these albums, Chet would collaborate with a variety of younger musicians from a wide spectrum of musical styles. Chet was seen as a legendary elder statesman by the entire music industry now, and there was no shortage of up-and-coming artists who were anxious to add a duet recording with Chet Atkins to their resume.

Chet and George Benson teamed up to record the song "Sunrise" for *Stay Tuned*, and that number was the one that Columbia chose to make the focal point of the album when it was first released. Not only was "Sunrise" chosen to be the opening track on *Stay Tuned*, but it was also released as a 45 single with an accompanying music video. In other words, Columbia was using "Sunrise" to aggressively market a "new" version of Chet Atkins.

"Sunrise" was a midtempo smooth jazz number written by George Benson and keyboardist Randy Goodrum, the well-known songwriter who had become one of Chet's close musical collaborators. Every last aspect of the song had a *very* strong smooth jazz vibe to it—its composition, tempo, arrangement and production gave it a modern sound that was unlike any song that Chet had ever recorded before.

Actually, "Sunrise" was by no means the only song on *Stay Tuned* that was a departure from Chet's catalog of recordings—most every song on the album was delivered in the style of modern-sounding smooth jazz. Columbia's efforts to reinvent Chet as a smooth jazz player were quite successful—"Sunrise" did not chart as a single, but *Stay Tuned* reached the number 12 spot on the U.S. jazz album charts and the number 145 spot on the U.S. pop album charts.

Let's go over the particulars of "Sunrise"—on the recording, Chet plays a very unusual guitar that came to be known as the "Peaver." The guitar was built by his longtime guitar sideman Paul Yandell to be used specifically as a recording instrument. The Peaver was constructed out of a Peavey T-60 body, a Fender Stratocaster neck, and EMG pickups. While the instrument might have looked very strange, it sounded great in the studio. On "Sunrise," Chet plays the Peaver in standard tuning, and he is joined by George Benson playing an electric guitar that is also in standard tuning. The two are accompanied by keyboards, bass, drums, percussion, and strings.

Chet Atkins and George Benson performing together at the Vanderbilt Plaza Hotel in Nashville, Tennessee, on February 13, 1985. This performance was arranged to promote the release of Chet's new Columbia Records album *Stay Tuned*. Note that Chet is playing the "Peaver," the customized guitar that he used to record the *Stay Tuned* song "Sunrise" with George.

Playing in the key of G, Chet opens the recording by rendering the tranquil melody of "Sunrise" along with simultaneously played harmony lines. The reason this melody is so soothing is because it is built around the chords of G major seventh, B flat major seventh, and F major seventh—and the major seventh is a particularly peaceful-sounding chord structure. A little less than two minutes into the recording, Chet steps back in order to let George take a solo break. George first delivers a wealth of solo lines that feature simultaneously played harmony patterns, and then he offers up some nimble, silky smooth single-note soloing. George turns the song back over to Chet, who closes out the recording by restating the song's melody.

"Sunrise" was the perfect recording to announce Chet's new, smooth jazz-based musical direction to the world—that said, however, the world still loved Chet when he played his guitar country-style. This fact was made very apparent by how well-received the sole country-sounding number off of *Stay Tuned* turned out to be—we'll discuss that number, "Cosmic Square Dance," next.

"Cosmic Square Dance"

Composers: Chet Atkins, Paul Yandell, Mark Knopfler. **Producer:** David Hungate. **Musicians:** Chet Atkins (guitar), Mark Knopfler (guitar), Mark O'Connor (fiddle), Paul Yandell (banjo), David Hungate (bass), Larrie Londin (drums), Paulinho da Costa (percussion). **Locations of Recording:** Larry Carlton Studios, Los Angeles,

California; C.A. Workshop, Nashville, Tennessee; Sound Shop Studios, Nashville, Tennessee. **Original Release:** *Stay Tuned* (Columbia album, 1985).

As we just noted in our discussion of "Sunrise," Chet's 1985 instrumental album *Stay Tuned* was essentially a musical summit meeting between Chet and a number of the 1980s' most prominent jazz and rock guitarists. The most well-known rock guitarist that appeared on the album was Mark Knopfler, the founder/frontman of the hugely successful British rock band Dire Straits. But in truth, Mark really did not offer up that much rock playing on *Stay Tuned*—instead, his most memorable contribution to the album was the country-style playing that he did with Chet on a song entitled "Cosmic Square Dance."

Chet and Mark wrote "Cosmic Square Dance" along with Paul Yandell, Chet's longtime guitar sideman. Paul also performed on the recording with Chet and Mark, contributing its banjo part. The song was a lighthearted midtempo jazz number that was infused with a strong country music sensibility. In fact, "Cosmic Square Dance" was very much crafted to live up to its name and have an infectiously fun "space age country" feel to it—the recording featured some undulating, otherworldly sounding keyboard parts, as well as square dance calls made by a robotic-sounding voice.

On "Cosmic Square Dance," Chet and Mark both play electric guitars in standard tuning out of the key of C, and they are accompanied by keyboards, fiddle, banjo, bass, drums, and percussion. Throughout the recording, Chet fingerpicks the song's catchy, country-sounding melody, and Mark answers his playing with a wealth of crisp solo lines. Chet and Mark are two guitarists with wonderfully distinctive styles of playing, and both of them found those distinctive styles through their fingerpicking—so it is a real treat to hear these two world-class fingerpickers trade guitar licks with each other.

Stay Tuned might have announced Chet's new, smooth jazz-based musical direction to the world, but his country-style playing with Mark on "Cosmic Square Dance" ended up garnering more attention than anything else on the album. At the Grammy Awards of 1985, the song won the Grammy Award for Best Country Instrumental Performance. Incidentally, Chet enjoyed working with Mark on *Stay Tuned* so much that the two would continue to musically team up over the next few years. In 1990, they would even record a full album together entitled *Neck and Neck*. We'll discuss two numbers off of that album, "Poor Boy Blues" and "So Soft, Your Goodbye," a bit later.

"Honolulu Blue"

Composers: Chet Atkins, John Knowles. **Producers:** Ronnie Foster, Darryl Dybka. **Musicians:** Chet Atkins (guitar). **Locations of Recording:** Yahama Research and Development Studio, Glendale, California; Galaxy Sound Studios, Hollywood, California; C.A. Workshop, Nashville, Tennessee. **Original Release:** *Street Dreams* (Columbia album, 1986).

After the success of "Stay Tuned," Chet decided to stick with the smooth jazz motif for his next Columbia album, which was given the title of *Street Dreams*. The album was an all-instrumental work that very much had a "1980s southern California" feel to it—it was recorded in 1986 at Yahama Research and Development Studio in Glendale, and Galaxy Sound Studios in Hollywood. However, like most all of the albums Chet had made over the past 30-plus years, a portion of *Street Dreams* was also recorded at his home studio in Nashville.

Unfortunately, the musical direction that had worked so well for Chet and Columbia on *Stay Tuned* fell a bit flat on *Street Dreams*. Chet was so determined to shape the album into a modern-sounding smooth jazz work that he chose to outfit most all of its songs with synthesizers and heavy drum tracks. This slick production tended to overwhelm Chet's time-honored style of playing—consequently, much of *Street Dreams* was left sounding decidedly generic.

However, Chet *did* allow himself plenty of playing room on the album's last song, which was entitled "Honolulu Blue." "Honolulu Blue" was a low-key, slightly bluesy number written by Chet and guitarist John Knowles, and it featured Chet playing with no accompaniment other than a keyboard that sounded a little like a steel guitar.

Chet Atkins with his Gibson Chet Atkins CE electric guitar in the mid–1980s.

On "Honolulu Blue," Chet plays his Gibson Chet Atkins CE guitar in the key of A. (The CE was the solidbody acoustic that Chet and Gibson designed together in the early 1980s.) Chet has the CE tuned in an unusual manner for the song—it is in standard tuning with the exception of his D string, which is tuned down a half step to D flat. This tuning allows him to leave that string open when he uses several variations of an A chord. Throughout the recording, Chet nicely renders the easygoing melody of "Honolulu Blue" along with a simultaneously played accompanying pattern. The steel guitar-like keyboard often joins in with his playing, which gives the song just a bit of a Hawaiian music feel.

Since Chet's playing so often took a back seat to slick production on *Street Dreams*, the album did not end up being as commercially or critically well-received as *Stay Tuned* had been. This would lead Chet to slightly change up the smooth jazz-oriented format he had been using for his next album project, which would end up being entitled *Sails*. We'll discuss two numbers off of that album, "Sails" and "Waltz for the Lonely," in the next two entries of this book.

"Sails"

Composers: John Hall, Johanna Hall. **Producers:** David Hungate, Chet Atkins. **Musicians:** Chet Atkins (guitar). **Locations of Recording:** C.A. Workshop,

Nashville, Tennessee; Sound Emporium, Nashville, Tennessee. **Original Release:** *Sails* (Columbia album, 1987).

As we just noted in our discussion of "Honolulu Blue," Chet's 1986 smooth jazz album *Street Dreams* had not been as well-received as his initial foray into smooth jazz, the 1985 album *Stay Tuned*, had been. So Chet decided to change up his musical direction a bit for his next album project—that album was an all-instrumental work released by Columbia Records in 1987, and it was given the title of *Sails*. Like *Street Dreams*, *Sails* contained a healthy sampling of smooth jazz numbers—but it also contained several songs that fell squarely into the category of new-age music. Far and away the most prominent new-age number on the album was its title track. "Sails" was a wonderfully peaceful guitar instrumental laden with soothing, nautical-themed sound effects such as ocean waves and seagulls.

"Sails" was written in the mid–1970s by the husband and wife songwriting team of John Hall and Johanna Hall. The Halls had originally crafted the song as a slow-tempoed vocal number about the restorative power of spending time out at sea. John Hall first recorded "Sails" with his well-known 1970s soft rock band Orleans—that recording was featured on the band's 1976 album *Waking and Dreaming*. (Incidentally, "Sails" was not the first Orleans song written by the Halls that Chet had recorded— he had performed a live instrumental version of the band's 1975 hit song "Dance with Me" on his 1980 live album *The Best of Chet on the Road … Live*.)

Chet is accompanied by guitar, keyboards and strings on his version of "Sails." (Unfortunately, the credits for *Sails* are not clear regarding just who the musicians are who play these parts.) Chet plays two separate guitar tracks on the recording— he plays a Hascal Haile classical guitar outfitted with a Baggs pickup on the guitar track that is heard throughout the song, and he plays his Del Vecchio Dinamico resonator on the solo guitar track that is heard in the middle of the song. Both guitars are played in standard tuning out of the key of A.

"Sails" is one of Chet's all-time most beautiful recordings. He renders the song's deeply peaceful melody to perfection both on his Hascal Haile and his Del Vecchio, and the sumptuous sound of those guitars on the recording is simply a joy to the ears.

Since Chet had decided to explore the genre of new-age music on *Sails*, he backed off from using as many synth and heavy drum tracks on the album as he had used on his previous record *Street Dreams*. "Sails" was a perfect example of this change in musical focus. And Chet fans warmly responded to this change, taking to *Sails* far more than they had taken to *Street Dreams*. We'll discuss one more number off of *Sails*, "Waltz for the Lonely," in the next entry of this book.

"Waltz for the Lonely"

Composers: Chet Atkins, Randy Goodrum. **Producers:** David Hungate, Chet Atkins. **Musicians:** Chet Atkins (guitar). **Locations of Recording:** C.A. Workshop, Nashville, Tennessee; Sound Emporium, Nashville, Tennessee. **Original Release:** *Sails* (Columbia album, 1987).

"Waltz for the Lonely" was another one of the numbers on *Sails* that moved away from the modern-sounding, smooth jazz-based music featured on Chet's previous album *Street Dreams*. The song was not an out-and-out new-age number with soothing sound effects like *Sails'* title track. (We discussed that track in detail in the previous entry.) But "Waltz for the Lonely" was very similar to "Sails" in that it was a quiet, reflective song, and it featured Chet playing with very subtly arranged backing tracks.

Like all of the songs featured on *Sails*, "Waltz for the Lonely" was an instrumental. The song was written by Chet and the well-known keyboardist/songwriter Randy Goodrum, one of Chet's closest musical collaborators over the past few years. "Waltz for the Lonely" was a waltz piece featuring an achingly beautiful melody that did indeed capture a feeling of great loneliness.

On "Waltz for the Lonely," Chet plays a Hascal Haile classical guitar outfitted with a Baggs pickup in standard tuning out of the key of C, and his sole accompaniment is a string section. He beautifully renders the song's haunting melody along with an array of simultaneously played, delicate backing patterns. Toward the end of the recording, he uses alternation (the technique of plucking a string repeatedly using more than one finger) to play a section of that melody. Both the sophisticated melodic structure and the instrumentation of "Waltz for the Lonely" make the song sound more like a classical chamber music piece than any other style of music.

Sails did not end up charting when it was first released by Columbia in 1987. Still, the album's tendency to use fewer synth and drum-heavy arrangements than Chet's previous album *Street Dreams* had used made it quite popular with his fans. And thanks to its standout tracks like "Sails" and "Waltz for the Lonely," *Sails* has continued to be held in high esteem by Chet fans throughout the years.

"I Still Can't Say Goodbye"

Composers: Robert Blinn, James Moore. **Producers:** Darryl Dybka, Chet Atkins. **Musicians:** Chet Atkins (guitar/vocals). **Location of Recording:** C.A. Workshop, Nashville, Tennessee. **Original Release:** *Chet Atkins, C.G.P.* (Columbia album, 1988), Columbia 38–07929 (Columbia 45 single, 1988).

Chet's 1988 release *Chet Atkins, C.G.P.* marked his fourth straight smooth jazz-based album for Columbia Records in as many years. (As we noted in our discussion of "East Tennessee Christmas" a bit earlier in this book, Chet had lightheartedly created a "C.G.P." degree for himself around the time he first started recording for Columbia—those initials stood for "Certified Guitar Player.") Like his previous three jazz albums, *Chet Atkins, C.G.P.* was mostly made up of instrumentals that featured modern-sounding synthesizer and heavy drum tracks. But the last song on the album was a remarkable break from this trend—*Chet Atkins, C.G.P.* closed with an emotional vocal number sung by Chet called "I Still Can't Say Goodbye."

"I Still Can't Say Goodbye" was composed in 1983 by songwriters Robert Blinn and Jimmy Moore, and it was about a man well into his own adult life who still actively grieved the loss of his father who had passed away many years earlier. At the beginning of the song, the man talked about trying on his dad's hat when he was a little boy, pretending to be his father. And at the end of the song, the man talked about how he had just recently seen a hat like his dad's in a Salvation Army store. Of course, he tried the hat on—after so many years without his father, after growing into adulthood himself, he was still trying to be like his dad.

To simply say that Chet was touched by Robert and Jimmy's song would be a huge understatement. *Here's* how touched he was by it—he recorded the song for

Chet Atkins, C.G.P., he dedicated that album to his own late father James Arley Atkins, and over the years he performed the song live during many of his television and concert appearances. And right before he would start playing the song, he would put on a white fedora hat that was just like the hat his father used to wear.

Throughout this book, I have purposefully avoided going into detail about Chet's personal life. After all, the book is not an in-depth biography of Chet, it is a book about his greatest recorded songs. But what I feel I need to say about "I Still Can't Say Goodbye" requires me to offer up some observations about Chet the man, not just Chet the musician.

Chet made no secret of the fact that his relationship with his father was at times very difficult—in fact, Chet openly discussed the tension that so often existed between him and James in his 1974 autobiography *Country Gentleman*. Since the father and son in "I Still Can't Say Goodbye" were portrayed as

Chet Atkins with a Gibson Chet Atkins CE electric guitar, late 1980s. Wearing a white fedora hat, he is about to perform the vocal number "I Still Can't Say Goodbye" from his 1988 Columbia album *Chet Atkins, C.G.P.*

having a constantly warm and loving relationship, Chet could not possibly have viewed the song as being totally autobiographical for him. But whatever problems that existed between Chet and his father did not stop Chet from really loving his dad and greatly missing him when he passed away—so Chet felt compelled to sing "I Still Can't Say Goodbye" as a tribute to James.

In truth, when one knows about the problems that Chet and his father had, it makes Chet's performance of "I Still Can't Say Goodbye" all the more poignant. By the time Chet recorded the song, he had reached the autumn of his own life—and when Chet sang that song, he made it clear that both time and trouble had not weakened his feelings for his dad in the least. "I Still Can't Say Goodbye" would have been a powerful message about family, love and grief no matter who ended up performing the song—but once Chet became the deliverer of that message, "I Still Can't Say Goodbye" became an even *more* profound and touching musical work.

Chet does play guitar on his recording of "I Still Can't Say Goodbye"—but since the song centers around his vocal performance, we'll discuss that first. Chet's singing on "I Still Can't Say Goodbye" is truly wonderful—and what makes it wonderful is the fact that his plain, earnest voice takes on an everyman quality that perfectly captures the universality of the song's lyrics. Incidentally, the number sounds as if it was recorded in front of a live audience—Chet delivers some remarks about his dad to that audience before the song starts, and applause is heard when the song ends. However, the credits for *Chet Atkins, C.G.P.* state that the album was solely recorded at C.A. Workshop, Chet's home studio in Nashville—so in all probability, "I Still Can't Say Goodbye" was a studio recording that was outfitted with an applause track to make it sound like a live recording.

At any rate, on "I Still Can't Say Goodbye," Chet plays his Gibson Chet Atkins CE guitar in standard tuning out of the key of G—his guitar is capoed at the 2nd fret, so it sounds as if he is playing out of the key of A. On the recording, he is nicely accompanied by keyboards and bass. (Unfortunately, the credits for *Chet Atkins, C.G.P.* are not clear regarding just who the musicians are who play these parts.)

When Columbia released *Chet Atkins, C.G.P.* in 1988, they also chose to release "I Still Can't Say Goodbye" as a 45 single. Neither the album nor the single charted when they were first released—but over the years, "I Still Can't Say Goodbye" came to be regarded as one of the most beautiful and emotionally moving recordings that Chet ever made. As we discussed earlier in this book, people had been making jokes about what a poor singer Chet was for many years—and Chet himself was one of those people. But this really was just a joke, because the truth was that Chet *had* made a bit of a mark for himself as a vocalist during his career. And the only proof that one really needs to support this statement is "I Still Can't Say Goodbye."

"Poor Boy Blues"

Composer: Paul Kennerley. **Producer:** Mark Knopfler. **Musicians:** Chet Atkins (guitar/vocals), Mark Knopfler (guitar/vocals), Paul Franklin (steel guitar), Guy Fletcher (bass), Larrie Londin (drums), Vince Gill (vocals). **Locations of Recording:** C.A. Workshop, Nashville, Tennessee; Sound Emporium, Nashville, Tennessee; Hillbilly Heaven, London. **Original Release:** *Neck and Neck* (Columbia album with Mark Knopfler, 1990), Columbia 38–73556 (Columbia single with Mark Knopfler, 1990).

By the late 1980s, Chet had recorded six albums for Columbia Records—but he still had yet to make an album for the label was that centered around country music, the style he had always been best-known for playing. His seventh Columbia album was entitled *Neck and Neck*, and it marked his return to his country music roots. *Neck and Neck* was a collaborative album with singer/guitarist Mark Knopfler released in late 1990, and most of its selections were decidedly country-flavored. Four of those selections were vocal numbers sung by Chet and Mark. Of course, the album did not mark the first time that Chet had worked with Mark—we discussed their Grammy-winning collaboration on the 1985 song "Cosmic Square Dance" earlier in the book.

Neck and Neck was definitely an album that celebrated Chet's past—almost half of its numbers were songs that Chet had recorded during his glory days at RCA Victor. (In fact, we've discussed Chet's original recordings of three of those numbers, "Yakety Axe," "Tears," and "I'll See You in My Dreams," earlier in this book.) But the album also featured some newly written songs as well. The most prominent of these songs was "Poor Boy Blues"—it was one of Chet and Mark's vocal numbers, and it was chosen to open the album.

The lyrics of "Poor Boy Blues" were about a poor boy hoping to win a girl's love, but the song had more than enough solo breaks thrown in to allow Chet and Mark to leisurely trade guitar licks. The song was credited to the English songwriter Paul Kennerley, but it was very obvious that Mark's songwriting style was its major inspiration. "Poor Boy Blues" was essentially a shameless imitation of Mark's 1985 Dire Straits hit "Walk of Life—both songs were basic three-chord, rockabilly style shuffle tunes out of the key of E.

"Poor Boy Blues" might not be particularly original, but it is very entertaining. On the recording, Chet plays a Gibson electric guitar in standard tuning, and Mark plays an electric guitar that is also in standard tuning.

Chet Atkins with a Gibson Chet Atkins Country Gentleman electric guitar, 1990.

Their singing and playing meshes together wonderfully, and they are supported by a great group of supporting musicians, including country superstar Vince Gill on backing vocals. In fact, "Poor Boy Blues" turned out so well that it earned Chet and Mark another Grammy. At the Grammy Awards of 1991, the song won the Grammy Award for Best Country Collaboration with Vocals.

"Poor Boy Blues" holds several other distinctions in Chet's storied recording career. It was on the last vinyl single ever released by Chet—the flip side of that single was "So Soft, Your Goodbye, the subject of this book's next entry. (After about 45 years of recording music, Chet had seen the age of mass-produced vinyl records basically come to its end.) And the release of the recording was accompanied by one of the relatively few official music videos that Chet ever made—that video featured Chet, Mark and a group of musicians performing the song together in an informal living room setting.

"Poor Boy Blues" did not end up charting as a single, but all of the attention that the song received certainly helped to promote the *Neck and Neck* album as a whole—consequently, the album turned out to be quite successful, reaching the number 27 spot on the U.S. country album charts.

"So Soft, Your Goodbye"

Composer: Randy Goodrum. **Producer:** Mark Knopfler. **Musicians:** Chet Atkins (guitar), Mark Knopfler (guitar), Mark O'Connor (violin), Guy Fletcher (keyboards). **Locations of Recording:** C.A. Workshop, Nashville, Tennessee; Sound Emporium, Nashville, Tennessee; Hillbilly Heaven, London. **Original Release:** *Neck and Neck* (Columbia album with Mark Knopfler, 1990), Columbia 38–73556 (Columbia single with Mark Knopfler, 1990).

Like "Poor Boy Blues," "So Soft, Your Goodbye" was one of the newly written songs featured on Chet and Mark Knopfler's 1990 collaborative album *Neck and Neck*. The song was a melancholy vocal number composed by the well-known keyboardist/songwriter Randy Goodrum, one of Chet's closest musical collaborators over the past few years. Chet and Mark chose to record "So Soft, Your Goodbye" as a guitar instrumental for *Neck and Neck*.

On "So Soft, Your Goodbye," Chet plays his Del Vecchio Dinamico resonator guitar in standard tuning, and Mark plays an electric guitar that is also in standard tuning. Accompanied by keyboards and violin, the two render the song's hauntingly beautiful melody mainly through single-note soloing. Chet and Mark basically trade solos with one another, but they do occasionally harmonize with one another's playing as well.

Chet and Mark's contemplative performances on "So Soft, Your Goodbye" make the recording one of the best that they ever did together. In fact, "So Soft, Your Goodbye" ended up being so memorable that it earned Chet and Mark yet *another* Grammy. At the Grammy Awards of 1991, the song won the Grammy Award for Best Country Collaboration with Vocals. This marked the first time that Chet had won more than one Grammy for his work on a single album.

"So Soft, Your Goodbye" was paired with "Poor Boy Blues" on Chet's last-ever vinyl single, which like the *Neck and Neck* album, was released by Columbia Records in 1990. Neither song from that single ended up charting—but since *both* of the songs on the single ended up being Grammy winners, the single certainly helped to promote the *Neck and Neck* album as a whole—consequently, the album turned out to be quite successful, reaching the number 27 spot on the U.S. country album charts.

"Sneakin' Around"

Composer: R.L. Kass. **Producers:** Chet Atkins, David Hungate, Jerry Reed. **Musicians:** Chet Atkins (guitar), Jerry Reed (guitar), Pat Bergeson (guitar), Darryl Dybka (keyboards), Terry McMillan (harmonica), David Hungate (bass), Larrie Londin (drums). **Location of Recording:** C.A. Workshop, Nashville, Tennessee. **Original Release:** *Sneakin' Around* (Columbia album with Jerry Reed, 1991).

You might have noticed that Jerry Reed's name has not come up in this book for quite some time now—after all, we had been regularly talking about him for so many pages, and then he just seemed to vanish. Well, Chet himself felt that Jerry kind of vanished from his life for a while. In his 2001 autobiography *Chet Atkins: Me and My Guitars*, Chet lamented the fact that he had lost touch both personally and professionally with Jerry during the late 1970s and most of the 1980s, because during that time Jerry was so focused on his very successful acting and singing career.

Happily, Chet and Jerry reconnected with each other for a new collaborative album project in the early 1990s—that album was entitled *Sneakin' Around*, and it was released by Columbia Records in late 1991. *Sneakin' Around* was the third full album that Chet and Jerry had made together, the first two being the RCA Victor releases *Me and Jerry* (1970) and *Me and Chet* (1972). (Earlier in this book, we discussed "Tennessee Stud" and "Cannonball Rag" from *Me and Jerry*, and "The Mad Russian" and "Nashtown Ville" from *Me and Chet*.)

Chet Atkins with Jerry Reed, 1991.

Sneakin' Around was basically a collection of country and light jazz-flavored guitar instrumentals—however, the album did also feature several novelty vocal numbers sung by Chet and Jerry. The record consisted almost entirely of songs that neither Chet nor Jerry had ever recorded before, with one notable exception—they laid down a great new version of Jerry's signature instrumental "The Claw." Chet and Jerry had both previously recorded "The Claw," but not together. Jerry first recorded it for his first RCA album called *The Unbelievable Guitar and Voice of Jerry Reed*, which was released in 1967. And Chet first recorded it for his 1973 RCA album *Alone*. (We are not going to discuss the Chet/Jerry *Sneakin' Around* version of "The Claw" in detail here, because we examined Chet's *Alone* version of the song earlier.)

Besides "The Claw," another one of *Sneakin' Around*'s standout numbers was its title track. "Sneakin' Around" was a catchy midtempo instrumental written by R.L. Kass that featured a intriguingly dissonant, minor-key based melody. That melody was punctuated by Jerry mysteriously whispering "sneakin' around" several times during the recording.

Chet plays a Gibson electric guitar in standard tuning on "Sneakin' Around," and he is joined by Jerry playing a classical guitar through a pickup that is also in standard tuning. Playing in the key of A minor, the two are accompanied by guitar, keyboards, harmonica, bass, and drums. Throughout the recording, Chet renders the song's slightly spooky melody along with a simultaneously played accompanying pattern. Jerry answers Chet's playing with a combination of inventive chord voicings and jittery-sounding staccato solo lines. Chet and Jerry briefly lay out in order to make room for nice lead breaks played by bassist David Hungate and guitarist Pat Bergeson.

Sneakin' Around was both an enjoyable album and a very welcome reunion of two undisputed legends of the guitar, so it was no surprise that it ended up quite well-received when it was first released. It reached the number 68 spot on the U.S. country album charts, and it netted a Grammy for Chet and Jerry—at the Grammy Awards of 1993, the album won the Grammy Award for Best Country Instrumental Performance. (This was Chet and Jerry's second joint Grammy win—in 1970, they had won in the same category for *Me and Jerry*.) Unfortunately, as the old saying goes, all good things must come to an end—*Sneakin' Around* would end up being the last work that Chet and Jerry would ever record together.

"Young Thing"

Composer: Chet Atkins. **Producers:** Chet Atkins, David Hungate. **Musicians:** Chet Atkins (guitar), Pat Bergeson (guitar), Randy Goodrum (keyboards), John Jarvis (keyboards), David Hungate (bass), Lonnie Wilson (drums). **Locations of Recording:** Javelina Studios, Nashville, Tennessee, C.A. Workshop, Nashville, Tennessee. **Original Release:** *Read My Licks* (Columbia album, 1994).

By the early 1990s, Chet had lost interest in framing his music within the genre of smooth jazz—that style had shaped most of his 1980s Columbia albums, but he decided to set it aside in favor of a musical direction that was much more eclectic. Nowhere was this fact more apparent than on his 1994 album *Read My Licks*. The album was similar to his 1985 smooth jazz album *Stay Tuned* in that it featured him sharing the spotlight with a number of prominent artists who were quite a bit younger than him—but it was very different from *Stay Tuned* in that it was difficult to categorize in terms of its musical style.

Simply put, *Read My Licks* was all over the map style-wise, and this was a very good thing. First off, the album featured Chet performing instrumental duets with a diverse group of guitarists including George Benson, Mark Knopfler, and Eric Johnson. (We've discussed George and Mark earlier in this book, but this is the first time we've mentioned Eric—he was the virtuosic rock guitarist best known for his 1990 Grammy-winning instrumental "Cliffs of Dover.")

Also, the album boasted the vocal work of two current country music superstars. Its title track featured Steve Wariner performing an amusing duet with Chet that involved both men singing, and then trading out several lines of their singing for some well-placed guitar licks. (As we noted earlier in this book, Steve worked as one of Chet's backing musicians in the late 1970s. He would eventually leave Chet's employment in order to have a hugely successful career of his own as a country singer/songwriter/guitarist.) And the lead vocals on Chet's rendition of the pop/jazz standard "After You've Gone" were performed by singer/songwriter Suzy Bogguss, who would record a collaborative album with Chet the same year that *Read My Licks* was released. (We'll be discussing both Suzy and her album with Chet entitled *Simpatico* just a bit later in the book.)

So *Read My Licks* rocked as hard as any album Chet ever made when he and Eric Johnson were playing their duet entitled "Somebody Loves Me Now." And it delivered timeless-sounding jazz when Chet and George Benson were trading solos on their relaxed cover of the Johnny Mercer-penned standard "Dream." *And* it featured Chet trading great country blues licks with Mark Knopfler on their duet entitled "Around the Bend." (Incidentally, "Around the Bend" was written by Chet and Jerry Reed.) *And* it included performances by the top-notch country music artists Steve Wariner and Suzy Bogguss.

Whew—all of this, and we still haven't gotten to Chet's finest moments on the record. *Read My Licks* opened with a Chet-penned instrumental entitled "Young Thing." The reason that he chose this title was because he had written it in honor of a longtime friend of his, guitarist Bill Young. Chet's idea for the song was to create a boogie-woogie style piano number, and then play that number on a guitar instead of a piano—so "Young Thing" was a swing-tempo song that featured a busy melody and a simultaneously played walking bass line.

Chet incorporated parts that sounded as if they were played by a brass instrument section into his recording of "Young Thing" in order to accentuate the song's boogie-woogie feel. These parts were not played by a real brass section—instead, they were played on electronic keyboards that could perfectly mimic the sound of brass instruments.

On "Young Thing," Chet plays a Gibson Chet Atkins Studio Classic guitar in standard tuning out of the key of E. (Incidentally, the Studio Classic was a modified version of Chet and Gibson's CE solidbody acoustic—we discussed the Studio Classic in detail in the second chapter of this book.) Accompanied by guitar, keyboards, bass, and drums, Chet deftly keeps his melody and walking bass part swinging through every note of the recording. "Young Thing" might have been inspired by boogie-woogie piano playing, but once Chet moves that style to his guitar, the song ends up having a strong 1950s rock and roll feel to it as well.

Read My Licks was released by Columbia Records in 1994—the album did not make the charts, but both its musical diversity and spectacular performances made it a favorite of Chet's longtime fans. Also, its opening track was singled out for special recognition—at the Grammy Awards of 1994, "Young Thing" won the Grammy Award for Best Country Instrumental Performance. We'll discuss one more number off of *Read My Licks*, "Vincent," in the next entry.

"Vincent"

Composer: Don McLean. **Producers:** Chet Atkins, David Hungate. **Musicians:** Chet Atkins (guitar). **Locations of Recording:** Javelina Studios, Nashville, Tennessee; C.A. Workshop, Nashville, Tennessee. **Original Release:** *Read My Licks* (Columbia album, 1994).

As we just noted in our discussion of "Young Thing," Chet's *Read My Licks* album had the ability to surprise listeners with its musical diversity from song to song. Toward the end of the album, he had delivered a masterful mix of country, rock, blues and jazz styles—but he still had some more musical brilliance that he wanted to share before he signed off. Stepping away from the country, rock, blues and jazz that had constituted the bulk of the album, he played one last number in the style of—well, in the style of just *Chet*. That last selection on *Read My Licks* was an exquisite instrumental version of singer/songwriter/guitarist Don McLean's classic folk song "Vincent." Chet played "Vincent" on his Gibson Chet Atkins Studio Classic guitar, and he was unaccompanied by any other musicians.

"Vincent" was a hauntingly beautiful vocal number about the tragic life of the famed late nineteenth-century poet Vincent Van Gogh, and the song had been played and sung to perfection by Don when he first recorded it in 1971. Chet loved Don's performance of "Vincent," and Chet grew to love performing the song as a solo instrumental guitar work. In fact, Chet had already had quite a long history with "Vincent" by the time he recorded it for *Read My Licks*. He first recorded a version of the number for his 1977 RCA Victor album *Me and My Guitar*—that version was quite lovely, and like his *Read My Licks* version, it featured him playing a nylon-string guitar, unaccompanied.

In the years following the release of *Me and My Guitar*, "Vincent" became a regular feature in both Chet's concert and television appearances. Since he continued to play the song so regularly over the years, his arrangement of it gradually began to change—it was invested with more and more subtle musical phrases that supported Don's unforgettable melody. Eventually Chet ended up refining his arrangement of "Vincent" to a point where he felt that a newly recorded version of it was in order.

On the *Read My Licks* "Vincent," Chet plays his Gibson Studio Classic out of the key of G. The guitar is in standard tuning, except for his two lowest strings—his low E string is tuned down to D, and his A string is tuned down to G. This tuning allows Chet to render much of the song's melody on his higher strings while simultaneously playing accompanying notes on his open lower strings. Simply put, Chet's *Read My Licks* performance of "Vincent" is one of his greatest masterpieces—his melody work, accompanying harmony lines, chord voicings, harmonic note passages, and subtle tempo shifts perfectly blend together to create a magnificent, richly layered musical landscape.

Chet was approaching his fiftieth year as a recording artist—and as evidenced by the incredibly high quality of "Vincent" and the rest of the songs found *Read My Licks*, he was showing no signs of slowing up just yet.

"One More for the Road"

Composers: Suzy Bogguss, Doug Crider, Chet Atkins. **Producers:** Suzy Bogguss, John Guess. **Musicians:** Chet Atkins (guitar), Suzy Bogguss (vocals), Matt Rollings (piano), Pat Bergeson (harmonica). **Locations of Recording:** Emerald Sound and Sound Stage, Nashville, Tennessee, Studio 6, Nashville, Tennessee; Javelina Studios, Nashville, Tennessee; Secret Sound, Nashville, Tennessee, The Plant, San Francisco, California. **Original Release:** *Simpatico* (Liberty Records album with Suzy Bogguss, 1994).

As we've noted a number of times, Chet's track record of making collaborative albums with other artists was a truly stellar one. By the mid–1990s, he had recorded albums with a list of famed performers including Hank Snow, Jerry Reed, Merle Travis, Les Paul, Doc Watson, and Mark Knopfler. But he still had yet to make a collaborative album with a female artist. In 1994, a woman's name was finally added to the list of Chet's album partners when he recorded *Simpatico* with country superstar Suzy Bogguss.

Suzy was a singer/songwriter who had enjoyed an incredibly successful country music career during the late 1980s and early 1990s. She and Chet first had first become friends at the beginning of her rise to popularity. Chet was so impressed with her talent that he penned the liner notes for *Somewhere Between*, her 1989 debut album for Capitol Records. Over the next few years, she notched a string of hit albums and singles—and during that time, she remained close with Chet both personally and professionally.

The two even performed and recorded together from time to time. For example, Suzy sang backing vocals on "Nifty Fifties," a song featured on Chet and Jerry Reed's 1991 collaborative album *Sneakin' Around*, and lead vocals on "After You've Gone," a song featured on Chet's 1994 album *Read My Licks*. (We just mentioned "After You've Gone" in our discussion of the *Read My Licks* number "Young Thing.")

Every number on *Simpatico* featured Suzy on lead vocals, and Chet on lead guitar. The album was very much a straight-up country album, and it contained a winning combination of old and new songs. One of the best of those new songs was "One More for the Road," an uptempo rockabilly flavored number celebrating a musician's life out on the road. "One More for the Road" was written by Suzy, Chet and Doug Crider. (Incidentally, Doug was not only a successful songwriter, but also Suzy's husband.)

On "One More for the Road," Chet plays a Gibson electric guitar in standard tuning out of the key of E. He and Suzy are backed by guitar, piano, harmonica, bass, and drums. As the song shuffles along at a good clip, Suzy sings about wanting to play one more tune for her audience before she and her band have to pack up and move on to the next town. She then turns the number over to Chet, who offers up a wealth of great rockabilly inspired soloing. Most of this soloing features lead lines rendered with simultaneously played accompanying patterns—however, he also throws in just a bit of nimble single-note lead work as well. In the middle of the recording, both Suzy and Chet step back in order to make room for a nice piano solo played by Matt Rollings.

Simpatico was released in late 1994 by Suzy's label, Liberty Records. The label also chose to release "One More for the Road" as a single at that time, so Suzy and Chet made a very enjoyable music video for the song. The video featured Suzy, Chet and the band playing the number in an ornate, 1940s-style hotel—that hotel's guests and staff ended up enjoying the song so much that they all ended up dancing to it together. "One More for the Road" did not end up charting as a single, but *Simpatico* reached the number 55 spot on the U.S. country album charts.

"Jam Man"

Composer: Chet Atkins. **Producer:** Chet Atkins. **Musicians:** Chet Atkins (guitar). **Location of Recording:** C.A. Workshop, Nashville, Tennessee. **Original Release:** *Almost Alone* (Columbia album, 1996).

Chet playing a Gibson Chet Atkins Country Gentleman electric guitar during a concert performance, mid–1990s.

As the old adage goes, most every entertainer would like to end a performance by "going out on a high note"—and that is exactly the manner in which Chet wrapped up his recording career as a whole. 1996 and 1997 ended up being the last two years that his health allowed him to actively record, and during that time he delivered a pair of albums that were every bit as satisfying and creative as anything he had ever done. The first of these albums was the 1996 release *Almost Alone*, which turned out to be his last-ever work as a solo artist. Twelve of the thirteen numbers on the album were instrumentals. (In a moment, we'll discuss *Almost Alone*'s lone vocal number just a bit.)

On *Almost Alone*, Chet returned to a theme that he had used as a starting point for several of his earlier albums, including the similarly titled *Alone* (1973)—that theme was performing a wide variety of songs basically unaccompanied by any other musicians. I use the word "basically" here because both *Alone* and *Almost Alone* actually *did* feature just a bit of accompaniment on them. That accompaniment was only used on a few songs found on each album, and it was always very spare—but it was accompaniment nonetheless.

At any rate, *Almost Alone* was a wonderful collection of thirteen recordings that really *did* feature Chet playing almost alone, and the album very much captured his genius in its full glory. Like so much of his best work, *Almost Alone* featured songs from so many different styles of music that it was hard to categorize—that is, unless you just categorized it as *Chet*. Fittingly, Chet's final work as a solo artist was also a deeply personal one—he wrote six of the album's twelve instrumental numbers, he co-wrote its lone vocal number, and the entire album was recorded at his home studio in Nashville.

One indication of how personal of a work *Almost Alone* was for Chet was the fact that three of the instrumentals he wrote for the album were directly inspired by his own circle of musical friends. "Maybelle" paid tribute to the guitar work of Maybelle Carter, "A Little Mark Musik" was written in the style of Mark Knopfler's playing, and "Waiting for Susie B." was named in honor of Suzy Bogguss.

Now, about the album's vocal number—it was a novelty song sung by Chet called "I Still Write Your Name in the Snow." Chet wrote the number with the well-known country songwriter Billy Edd Wheeler, and it was undoubtedly among the silliest pieces of music that either man had ever created. The song was about a man who sentimentally wrote his lost love's name in the snow in a most unusual and unsanitary manner. (In the interest of good taste, the song avoided going into *too* much detail regarding just what that man's writing utensil was.)

"I Still Write Your Name in the Snow" definitely proved that Chet never lost his penchant for creating novelty records from the beginning of his career right up until its very end. Incidentally, the song featured a laughter and applause track to make it sound as if it had been recorded in front of a live audience, but it had been recorded at C.A. Workshop just like the rest of the album.

Among the best of Chet's six instrumental originals found on *Almost Alone* was a song he entitled "Jam Man." The song featured a very catchy, minor-key based melody that captured not so much a sense of foreboding, but rather a sense of mischievous fun. The reason that Chet chose the title of "Jam Man" for the song was because he had used an audio looping device called the JamMan, manufactured by the Lexicon company, in order to record it. The JamMan looper allowed Chet to instantly layer a number of guitar parts over the recording's initially played guitar part.

On "Jam Man," Chet plays a Gibson electric guitar in the key of A minor, and he is unaccompanied by any other musicians. Cruising along at a moderate shuffle tempo, he starts out the recording by rendering the song's initial melody along with a simultaneously played accompanying pattern. As the recording goes on, Chet uses the JamMan to layer in more and more guitar parts over his original guitar part—these new parts make the song's melody increasingly complex. Plus, some of the new parts that Chet layers in are harmony parts for that ever-more complex melody—so the song begins to sound as if it is being played by some sort of grand, otherworldly guitar orchestra.

The overall sound of "Jam Man" is made even a bit more quirky by the fact that Chet uses fairly heavy distortion on several of the song's guitar parts. Obviously, Chet almost *never* outfitted his guitar sound with any kind of distortion—so it is quite a bit of a novelty to hear him throw some real grind into his soloing. Chet's overdubbed and distorted guitars shape "Jam Man" into one of his most pronounced rock and roll-style recordings.

Almost Alone was moderately successful when it was first released by Columbia, reaching the number 74 spot on the U.S. country album charts. And "Jam Man" was singled out for special recognition—at the Grammy Awards of 1997, the song won the Grammy Award for Best Country Instrumental Performance. This marked Chet's fourteenth Grammy win, as well as the very last of his career.

"Happy Again"

Composer: Chet Atkins. **Producer:** Chet Atkins. **Musicians:** Chet Atkins (guitar). **Location of Recording:** C.A. Workshop, Nashville, Tennessee. **Original Release:** *Almost Alone* (Columbia album, 1996).

It would be a difficult task to pick just which of the half-dozen instrumentals that Chet wrote and recorded for his 1996 Columbia Records album *Almost Alone* turned out to be the best of the bunch, because they were *all* so good. However, most Chet fans would likely view "Happy Again" as a serious contender for the top of that list. "Happy Again" was a perfectly titled song, because it was truly such a happy-sounding number. (Incidentally, Chet publicly stated that he was inspired to write the number after successfully coming through a serious health scare.) The song's bright, memorable melody gave it the feel of a timeless standard—in other words, it did not sound like a brand-new composition nearly as much as it sounded like a famed Tin Pan Alley work, or a well-loved selection from a classic movie musical.

On "Happy Again," Chet plays a Gibson Chet Atkins Studio Classic guitar in standard tuning out of the key of A. As is the case with most all of the other songs found on *Almost Alone*, he is unaccompanied by any other musicians. He opens the number by playing a few slow melodic lines that even sound just a bit bluesy—but then he literally and figuratively shakes off those blues by taking up the song's ebullient main melody at a jaunty pace. Throughout the entire recording, he renders that melody along with a simultaneously played accompanying pattern.

"Happy Again" is another one of those remarkable Chet recordings where he somehow finds a way to make his playing both tremendously exciting and deeply peaceful at the same time. As we just noted in our discussion of "Jam Man," *Almost Alone* would turn out to be Chet's last-ever solo album—its wonderful songs like "Happy Again" proved that he was going out while he was truly still at the top of his game.

"Ave Maria"

Composer: Franz Schubert. **Producer:** Chet Atkins. **Musicians:** Chet Atkins (guitar), the Nashville String Machine (strings). **Location of Recording:** C.A. Workshop, Nashville, Tennessee. **Original Release:** *Almost Alone* (Columbia album, 1996).

In this book's previous two entries, we've discussed songs that Chet wrote and recorded for his last-ever solo release *Almost Alone*. Far and away the most well-known song on that album that Chet did *not* write was the famed nineteenth-century composer Franz Schubert's vocal piece "Ave Maria." Chet arranged "Ave Maria" as an instrumental for solo guitar, and then recorded it with string accompaniment provided by the Nashville String Machine.

Interestingly, Schubert did not originally compose "Ave Maria" as the song that is now known and loved the whole world over. The piece was originally titled "Ellens Gesang III," which in English means "Ellen's Third Song"—and it was part of a much larger musical work by Schubert entitled *Liederzyklus vom Fraulein vom See*. That work was a seven-song collection that set Walter Scott's 1810 epic poem *The Lady of the Lake* to music. In "Ellens Gesang III," the character of Ellen sang a prayer to the Virgin Mary. (Incidentally, Ellen was the character who was known as The Lady of the Lake in both Scott's poem and Schubert's musical work.)

Ellen's prayer to the Virgin Mary in "Ellens Gesang III" evidently led someone to think of pairing Schubert's exquisite composition with *Ave Maria*, the traditional Roman Catholic prayer spoken in Latin. As generation after generation went by, "Ellens Gesang III" became far more widely known as "Ave Maria"—in fact, nowadays most people just incorrectly assume that "Ave Maria" is the original musical work that Schubert intended to write.

Incidentally, Chet had recorded a version of "Ave Maria" much earlier in his career—that recording was featured on *Class Guitar*, his 1967 RCA Victor album consisting entirely of classical guitar instrumentals. Chet's *Class Guitar* version of the song was very enjoyable, but its arrangement definitely did not have the same level of musical complexity that his *Almost Alone* version had.

On the *Almost Alone* version of "Ave Maria," Chet plays a Gibson Chet Atkins Studio Classic guitar in the key of G. His low E string is tuned down to D, his A string is tuned down to G, and his D, G, B and high E strings are unchanged from standard tuning. This tuning allows Chet to render much of the song's melody on his higher strings while simultaneously playing accompanying notes on his open lower strings. Throughout the recording, The Nashville String Machine supports Chet's playing with just the right amount of string accompaniment. Chet's performance of "Ave Maria" treats Schubert's timeless masterpiece with the reverence it deserves—every note he plays is both very stately and very beautiful.

"Ave Maria" was chosen to close *Almost Alone* when the album was released by Columbia Records in 1996—so the song ended up being the last song on Chet's last-ever solo album. If Chet's career as a solo recording artist had to come to an end, his masterful rendition of such a revered musical work was as perfect of an ending as one could ever imagine.

"Dixie McGuire"

Composer: Tommy Emmanuel. **Producer:** Chet Atkins. **Musicians:** Chet Atkins (guitar), Tommy Emmanuel (guitar, bass, brushes), Randy Goodrum (keyboards). **Location of Recording:** C.A. Workshop, Nashville, Tennessee. **Original Release:** *The Day Finger Pickers Took Over the World* (Columbia album with Tommy Emmanuel, 1997).

Since so many of the wonderful albums Chet had made throughout his career were collaborative works with other artists, it was perfectly fitting that the very last album he ever made would be a collaborative one. Chet teamed up with Australian guitar virtuoso Tommy Emmanuel to record *The Day Finger Pickers Took Over the World*, which was released by Columbia Records in 1997.

Tommy was born into a musical family in the mid–1950s, and well before he was ten years old, he was touring all over Australia with them as a guitarist. Around this time, Tommy first heard Chet play, and Chet became Tommy's greatest musical inspiration. Tommy's musical career continued on an upward trajectory as he grew into adulthood, and he first established contact with Chet by writing him letters. Chet wrote back to Tommy, encouraging him to keep honing his guitar skills. As the years went by, Chet became very impressed by Tommy's incredible talent as a guitarist, and the two men eventually grew to be close personal friends.

By the time Chet and Tommy decided to make a collaborative album together, Chet was in very poor health. As we discussed in the first chapter of this book, Chet was diagnosed with colon cancer back in 1973. His treatment allowed him to maintain his health for over two decades, but in the mid–1990s his cancer returned. So when he and Tommy began work on their album, he knew that it would be a difficult process to see the project through to completion. Of course, the fact that Chet could record the album at his own home studio helped matters tremendously—so he kept working on it when his health allowed him to, and eventually he and Tommy were able to deliver a great finished product to Columbia Records.

The Day Finger Pickers Took Over the World was an intimate collection of eleven songs, most of them acoustic guitar instrumentals. The album leaned toward country more than any other style, but it still had quite a bit of a jazz sensibility to it as well. In addition to its instrumentals, the album also featured several novelty vocal numbers sung by Chet and Tommy. One of those numbers was the album's title track, which told the story of fingerpicking guitarists taking over the world with their music. (Incidentally, "The Day Finger Pickers Took Over the World" was originally written as "The Day Bass Players Took Over the World" by Emily Kaitz and Dave Pomeroy, and Chet rewrote the lyrics of the song to reflect his own musical specialty.)

One of the album's standout tracks was "Dixie McGuire," a catchy midtempo instrumental that Tommy had written back in 1977 for the daughter of one of his good friends. The song featured a jazzy, easygoing melody that gave Chet and Tommy the perfect opportunity to play off of each other.

On "Dixie McGuire," Chet plays his Del Vecchio Dinamico resonator guitar in standard tuning, and Tommy plays an acoustic guitar that is also in standard tuning. Tommy provides a good deal of their

Chet Atkins with Tommy Emmanuel, 1997.

accompaniment on the recording—on separate tracks, he plays bass and drums. In fact, the only other musician besides Chet and Tommy on the recording is Chet's longtime musical collaborator, keyboardist Randy Goodrum.

Tommy opens the recording by rendering the song's melody along with a simultaneously played accompanying pattern in the key of D. Chet then joins the recording, adding harmony lines to Tommy's melody playing. The song moves to the key of E, and Chet takes a relaxed solo break. After Chet's solo, the song returns to the key of D, and Tommy and Chet close out the recording by restating their respective melody and harmony parts.

The Day Finger Pickers Took Over the World did not end up charting when it was first released by Columbia—but in truth, the album really did not need any sort of commercial achievement to make it a rousing success. First off, it was a triumph simply because it was a great collection of songs played by two of the world's premier guitarists. But even more importantly, it was a triumph because it tastefully and joyfully closed out the incredible recording history of Chet Atkins. We'll discuss one more song from *The Day Finger Pickers Took Over the World*, "Smokey Mountain Lullaby," in the next entry of this book.

"Smokey Mountain Lullaby"

Composer: Chet Atkins. **Producer:** Chet Atkins. **Musicians:** Chet Atkins (guitar), Tommy Emmanuel (guitar), Randy Goodrum (keyboards), Giles Reeves (bass, strings). **Location of Recording:** C.A. Workshop, Nashville, Tennessee. **Original Release:** *The Day Finger Pickers Took Over the World* (Columbia album with Tommy Emmanuel, 1997).

The story of Chet and Tommy Emmanuel's recording of "Smokey Mountain Lullaby" is both an amazing and very poignant one. The song was the last number that they recorded for their 1997 album *The Day Finger Pickers Took Over the World*, and they very fittingly chose it to be the album's closer.

"Smokey Mountain Lullaby" was a delicately beautiful, slow-tempoed instrumental originally written and recorded by Chet for one of his more unusual musical projects. In 1993, he teamed with the famed singer/songwriter Amy Grant to record an album based on the Christmas-themed children's book *The Gingham Dog and the Calico Cat* by Eugene Field. On *The Gingham Dog and the Calico Cat* album, Amy narrated the book's story, and Chet performed a number of guitar instrumentals to accompany her narration. "Smokey Mountain Lullaby" was the last of Chet's instrumentals featured on that album.

Chet and Tommy needed one more number for *The Day Finger Pickers Took Over the World*, and Chet had the idea to shape "Smokey Mountain Lullaby" into a duet for them to play. But the problem was that Chet's health had taken a very serious downturn due to his struggle with cancer—doctors had discovered a tumor in his brain that would have to be removed immediately. So it was going to be difficult for them to find a way to get the song recorded for the album.

Tommy has publicly told the story of the recording of "Smokey Mountain Lullaby" for *The Day Finger Pickers Took Over the World* many times over the years, so I don't think he will mind at all if I paraphrase that story here. The night before Chet's surgery, Chet woke up Tommy at 3:00 a.m. to ask him if they could try to record the song right then and there. Tommy was staying at Chet's home while they were making the album, so all they had to do to get ready to record was to walk from their bedrooms into Chet's home studio—in their pajamas, mind you.

So in the middle of the night, these two great friends grabbed their guitars and sat down to record one final number for their album. And they only had a ridiculously brief window of opportunity to get the song down just right—after all, Chet's surgery was just a few hours away, and it would leave him in no condition to play at the high level he was accustomed to for quite some time. They got set up, Chet pushed the "record" button, and in just one take they created an indescribably beautiful piece of music.

On "Smokey Mountain Lullaby," Chet plays his Ramirez classical guitar, an instrument he only occasionally used on any of his recordings. He plays the song in the key of G, but the Ramirez is tuned in a decidedly unusual manner—this manner will be a bit difficult to explain, but I'll give it a try here. Sometimes when Chet would play in the key of G, he would tune his low E string down to D, his A string down to G, and his D, G, B and high E strings would remain unchanged from standard tuning. This tuning would allow Chet to render much of a song's melody on his higher strings while simultaneously playing accompanying notes on his open lower strings.

Chet uses this tuning configuration on "Smokey Mountain Lullaby"—but all of the strings on the Ramirez are tuned down a whole step from D-G-D-G-B-E to C-F-C-F-A-D. So when Chet plays "Smokey Mountain Lullaby" in the key of G, it sounds as if he is playing the song in the key of F. On the recording, Chet is joined by Tommy playing an acoustic guitar. I won't try to venture a guess as to Tommy's tuning on the song—most of his guitar work consists of single-note soloing, so it is hard to tell if his guitar is changed up at all from standard tuning.

Backed by keyboards, bass and strings, Chet and Tommy's guitar parts move as one on "Smokey Mountain Lullaby." They render the song's lovely melody with an empathy for each other's playing that is deeply moving. Incidentally, that melody is often built around peaceful-sounding major seventh chords, so the song really *does* sound as if it could be a lullaby. It seems quite appropriate that Chet and Tommy recorded "Smokey Mountain Lullaby" in the middle of the night, because the song very much captures the feeling of a gorgeous, tranquil dream.

Sadly, the recording of "Smokey Mountain Lullaby" ended up marking the end of Chet's incredible recording career—his health never allowed him to fully resume his musical activities after *The Day Finger Pickers Took Over the World* was released in 1997. He would perform live a few more times over the next two years before his battle with cancer really began to overtake him—but after over fifty years of creating extraordinary music in the studio, Chet's work as a recording artist was finally done.

"Mr. Bojangles"

Composer: Jerry Jeff Walker. **Producer:** Chet Atkins. **Musicians:** Chet Atkins (guitar). **Location of Recording:** C.A. Workshop, Nashville, Tennessee. **Original Release:** *Solo Sessions* (CGP album, 2003).

We'll close out our journey through the history of Chet's recording career with a wonderful postscript. Since the early 1980s, Chet had been periodically recording solo guitar instrumentals at his home studio—and these recordings never ended up being featured on any of his Columbia Records albums. Some of these recordings were newly arranged versions of songs that Chet had previously recorded and released, and some of them were of songs that he had *never* recorded or released in any other form. All of them had one thing in common—they featured Chet playing unaccompanied by any other musicians.

Just what Chet would have ever ended up doing with this collection of recordings will always remain a bit of a mystery—in fact, it is even somewhat hard to guess why he even made the recordings in the first place. Some of them might have been laid down in order to work out arrangements of songs that he did plan on formally recording. (We'll discuss that hypothesis in more detail in just a moment.) Some of them might have been laid down in order to test out the sound of a particular guitar or piece of audio equipment. Some of them might have been laid down simply because Chet had an arrangement of a song that he really wanted to record, even if that song was not going to meet the needs whatever album project he was working on at the time.

At any rate, by the time Chet passed away on June 30, 2001, he had amassed a marvelous collection of solo guitar recordings that very few people had ever heard. Thankfully, Chet's family realized how much his fans would enjoy these recordings, so they made plans to compile them for a formal album release. This album was assembled by a group of people who had been very close to Chet both personally and professionally for many years. It was engineered by Mike Poston, who had been engineering Chet's albums since the early 1980s. And it was mastered by Chet's grandson Jonathan Russell, who had worked on mastering the last several albums that Chet had made for Columbia. Finally, Chet's longtime guitar sideman Paul Yandell served as the album's creative consultant.

The album that this distinguished team put together was entitled *Solo Sessions*, and it was released in 2003 by an Atkins family created label dubbed "CGP Records." (Of course, the label's name was inspired by the "Certified Guitar Player" degree Chet had lightheartedly bestowed on himself two decades earlier.) *Solo Sessions* featured a whopping 28 numbers, and they all had an intimacy to them that made listeners feel as if they were sitting right next to Chet as he played.

The song I have chosen to discuss from *Solo Sessions* is "Mr. Bojangles," and I have chosen it for two main reasons. First, it is a wonderful version of a song that Chet loved to play for many years. Second, this particular recording might shed a bit of light on many of the other recordings that ended up being featured on *Solo Sessions*.

"Mr. Bojangles" was a melancholy country story song about an elderly street dancer who had long grieved for his dog that had passed away many years before. The number was written and recorded in 1968 by country singer Jerry Jeff Walker, but the most well-known version of it was recorded by the Nitty Gritty Dirt Band for their 1970 album *Uncle Charlie & His Dog Teddy*. The Nitty Gritty Dirt Band's version reached the top ten on the U.S. pop single charts the following year. "Mr. Bojangles" was an unusual hit single in the age of rock and roll, considering the fact that most of the song was performed in waltz time.

Chet very quickly took a strong liking to "Mr. Bojangles" after first hearing it—he recorded an instrumental version of the song with a full band for his 1973 RCA Victor album *Superpickers*, and he also performed it live during many of his concert appearances. As the years went by, the song obviously remained one of Chet's all-time favorites, because he chose to record a new version of it for his last-ever solo album, the 1996 Columbia release *Almost Alone*. The *Almost Alone* version of "Mr. Bojangles" featured Chet playing with no accompaniment other than a string arrangement performed by The Nashville String Machine.

This is where Chet's *Solo Sessions* version of "Mr. Bojangles" fits into the story. The arrangement Chet used for his *Solo Sessions* version of the song is strikingly similar to the arrangement he used for the *Almost Alone* version—so it seems entirely possible that the *Solo Sessions* version was originally recorded in order to help him work out his *Almost Alone* arrangement of the song. Perhaps the *Solo Sessions* version of "Mr. Bojangles" was even given to The Nashville String Machine so that they could work out their string arrangement for the *Almost Alone* version of the song.

These theories would seem to be supported by the fact that there is a noticeable casualness to Chet's *Solo Sessions* version of "Mr. Bojangles"—for instance, the recording is played at a substantially quicker tempo than the *Almost Alone* version. That said, however the *Solo Sessions* version of the song is still a tremendous recording. On the number, Chet plays one of his classical guitars outfitted with a pickup, and that guitar is in standard tuning. Playing in the key of C, Chet delivers a heartfelt rendition of the song that features the perfect balance of melody work, accompanying patterns, and inventive chord voicings.

If the *Solo Sessions* "Mr. Bojangles" was in fact a "rough draft" recording like I just suggested, then maybe a number of the other *Solo Sessions* recordings were "rough drafts" too. At any rate, no matter *what* Chet ever planned on doing with the *Solo Sessions* recordings, one thing about them is certain—they provide a wonderfully intimate view of Chet's musical genius.

And with those thoughts, we have finished our journey through the major highlights of Chet Atkins' incredible recording career, all the way from his first officially released record "Guitar Blues (Pickin' the Blues)" to the final song on his final album, "Smokey Mountain Lullaby." And Chet even gave us an encore with CGP's 2003 release of *Solo Sessions*.

What an awe-inspiring journey it has been—and in reality, the music we have covered in this book is really only the tip of the iceberg. Chet's recorded legacy as a guitarist spans over fifty years, and hundreds upon hundreds of songs drawn from almost every conceivable style of music—it is a legacy that is truly unmatched in the history of modern musical entertainment.

I must admit that I'm having a hard time finding the right words to close out this book—I have loved Chet's music for most all of my life, and it has been a truly incredible experience to study his work in such great detail over this past year or so. I hope that all of you who are reading these words have enjoyed the end result of my efforts.

I opened this book with words of thanks directed beyond our earthly realm to Mister Guitar himself, and it seems to me that it would be very appropriate to close the book in the exact same way. Thanks for all of the great music, Chet.

Appendix: The Songs

Alphabetically

"Alabama Jubilee," *The Pops Goes Country*, RCA Victor album, 1966 (with Arthur Fiedler and the Boston Pops)
"Alley Cat," *Teen Scene*, RCA Victor album, 1963
"Arkansas Traveler," *Chet Atkins in Three Dimensions*, RCA Victor album, 1955
"Avalon," *Chester and Lester*, RCA Victor album, 1976 (with Les Paul)
"Ave Maria," *Almost Alone*, Columbia album, 1996
"Baby's Coming Home," *Chet Atkins Picks on Jerry Reed*, RCA Victor album, 1974
"The Bells of St. Mary's," RCA Victor 20-5300 78 single, RCA Victor 47-5300 45 single, 1953
"Black Mountain Rag," *Pickin' My Way*, RCA Victor album, 1971, RCA Victor 74-0536 45 single, 1971
"Blue Angel," *Hometown Guitar*, RCA Victor album, 1968, RCA Victor 47-9578 45 single, 1968
"Boo Boo Stick Beat," RCA Victor 47-7589 45 single, 1959, *Teensville*, RCA Victor album, 1960
"Boogie Man Boogie," RCA Victor 21-0367 78 single, RCA Victor 48-0367 45 single, 1950
"Brahms' Lullaby," *Reminiscing*, RCA Victor album, 1964 (with Hank Snow)
"Bug Dance," RCA Victor 20-2692 78 single, 1947
"Canned Heat," RCA Victor 20-2472 78 single, 1947
"Cannonball Rag," *Me and Jerry*, RCA Victor album, 1970 (with Jerry Reed)
"Caravan" *Chester and Lester*, RCA Victor album, 1976 (with Les Paul)
"Cascade" *Me and My Guitar*, RCA Victor album, 1977, RCA Victor PB-11071 45 single, 1977
"Centipede Boogie," RCA Victor 21-0139 78 single, RCA Victor 48-0142 45 single, 1949
"Chinatown, My Chinatown," RCA Victor 20-4896 78 single, RCA Victor 47-4896 45 single, 1952
"Chopin Waltz No. 10 in B Minor," *My Favorite Guitars*, RCA Victor album, 1964
"City Slicker," RCA Victor 20-5484 78 single, RCA Victor 47-5484 45 single, 1953
"The Claw," *Alone*, RCA Victor album, 1973
"El Condor Pasa," *For the Good Times and Other Country Moods*, RCA Victor album, 1971
"Cosmic Square Dance," *Stay Tuned*, Columbia album, 1985
"Country Gentleman," RCA Victor 20-5300 78 single, RCA Victor 47-5300 45 single, 1953
"El Cumbanchero," *Hi-Fi in Focus*, RCA Victor album, 1957
"Darling, Je Vous Aime Beaucoup," *Pickin' the Hits*, RCA Victor Extended Play 45, 1955
"Dixie McGuire," *The Day Finger Pickers Took Over the World*, Columbia album, 1997 (with Tommy Emmanuel)
"Dizzy Strings," RCA Victor 20-3006 78 single, 1947
"Django's Castle," RCA Victor 47-7589 45 single, 1959, *Teensville*, RCA Victor album, 1960
"Do I Ever Cross Your Mind," *The Best of Chet Atkins and Friends*, RCA Victor album, 1976
"Downhill Drag," RCA Victor 20-5704 78 single, RCA Victor 47-5704 45 single, 1954
"Drive In," *Solo Flights*, RCA Victor album, 1968
"East Tennessee Christmas," *East Tennessee Christmas*, Columbia album, 1983
"The Entertainer," RCA Victor PB-10046 45 single, 1974, *Chet Atkins Goes to the Movies*, RCA Victor album, 1976

"Fiddlin' Around," *Superpickers*, RCA Victor album, 1973, RCA Victor APBO-0146 45 single, 1973
"Foggy Mountain Top," *Chet*, RCA Camden album, 1967
"Freight Train," *Guitar Country*, RCA Victor album, 1964, RCA Victor 47-8342 45 single, 1964
"Frog Kissin'," *The Best of Chet Atkins and Friends*, RCA Victor album, 1976, RCA Victor PB-10614 45 single, 1976
"From Nashville with Love," *From Nashville with Love*, RCA Victor album, 1966, RCA Victor 47-8781 45 single, 1966
"Gallopin' on the Guitar," RCA Victor 21-0021 78 single, 1949
"Good-Bye Blues," RCA Victor 20-4491 78 single, RCA Victor 47-4491 45 single, 1952
"Guitar Blues (Pickin' the Blues)," Bullet 617 78 single, 1946
"Happy Again," *Almost Alone*, Columbia album, 1996
"Hidden Charm," RCA Victor 20-7048 78 single, RCA Victor 47-7048 45 single, 1957
"Honolulu Blue," *Street Dreams*, Columbia album, 1986
"Hot Mocking Bird," *Chet Atkins' Workshop*, RCA Victor album, 1961, RCA Victor 47-7847 45 mono single, 1961, RCA Victor 37-7847 Compact 33 single, 1961
"I Still Can't Say Goodbye," *Chet Atkins, C.G.P.*, Columbia album, 1988, Columbia 38-07929 45 single, 1988
"I'll See You in My Dreams," *The Atkins-Travis Traveling Show*, RCA Victor album, 1974 (with Merle Travis)
"I'm Forever Blowing Bubbles," *Mister Guitar*, RCA Victor album, 1959
"I've Been Working on the Guitar," RCA Victor 20-2876 78 single, 1947
"Imagination," RCA Victor 20-4925 78 single, RCA Victor 47-4925 45 single, 1952
"Indiana (Back Home in Indiana)," *A Session with Chet Atkins*, RCA Victor album, 1954
"It Ain't Necessarily So," *The Most Popular Guitar*, RCA Victor album, 1961
"It Don't Mean a Thing (If It Ain't Got That Swing)," *Guitar Monsters*, RCA Victor album, 1978 (with Les Paul)
"Jam Man," *Almost Alone*, Columbia album, 1996
"Jingle Bell Rock," *Christmas with Chet Atkins*, RCA Victor album, 1961, RCA Victor 47-7971 45 single, 1961
"Jitterbug Waltz," *Chet Atkins in Hollywood*, RCA Victor album, 1959
"Kentucky Derby," RCA Victor 20-5704 78 single, RCA Victor 47-5704 45 single, 1954
"Kicky," *Progressive Pickin'*, RCA Victor album, 1964
"A Little Bit of Blues," *Guitar Country*, RCA Victor album, 1964
"Liza," *Finger-Style Guitar*, RCA Victor album, 1956
"Londonderry Air," *Alone*, RCA Victor album, 1973
"Love Song of Pepe Sanchez," *The First Nashville Guitar Quartet*, RCA Victor album, 1979, RCA Victor PB-11523 45 single, 1979 (with the First Nashville Guitar Quartet)
"Lover Come Back to Me," *Pickin' My Way*, RCA Victor album, 1971
"The Mad Russian," *Me and Chet*, RCA Victor album, 1972 (with Jerry Reed)
"Main Street Breakdown," RCA Victor 21-0329 78 single, RCA Victor 48-0329 45 single, 1950
"Malagueña," *Finger-Style Guitar*, RCA Victor album, 1956
"The Masterpiece," *Chet Atkins Picks on the Hits*, RCA Victor album, 1972
"Mayan Dance," *Caribbean Guitar*, RCA Victor album, 1962
"Medley: The Battle of New Orleans/Sugarfoot Rag," *Chet Atkins Picks on the Pops*, RCA Victor album, 1969 (with Arthur Fiedler and the Boston Pops)
"Michelle," *Chet Atkins Picks on the Beatles*, RCA Victor album, 1966
"Minute Waltz," *Chet Atkins in Three Dimensions*, RCA Victor album, 1955
"Mr. Bojangles," *Solo Sessions*, CGP, 2003
"Mister Sandman," RCA Victor 20-5956 78 single, RCA Victor 47-5956 45 single, 1955
"Mountain Melody," RCA Victor 21-0440 78 single, RCA Victor 48-0440 45 single, 1951
"Nagasaki," *Chet Atkins at Home*, RCA Victor album, 1958
"Nashtown Ville," *Me and Chet*, RCA Victor album, 1972 (with Jerry Reed)
"The Night Atlanta Burned," *The Night Atlanta Burned*, RCA Victor album, 1975, RCA Victor PB-10346 45 single, 1975 (with the Atkins String Company)
"Ochi Chornya (Dark Eyes)," *Chet Atkins in Three Dimensions*, RCA Victor album, 1955

Appendix: The Songs (Alphabetically)

"Oh! By Jingo, Oh! By Gee! (You're the Only Girl for Me)," *Stringin' Along with Chet Atkins*, RCA Victor album, 1956
"The Old Buck Dance," RCA Victor 21-0165 78 single, RCA Victor 48-0173 45 single, 1950
"The Old Rugged Cross," *Chet Atkins Plays Back Home Hymns*, RCA Victor album, 1962
"On My Way to Canaan's Land," *Reflections*, RCA Victor album, 1980, RCA Victor PB-12138 45 single, 1980 (with Doc Watson)
"One Mint Julep," *Teensville*, RCA Victor album, 1960, RCA Victor 47-7684 45 mono single, 1960, RCA Victor 61-7684 45 stereo single, 1960
"One More for the Road," *Simpatico*, Liberty Records, 1994 (with Suzy Bogguss)
"Orange Blossom Special," *Country After All These Years*, RCA Victor album, 1981
"The Peanut Vendor," *The Other Chet Atkins*, RCA Victor album, 1960
"Poison Love," *C.B. Atkins and C.E. Snow by Special Request*, RCA Victor album, 1969 (with Hank Snow)
"Polka Dots and Moonbeams," *Standard Brands*, RCA Victor album, 1981 (with Lenny Breau)
"Poor Boy Blues," *Neck and Neck*, Columbia album, 1990, Columbia 38-73556 single, 1990 (with Mark Knopfler)
"The Poor People of Paris (Jean's Song)," RCA Victor 20-6366 78 single, RCA Victor 47-6366 45 single, 1956
"Prancin' Filly," *Music From Nashville, My Home Town*, RCA Camden album, 1966
"Prissy," RCA Victor 47-8927 45 single, 1966
"Rainbow," RCA Victor 20-4491 78 single, RCA Victor 47-4491 45 single, 1952
"Sails," *Sails*, Columbia album, 1987
"Salty Dog Rag," *Down Home*, RCA Victor album, 1962
"Satan's Doll" *Progressive Pickin',* RCA Victor album, 1964
"Scare Crow," *Our Man in Nashville*, RCA Victor album, 1963
"Silver Bell," RCA Victor 20-5995 78 single, RCA Victor 47-5995 45 single, 1955 (with Hank Snow)
"Slinkey," *Mister Guitar*, RCA Victor album, 1959
"Smokey Mountain Lullaby," *The Day Finger Pickers Took Over the World*, Columbia album, 1997 (with Tommy Emmanuel)
"Sneakin' Around," *Sneakin' Around*, Columbia album, 1991 (with Jerry Reed)
"Snowbird," *For the Good Times and Other Country Moods*, RCA Victor album, 1971, RCA Victor 47-9956 45 single, 1971
"So Soft, Your Goodbye," *Neck and Neck*, Columbia album, 1990, Columbia 38-73556 single, 1990 (with Mark Knopfler)
"The Stars and Stripes Forever," *The Best of Chet on the Road...Live*, RCA Victor album, 1980
"Steeplechase Lane," *Yestergroovin',* RCA Victor album, 1970, RCA Victor 47-9827 45 single, 1970
"Sunrise," *Stay Tuned*, Columbia album, 1985, Columbia 38-04859 45 single, 1985
"Swanee River," *The Guitar Genius*, RCA Camden album, 1963
"Swedish Rhapsody," *Finger-Style Guitar*, RCA Victor album, 1956
"Sweet Georgia Brown," *The Best of Chet Atkins and Friends*, RCA Victor album, 1976
"Take Five," *Alone*, RCA Victor album, 1973
"A Taste of Honey," *It's a Guitar World*, RCA Victor album 1967
"Tears," *Chet Atkins Picks the Best*, RCA Victor album, 1967
"Teensville," *Teensville*, RCA Victor album, 1960, RCA Victor 47-7684 45 mono single, 1960, RCA Victor 61-7684 45 stereo single, 1960
"Tennessee Rag/Beaumont Rag," *Reflections*, RCA Victor album, 1980, RCA Victor PB-12138 45 single, 1980 (with Doc Watson)
"Tennessee Stud," *Me and Jerry*, RCA Victor album, 1970 (with Jerry Reed)
"Terry on the Turnpike," *The Best of Chet Atkins and Friends*, RCA Victor album, 1976
"Theme from a Dream," *Chet Atkins in Hollywood*, RCA Victor album, 1959
"Theme from *The Dark at the Top of the Stairs*," RCA Victor 47-7796 45 mono single, 1960, RCA Victor 61-7796 45 stereo single, 1960

"Theme from *Zorba the Greek*," *Lover's Guitar* RCA Victor album, 1969, RCA Victor 47-9725 45 single, 1969
"The Third Man Theme," RCA Victor 20-4925 78 single, RCA Victor 47-4925 45 single, 1952
"Tiger Rag," *Hi-Fi in Focus*, RCA Victor album, 1957
"Trambone," RCA Victor 20-6796 78 single, RCA Victor 47-6796 45 single, 1957
"Vincent," *Read My Licks*, Columbia album, 1994
"Walk Don't Run," *Hi-Fi in Focus*, RCA Victor album, 1957
"Waltz for the Lonely," *Sails*, Columbia album, 1987
"Wheels," *Travelin',* RCA Victor album, 1963
"When You Wish Upon a Star," *Pickin' My Way*, RCA Victor album, 1971
"Wildwood Flower," RCA Victor 20-5638 78 single, RCA Victor 47-5638 45 single, 1954
"Wimoweh," *My Favorite Guitars*, RCA Victor album, 1964
"Windy and Warm," *Down Home*, RCA Victor album, 1962
"Yakety Axe," *More of That Guitar Country*, RCA Victor album, 1965, RCA Victor 47-8590 45 single, 1965
"Yankee Doodle Dixie," *Chet Atkins at Home*, RCA Victor album, 1958
"Yellow Bird," *Class Guitar*, RCA Victor album, 1967
"You're Just in Love," *Chet Atkins at Home*, RCA Victor album, 1958
"Young Thing," *Read My Licks*, Columbia album, 1994

Bibliography

Atkins, Chet, and Michael Cochran. *Chet Atkins: Me and My Guitars*. West Plains, MO: Russ Cochran, 2001.

Atkins, Chet, with Bill Neely. *Country Gentleman*. Chicago: Henry Regnery, 1974.

Bacon, Tony. *50 Years of Gretsch Electrics*. San Francisco: Backbeat, 2005.

_____, and Paul Day. *The Gretsch Book: A Complete History of Gretsch Electric Guitars*. San Francisco: Miller Freeman, 1996.

Ball, Edward. *Gretsch 6120: The History of a Legendary Guitar*. Arglen, PA: Schiffer, 2010.

Bratic, Deyan, and John McClellan. *Chet Atkins in Three Dimensions, Volume 1: 50 Years of Legendary Guitar*. Pacific, MO: Mel Bay, 2003.

_____. *Chet Atkins in Three Dimensions, Volume 2: 50 Years of Legendary Guitar*. Pacific, MO: Mel Bay, 2010.

Chintala, John. *Chet Atkins: A Complete Guide to "Mister Guitar."* Kindle edition. CHI, 2013.

Kienzle, Rich. Notes to *Chet Atkins, Galloping Guitar*. Four-CD set. Bear Family BCD 15714 (1993).

_____. Notes to *Chet Atkins, Mr. Guitar*. Seven-CD set. Bear Family BCD 16539 (2004).

Kingsbury, Paul. Notes to *Chet Atkins, The RCA Years*. Two-CD set. RCA 07863 61095-2 (1992).

Rumble, John W., ed. *Chet Atkins: Certified Guitar Player*. Nashville: Country Music Foundation Press, 2011.

Scott, Jay. *The Guitars of the Fred Gretsch Company*. Fullerton, CA: Centerstream, 2012.

Index

All recorded songs or collections of recorded songs found in this index are Chet Atkins releases unless otherwise indicated. Numbers in ***bold italics*** indicate pages with photographs.

ABC Television Network 13, 64
Abraham Lincoln on Screen (2009 book) 2
Acuff, Roy 8
Adams, A. Emmett 45
"After You've Gone" (song on 1994 album *Read My Licks*) 187, 189
"Alabama Jubilee" (song on 1954 album *A Session with Chet Atkins*) 117
"Alabama Jubilee" (song on 1966 album *The Pops Goes Country*) 117, 131
Albertine, Charles 107
Alfvén, Hugo 67
"All I Have to Do Is Dream" (Everly Brothers single track, 1958) 46, 84
Allen, Rosalie 44
"Alley Cat" (Frank Bjorn single track, 1962) 106
"Alley Cat" (song on 1963 album *Teen Scene*) 106
Almost Alone (1996 album) 190, 191, 192, 193
Alone (1973 album) 146, 147, 148, 149, 186, 190
Alpert, Herb 122
The Amazing Chet Atkins (1955 album) 91
American Civil War 78, 154
American Federation of Musicians 10, 31, 32
"American Song" (song on 2006 *Rich Meaty Taste* album *Thank You So Much*) 2

And Then Came ... Chet Atkins (1979 album) 168
The Andrews Sisters 41
The Anita Kerr Singers 91, 92, 93, 99, 100, 107, 115, 129
"Arkansas Traveler" (song on 1955 album *Chet Atkins in Three Dimensions*) 60, 61
Armstrong, Louis 45, 61
Arnold, Eddy 47, 135
"Around the Bend" (song on 1994 album *Read My Licks*) 187
Atkins, Billie Rose 32
Atkins, Chester Burton "Chet": awards received for musical work 16, 17, 19, 125, 136, 139, 151, 153, 156, 157, 171, 177, 183, 184, 186, 188, 192; birth 5; childhood 5, 6; creation of the honorary C.G.P. degree 18, 173, 180, 197; death 2, 19, 197; decision to leave RCA Victor for Columbia Records 17, 171, 172, 173; endorsement of the Gibson Guitar Corporation 5, 17, 18, 23, 24, 47, 173; endorsement of the Gretsch Company 1, 5, 12, 17, 18, 20, 21, 22, 23, 24, 47, 55; experiments with new guitar and recording technology 15, 18, 23, 24, 39, 40, 88, 89; fiddle playing 6, 7; fingerpicking guitar style 7, 29, 94; Grammy Awards 16, 125, 136, 139, 151, 153, 156, 157, 171, 177, 183, 184, 186, 188,

192; guitar instructional material created by 19; health problems 6, 17, 19, 194, 195, 196; induction into the Country Music Hall of Fame 17, 153; interest in creating novelty records 49, 50, 79, 89, 191; legacy 2, 5, 198; musical styles 5; nickname of "Chet" 9, 27; nickname of "Mister Guitar" 5, 87; personality 20; photographs ***28, 38, 52, 63, 88, 90, 93, 112, 123, 126, 133, 160, 176, 178, 181, 183, 185, 190, 194***; record producing career 13, 14, 17, 48, 50, 76, 118; recording practices 26, 66, 78, 79, 95, 135, 174, 196, 197, 198; relationship with father James 181; singing 10, 29, 32, 35, 41, 52, 133, 134, 158, 182; songwriting 11, 12; superlick 110, 127, 128, 139, 140, 156; television performances 13, 16, 19
Atkins, Ida Sharp 5
Atkins, James Arley 5, 123, 181
Atkins, Jim 5, 6, 7, 8, 10, 20, 31, 32, 39, 40, 80, 81, 82
Atkins, Leona 8, 9
Atkins, Lowell 6
Atkins, Merle 9
The Atkins String Company 154
The Atkins-Travis Traveling Show (1974 album) 136, 150, 151, 152
Atlanta, Georgia 32, 33, 154

"Avalon" (Al Jolson single track, 1921) 156
"Avalon" (song on 1955 Extended Play 45 *Chet Atkins and His Guitar*) 156, 157
"Avalon" (song on 1976 album *Chester and Lester*) 156, 157
Ave Maria (prayer) 193
"Ave Maria" (song on 1967 album *Class Guitar*) 193
"Ave Maria" (song on 1996 album *Almost Alone*) 192, 193

"Baby's Coming Home" (song on 1974 album *Chet Atkins Picks on Jerry Reed*) 145, 152
Bach, Johan Sebastian 94
Baez, Joan 107
Baggs guitar pickups 179
Baldwin Prismatone guitar pickups 129, 159, 161
Ballard, Pat 56
The Batman Filmography (2013 book) 2
"The Battle Hymn of the Republic" (traditional song) 153
"The Battle of New Orleans" (Johnny Horton single track, 1959) 131
Baxter, Les 64
Beal, Joe 99
Bear Family Records 29, 50, 52, 86, 90, 98
The Beasley Singers 41, 42
The Beatles 1, 15, 16, 22, 71, 106, 119, 121
The Bells of St. Mary's (1945 film) 45
"The Bells of St. Mary's" (single track, 1953) 45, 46, 47, 65
"The Bells of St. Mary's" (song on 1974 album *Superpickers*) 46
Bennard, George 105
The Benny Hill Show (television program) 116
Benson, George 18, 175, **176**, 187
Bergeson, Pat 186
Bergman, Alan 126
Berlin, Irving 76
Bernie, Ben 162
Berry, Chuck 80
The Best Chet Yet (1955 album) 91
The Best of Chet Atkins and Friends (1976 album) 157, 158, 159, 160, 161, 162, 163, 172
The Best of Chet on the Road ... Live (1980 album) 106, 108, 130, 167, 168, 179
Bigsby guitar pickups 20
Biviano, Joe 31, 32
Bjorn, Frank 106
"Black Mountain Rag" (1952 single) 44, 140, 141, 142
"Black Mountain Rag" (song on 1956 album *Stringin' Along with Chet Atkins*) 65, 141, 142
"Black Mountain Rag" (song on 1971 album *Pickin' My Way*) 2, 44, 141, 142, 143
Blanchard, Lowell 7
"Blind Willie" (song on 1980 album *The Best of Chet on the Road ... Live*) 168
"Blue Angel" (song on 1968 album *Hometown Guitar*) 129, 130
"Blue Angel" (song on 1980 album *The Best of Chet on the Road ... Live*) 130
Bogguss, Suzy 19, 187, 189, 190, 191
"Boo Boo Stick Beat" (song on 1960 album *Teensville*) 89, 90, 91
"Boo Boo Stick Beat" (unreleased track, 1959) 90
"Boogie Man Boogie" (single track, 1950) 35, 36, 37, 133
Boothe, Jim 99
Boston, Massachusetts 117, 118, 131
The Boston Pops 16, 102, 117, 118, 131, 132, 138, 170
Boyd, Liona 149, 165
Brahms, Johannes 113
"Brahm's Lullaby" (song on 1964 album *Reminiscing*) 113, 114, 132
Bream, Julian 165
Breau, Lenny 17, 161, 162, 163, 172
Brockman, James 82
Brooklyn, New York 11, 20
Brown, Lew 65
"Brown Eyes Cryin' in the Rain" (single track, 1946) 9, 27, 60
Brown Radio Productions, Nashville, Tennessee 37, 38, 40, 42, 48, 57
The Browns 84
Bryan, Alfred 39

Bryant, Boudleaux 12, 46, 50, 53, 84, 156
Bryant, Felice 46
"Bug Dance" (single track, 1947) 30
Bullet Records 9, 27, 28, 60
Burke, Johnny 172
Burns, Kenneth "Jethro" 8, 32, 33, 34, 35, 36, 37, 46, 47, **52**, 53, 113, 156
Butts, Ray 24, 57
"Bye Bye Love" (Everly Brothers single track, 1957) 46, 84
Byrd, Jerry 46, 65

C.A. Workshop, Nashville, Tennessee 166, 170, 182, 191
Cadence Records 84
Call Me Madam (1950 musical) 76
Call Me Madam (1953 film) 76
"The Call to the Post" (traditional song) 50
Campbell, Archie 7
Campbell, Paul 112
"Canned Heat" (single track, 1947) 20, 29, 30
"Cannonball Rag" (song on 1970 album *Me and Jerry*) 136
"Cannonball Rag" (song on 1974 album *The Atkins-Travis Traveling Show*) 137, 185
Capitol Records 9, 29, 189
"Caravan" (Duke Ellington single track, 1937) 155
"Caravan" (song on 1950 Les Paul album *The New Sound*) 155
"Caravan" (song on 1954 album *A Session with Chet Atkins*) 155
"Caravan" (song on 1976 album *Chester and Lester*) 154, 155, 156
Caribbean Guitar (1962 album) 103
Carlisle, Bill 7
Carter, A.P. 127
Carter, Anita 10, 34, 35, 36, 37
Carter, Helen 10, 34, 35
Carter, June 10
Carter, Maybelle 10, 127, 191
Carter Family 51, 127
The Carter Sisters 10, 11, 20, 34, 37, 48
"Cascade" (song on 1977 album *Me and My Guitar*) 159, 160, 161

Index

Casey, Kenneth 162
C.B. Atkins and C.E. Snow by Special Request (1969 album) 106, 114, 132, 134
CBS Special Products 58, 153
Ceará, Brazil 22, 111, 129
"Centipede Boogie" (single track, 1949) 33, 34
CGP Records 197
"Cherry Pink and Apple Blossom White" (song on 1955 Extended Play 45 *Pickin' the Hits*) 58
Chester and Lester (1976 album) 17, 155, 156, 157, 164
Chet (1967 album) 127, 128
Chet Atkins and His Guitar (Extended Play 45, 1955) 157
Chet Atkins Appreciation Society 18
Chet Atkins at Home (1958 album) 14, 76, 77, 78, 130
Chet Atkins, C.G.P. (1988 album) 180, 181, 182
Chet Atkins Fan Club 12
Chet Atkins' Gallopin' Guitar (1953 album) 11, 33, 42, 43, 44, 50, 54, 65, 140, 141
Chet Atkins Goes to the Movies (1976 album) 152, 153
Chet Atkins in Hollywood (1959 album) 22, 83, 84, 85, 86, 87, 97, 98, 101
Chet Atkins in Three Dimensions (1955 album) 14, 22, 59, 60, 61, 62, 69, 94, 148
Chet Atkins: Me and My Guitars (2001 book) 12, 19, 66, 172, 184
Chet Atkins Picks on Jerry Reed (1974 album) 135, 145, 152
Chet Atkins Picks on the Beatles (1966 album) 15, 16, 118, 120, 121
Chet Atkins Picks on the Hits (1972 album) 146
Chet Atkins Picks on the Pops (1969 album) 117, 131
Chet Atkins Picks the Best (1967 album) 124, 125, 136
Chet Atkins Plays Back Home Hymns (1962 album) 105
Chet Atkins Plays Great Movie Themes (Compact 33 Double EP, 1961) 98
Chet Atkins' Workshop (1961 album) 14, 15, 95, 96, 99
Chicago, Illinois 10, 29, 34, 35, 36, 52, 156

"Chinatown, My Chinatown" (single track, 1952) 44, 45, 46
Chopin, Frédéric 60, 114
"Chopin Waltz No. 10 in B Minor" (song on 1964 album *My Favorite Guitars*) 114, 115
The Chordettes 12, 56, 57
"Choucoune" (traditional song) 125
Christmas with Chet Atkins (1961 album) 99, 100, 173, 174
Cincinnati, Ohio 6, 8
"City Slicker" (single track, 1953) 48, 49, 50
Class Guitar (1967 album) 125, 126, 127, 193
"The Claw" (song on 1967 Jerry Reed album *The Unbelievable Guitar and Voice of Jerry Reed*) 186
"The Claw" (song on 1973 album *Alone*) 146, 147, 186
"The Claw" (song on 1991 album *Sneakin' Around*) 147, 186
"Cliffs of Dover" (Eric Johnson single track, 1990) 187
The Clovers 91
Cobb, George L. 117
Cochran, Michael 19
Cochran, Russ 19
Cogswell, Wayne 92
Cole, Nat "King" 58
Columbia Records 17, 18, 19, 23, 26, 79, 87, 100, 104, 173, 174, 175, 180, 182, 185, 186, 188, 192, 194, 195, 197, 198
Columbus, Georgia 6, 7
Columbus, Ohio 1, 2
El Condor Pasa (1913 musical play) 137
"El Condor Pasa" (song on 1970 Simon and Garfunkel album *Bridge over Troubled Water*) 138
"El Condor Pasa" (song on 1971 album *For the Good Times and Other Country Moods*) 137, 138, 139
"Copper Kettle" (song on 1964 album *Guitar Country*) 110
Copper Ridge Holiness Church, Luttrell, Tennessee 169
"Cosmic Square Dance" (song on 1985 album *Stay Tuned*) 176, 177, 182
Cotten, Elizabeth 107

Country After All These Years (1981 album) 170, 171
Country All-Stars 53, 113
Country and Western Caravan (1954 album) 78, 170
Country Gentleman (1974 book) 17, 48, 181
"Country Gentleman" (single track, 1953) 2, 12, 14, 46, 47, 48, 53
"Country Gentleman" (song on 1959 album *Mister Guitar*) 48, 83, 87
"Country Gentleman" (song on 1966 album *The Pops Goes Country*) 48, 117
The Country Hams 121
Country Music Association 16
Country Music Hall of Fame, Nashville Tennessee 17, 153
Coursey, Farris 63, 75
Cramer, Floyd 16, 70, 71, 88, 90, 93, 101, 105, 108, 109, 121, 138, **160**
Creatore, Luigi 112
Crider, Doug 189
Crooks, Bob 24
Crosby, Bing 45
"El Cumbanchero" (song on 1957 album *Hi-Fi in Focus*) 71, 72, 74, 86

Dadi, Marcel 108
"Dance with Me" (song on 1980 album *The Best of Chet on the Road ... Live*) 179
D'Angelico, John 11, 20
D'Angelico Excel model guitar 11, 20, **38**, 39, 40, 41, 42, 43, 44, 45, 46, 47, 48, 50, 51, **52**, 53
"Danny Boy" (traditional song) 148
The Dark at the Top of the Stairs (1960 film) 97
"Darling, Je Vous Aime Beaucoup" (Nat "King" Cole single track, 1955) 58
"Darling, Je Vous Aime Beaucoup" (song on 1955 Extended Play 45 *Pickin' the Hits*) 58, 59
The Dave Brubeck Quartet 147, 148
The Day Finger Pickers Took Over the World (1997 album) 19, 194, 195, 196
"The Day Finger Pickers Took Over the World" (song on 1997 album *The Day Finger*

Pickers Took Over the World) 194
DeArmond guitar foot pedals 15, 88, 89, 90, 91, 92
DeArmond guitar pickups 20, 33, 34
DeCosta, Harry 72
Del Vecchio Dinamico guitars 22, 23, 111, **123**, 129, 130, 135, 179, 184, 194
Denver, Colorado 9, 29
Desmond, Paul 147
DeSylva, Buddy 156
Dill, Danny 38
Dire Straits 177, 183
"Dixie" (traditional song) 78, 154
"Dixie McGuire" (song on 1997 album *The Day Finger Pickers Took Over the World*) 193, 194, 195
Dixon, Mort 77
"Dizzy Strings" (single track, 1947) 20, 31, 32
"Django's Castle" (song on 1960 album *Teensville*) 86, 87, 88, 89, 90, 91
"Do I Ever Cross Your Mind" (song on 1976 album *The Best of Chet Atkins and Friends*) 23, 162, 163
"Do I Ever Cross Your Mind" (song on 1982 Dolly Parton album *Heartbreak Express*) 163
"Do I Ever Cross Your Mind" (song on 1990 album *Heroes & Friends*) 164
Dorsey, Tommy 45, 172
Down Home (1962 album) 100, 101, 102
"Down Home" (song on 1963 album *Our Man in Nashville*) 104
"Downhill Drag" (single track, 1954) 52, 53, 156
"Dream" (song on 1994 album *Read My Licks*) 187
Driftwood, Jimmy 131, 135
"Drive In" (song on 1968 album *Solo Flights*) 128
Drusky, Roy 124
Durand, Oswald 125, 126

East Tennessee Christmas (1983 album) 100, 101, 174
"East Tennessee Christmas" (song on 1983 album *East Tennessee Christmas*) 173, 174, 180

EchoSonic guitar amplifiers 24, 57
Eddy, Duane 71
Edwards, Cliff 143
"Ellens Gesang III" (song from *Liederzyklus vom Fraulein vom See*) 193
Ellington, Duke 155, 164
EMG guitar pickups 175
Emmanuel, Tommy 19, **194**, 195, 196
Emmett, Daniel Decatur 78
"Empty Slippers" (1940s demo recording) 28
"The Entertainer" RCA Victor PB-10046 45 single, 1974 (song on 1976 album *Chet Atkins Goes to the Movies*) 19, 152, 153
"The Entertainer" (song on 1990 album *The Magic of Chet Atkins*) 153
"Entrance of the Gladiators" (march) 116
essential guitar theory 25
essential recording technology theory 25, 26
Evening at Pops (television program) 16, 132
The Evening Birds 112
The Everly Brothers 84

Fabric, Bent 106
Faith, Percy 67
Farnon, Dennis 83, 84, 85, 86
Faulkner, Sanford C. 60
Fender guitar amplifiers 79
Fender Stratocaster guitar model 175
Ferron, Jim 18
"Fiddlin' Around" (song on 1973 album *Superpickers*) 149, 150
Fiedler, Arthur 16, 102, 117, 118, 131, 138, 170
Field, Eugene 195
Fields, Don 12
Fields, Dorothy 41
Fields, Margaret 12
Finger-Style Guitar (1956 album) 14, 66, 67, 68, 69
The First Nashville Guitar Quartet 165, 166
The First Nashville Guitar Quartet (1979 album) 165, 166
Flatt, Lester 127
"Foggy Mountain Top" (song on 1967 album *Chet*) 127, 128
Foley, Red 8, 9, 47, 101, 131

"For Dad and Chet" (song on 2006 Rich Meaty Taste album *Thank You So Much*) 2
For the Good Times and Other Country Moods (1971 album) 137, 138, 139
For the Good Times and Other Country Moods (Ray Price single track, 1970) 137
Ford, Mary 39
Foster, Stephen 81
Four Venezuelan Waltzes (collection of compositions for guitar) 103
Fox, Curly 141
Fox Theatre, Atlanta, Georgia 32
"Freight Train" (song on 1964 album *Guitar Country*) 107, 108, 110
"Freight Train/Chattanooga Train" (song on 1980 album *The Best of Chet on the Road ... Live*) 108
"Frog Kissin'" (song on 1976 album *The Best of Chet Atkins and Friends*) 157, 158, 168
From Nashville with Love (1966 album) 119, 122
"From Nashville with Love" (song on 1966 album *From Nashville with Love*) 118, 119, 120
Fučík, Julius 116
Furber, Douglas 45

Galaxy Sound Studios, Hollywood, California 177
Gallagher guitars 169, 170
Gallopin' Guitar News (Chet Atkins Fan Club newsletter) 12
"Gallopin' on the Guitar" (single track, 1949) 11, 12, 20, 32, 33, 34, 36, 46, 65, 81
Galloping Guitar: The Early Years (1993 CD set) 50, 52
Garland, Hank 131
Garvin, Karl 98
Gershwin, George 69, 98
Gershwin, Ira 69, 98
Get Started on the Guitar (1986 book/video set) 19
"Get Up and Go" (unreleased track, 1954) 52
Gibson Chet Atkins CE model guitar 18, 24, 58, 153, **178**, **181**, 182
Gibson Chet Atkins Country

Gentleman model guitar 14, 24, 47, ***183***, ***190***
Gibson Chet Atkins Studio Classic model guitar 24, 187, 188, 192, 193
Gibson Guitar Corporation 5, 14, 17, 18, 23, 24, 47, 58, 153, 173, 178, 187
Gibson L-7 model guitar 20, 31, 35
Gibson L-10 model guitar 8, 20, 27, ***28***, 29, 30, 33, 34, 35, 36, 37
Gibson Les Paul model guitar 155, 157, 164
Gilbert, L. Wolfe 94
Gill, Vince 20, 183
Gimble, Johnny 149, 150, 154
The Gingham Dog and the Calico Cat (children's book) 195
The Gingham Dog and the Calico Cat (1993 album) 195
"The Girl I Left Behind" (traditional song) 54
Glendale, California 177
"Good-Bye Blues" (single track, 1952) 40, 41, 42, 45, 46, 66, 143
Goodrum, Randy 171, 175, 180, 184, 195
Gordy, John 54, 101
"La Goualante du Pavre Jean" (Edith Piaf single track, 1954) 62
Grand Ole Opry (Nashville, Tennessee concert series) 8, 9, 1113, 20, 37
Grant, Amy 195
Grappelli, Stephane 124, 125
Grean, Charles 31, 32, 34, 46, 47
Great Hits of the Past (1983 album) 173
Gretsch Chet Atkins Country Gentleman model guitar 14, 15, 21, 22, 23, 24, 47, 80, 81, 97, ***88***, ***90***, ***93***, 111, ***112***, 120155, 157, ***160***, 164
Gretsch Chet Atkins Nashville model guitar 1, 2, 23, ***133***
Gretsch Chet Atkins Super Axe model guitar 23
Gretsch Chet Atkins Tennessean model guitar 15, 22, 120
Gretsch Company 1, 5, 12, 14, 15, 17, 18, 20, 21, 22, 23, 24, 47, 54, 55, 80, 81, 87, 120, 173

Gretsch 6120 Chet Atkins Hollow Body model guitar 12, 21, 22, 23, 54, 64, 66, 67, 68, 81, 82, 83
Gretsch 6121 Chet Atkins Solid Body model guitar 12, 21, 54
Gretsch Super Chet model guitar 23
Greubel, John 117, 122
"Guitar Blues (Pickin' the Blues)" (single track, 1946) 9, 27, 60, 198
Guitar Country (1964 album) 107, 108, 115, 129, 131, 132
The Guitar Genius (1963 album) 82
Guitar Monsters (1978 album) 17, 157, 164, 165
The Guitar of Chet Atkins (1996 book/video set) 19

Haile, Hascal 23, 24, 163
Hall, Joanna 179
Hall, John 179
Hammerstein, Oscar, II 73, 140
"Hangover Blues" (single track, 1952) 50
"Happy Again" (song on 1996 album *Almost Alone*) 192
Harline, Leigh 143
Harman, Buddy 67, 68, 70, 80, 89, 90
Harrison, George 1, 15, 16, 22, 119, 120
Hascal Haile guitars 23, 24, 163, 169, 170, 179, 180
Hauser, Randy 167, 171
Haynes, Henry "Homer" 8, 32, 34, 35, 36, 37, 46, 47, ***52***, 53, 113, 156
Heartbreak Express (1976 Dolly Parton album) 163
"Heartbreak Hotel" (Elvis Presley single track, 1956) 13, 70
Heartland Music 58, 153
Hee Haw (television program) 16
Helms, Bobby 99, 100
Hernández, Rafael 71
Heroes & Friends (1990 Randy Travis album) 164
Hi-Fi in Focus (1957 album) 14, 71, 72, 73, 74, 85, 86
"Hidden Charm" (single track, 1957) 74, 75, 115
Holly, Buddy 106
Hollywood, California 83, 84, 85, 97, 150

Homer and Jethro 8, 11, 32, 34, 35, 36, 37, 46, 47, ***52***, 53, 65
Hometown Guitar (1968 album) 129, 130, 162
"Honolulu Blue" (song on 1986 album *Street Dreams*) 177, 178, 179
Horowitz, Vladimir 167
"Hot Mocking Bird" (song on 1961 album *Chet Atkins' Workshop*) 95, 96, 97
"How's the World Treating You" (Eddy Arnold single track, 1953) 47
Hubbard, Jerry Reed *see* Reed, Jerry
Hubbard, Priscilla 124, 129
Hum and Strum Along with Chet Atkins (1959 album) 87, 173
Hungate, David 186
Hurta, Charles 29, 30

"I Still Can't Say Goodbye" (song on 1988 album *Chet Atkins, C.G.P.*) 180, 181, 182
"I Still Write Your Name in the Snow" (song on 1996 album *Almost Alone*) 191
"I'll See You in My Dreams" (Isham Jones/Ray Miller Orchestra single track, 1925) 150
"I'll See You in My Dreams" (song on 1968 Merle Travis album *Strictly Guitar*) 151
"I'll See You in My Dreams" (song on 1974 album *The Atkins-Travis Traveling Show*) 150, 151, 182
"I'll See You in My Dreams" (song on 1990 album *Neck and Neck*) 151, 182
"I'll Twine 'Mid the Ringlets" (traditional song) 51
"I'm Forever Blowing Bubbles" (song on 1959 album *Mister Guitar*) 21, 82, 83, 87
"Imagination" (single track, 1952) 43, 44, 50, 141
"In the Mood" (song on 1956 album *Finger-Style Guitar*) 70
Los Incas 137, 138
"Indian Love Call" (single track, 1950) 38
"Indiana (Back Home in Indiana)" (song on 1954 album *A Session With Chet Atkins*) 53, 54

"Indiana (Back Home in Indiana)" (song on 1963 album *Teen Scene*) 55
Los Indios Tabajaras 22, 23, 111, 129
Innis, Louis 50
Irving, Maud 51
Isaacs, Bud 54, 96
"It Ain't Necessarily So" (song on 1961 album *The Most Popular Guitar*) 98
"It Don't Mean a Thing (If It Ain't Got That Swing)" (song on 1964 album *My Favorite Guitars*) 164
"It Don't Mean a Thing (If It Ain't Got That Swing)" (song on 1978 album *Guitar Monsters*) 157, 164, 165
It's a Guitar World (1967 album) 121, 122
"I've Been Working on the Guitar" (single track, 1947) 20, 30, 31

"Jam Man" (song on 1996 album *Almost Alone*) 190, 191, 192
JamMan (audio looping device) 191
Jerome, William 45
"Jessie" (song on 1959 album *Mister Guitar*) 79
"Jingle Bell Rock" (Bobby Helms single track, 1958) 99, 100
"Jingle Bell Rock" (song on 1961 album *Christmas with Chet Atkins*) 99, 100
"Jingle Bell Rock" (song on 1983 album *East Tennessee Christmas*) 100
"Jingle Bells" (single track, 1955) 99
"Jingle Bells" (song on 1961 album *Christmas with Chet Atkins*) 100
"Jitterbug Waltz" (single track, 1951) 39, 85, 86
"Jitterbug Waltz" (song on 1959 album *Chet Atkins in Hollywood*) 39, 85
"Jitterbug Waltz" (unreleased track, 1957) 86
Johannesburg, South Africa 105
Johnson, Arnold 41
Johnson, Eric 187
Johnson, Leona 8
Johnson, Lois 8
Jolson, Al 45, 69, 156

Jones, Isham 150
Joplin, Scott 19, 152
Juan Estruch guitars 22, 111, 114, 119, 127, 129, 131, 159, 161

Kahn, Gus 69, 150
Kaitz, Emily 194
Kalb, Buddy 158, 168
Karas, Anton 42
Kass, R.L. 186
Keeler, Ruby 69
Keillor, Garrison 18, 20
Keith, Leslie 141
Kellette, John 82
Kenbrovin, Jan 82
Kendis, James 82
Kennerly, Paul 183
"Kentucky Derby" (single track, 1954) 49, 50, 51, 53, 79
Kerr, Anita 91, 92, 129
Klein, Augie 29, 30
"Kicky" (song on 1964 album *Progressive Pickin'*) 110, 111
Klugh, Earl 18, 175
KMMJ-AM, Grand Island, Nebraska 6
Knopfler, Mark 18, 19, 116, 125, 151, 175, 177, 182, 183, 184, 187, 189, 191
Knowles, John 19, 149, 153, 165, 174
Knoxville, Tennessee 5, 7, 10, 28
KOA-AM, Denver, Colorado 9, 10
Kristofferson, Kris 137
KWTO-AM, Springfield, Missouri 9, 10, 11, 27, 37

The Lady of the Lake (epic poem) 193
Laird, Elmer 132
Lambert, Buck 31, 32
Lanham, Roy 60, 61
Lauro, Antonio 103
Lawrence, Jack 62
Lecuona, Ernesto 67
Lennon, John 15, 119, 120
Leoncavallo, Ruggero 137
Les Paul Trio 7
"Let It Be Me" (Everly Brothers single track, 1960) 84
"Let It Be Me" (song on 1959 album *Chet Atkins in Hollywood*) 84
Lexicon Company 191
Liberty Records 190
Liederzyklus vom Fraulein vom See (song collection) 193

Lima, Antenor 22, 129
Lima, Nato 22, 23, 111, 123, 129
"Limelight" (song on 1959 album *Chet Atkins in Hollywood*) 98
"The Lion Sleeps Tonight" (Tokens single track, 1961) 112
"Listen to the Mockingbird" (traditional song) 96
"A Little Bit of Blues" (song on 1964 album *Guitar Country*) 107, 108, 109, 110
"A Little Mark Musik" (song on 1996 album *Almost Alone*) 191
"Liza (All the Clouds'll Roll Away)" (Al Jolson single track, 1929) 69
"Liza" (song on 1956 album *Finger-Style Guitar*) 68, 69, 70
London, Larrie 147, 148
"Londonderry Air" (song on 1955 album *Chet Atkins in Three Dimensions*) 148
"Londonderry Air" (song on 1973 album *Alone*) 148, 149
"Londonderry Air" (song on 1979 album *The First Nashville Guitar Quartet*) 149
The Lone Ranger 50
Los Angeles, California 129, 172
Loudermilk, John D. 89, 90, 102, 118, 154
"Love Song of Pepe Sanchez" (song on 1979 album *The First Nashville Guitar Quartet*) 165, 166
"Lover Come Back to Me" (single track, 1952) 140
"Lover Come Back to Me" (song on 1971 album *Pickin' My Way*) 140, 141
"Lover Come Back to Me" (song on 1976 album *Chester and Lester*) 141
Lover's Guitar (1969 album) 130, 131
"Lullaby of the Leaves" (song on 1957 album *Hi-Fi in Focus*) 74
Luttrell, Tennessee 5, 6, 169

MacLellan, Gene 139
"The Mad Russian" (song on 1972 album *Me and Chet*) 137, 144, 145, 185

Madden, Edward 55
The Magic of Chet Atkins (1990 album) 57, 58, 153
Magness, Tommy 141
"Main Street Breakdown" (single track, 1950) 11, 12, 20, 33, 35, 36, 65, 81
Málaga, Spain 67
"Malagueña" (song on 1956 album *Finger-Style Guitar*) 66, 67, 70
"Manoir de Mes Reves" (Django Reinhardt single track, 1942) 88, 89
"Maria Elena" (Los Indios Tabajaras single track, 1963) 22, 111
"Maria Elena" (song on 1960 album *The Other Chet Atkins*) 22, 23, 110, 111
Marlow, Ric 121
Martin D-45 model guitar 150
"The Masterpiece" (song on 1972 album *Chet Atkins Picks on the Hits*) 145, 146
Masterpiece Theatre (television program) 146
"Mayan Dance" (song on 1962 album *Caribbean Guitar*) 102, 103, 104
"Maybelle" (song on 1996 album *Almost Alone*) 191
"Mbube" (Evening Birds single track) 112
McCarthy, Mac 52
McCartney, Paul 15, 71, 119, 120, 121
McCoy, Charlie 101, 116, 120, 127, 149, 150
McGuire, Dorothy 97
McHugh, Jimmy 41
McLean, Don 188
McMillan, Dutch 27
McMillan, Terry 171
McTell, Blind Willie 168
Me and Chet (1972 album) 137, 144, 145, 185
Me and Jerry (1970 album) 135, 136, 137, 144, 185, 186
Me and My Guitar (1977 album) 159, 160, 188
"Me and My Guitar" (song on 1977 album *Me and My Guitar*) 159
"Medley: The Battle of New Orleans/Sugarfoot Rag" (song on 1969 album *Chet Atkins Picks on the Pops*) 118, 131, 132
"Meet Mr. Callaghan" (song on 1959 album *Chet Atkins in Hollywood*) 98
Mercer, Johnny 187
Merman, Ethel 76
Methodist Television, Radio & Film Commission, Nashville, Tennessee 14, 57, 74, 76
Miami, Florida 170
"Michelle" (song on 1965 Beatles album *Rubber Soul*) 71, 119, 120
"Michelle" (song on 1966 album *Chet Atkins Picks on the Beatles*) 118, 119, 120, 121
"Midnight" (Red Foley single track, 1952) 46, 47
Milburn, Richard 96
Milchberg, Jorge 137
Miller, Mitch 87
Mills, Irving 155, 164
The Mills Brothers 41, 45, 72
Minnesota Public Radio 18
"Minuet (from French Harpsichord Suite) and Prelude (from Six Short Preludes)" (song on 1955 album *Chet Atkins in Three Dimensions*) 94
"Minute Waltz" (song on 1955 album *Chet Atkins in Three Dimensions*) 59, 60, 61
"Misery Loves Company" (Porter Wagoner single track, 1962) 104
Mister Atkins If You Please (1955 album) 91
"Mr. Bojangles" (song on 1970 Nitty Gritty Dirt Band album *Uncle Charlie & His Dog Teddy*) 197
"Mr. Bojangles" (song on 1973 album *Superpickers*) 197
"Mr. Bojangles" (song on 1996 album *Almost Alone*) 198
"Mr. Bojangles" (song on 2003 album *Solo Sessions*) 196, 197, 198
Mister Guitar (Chet Atkins Appreciation Society newsletter) 18
Mister Guitar (1959 album) 22, 48, 79, 80, 82, 83, 87
Mister Guitar: The Complete Recordings (2004 CD set) 29, 86, 90, 98
"Mister Lucky" (song on 1974 album *Chet Atkins Picks on Jerry Reed*) 152
"Mister Sandman" (single track, 1955) 12, 13, 24, 56, 57
"Mister Sandman" (song on 1990 album *The Magic of Chet Atkins*) 57, 58
Mitchell, Priscilla 124
Modern Jazz Quartet 73
The Monkees 1
Monnot, Marguerite 62
Monton, Michel Mauleart 125, 126
Monument Records 116
Moore, Bob 70, 72, 89, 90
Moore, Jimmy 180
More of That Guitar Country (1965 album) 115, 116, 129
Morel, Jorge 126, 148
The Most Popular Guitar (1961 album) 98, 99, 101
"Mountain Melody" (single track, 1951) 37, 38, 39
Mouret, Jean-Joseph 146
Murray, Anne 139
Music City Music Hall, Nashville, Tennessee 166, 167, 169, 170
Music from Nashville, My Home Town (1966 album) 122, 123
My Brother Sings (1959 unreleased album) 80, 81, 82, 83, 87
My Favorite Guitars (1964 album) 22, 23, 111, 112, 113, 114, 115, 119, 121, 123, 164
Myrick, Weldon 149, 150

"Nagasaki" (song on 1958 album *Chet Atkins at Home*) 77
"Nashtown Ville" (song on 1972 album *Me and Chet*) 137, 145, 185
Nashville, Tennessee 8, 9, 11, 12, 14, 18, 19, 24, 26, 27, 37, 38, 40, 42, 43, 48, 50, 51, 53, 55, 56, 58, 59, 60, 61, 66, 68, 70, 71, 72, 73, 74, 75, 77, 78, 79, 80, 82, 84, 86, 87, 88, 90, 91, 92, 95, 96, 98, 99, 101, 102, 103, 104, 105, 106, 107, 108, 109, 110, 111, 113, 114, 115, 118, 120, 121, 123, 124, 125, 127, 128, 129, 130, 132, 134, 135, 136, 137, 139, 140, 141, 142, 144, 145, 146, 147, 149, 150, 152, 153, 154, 155, 156, 158, 159, 160, 161, 163, 164, 166, 167, 168, 169, 170, 176, 178, 182, 191
The Nashville Network 19
Nashville String Band 53

Nashville String Machine 193, 198
"Natalia" (composition for guitar) 103
National Academy of Recording Arts and Sciences 16
National Barn Dance (WLS-AM radio program) 6
NBC Broadcasting Corporation 8, 9, 13, 64
Neck and Neck (1990 album) 116, 125, 177, 182, 183, 184
Neely, Bill 17, 48
The New Moon (1928 operetta) 73, 144
New York City, New York 8, 10, 30, 31, 39, 40, 43, 45, 46, 65, 85, 141, 146, 170
Newman, Paul 153
Newton, Ernie 50
"Nifty Fifties" (song on 1991 album *Sneakin' Around*) 189
The Night Atlanta Burned (1975 album) 153, 154, 165
"The Night Atlanta Burned" (song on 1975 album *The Night Atlanta Burned*) 153, 154, 165
The Nitty Gritty Dirt Band 197

"Ochi Chornya (Dark Eyes)" (song on 1955 album *Chet Atkins in Three Dimensions*) 61, 62
O'Connor, Donald 76
"Oh! By Jingo, Oh! By Gee! (You're the Only Girl for Me)" (song on 1956 album *Stringin' Along with Chet Atkins*) 43, 54, 64, 65, 66, 79
"The Old Buck Dance" (single track, 1950) 34, 35, 133
"The Old Grey Mare" (traditional song) 50
"The Old Rugged Cross" (song on 1962 album *Chet Atkins Plays Back Home Hymns*) 105
Olympia, Theatre, Paris, France 166
"On My Way to Canaan's Land" (song on 1980 album *Reflections*) 168, 169, 170
"One Mint Julep" (Clovers single track, 1952) 91
"One Mint Julep" (song on 1960 album *Teensville*) 91, 92, 93
"One More for the Road" (song on 1994 album *Simpatico*) 189, 190
"Orange Blossom Special" (song on 1966 album *The Pops Goes Country*) 170
"Orange Blossom Special" (song on 1981 album *Country After All These Years*) 170, 171
The Original Dixieland Jazz Band 54, 72
Orleans 179
Osborne, Sonny 127
The Other Chet Atkins (1960 album) 15, 22, 23, 93, 94, 95, 110, 111, 125
Our Man in Nashville (1963 album) 104, 105, 108

"Paddy on the Turnpike" (traditional song) 160
Pagliacci (1892 opera) 137
Paris, France 166, 167, 168
Parton, Dolly 23, 163, 164, 166, 169
The Passing Show of 1918 (1918 musical) 82
Patrick, DiAnne 23, 163
Paul, Les 7, 8, 17, 20, 39, 40, 155, 156, 161, 164, 165, 168, 189
PBS Television Network 16, 132, 146
"The Peanut Vendor" (single track, 1957) 94
"The Peanut Vendor" (song on 1960 album *The Other Chet Atkins*) 93, 94, 95, 110
Pearl, Minnie 169
Peaver custom guitar 175, **176**
Peavey T-60 model guitar 175
"Peeping Tom" (unreleased track, 1952) 50
Pell, John 149, 165, 166
Peretti, Hugo 112
A Perfect Match (1962 Johnny Smith/Art Van Damme album) 109
Peter, Paul and Mary 107
Petty, Norman 105
Piaf, Édith 62
Pickin' My Way (1971 album) 44, 140, 141, 142, 143, 144
Pickin' the Hits (1955 Extended Play 45) 58, 59
Pinkard, Maceo 162
Pinocchio (1940 film) 143
Please Please Me (1963 Beatles album) 122
"Poison Love" (song on 1969 album *C.B. Atkins and C.E. Snow by Special Request*) 114, 132, 133, 134
"Polka Dots and Moonbeams" (song on 1981 album *Standard Brands*) 162, 171, 172
Pomeroy, Dave 194
"Poor Boy Blues" (song on 1990 album *Neck and Neck*) 177, 182, 183, 184
"The Poor People of Paris (Jean's Song)" (single track, 1956) 13, 62, 63, 64, 74, 75
"The Poor People of Paris" (Les Baxter single track, 1956) 64
The Pops Goes Country (1966 album) 48, 102, 117, 118, 131, 170
Porgy and Bess (1935 opera) 98
Porter, Bill 99
Poston, Mike 197
Potter, Dale 54
A Prairie Home Companion (radio program) 18, 19
"Prancin' Filly" (song from the 1966 album *Music from Nashville, My Home Town*) 122, 123
Presley, Elvis 13, 70, 75
Preston, Robert 97
Price, Ray 137
"Prissy" (single track, 1966) 124
Pritcher, Mark 18
Progressive Pickin' (1964 album) 109, 110, 111
The Purina Grand Ole Opry (television program) 13, 54
Pursell, Bill 110, 111

Radio Recorders Annex Studio, Hollywood, California 83, 84, 85
"Rainbow" (single track, 1952) 39, 40, 47
"Rainbow" (song on 1959 album *Mister Guitar*) 39, 83, 87
Raleigh, North Carolina 8
Ramirez classical guitars 196
Randolph, Boots 16, 88, 89, 92, 101, 115, 116, 124, 138, **160**, 161, 163
Rao, Harihar 121
Ray Miller Orchestra 150
RCA Camden 82, 123, 127
RCA Victor Corporation 9, 10, 13, 14, 17, 18, 23, 26, 29, 30, 31, 32, 33, 34, 35, 36, 37, 39, 40, 41, 42, 43, 44, 45, 46,

47, 48, 49, 50, 51, 52, 53, 54, 55, 56, 57, 58, 59, 60, 61, 62, 64, 65, 66, 68, 70, 71, 72, 73, 74, 75, 76, 77, 78, 79, 80, 81, 82, 83, 84, 85, 86, 87, 88, 89, 90, 91, 92, 93, 94, 95, 96, 97, 98, 99, 100, 101, 102, 103, 104, 105, 106, 107, 108, 109, 110, 111, 113, 114, 115, 116, 118, 120, 121, 122, 123, 124, 125, 127, 128, 129, 130, 131, 132, 134, 135, 136, 137, 138, 139, 140, 141, 142, 144, 145, 146, 147, 149, 150, 151, 152, 153, 154, 155, 156, 158, 159, 160, 161, 163, 164, 165, 167, 168, 169, 170, 171, 172, 173, 174, 175, 182, 185, 186, 193, 197

Read My Licks (1994 album) 186, 187, 188, 189

"Read My Licks" (song on 1994 album *Read My Licks*) 187

Redford, Robert 153

Reed, Jerry 16, 19, 104, 110, 123, 124, 125, 128, 129, 134, 135, 136, 137, 144, 145, 147, 150, 151, 152, 159, 161, 168, 184, **185**, 186, 187, 189

Reeves, Jim 105

Reflections (1980 album) 17, 23, 169, 170

Reinhardt, Django 8, 11, 29, 32, 33, 36, 58, 61, 88, 89, 124, 125, 151, 161

Reinhart, Larry 1

Relaxin' with Chet (1968 album) 130

Reminiscing (1964 album) 113, 114, 132

"Reminiscing" (single track, 1956) 113

Rich, James "Spider" 74, 115

Rich Meaty Taste 2

Richmond, Virginia 9

Riddle, Jimmy 70, 71

Robbins, Hargus "Pig" 150

Robles, Daniel Alomia 137

"Rocky Top" (Osborne Brothers single track, 1967) 46

Rollings, Matt 190

Romberg, Sigmund 73, 140

"Rondeau from *Symphonies and Fanfares for the King's Supper*" (orchestral fanfare) 146

Rose, Vincent 156

Rouse, Irving T. 170

Rubber Soul (1965 Beatles album) 120

Russell, Jonathan 197

Ryman Auditorium, Nashville, Tennessee 9, 19

Sablon, Jean 58

Sails (1987 album) 178, 179, 180

"Sails" (song on 1976 Orleans album *Waking and Dreaming*) 179

"Sails" (song on 1987 album *Sails*) 178, 179, 180

"Salty Dog Rag" (Red Foley single, 1952) 101

"Salty Dog Rag" (song on 1962 album *Down Home*) 100, 101

Sand, Kirk 24

"Satan's Doll" (song on 1964 album *Progressive Pickin'*) 109, 110, 128

"Scare Crow" (song on 1963 album *Our Man in Nashville*) 103, 104, 108

Schubert, Franz 193

Schwartz, Jean 45

Scott, Bobby 121

Scott, Walter 193

Scruggs, Earl 127

Seaboard Air Line Railroad 170

Sears and Roebuck Company 6

Seeger, Mike 107

Seeger, Pete 107, 112

Segovia, Andrés 103, 165

A Session with Chet Atkins (1954 album) 21, 53, 54, 55, 96, 149, 155

Shaw, Artie 73

Sholes, Stephen H. 9, 10, 13, 14, 29, 30, 31, 48, 75, 138

Shook, Jack 27

Shook, Jerry 150

Show Girl (1929 musical) 69

Silver 50

Silver, Lisa 154

"Silver Bell" (single track, 1955) 13, 55, 56, 57, 113, 114

Siman, Si 9, 27

Simon and Garfunkel 137, 138

Simóns, Moisés 94

Simpatico (1994 album) 187, 189, 190

Sinatra, Frank 172

Sing-Along with Mitch (1950s album series) 87

"Slinkey" (song on 1959 album *Mister Guitar*) 79, 80, 81, 87

Slinky (children's toy) 79

Slone, Gene 159

Smith, Johnny 73, 109

"Smokey Mountain Lullaby" (song on 1993 album *The Gingham Dog and the Calico Cat*) 195

"Smokey Mountain Lullaby" (song on 1997 album *The Day Finger Pickers Took Over the World*) 195, 196

Sneakin' Around (1991 album) 147, 184, 185, 186

"Sneakin' Around" (song on 1991 album *Sneakin' Around*) 184, 185, 186

Snow, Hank 13, 16, 55, 56, 106, 113, 114, 132, 133, 134, 168, 189

"Snowbird" (Anne Murray single track, 1970) 139

"Snowbird" (song on 1971 album *For the Good Times and Other Country Moods*) 138, 139

"So Soft, Your Goodbye" (song on 1990 album *Neck and Neck*) 177, 183

Society of European Stage Authors and Composers (SESAC) 91

"Softly, as in a Morning Sunrise" (song from the 1928 operetta *The New Moon*) 73

Solid Gold '68 (1968 album) 130, 134, 146

Solid Gold '69 (1969 album) 130, 146

Solid Gold '70 (1970 album) 130, 146

Solo Flights (1968 album) 128, 143

Solo Sessions (2003 album) 197, 198

"Somebody Loves Me Now" (song on 1994 album *Read My Licks*) 187

Somewhere Between (1989 Suzy Bogguss album) 189

Songs of America (musical history program) 2

Sosenko, Anna 58

Sousa, John Phillip 167

Springfield, Missouri 9, 10, 27

"Squirrelly" (song on 1974 album *Chet Atkins Picks on Jerry Reed*) 152

Standard Brands (1981 album) 17, 162, 172, 173

Standel guitar amplifiers 24, 93

"The Stars and Stripes For-

ever" (song on 1980 album *The Best of Chet on the Road ... Live*) 166, 167, 168
Stars of the Grand Ole Opry (television program) 13
Stay Tuned (1985 album) 18, 175, 176, 177, 178, 187
"Steeplechase Lane" (song on 1970 album *Yestergroovin'*) 134, 135
"Steeplechase Lane" (song on 1974 album *Chet Atkins Picks on Jerry Reed*) 135, 152
Steiner, Max 97
Stevens, Ray 158, 168
The Sting (1973 film) 153
Street Dreams (1986 album) 177, 178, 179
Strevel, Willie 6
String Dustin' (1953 Country All-Stars album) 53, 113
Stringin' Along with Chet Atkins (1953 album) 43, 54, 64, 65
Stringin' Along with Chet Atkins (1956 album) 43, 54, 64, 65, 66, 141
Strzelecki, Henry 117, 128
"Sugarfoot Rag" (Hank Garland single track, 1949) 131
"Sugarfoot Rag" (song on 1964 album *Guitar Country*) 131, 132
Suite Andalucia (piano suite) 67
Sullivan, Maxine 61
"Sunrise" (song on 1985 album *Stay Tuned*) 174, 175, 176, 177
Sunshine, Marion 94
Superpickers (1973 album) 46, 149, 150
"Swanee River" (song on 1963 album *The Guitar Genius*) 21, 80, 81, 82
"Swanee River" (traditional song) 81
Swanson, Holly 53
"Swedish Rhapsody" (Percy Faith single track, 1953) 67, 68
"Swedish Rhapsody" (song on 1956 album *Finger-Style Guitar*) 67, 68, 70
Swedish Rhapsody No. 1, Midsommarvaka (symphonic rhapsody) 67, 68
"Sweet Georgia Brown" (Ben Bernie single track, 1925) 162
"Sweet Georgia Brown" (song on 1968 album *Hometown Guitar*) 162
"Sweet Georgia Brown" (song on 1976 album *The Best of Chet Atkins and Friends*) 161, 162, 172
Symphony Hall, Boston Massachusetts 117, 131

"Take Five" (Dave Brubeck Quartet single track, 1959) 148
"Take Five" (song on 1973 album *Alone*) 147, 148
"A Taste of Honey" (Herb Alpert and the Tijuana Brass single track, 1965) 122
A Taste of Honey (1957 play) 121
"A Taste of Honey" (song on 1963 Beatles album *Please Please Me*) 122
"A Taste of Honey" (song on 1967 album *It's a Guitar World*) 121, 122
Taylor, James 159
Taylor, Robert 154
"Tears" (song on 1967 album *Chet Atkins Picks the Best*) 124, 125, 136, 182
"Tears" (song on 1990 album *Neck and Neck*) 125, 182
Teen Scene (1963 album) 55, 106
Teensville (1960 album) 14, 15, 87, 88, 89, 91, 92, 93, 106
"Teensville" (song on 1960 album *Teensville*) 92, 93
"Tennessee Rag/Beaumont Rag" (song on 1980 album *Reflections*) 169, 170
"Tennessee Stud" (song on 1970 album *Me and Jerry*) 135, 136, 185
"Terry on the Turnpike" (song on 1976 album *The Best of Chet Atkins and Friends*) 159, 160, 161
Thank You So Much (2006 Rich Meaty Taste album) 2
"Theme from a Dream" (song on 1959 album *Chet Atkins in Hollywood*) 83, 84, 85
"Theme from *Picnic*" (song on 1959 album *Chet Atkins in Hollywood*) 98
"Theme from *The Dark at the Top of the Stairs*" (single track, 1960) 97, 98
"Theme from *Zorba the Greek*" (song on 1969 album *Lover's Guitar*) 130, 131

Theodorakis, Mikis 130
The Third Man (1949 film) 42
"The Third Man Theme" (single track, 1952) 42, 43, 44, 54, 140
"The Third Man Theme" (song on 1956 album *Stringin' Along with Chet Atkins*) 43
Thomas Productions, Nashville, Tennessee 48, 50, 51, 53, 55, 57
Thompson, Bob 97
Thompson, Shorty 9, 10, 29
"The Three Bells" (Browns single track, 1959) 84
"The Three Bells" (song on 1959 album *Chet Atkins in Hollywood*) 84
"Tiger Rag" (Mills Brothers single track, 1931) 72
"Tiger Rag" (song on 1957 album *Hi-Fi in Focus*) 72, 73, 86
The Tijuana Brass 122
Tizol, Juan 155
The Today Show (television program) 13, 63, 64
The Tokens 112
Tommy Dorsey Orchestra 172
Toombs, Rudolph 91
"Trambone" (single track, 1957) 69, 70, 71, 88, 94, 119
"Trambone" (song on 1962 album *Down Home*) 71, 101
Travelin' (1963 album) 105, 106
Travis, Merle 6, 7, 8, 9, 10, 29, 30, 32, 41, 52, 116, 136, 138, 150, 151, 152, 161, 168, 169
Travis, Randy 164
"Tweedlee Dee" (song on 1955 Extended Play 45 *Pickin' the Hits*) 58
"Twelfth Street Rag" (single track, 1953) 65

The Unbelievable Guitar and Voice of Jerry Reed (1967 Jerry Reed album) 186
Uncle Charlie & His Dog Teddy (1970 Nitty Gritty Dirt Band album) 197

"Vals Criollo" (composition for guitar) 103
Van Damme, Art 109
Vanderbilt Plaza Hotel, Nashville, Tennessee 176
Van Duser, Guy 167
Van Gogh, Vincent 188
Van Heusen, Jimmy 172

Vaughn, George 131
The Ventures 74
"Vesti la Giubba" (aria from *Pagliacci*) 137
"Vincent" (Don McLean single track, 1971) 188
"Vincent" (song on 1977 album *Me and My Guitar*) 188
"Vincent" (song on 1994 album *Read My Licks*) 188, 189
Vincent, Nat 82
Von Tizer, Albert 65

Wagoner, Porter 104, 169
"Waiting for Susie B" (song on 1996 album *Almost Alone*) 191
"Wake Up Little Susie" (Everly Brothers single track, 1957) 84
Waking and Dreaming (Orleans album, 1976) 179
"Walk Don't Run" (song on 1957 album *Hi-Fi in Focus*) 73, 74, 109
"Walk Don't Run" (Ventures single track, 1959) 74
"Walk of Life" (Dire Straits single track, 1985) 183
Walker, Jerry Jeff 197
"Walking in the Park with Eloise" (Country Hams single track, 1974) 121
Waller, Fats 39, 85
"The Wallflower (Dance with Me, Henry)" (song on 1955 Extended Play 45 *Pickin' the Hits*) 58
The Walt Disney Company 143
"Waltz for the Lonely" (song on 1987 album *Sails*) 178, 179, 180
"The Waltz in D-flat Major, Op. 64, No. 1" (waltz for solo piano) 59, 60
"Waltz Number 3" (composition for guitar) 103
"Waltz Op. 69, No. 2" (waltz for solo piano) 114
Wariner, Steve 20, 171, 187
Waring, Fred 8
Warren, Harry 77
Washington, Ned 143
Watson, Doc 17, 23, 168, 169, 170, 189
Weatherly, Frederic 148

The Weavers 112
Webb, Runyan 125
Webster, Jimmie 12, 21
Webster, Joseph Philbrick 51
Weiss, George David 112
Wells, Ruby 57
Wenrich, Percy 39, 55
Wheeler, Billy Edd 191
"Wheels" (song on 1963 album *Travelin'*) 105, 106
"Wheels" (song on 1969 album *C.B. Atkins and C.E. Snow by Special Request*) 106
"Wheels" (song on 1980 album *The Best of Chet on the Road ... Live*) 106
"When You Wish Upon a Star" (song on 1968 album *Solo Flights*) 143
"When You Wish Upon a Star" (song on 1971 album *Pickin' My Way*) 142, 143, 144
"When You Wish Upon a Star" (song on 1980 album *The Best of Chet on the Road ... Live*) 144
"Why Don't You Leave Me Alone" (1940s demo recording) 28
"Wiegenlied: Guten Abend, gute Nacht" (lullaby) 113
"Wildwood Flower" (single track, 1954) 51
"Wildwood Flower" (traditional song) 6, 51
William Tell Overture 50
"Wimoweh" (song on 1964 album *My Favorite Guitars*) 111, 112, 113, 115, 123
"Wimoweh" (Weavers single track, 1952) 112
"Windy and Warm" (single track, 1961) 102
"Windy and Warm" (song on 1962 album *Down Home*) 101, 102, 118
"Windy and Warm" (song on 1966 album *The Pops Goes Country*) 102, 117
Wings 121
Winner, Septimus 96
WLS-AM, Chicago, Illinois 6
WLW-AM, Cincinnati, Ohio 6, 8
WNOX-AM, Knoxville, Tennessee 7, 8, 10, 28
Work It Out with Chet Atkins C.G.P. (1983 album) 173

WPTF-AM, Raleigh, North Carolina 8
WRBL-AM, Columbus, Georgia 7
Wright, Lenny 121
WRVA-AM, Richmond, Virginia 9, **28**
WSM-AM, Nashville, Tennessee 9, 11, 27, 37

Yahama Research and Development Studio, Glendale, California 177
"Yakety Axe" (song on 1965 album *More of That Guitar Country*) 16, 115, 116, 182
"Yakety Axe" (song on 1990 album *Neck and Neck*) 116, 117, 182
"Yakety Sax" (Boots Randolph single track, 1963) 16, 115, 116
Yandell, Paul 16, 20, 144, 147, 148, 150, 154, 155, 171, 175, 177, 197
"Yankee Doodle" (traditional song) 77, 78
"Yankee Doodle Dixie" (song on 1954 album *Country and Western Caravan*) 78
"Yankee Doodle Dixie" (song on 1958 album *Chet Atkins at Home*) 77, 78
Yellen, Jack 117
"Yellow Bird" (Arthur Lyman Group single track, 1961) 126
"Yellow Bird" (song on 1962 album *Caribbean Guitar*) 126
"Yellow Bird" (song on 1967 album *Class Guitar*) 125, 126, 127
"Yesterday" (song on 1966 album *Chet Atkins Picks on the Beatles*) 120
Yestergroovin' (1970 album) 134, 152
Young, Bill 187
"Young Thing" (song on 1994 album *Read My Licks*) 186, 187, 189
"You're Just in Love" (song on 1958 album *Chet Atkins at Home*) 75, 76, 77

Zorba the Greek (1964 film) 130

www.ingramcontent.com/pod-product-compliance
Ingram Content Group UK Ltd.
Pitfield, Milton Keynes, MK11 3LW, UK
UKHW050529150426
5217IPUK00026B/1860